ARTHUR J MARDER was a meticulous researcher, teacher and writer who, born in 1910, was to become perhaps the most distinguished historian of the modern Royal Navy. He held a number of teaching posts in American universities and was to receive countless honours, as well as publish some fifteen major works on British naval history. He died in 1980.

BARRY GOUGH, the distinguished Canadian maritime and naval historian, is the author of *Historical Dreadnoughts: Arthur Marder, Stephen Roskill and the Battles for Naval History*, and contributed new introductions to Marder's five-volume history of the Royal Navy in the First World War, *From the Dreadnought to Scapa Flow*, all recently published by Seaforth Publishing.

Winston Churchill, First Lord of the Admiralty, 14 October 1939

FROM THE
DARDANELLES
TO
ORAN

STUDIES OF THE ROYAL NAVY
IN WAR AND PEACE 1915–1940

ARTHUR J MARDER
INTRODUCTION BY BARRY GOUGH

Naval Institute Press
Annapolis

Seaforth
PUBLISHING

THE MAPS
Large-scale versions of the maps located at the back
can be downloaded from the book's page
on the publishers' websites.

Copyright © Arthur J Marder 1974

Introduction copyright @ Barry Gough 2015

First published in Great Britain in 2015 by
Seaforth Publishing,
Pen & Sword Books Ltd,
47 Church Street,
Barnsley S70 2AS

Published and distributed in the
United States of America and Canada by the
Naval Institute Press,
291 Wood Road, Annapolis,
Maryland 21402–5034

British Library Cataloguing in Publication Data
A catalogue record for this book is available from the British Library

Library of Congress Control Number: 2015938192

(UK) ISBN 978 1 84832 252 3
(US) ISBN 978 1 59114 585 1

Printed and bound in Great Britain by CPI Group (UK) Ltd, Croydon, CR0 4YY

To

the memory of

JOHN CRESWELL

Captain, R.N.
gentleman, scholar
and dear friend

Introduction

L ONG will Arthur Jacob Marder (1910–1980) be remembered
for his five-part *From the Dreadnought to Scapa Flow: The Royal
Navy in the Fisher Era, 1904–1919* (original edition 1961–
1970; reprinted by Seaforth Publishing, 2013–2014, with
introductions for each volume by myself). That work is today
classified by the naval historical profession as 'core history',
although well might it be regarded (across the larger canvas of
historical enterprise) as a classic of historical research and writing.
Marder came to the Admiral Sir John Fisher era of British naval
history, 1904–1920, when the official documents were finally
released to him. In the meantime, he had published *The Anatomy
of British Sea Power: A History of British Naval Policy in the Pre-
Dreadnought Era* (1940; English edition, 1941). Then he had edited
the diaries of Admiral Sir Herbert Richmond, *Portrait of an Admiral:
The Life and Papers of Sir Herbert Richmond* (1952). He also produced
three volumes of Fisher's edited letters *Fear God and Dread Nought*.
Taken altogether these formed a significant contribution to the
corpus of history especially on the lead up to the First World War
and the direction of that conflict at sea, and in doing so they raised
the standard of naval history. That these books were written by an
American provided not a little amusing comment by the British.
And that his last name carried the initial 'M' as did that of US
Admirals Alfred Thayer Mahan and Samuel Elliott Morison,
likewise attracted idle chatter.

By 1970 and the time Marder had come to the completion of his
From the Dreadnought to Scapa Flow he had been employed on
historical enterprises for almost four decades. And as of that year he
knew in his inner heart that he was exhausted, as his correspondence with Oxford University Press discloses. His spirited and
furious production of these several works completed at breakneck
speed, his other academic obligations (for he carried heavy teaching
obligations, graduate and undergraduate), his mid-career switch
in university affiliation from Hawaii to Southern California, and
then a climactic, triumphant year at Baillol College, Oxford, as
Eastman Professor spelled an accumulation of pressures amount-
ing to a personal crisis that he could not ignore. Exhausted and
perhaps in despair, he wrote to his publisher, Geoffrey Hunt, at
Oxford University Press and said he could do no more.

The ever solicitous Hunt decided to leave Marder well enough alone and to await the course of events. Sure enough in early April 1971 he received a letter from Marder in sunny California announcing that he had had further thoughts. 'I was deadly serious a year ago, and in my last letter, when I told you that I had written my last book.' As he now explained, no subject appealed to him sufficiently: the interwar period would have been 'the logical thing to do, that is till [Captain Stephen] Roskill moved in. (*Entre nous*, Vol. I of his *Naval Policy [Between the Wars]* is a horror. Still he has pre-empted the period.') Then, Marder went on, he needed more time for his teaching and for his family. However, if Hunt were willing to publish a different sort of book, Marder was prepared to explain what he had in mind. 'I could be persuaded to do a book of essays and articles,' he said, and by these he meant a mix of published and unpublished pieces. He gave a long list of possibilities, including a seminal article on early Japanese seapower that he had published in the *American Historical Review* in 1945, based on some Japanese materials. Another prospective item was his delightful and (still) unpublished 'That Hamilton Woman,' all about Horatio Lord Nelson and Emma Hamilton, an engrossing story of that ever so promising book, not yet written, 'The Women Behind the Fleet.'

Such was Marder's reputation and such were the sales of his books that Hunt jumped at the prospect. Hunt had rich pickings from which to choose. In the end, these five were to make up the new volume: 1. 'The Dardanelles Revisited: Further Thoughts on the Naval Prelude'; 2. 'The Influence of History on Sea Power: The Royal Navy and the Lessons of 1914–1918'; 3. 'The Royal Navy and the Ethiopian Crisis of 1935–1936'; 4. 'Winston is Back': Churchill at the Admiralty, 1939–1940'; and 5. 'Oran, 3 July 1940: Mistaken Judgement, Tragic Misunderstanding, or Cruel Necessity?' As is explained below, each of the five has a history of its own, and only the last of these (and the major) was truly original in the sense that it had not appeared before in earlier form. That having been said, each of the five constitutes a commentary on the Royal Navy in those very circumstances that tested its very mettle, during war or in phases of peace. Because Marder was fascinated by 'the war behind the war', the last three chapters give insights into the relationships of statesmen and admirals, naval administration, and the higher management of war. As to the first two, and with which this engaging book commences, Marder was returning to his earlier preoccupations, in turn: What lessons had the Admiralty and the Navy learned from the First World War? What had separated British forces from a victory at the Dardanelles?

Marder re-examined the Dardanelles/Gallipoli campaign in the period mid-February to late April 1915 – that is, from its inception to when landings took place at Cape Helles and Anzac. Two situations presented themselves to the Navy to force the Straits and, as a consequence, dominate the Bosporus, threaten Constantinople and, it was to be hoped, drive Turkey out of the war. Had, first, the enemy forts been destroyed at the Narrows entrance the enemy minefields might have been swept and the unrestricted fairway opened. The tragedy here lay in the fact that seaplanes were unable to render effective assistance in spotting the fall of shot from the powerful HMS *Queen Elizabeth*. Marder charges that Admiral Sir Sackville Hamilton Carden, then naval commander in chief, dissipated his naval air assents and squandered stocks of ammunition. Had the forts been put out of action a different result would have eventuated. Had, second, the minesweeping force under Commodore Roger Keyes, then Chief of Staff to Admiral Sir John de Robeck, now commander in chief, been properly employed as it could have been after a successful air attack an altogether different result would have occurred at the Narrows. Marder's views on the Dardanelles differed somewhat from what he had written in *From the Dreadnought to Scapa Flow Vol. 2: The War Years to the Eve of Jutland*. Such opinions as he now expressed were based on the so-called Mitchell Report (named for Commodore F.H. Mitchell, president of the committee appointed to investigate the Dardanelles campaign) and on the papers of Group Captain H.A. Williamson, second-in-command and senior flying officer in the carrier *Ark Royal* at the Dardanelles. Captain L.A.K. Boswell, who served in trawlers and helped in fitting out destroyers as sweepers, provided minesweeping retrospectives. This chapter reflected Marder's zeal for finding new sources and seeking out informants (for he was an early practitioner of oral history). Such estimations as to possible Turkish responses in the event of a breakthrough remain speculative. The might-of-beens continue to accumulate. It was a near-run thing – in defeat – and it engrossed Marder to his last days. Marder, we note a little sadly, did not extend his analysis to the autumn of 1915, a pity, for after the Suvla landings attempts by Keyes when he returned to London to argue for a naval attempt proved unsuccessful. Such an attempt would have at least brought higher chances of success. Moreover, had specially designed vessels been made available perhaps running the Narrows might have brought about the desired result. Then again, by this time, Bulgaria had entered the war on the side of the Central Powers and rail communications had been opened between Germany and Constantinople. The Dardanelles was a graveyard of Allied possibilities and efforts, and it took Churchill and Fisher out of the active affairs of the war. Thereafter the Dardanelles Commission inquiry into the origin, inception and conduct of operations refought the episode and reported to Parliament. The conclusion was telling: 'If, however, the result of our investigations should assist in bringing about such an improvement in organization and management as will render impossible a recurrence of events as sad as those with which we have had to deal, the work of the Commission will not have been in vain.'

In his second chapter, 'The Influence of History on Sea Power' – all about the British naval lessons of the First World War – Marder sought to examine and to elucidate 'lessons learned' by the Admiralty and the Navy. We sense that his findings made him sorely disappointed. British failures to learn from the First influenced the conduct of the Second. Such naval staff work and command courses as there were tended to focus on Jutland and to prepare for another great fleet action. Naval aviation was not developed, as it should have been. Bold thinking and forthright criticism were not welcome at the Admiralty, he says. The stringencies of the Ten Year Rule (no major war for ten years) were a formidable factor. We get the feeling in reading this retrospective that despite the appalling losses and failures of the Navy in the First World War reticence and conservatism were the predominant features of naval thinking in the interwar interval. Certainly the establishment of the Naval Staff College at Greenwich in 1919 reflected one lesson happily learned, or as Admiral Lord Beatty, the First Sea Lord, put it at the time, 'Such naval disasters as occurred during the war were the direct result of the lack of sufficient and efficient staff.' An interesting sidelight to this chapter's subject may be given from Marder's own later experience. In the 1970s while researching what became known as *Old Friends, New Enemies*, all about the relationship of the Royal Navy and the Imperial Japanese Navy, Marder visited the naval academy Etajima and found there to his pleasant surprise that his 'The Influence of History on Sea Power' had been translated into Japanese and was required reading by all staff and students. What Japanese naval academy staff and students had learned from their own recent experiences in the First and Second World Wars must have been of interest to Marder. At Etajima the spirit of Nelson lived. As for the Japanese, they regarded Marder as the reincarnation of Admiral Mahan, who in his several books had taken as his theme the influence of sea power upon history.

In examining the Ethiopian crisis of the mid-1930s Marder moved to less speculative matters. He exploited very rich Admiralty papers recently released into the public realm. Here was new material with all sorts of fresh insights into British naval and foreign policy realities. He showed how British naval weakness limited Britain's ability to respond to Italian actions. Overstretched by obligations, notably in the Far East, the Admiralty took the position that really Britain was acting on the assumption of a one-power standard. The Mediterranean needed to be made secure, and Admiral Lord Chatfield, First Sea Lord, was acutely conscious of the folly of creating a danger on the main line of communications to the Far East. The 'moral motive' of dealing with the Italians without a guarantee of French support was a contingent factor. As Marder explains, when the Rhineland crisis occurred in 1936, insufficient naval force existed in Home waters while other obligations had to be met in the form of protecting British trade and preventing a possible German bombardment of British coasts. It was impossible, then, for Britain to fight simultaneously in Asian waters against Japan and in Home waters against Germany unless Britain could count on a friendly, or at least, neutral Italy. Such talk as went on in the well-intentioned League of Nations had to be matched by firm action, but that was impossible against the rising calculation of a hostile alliance of Japan, Italy and Germany. This chapter represents Marder's highest capacities as a writer of historical articles, and in its preparation the work in question had had the benefit of the guidance at the *American Historical Review* of its editor Robert Webb, the English historian, and prominent, judicious anonymous reviewers. The author made slight additions to the original. Marder also included as an appendix his discussion of a naval war plan, much of it concerned with Fleet Air Arm prospects and possibilities.

Chapter 4, 'Winston is Back' – all about the return of Churchill to the Admiralty and his tenure there until relieved by his own nominated successor, A.V. Alexander – will always be of compelling interest. Some readers of this book will consider it 'the main event.' At the same time, by no means is it a piece without criticism, for it is so very much a clear defence of Churchill and almost appears to be so as a partisan effort. One almost feels as if Marder is protesting too much. On the other side of the ledger, however, this chapter is a fine example of the historian proving his case by truly a remarkable body of evidence duly laid on, layer upon layer.

The title comes from the famous message flashed to the fleet upon Churchill's return to the Admiralty on 3 September 1939. Whether that message was greeted with cheers or groans (or perhaps both, in whole or part) is not known. Given what we now know about his domineering actions and meddling in the First World War, even against the powerful Lord Fisher, and what he did to dominate admirals, generals, chiefs of staff and underlings in the Second, it seems entirely unique and unusual that we should be given such a picture of Churchill *not* dominating the Admiralty and *not* interfering with commands at sea. Marder states his position clearly, and he marshals all his facts to sustain his thesis. 'The fact is that, notwithstanding his great influence as First Lord (for better or worse), he did not dominate his professional advisers' (p. 109). The work had first been published as a supplement to *The English Historical Review* in 1972.

Marder defended Churchill against charges of interference. And he defended Admiral Sir Dudley Pound, First Sea Lord at the beginning of the war until his death in October 1943. 'Pound feared neither God, man, nor Winston Churchill.' Marder's view is that he did not interfere with Pound. The story behind this is of interest, and I have written about it more fully in *Historical Dreadnoughts*.

It turns out that Marder's cartographer, Noel Atherton, had been telling his brother-in-law, Sir Eric Seal, all about Marder's work on his 'W.C.' project, with all its intriguing possibilities. Marder – as was his technique – had already opened an extensive correspondence with professional naval and civil servants who knew about those years. Now at the eleventh hour new information was unexpectedly provided. Seal's letter, and subsequent exchange of letters, was something volunteered, out of the blue. Seal had served at the Admiralty before the war; he became Churchill's private secretary at the beginning of the war.

In replying to Seal's first letter, Marder, who did not then have a publisher for the intended article, explained to his new correspondent that his problem was keeping his narrative within word limits. He was struggling with two alternatives: treating the whole story of Churchill at the Admiralty by thinning the various segments, or singling out for adequate treatment what he considered to be the most important part of his tenure – the strategic ideas, influence on naval operations – with Norway as the centre piece. At this stage he had intended an article for the *English Historical Review*. Seal wrote: 'May I say that I think that I am almost the sole survivor of those who were close to Winston as First Lord senior enough to know what it was all about, and I feel a corresponding responsibility.' Seal recounted how Churchill, when reading the draft text, had become disturbed by Stephen Roskill's official *War at Sea*, 'which enlarged upon the undoubted fact that the Admiralty had intervened seriously in Naval operations in the early years and suggested, quite falsely, that the prime factor in this was Churchill's influence as First Lord.' When the text of Roskill's *War at Sea*, Volume 1, came to the Cabinet Committee for approval in advance of publication, Churchill, then prime minister, had become alarmed by Roskill's inference that the First Lord had meddled in naval operations in Norway. Seal had been sent at Churchill's request to examine the Norway campaign records; he had found that there was no undue interference on the part of the First Lord. In the end, the irritated and emotionally exhausted Roskill was obliged to make some changes. Only then was the work released for printing and binding. This was 1954 and Seal had not forgotten. Nor had Roskill.

Seal held that interference from Whitehall was not Churchill's work but the spontaneous action of the Naval Staff and in particular Admiral Sir Dudley Pound and Vice Admiral Sir Tom Phillips.

The plain fact of the matter was that Dudley Pound, who had recently been C in C Med, found it very difficult to keep his hands off the the control of the fleet, and he certainly had more and better information. But much suspicion attached to Winston, partly as an echo of the Dardanelles, and partly because it was generally known that he was always in the War Room, to which he was irresistibly attracted. Being aware of the Dardanelles legend, I was very alert to the problem. I am quite satisfied that Winston took scrupulous care not to transgress the proper limits of Naval and Political responsibility, and not to force his view on any professional decision.

Reading Marder's account we can see Seal's influence on every page. 'Read this account and shudder,' commented the *Navy News*, July 1972, when the article first appeared. 'The factual account of Churchill's forays into professional realms, and the general muddle of the early war months, require the reader to remind himself constantly of Winston's morale-building influence, lest the conclusions become distorted.'

Roskilll read Marder's account and became distressed, not least because Seal's investigation in the files, at Churchill's request, had exposed a story still kept secret in the Cabinet Papers about the official military histories. What alarmed Roskill most was Marder's printing of a damaging segment of the Seal letter to Marder (see pp. 169–70 below and note 136). This accused Roskill of, among other things, 'near malice' towards Churchill, as Seal put it. Roskill, we know from his private papers, consulted his solicitor who remarked that the charge was unquestionably libelous. No legal action was pressed, but Roskill prepared a rebuttal to Marder's attack. This the editor of the *English Historical Review* declined to publish and so it eventually appeared in the more friendly *RUSI Journal*. Roskill disputed the value of Marder's witnesses to history, notably Seal. He thought Seal not a reliable source inasmuch as so much had transpired between Seal's investigation on Churchill's behalf into Roskill's account of the Norway campaign and Marder's revisiting of the same topic. Of this reply, Marder told Peter Kemp, the former Admiralty Librarian, that although he found Roskill's broadside interesting, provocative and amusing in places it told him more about Roskill than of Winston as First Lord. Marder's reply to Roskill's repost will be found below, in his long appendix entitled 'Musings on a Bolt from Olympus.' Marder buttressed his arguments about Churchill with two further and larger points that he felt had escaped historians of the war. These, he said, put Churchill's role and methods in proper historical perspective.

The first was that the Navy was not an expensive toy placed at the disposal of admirals in wartime: it was an instrument of national policy. Churchill had a clear idea of what the Navy could do, and Pound was in accord with this view. The second was that because Churchill was an historian of considerable merit, 'It could not have escaped him that throughout English naval history, when the admirals had been left to their own devices, they had made a mess of things, and that it was only when there had been strong political direction at the top, as in the Seven Years War and the Napoleonic War, that the Navy had really achieved the full measure of its capability.' Marder tipped the scale in favour of the professionals yet at the same time concluded that Churchill did not dominate his professional advisors. Did, therefore, Churchill infuse a new climate of morale into the administration of the Navy? Was this his greatest gift? And was Pound immune to Churchill's independent judgments and schemes that others classified as ill thought out?

Professor Bryan Ranft of Kings College London, a ranking authority on naval historical matters, wondered if there might not have existed a more complex relationship between Churchill and Pound than that of simple dominance of the sailor by the statesmen. Perhaps on occasion one of them might prevail; on other occasions there could be a clash of opinion. Pound's professional pragmatism was bound to clash with Churchill's obsession for offensive action. 'Which view prevailed on particular occasions depended on the totality of circumstances of which personalities were only a part,' suggested Ranft. He went further:

> Disagreement between such eminent scholars raises important questions of historiography. To what extent does the available evidence permit precise answers to the matters in dispute? What different criteria should be applied to the interpretation of official documents and personal papers, and, most important of all, to contemporary historians, what measure of reliability can be applied to the reminiscences of those once employed in great matters?

Marder's final study, the main event, offered the first fully documented published account of the British attack on the French warships at Oran. The whole episode is an extraordinary episode, or series of episodes. No dramatist could ever have conceived of it. The human dimensions run deep and are charged with pathos and sympathy. There is the sense of the inevitable, too. If the end result was never in doubt to Churchill, to almost everyone else the whole was problematic, fraught with difficulty and even regarded as morally reprehensible. Marder had always wondered if a more skilful handling of negotiations might have avoided all the bloodshed and the bitterness. 'It was an absolutely bloody business to shoot up those Frenchmen who showed the greatest gallantry,' commented Admiral Sir James Somerville of Force H which steamed from Gibraltar to execute orders from London (if last attempt naval diplomatic relations with the French admiral failed, which they did). Did Churchill really have realistic fears about Germany using the French warships? Marder makes a convincing case that the respective governments and their respective naval negotiators could not avoid the calamity. Churchill was ruthless. Perhaps he exaggerated the danger of the French fleet falling into enemy hands. He acted under the pressure of circumstances and at a time of great British weakness. Britain's fortunes and prestige were then at their lowest ebb. The attack was 'a cruel necessity.'

In all, Marder provided a well-proportioned analysis of the diplomatic background with a detailed account by the sailors on the spot. Churchill, in his history of the event, described the arc of the story as a Greek tragedy and in his analysis Marder follows equally strongly. Here is Marder at his best – a master of his sources, specific in his definition of the historian's tasks, organized in his narrative, and capable of telling a story with conviction and appeal. Incidentally, it may be noted that this work on Oran was followed on by another dynamic work, this time in book form: *Operation Menace': The Dakar Expedition and the Dudley North Affair* (1976). After this he turned to his study of the Royal Navy and the Imperial Japanese Navy.

Marder died in 1980 in his seventieth year. He did not see *Old Friends, New Enemies* in print. His friend Peter Kemp, naval officer and historian of note, paid him the great compliment of calling Marder the supreme historian. What Kemp identified in Marder, many others had witnessed first hand: first, Marder's great courage in redoing that segment of *From the Dreadnought to Scapa Flow* lost to the incinerator in consequence of janitorial error, and, second, Marder's great happiness in his work. Kemp stated that Marder demonstrated a marked modesty, and he was right, for modesty was the handmaiden of Marder's simplicity of approach and his insistence on forming no preconceived notions, let alone conclusions. He had opposed military historians 'of the drum and bugle type' and had sought something much more comprehensive, something more substantial. He liked to cite Homer's 'After the event any fool can be wise.'

Right to the end Marder defended his historical method of using details and particulars to sustain a powerful narrative. In his journal articles and book chapters he was necessarily more constrained, owing to circumstances. Resisting any desire to tilt at historical windmills or take on the theories of other historians, Marder stuck to the historical records. Of course, he was not faultless in the selection of materials, and on occasion he failed to weigh correctly the testimony of various informants; in certain cases or episodes, he may be said to have gone overboard by the needless recounting of supporting evidence. In disputatious matters he liked to have the last word. But these, his critics noted, did not appreciably weaken his great work. It is a fascinating fact that those who endeavour to rework his historical corpus deal almost exclusively with only the first three volumes of *From the Dreadnought to Scapa Flow* and then only on specific aspects. The feud between Marder and Roskill may provide titillations for the naval historians who know those times or have followed these by reputation. But it is not the essential factor in how we judge historians of Marder's elevated class or Roskill's either. Roskill had put it best, in 1966, when he wrote graciously about Marder: 'fortune had smiled on the Royal Navy when a scholar of Marder's distinctions and abilities had come along to write its history.' That is why Marder still commands our attention.

[Sources: Reviews of *From the Dardanelles to Oran* include Paul Halpern, 'Naval Topics, 1915–1940,' *Reviews in European History*, September 1976; Bryan Ranft, 'Naval Historians at War, '*RUSI Journal*, March 1975; and Stephen Roskill, 'Naval Engagements,' *Times Literary Supplement*, 13 December 1974. Marder's letter to Geoffrey Hunt, 31 March 1971, is in the Marder papers, University of California, Irvine, as is the Seal-Marder correspondence of 1971 on the Pound-Churchill relationship. Stephen Roskill's rejoinder to Marder's 'Winston is Back' (as it first appeared in the *English Historical Review*, Supplement 5, 1972) is published as 'Marder, Churchill, and the Admiralty,' *RUSI Journal*, December 1972. See also, Roskill, *Churchill and the Admirals* (1977). Discussion of differences between Marder and Roskill (and also Roskill's difficulties with Churchill over the Norway campaign and other naval operations) may be followed in Barry Gough, *Historical Dreadnoughts: Arthur Marder, Stephen Roskill and Battles for Naval History* (Barnsley: Seaforth, 2010). This last contains a comprehensive bibliography of Marder's works and, necessarily, one of his sparring partner Roskill.]

BARRY GOUGH,
Victoria, BC, Canada

Preface

THE five chapters in this volume represent something old, something new. A short version of the first, 'The Dardanelles Revisited: Further Thoughts on the Naval Prelude', was read at the Conference on Naval Studies at the University of Western Ontario in March 1972. It has been printed in A. M. J. Hyatt (ed.), *Dreadnought to Polaris: Maritime Strategy since Mahan* (Toronto, Copp Clark, 1973), pp. 30–46, 121–3. I have revised and considerably expanded this essay on one of the most fascinating 'ifs' of twentieth-century history.

Chapter 2, 'The Influence of History on Sea Power: the Royal Navy and the Lessons of 1914–1918', constituted, in its original form, my presidential address at the annual meeting of the Pacific Coast Branch of the American Historical Association in Santa Barbara, California, August 1972. It appeared in the *Pacific Historical Review*, xlvi (Nov. 1972), 413–43. I have reworked and expanded that version. The subject, I must say, is a difficult one and raises large issues which do not lend themselves to easy answers.

Chapter 3, 'The Royal Navy and the Ethiopian Crisis of 1935–1936', originally appeared in the *American Historical Review*, lxxv (June 1970), 1327–56. I have added some new material. The subject is one that had intrigued me ever since those far-off days in the England of 1935–6, when I was working on my doctoral thesis. For a generation and more I wondered about the degree to which naval considerations affected, and handicapped, the makers of British foreign policy during the crisis. I accordingly lost no time in examining the relevant documents when they were made available to me in the later sixties.

Chapter 4, '"Winston is Back": Churchill at the Admiralty, 1939–1940', was first printed as Supplement 5 of the *English Historical Review* (Longman, 1972). Having years ago studied Churchill as First Lord of the Admiralty in his first tenure of that office (1911–15), I was curious as to how he had comported himself as First Lord a second time a quarter of a century later. My *EHR* study has been enlarged somewhat, particularly through the addition of an appendix answering certain criticisms.

Chapter 5, 'Oran, 3 July 1940: Mistaken Judgement, Tragic Misunderstanding, or Cruel Necessity?', is an entirely new study. The subject had haunted me ever since the event itself, and I was determined some day to get to the bottom of it, or as closely as I could.

All five chapters deal with more or less controversial subjects, which is one reason why I have so enjoyed the research and, but for the sad episode of Oran, the writing.

I am profoundly grateful to my old friends Vice-Admiral Sir Peter Gretton, the late Captain John Creswell, and Lieutenant-Commander P. K. Kemp for reading the chapters in various states of completion and making all manner of constructive comment, and to all my informants (they are mentioned in the first footnote of each chapter), who provided the sort of information that one cannot find in documents or books. At the same time I must absolve them, as well as the three readers, from any responsibility for the opinions expressed in the text or for any errors that remain.

I owe a special vote of thanks to those who made important primary source material available: Dr. Brian Bond (typescript copy of the Pownall diaries of 1935–6), Lady Edwards (the diaries of Admiral Sir Ralph Edwards), Mrs. J. H. Godfrey (the personal papers of Admiral J. H. Godfrey), the second Lord Keyes (the papers of Admiral of the Fleet Lord Keyes), Mr. and Mrs. Stephen Lloyd (extracts from the Neville Chamberlain papers bearing on Oran), Mrs. Donald McLachlan (Donald McLachlan's records of his interviews with scores of senior naval officers and others for his projected biography of Sir Dudley Pound), Commander J. A. F. Somerville (the papers of Admiral of the Fleet Sir James Somerville), Lady Seal and the late Sir Eric Seal (the latter's unpublished autobiography), Dr. Friedrich Stahl, Head of the Bundesarchiv-Militärarchiv, and Kapitän zur See Dr. Friedrich Forstmeier, Head of the Militärgeschichtliches Forschungsamt, with the assistance of Leutnant, FGN, Jürgen Heibei (World War II records of the German Ministry of Marine), Mr. Warren Tute (Admiral Gensoul's post-Oran reports), and Dr. Weinandy, of the Foreign Office of the Federal German Republic (Wangenheim correspondence of March–April 1915).

I also wish to express my warm thanks to the following: the University of California, Irvine, for grants which have made the research painless; Mr. Noel Atherton, for his skilful preparation of the charts, with the able assistance of Captain John Creswell; Rear-Admiral P. N. Buckley, Head of Naval Historical Branch and Naval Librarian, Ministry of Defence, for making certain material available, and, together with Commander R. C. Burton, Mr. J. D. Lawson, Captain Donald Macintyre, and Miss V. Riley of his staff, for handling a flow of queries with dispatch and good humour; and, similarly, as regards queries, Mr. A. D. Childs, Deputy Librarian of Churchill College, and Miss Angela Raspin, the Archivist,

Mr. A. W. H. Pearsall, Custodian of Manuscripts, the National Maritime Museum, and Dr. E. K. Timings, Head of the Search Department, and Messrs. N. E. Evans and Michael Roper, of the Public Record Office; Messrs. Roger Berry and George Raulin, of the University of California, Irvine, Library staff, and my colleague Professor Henri Diament, for being helpful in so many ways; Mrs. Mary Z. Pain, for putting at my disposal the late Commander M. G. Saunders's notes for a book on the French Fleet from Oran to Toulon; Dr. Jun Tsunoda, the distinguished Japanese historian, for information on the Japanese Fleet at the time of the Ethiopian Crisis; Mr. Ludovic Kennedy, for sharing some research findings from his forthcoming book on the *Bismarck*; Miss Cathy Smith, the Incomparable, for once more waving a wand over my hieroglyphs and producing a neat typescript; and Miss Elizabeth Knight and Miss Helen McKenzie, of the staff of Oxford University Press, London, the former for acting as midwife to the present book, and the latter for her willing secretarial services.

Grateful acknowledgement is made for permission to quote from the copyright material indicated: Cassell and Co. Ltd. and Houghton Mifflin Company, from Winston Churchill, *The Second World War*, Vols. i, *The Gathering Storm*, and ii, *Their Finest Hour*; the Clarendon Press, from Admiral Sir Herbert Richmond, *Statesmen and Sea Power*; the second Lord Ironside, from *The Ironside Diaries, 1937–1940* (Constable & Co., Ltd.); Eyre & Spottiswoode (Publishers) Ltd. and E. P. Dutton & Co., Inc., from *The Naval Memoirs of Admiral of the Fleet Sir Roger Keyes*; Her Majesty's Stationery Office, from Captain S. W. Roskill, *The War at Sea*; Mr. Willoughby Pownall-Gray and Leo Cooper Ltd., from Brian Bond (ed.), *Chief of Staff*; and the United States Naval Institute, Annapolis, Maryland, from Rear-Admiral Paul Auphan and Jacques Mordal, *The French Navy in World War II*.

Transcripts of Crown-copyright records in the Public Record Office appear by permission of the Controller of H.M. Stationery Office.

ARTHUR J. MARDER

Irvine, California
August 1973

Abbreviations used in the text

(whether official or in common Service usage)

AA	anti-aircraft
ACNS	Assistant Chief of Naval Staff
A/S	anti-submarine
C-in-C	Commander-in-Chief
CID	Committee of Imperial Defence
CIGS	Chief of the Imperial General Staff
CNS	Chief of Naval Staff (First Sea Lord)
CO	Commanding Officer
COS	Chief of Staff to a Flag Officer Commanding, *or* Chiefs of Staff
DA/SW	Director of Anti-Submarine Warfare Division
DCNS	Deputy Chief of Naval Staff
DDOD(H)	Deputy Director of Operations Division (Home)
DNI	Director of Naval Intelligence
DNO	Director of Naval Ordnance
D of P	Director of Plans
NID	Naval Intelligence Division
RA	Royal Artillery
RAF	Royal Air Force
RM	Royal Marines
RN	Royal Navy
RNVR	Royal Naval Volunteer Reserve
S/M	submarine
VCNS	Vice Chief of Naval Staff
V/S	visual signal
W/T	wireless telegraphy

Contents

PREFACE   *page* vii

CHAPTER I. *The Dardanelles Revisited: Further Thoughts on the
Naval Prelude*   I

Scope of the chapter—The two fundamental errors preceding the operation—
The Turkish defences at the Dardanelles—Torpedoes—Floating mines—Guns
v. forts—The importance of air spotting—*Ark Royal* and her seaplanes—Their
misuse on 4 March—Air spotting for the *Queen Elizabeth*, 5 March—Post-
mortem on air spotting—The Turkish minefields—Failure of the minesweepers
—The reasons—De Robeck relieves Carden—The attack on the Narrows forts,
18 March—Line II of the minefields—The state of Turkish morale—De
Robeck's initial feelings—He changes his mind, 22 March—Churchill appeals
to de Robeck—His later criticism of the Admiral—Keyes and Sandford see hope
in the new minesweeping force—Effectiveness of the destroyer sweepers on
25–27 April—If the fleet had tried again in mid-April—Supposing the fleet had
anchored off Constantinople—How the Turks and Germans visualized the
scenario—The lost opportunity of April.

CHAPTER II. *The Influence of History on Sea Power: the Royal
Navy and the Lessons of 1914–1918*   33

Purpose of the chapter—The 'Young Turks' look forward to post-war reform—
Post-war committees—The work of the Naval Staff College—The Tactical
School is founded—The *Naval War Manual*—Post-war reforms—Improvement
in inter-Service co-operation—Neglect of the larger problems and lessons of
the war—The convoy system in the inter-war period—Explanation of the indifferent attitude towards convoy—Admiralty views on convoy are summed
up by the Parliamentary and Financial Secretary in 1935—Convoy developments in 1937–8—Wartime results of the pre-war attitude towards convoy—
The role of naval aircraft in convoy is forgotten between the wars—Unaware-
ness of the 'law of convoy size'—The Navy is unprepared for U-boat night
surface attacks—The question of convoy escort dispositions—The inter-war
obsession with a fleet action—Q-ships are revived in the Second World War—
Magnetic mines—Paravanes—The wastefulness of the Northern Mine Barrage
—Aircraft in minesweeping—The sorry state of Scapa's defences in 1939—
The lag in the development of combined operations—The tactical lessons of
the First World War are not completely absorbed—The problem of over-
centralization at the Admiralty—The failure to develop naval aviation—The
battleship complex and the Fleet Air Arm—Reasons for the neglect of the
lessons of 1914–18—Conclusions.

CHAPTER III. *The Royal Navy and the Ethiopian Crisis of
1935–1936*   64

Purpose of the chapter—The Services enter the Ethiopian picture—The Chiefs
of Staff warn against precipitating hostilities with Italy—Their admonitions
guide the Foreign Office—The emergency Cabinet of 22 August orders precautionary measures—Admiralty policy on sending reinforcements to the
Mediterranean—The problem of Malta's vulnerability—The Mediterranean

Fleet is sent to Alexandria—Hoare addresses the League Assembly, 11 September—Naval preparations are intensified during September—Purpose of the build-up in the Mediterranean—The Italians begin the invasion of Ethiopia, 3 October—The League Assembly votes sanctions—Failure of attempts to effect a military détente—Fear of an Italian 'mad-dog act'—Chatfield, the First Sea Lord: characteristics, influence, ideas—Comparative figures for the British and Italian fleets in the Mediterranean and Red Sea—Confidence of the Admiralty and Mediterranean Fleet—The C-in-C, Fisher, and his Chief of Staff, Pound—The naval war plan—Fisher is prepared to close the Suez Canal—The Admiralty opposes a strong sanctions policy—Britain's Far Eastern responsibilities and the Japanese threat—The fear of sustaining serious losses and damage in a war with Italy—The Navy and the air threat—The efficiency of the Fleet is a factor—The Admiralty are unable to count on active French naval and air co-operation—The effect of the Rhineland Crisis—Admiralty pressure on the Foreign Office to ease the naval situation—The state of war readiness ends, June–July 1936—Post-mortem: Was 'faint-heartedness' responsible for Britain's sanctionist position?—The principal lessons of the crisis for the Navy.

Appendix. A note on the Naval War Plan.   101

CHAPTER IV.   *'Winston is Back': Churchill at the Admiralty,
1939-40*   105

Churchill returns to the Admiralty, 3 September 1939—He stimulates the Admiralty and the Fleet—Love of job—Rights and responsibilities—Relations with his professional advisers—Churchill and Pound—Churchill's relations with the sailors afloat—His interest in personnel questions—and defensive devices: dummy ships, the 'Naval Wire Barrage', the antidote to magnetic mines—Churchill and capital-ship construction policy—Appreciates importance of trade defence—Attitude towards convoy—Supports a Northern Mine Barrage—Churchill and the statistics of U-boat kills—He presses for the use of southern Irish bases—His Mediterranean policy—His anxiety over the defences of Scapa—The problem of the Home Fleet's base—His itch for the offensive—He secures approval for 'trench-cutting tanks'—Churchill and 'Operation Royal Marine'—His role in naval strategy and operations—Takes a keen interest in the *Graf Spee* operation—His decisive intervention in the *Altmark* operation—Churchill and 'Operation Catherine'—His Baltic strategy: the problem of the Swedish iron ore—His ideas and initiatives in the Norwegian campaign—The bizarre Keyes *entr'acte*—A balance sheet of the campaign—An analysis of Churchill's role in the campaign—The Navy's faith in a warship's AA defences—Churchill's alleged interference with the naval side of the campaign—A reply to his critics—Churchill becomes Prime Minister, 10 May—and maintains his profound interest in the naval war—A summary of his time at the Admiralty.

Appendix. Musings on a Bolt from Olympus.   173

CHAPTER V.   *Oran, 3 July 1940: Mistaken Judgement, Tragic
Misunderstanding, or Cruel Necessity?*   179

Interest of the subject—The French military collapse, June 1940—The French Navy remains a powerful force—Anglo-French naval co-operation—The vital importance to the British of the disposition of the French Fleet—The problem is under serious discussion from 7 June—Assurances are sought from the

French—The French contemplate an armistice with Germany—Reynaud's telegram to Churchill, 15 June—The War Cabinet's reply, 16 June—The dramatic offer of complete union—A new French Government is formed under Pétain—It asks the Germans for armistice terms and assures the British *re* the Fleet, 17 June—Churchill's last appeal—Darlan's views and volte-face—Further assurances as regards the Fleet—Pound and Alexander confer with Darlan in Bordeaux, 18 June—and are 'apparently satisfied'— French Admiralty instructions to the Fleet, 18 June—Hitler's 'principles' in framing an armistice—The desiderata of the German Naval War Staff— Hitler meets Mussolini in Munich, 17–18 June—The armistice negotiations, 21–22 June: Article 8 and the French counterproposals—The British Ambassador precipitately leaves Bordeaux—as does the Naval Mission: significance —The War Cabinet's discussion on the 22nd—Final appeals to Darlan—The three meetings of the War Cabinet during 24 June: a decision is postponed— The concerted attempt to determine French naval opinion—The intensified Anglophobia in Bordeaux—French naval grievances: their ships in British ports and at Alexandria—Churchill's Commons speech of 25 June— '*Contrôle*', a problem in semantics—The Darlan factor in British calculations— Churchill sees important political advantages in a bold policy—American support is needed—The decisive War Cabinet, 27 June—Churchill is the driving force behind 'Catapult'—The attitude of Alexander, Pound, and Phillips— The Joint Planners have no enthusiasm for 'Catapult'—But the Chiefs of Staff back the War Cabinet, 30 June—The Germans accept a modification of Article 8—British naval preparations—Somerville is given command of Force H—He has no premonition of a grand tragedy—He confers with his officers at Gibraltar—and communicates their reservations to the Admiralty —The four 'most secret' Admiralty messages of 2 July—Somerville discusses his plans with his officers—Force H steams towards Oran, 2–3 July—The destroyer *Foxhound* is sent on ahead—French naval strength at Mers-el-Kébir and Oran—Pen portraits of Holland and Gensoul—The Holland– Gensoul sparring—Gensoul agrees to receive Holland—Why Gensoul had changed his mind—The discussion in the *Dunkerque*—Reflections on the events of 3 July—Somerville opens fire—The action—Escape and chase of the *Strasbourg*—The torpedo bombers attack the *Dunkerque*, 6 July—The surprise seizure of the French ships in British Home ports, 3 July—The unpleasant aftermath—Cunningham and Force X at Alexandria, 3–4 July— British policy post-3 July *re* French warships—The *Rigault de Genouilly* is sunk, 4 July—and the *Richelieu* damaged at Dakar, 8 July—The performance of the fleet at Mers-el-Kébir—Somerville is sickened by the action—Admiral North relieves his feelings—and is put down by the Admiralty—Churchill reports to the House of Commons, 4 July—British press and naval reaction to Mers-el-Kébir—Reactions in Vichy—The Joint Planners and Service Chiefs report on the 'implications of French hostility'—Mers-el-Kébir embarrasses the British war effort—The German reaction—The gains to Britain, naval and moral—The French case—How the situation looked to the British leaders *at the time*—The factor of German capabilities and intentions—Were the misunderstandings tragic?—The real tragedy of Mers-el-Kébir.

INDEX   289

List of illustrations

Ranks and appointments are those held at the dates mentioned, and the photographs, where not precisely dated, are from the same period

Winston Churchill, First Lord of the Admiralty, 14 October 1939   *Frontispiece*

facing page

I Aboard HMS *Triad* at the Dardanelles, 17 October 1915. *Left to right*: Commodore Roger Keyes (Chief of Staff to de Robeck), Acting Vice-Admiral Sir John de Robeck (C-in-C, Eastern Mediterranean Squadron), and General Sir Ian Hamilton (C-in-C, Mediterranean Expeditionary Force)   14

IIa Admiral Sir Ernle Chatfield, C-in-C, Atlantic Fleet, 1929–30   15

 b Admiral Sir William Fisher, C-in-C, Mediterranean Fleet, 1932–6   15

III Winston Churchill, First Lord of the Admiralty, with King George VI and Queen Elizabeth, and Neville Chamberlain, meeting relatives of men of HMS *Exeter* who were killed in the River Plate action, when men of the *Exeter* and *Ajax* marched through London, *en route* to the Guildhall, 23 February 1940   46

IV Admiral of the Fleet Sir Dudley Pound, First Sea Lord and Chief of Naval Staff, between (*left to right*) Air Chief Marshal Sir Cyril Newall (Chief of Air Staff) and General Sir Edmund Ironside (Chief of Imperial General Staff), arriving for a War Cabinet meeting at No. 10 Downing Street, 27 September 1939   47

Va Admiral Sir Andrew Cunningham, C-in-C, Mediterranean Fleet, 1939–42   238

 b Captain Cedric Holland, Commanding HMS *Ark Royal*, 1940–1   238

VI Vice-Admiral Sir James Somerville, Commanding 'Force H', 1940–2, in his cabin with his Siamese cat 'Figaro', who always accompanied Somerville on board his ships   239

VIIa Vice-Admiral Marcel Gensoul, C-in-C, Atlantic Fleet (Force de Raid), 1938–40   270

 b Admiral of the Fleet François Darlan, C-in-C, French Fleet, 1939–40; Minister of Marine, 1940–2   270

 c General view of Mers-el-Kébir shortly before 3 July   270

xvi   *List of illustrations*

VIIIa The *Bretagne* on fire after the bombardment and beginning
to sink   271

  b Admiral Gensoul at the funeral of the 'victims' of the action
at Mers-el-Kébir, held on 5 July 1940 (see p. 275)   271

Illustration in text

The 'round robin' from the Captain and officers of the
Dunkerque sent to Admiral Somerville, July/August 1940,
after the action at Mers-el-Kébir   277

Acknowledgements

The author and publishers are grateful to the following for their kind permission to
reproduce the illustrations in this book:

Lord Chatfield, II*a*; Mrs. Cedric Holland, V*b*; Imperial War Museum, I, VI; Musée de
la Marine, Paris, VII, VIII; Radio Times Hulton Picture Library, frontispiece, III,
IV, V*a*.

The letter on page 277 is reproduced by permission of Commander John Somerville.

List of Charts

at end of book

---

1. The Dardanelles and Sea of Marmora: February–April 1915

2. The Mediterranean: 1935–40

3. The North Sea and the Baltic

4. Mers-el-Kébir: 3 July 1940: Positions of French ships at start of action (5.54 p.m.) and subsequent movements

5. Mers-el-Kébir: 3 July 1940: Force H and escape of the *Strasbourg*

Chapter One

The Dardanelles Revisited

Further Thoughts on the
Naval Prelude[1]

(Chart 1)

THIS chapter is not concerned with the genesis of the Dardanelles campaign (although I consider it the one imaginative
strategic idea of the war on the Allied side) or the preliminary
moves. Its scope is the naval facets of the opening phase of the
operation, from the initial bombardment of 19 February to 25
April, when the Army took over the principal role, with the thrust
on what went wrong and why, and some second-guessing on
what might have been done. The naval side of the Dardanelles is
second only to Jutland in the longevity and passion of the controversy which it has aroused among naval historians. It must always
be a fascinating subject, if a tragic one from the British point of

[1] This essay is based on fresh thinking since I prepared volume ii of my *From the
Dreadnought to Scapa Flow* (1965), stimulated by materials that were either unknown
or unavailable to me then, more especially the massive and highly significant
'Mitchell Report' (copy in the Naval Historical Library, Ministry of Defence), in which
the essential facts are lost in a mass of verbiage and a faulty layout (*Report of Committee Appointed to Investigate the Attacks Delivered on and the Enemy Defences of the
Dardanelles Straits, 1919*, C.B. 1550, 10 Oct. 1919, but printed in April 1921: Commodore F. H. Mitchell was President of the Committee); the de Robeck MSS. (Churchill
College, Cambridge), which proved somewhat disappointing (there is little new
material of consequence *from* de Robeck); and the unpublished memoirs of Group-
Captain H. A. Williamson (Churchill College), which will be cited without reference
to title or pagination. Additionally, I have profited greatly from a fresh examination
of the *Proceedings of the Dardanelles Commission*, and from an extensive correspondence
with Williamson and Captain L. A. K. Boswell, R.N. Williamson, a pioneer in naval
aviation, was Second-in-Command and Senior Flying Officer in the seaplane carrier
HMS *Ark Royal* during the critical first weeks of the operation. Boswell, who served
at the Dardanelles in 1915 (he was a midshipman in HMS *Irresistible*, landed three
times with demolition parties, served as a volunteer in a minesweeping trawler, and
assisted in fitting the destroyers as minesweepers), has made a careful study of the
naval side. Air Chief Marshal Sir Christopher Courtney and Marshals of the Royal
Air Force Sir William Dickson and Sir John Slessor sent me helpful notes on the air
aspects of this chapter.

view, for there are so many points and aspects on which there can never be any cast-iron verdicts.

Two fundamental errors preceded the actual commencement of the operation. The naval bombardment of the outer defences of the Dardanelles by the battle cruiser *Inflexible* on 3 November 1914 did scant damage, but it prompted the Turks immediately to accelerate their programme for strengthening the coast defences of the Straits by multiplying the gun defences, laying additional minefields, adding searchlights, and so forth. The second basic error was the conception that slow minesweeping trawlers could clear a passage up to and through the Narrows to enable the fleet to reach the Marmora. This will be treated in detail below. Many critics at the time and since have asserted that the gravest error of all was the conception of a purely naval enterprise, which stemmed from the badly worded War Council recommendation of 13 January 1915 (the Navy should 'bombard and take the Gallipoli Peninsula, with Constantinople as its objective'), which was accepted by the Admiralty on 28 January. It is a fact that the Navy would have preferred to wait until troops were available and a combined assault could be mounted. 'From Lord Fisher [First Sea Lord] downwards every naval officer in the Admiralty who is in the secret believes that the Navy cannot take [i.e. pass?] the Dardanelles without troops. The First Lord [Churchill] still professes to believe that they can do it with ships . . .'[2] But *was there* a need for troops? The essential purpose of this chapter is to show that the Navy might well have succeeded by itself in forcing the Straits and knocking the Turks out of the war. The first opportunity presented itself early in March, the second and more promising, in mid-April.

The Turkish defences at the Dardanelles consisted of four principal elements: the forts, the minefields (and minefield and mobile howitzer batteries), torpedoes, and floating mines. The last two were of secondary importance, though the moored mines exercised an influence on Vice-Admiral de Robeck's decisions after 18 March. The torpedo defences of the Straits consisted of only three 18-inch tubes (two torpedoes available for each tube) housed in a shed on the pier at Kilid Bahr; only one of them could fire a torpedo across the mile width of the Narrows (the other two, barely half-way). 'The tubes at Kilid Bahr were, however, never located by the seaplanes and reports were frequently being received that more torpedo tubes were being placed. There was, therefore, no *certainty*

[2] Lieutenant-Colonel M. P. A. Hankey (Secretary to the War Council) to A. J. Balfour, 10 Feb. 1915, Balfour MSS., Add. MS. 49703 (British Museum).

as to the strength of the torpedo defences and no apparent reason why, by the use of concrete under-water positions, numbers of hidden and completely protected torpedo positions should not have existed. Moreover, few ships had nets; these were at best an uncertain protection and a great danger to the propellers underway.'[3] This uncertainty was not relieved by the fact that the Turks fired no torpedoes during the operation.

It was known that the Turks had about 35 Ramis-type floating mines (the explosive was 165 lb. of TNT). They sent 16 of them down on 1, 7, and 17 March without achieving any success. On 18 March a small steamer was standing by just above the Narrows with some 20 mines on board, but none was laid. The Navy had picked up a sample and discovered that a light surface sweep could deal with them by chopping off the float, and so sinking the mine. 'It was considered quite possible that the Turks might wait until the Fleet was committed to a break through and then launch floating mines in large numbers. . . . It is difficult to estimate what would have been the effect of a hundred or so floating mines amongst the Fleet once committed to a break through.'[4] It is, in fact, likely that they would all have been decapitated by the surface sweeps before they reached the battleships. The losses on 18 March, we shall see, were attributed to floating mines.

This left the forts and the minefields. The intention at first was to overcome the forts with naval gunfire, *then* sweep up the mines, and thereby open the way for the fleet to reach Constantinople. A naval bombardment on 25 February silenced the forts at each side of the entrance to the Straits. Then came the bombardment of the intermediate defences in the first days of March: the thirty-six mobile howitzers (mainly 5·9-inch) and twenty-four mortars (mostly 8·2-inch). Incapable of hitting a moving target, their function was to hit any anchored ships they could reach, thus keeping them on the move. They were not intended to protect the minefields, which task was assigned to the minefield batteries (see below). Although the bombardment of the intermediate defences

[3] Mitchell Report, p. 493. But the Report states (p. 494): 'The main value of the torpedo defences was their indirect influence in deterring a rush by the Fleet. In actual fact, however, the Fleet was prepared to accept the risk and the torpedo defences were not the cause of the Fleet's change of plan [22 March] . . . .'

[4] ibid., p. 491. The Turks had no factory or know-how to make such additional torpedo tubes as suggested by the Mitchell Report, or to make the hundred or so floating mines. Little help could be counted on from Germany, since transmission of war *matériel* to combatants through neutral countries was forbidden. (Hence the inability, too, of the Turks to get more Krupp shell for the forts, on which see below.) Once Bulgaria was in the war (October 1915), they could get what they liked, of course.

was not decisive, on 5 March the fleet initiated the next phase, whose objective was the silencing of the forts at the Narrows with their fixed batteries of heavy guns. The most modern were 35-cal. hand-loaded Krupp guns of 1885: two 14-inch and six 9·4-inch on the European side, and three 14-inch and eight 9·4-inch on the Asiatic side. They took 4–5 minutes to load by hand, compared to 45 seconds for the 12-inch guns of the battleships, loaded by hydraulic machinery, and 10 seconds for their 6-inch. The ships had the further advantage that, whereas the elementary fire-control system of the forts was not designed to hit a moving target, the ships accurately allowed for the current and their movement between salvoes. In short, the improved gun-power in recent years was entirely to the advantage of the fleet in a duel with these forts.

At the same time the Fleet, which had concentrated before the war on gunnery and torpedo practices for a fleet action, worked under certain disadvantages, as it had never practised firing at shore targets (and did not do so until the 1920s). Also, although the fire of the Turkish mobile howitzer batteries from concealed positions on both sides of the Straits, abreast of the ships, was never more than an irritation, by preventing the ships from anchoring it made accurate fire more difficult. This, in turn, necessitated the expenditure of more ammunition than could be spared. In the next place, only direct hits could destroy the guns of a fort: the possibility of achieving this at 12,000 yards was estimated by the Mitchell Committee at no better than 2 to 3 per cent. This, too, pointed to the need for a plentiful supply of ammunition that was not available before April. Finally, the capital ships themselves, apart from the dreadnought *Queen Elizabeth* and the battle cruiser *Inflexible*, were old, pre-dreadnought units, not fitted with the most modern gunnery appliances, and with crews composed mainly of reservists and young ratings.

The Narrows forts could have been silenced by ships attacking from inside the Straits by direct fire.[5] The gunlayers could see the target but required air spotting to correct the range, which was not possible from a ship, or ground position, at right angles to the line of fire. The alternative was to attack the forts by ships firing over the Gallipoli peninsula—that is, indirect fire—with a flank-spotting battleship inside the Straits, in sight of the forts, to spot for range, and an aircraft to spot for direction. (Using a battleship inside the Straits to spot for range was a refinement, but it was not

[5] Direct fire, for the uninitiated, is when you can see the target; indirect fire is when you cannot. The former, generally speaking, is flat trajectory fire; the latter generally means high-angle fire.

necessary, as an aircraft could give both range and direction corrections.) Firing over the peninsula was the more promising way, since the weaknesses of the gun defences at the Narrows lay in their vulnerability to indirect fire over the peninsula, though only the flagship, the *Queen Elizabeth*, had sufficient range for this. Firing from the direction of Gaba Tepe, she could bombard the forts with accuracy, given *efficient aircraft spotting and sufficient ammunition*, since she could anchor outside the range of the howitzers. The guns of the forts, designed on the expectation of attack from inside the Straits, would present almost a broadside target to indirect fire over the peninsula. This was 'about four times as favourable as the "end on" target presented when attacking from inside the Straits. The forts were further unprotected against an attack of this description from the rear.'[6] The European forts were particularly vulnerable.

With indirect firing, as in the case of a ship off Gaba Tepe firing over the peninsula, air spotting for direction was highly desirable. The gunlayer could not see the target, and had to lay his gun on some object believed to be in the right direction, and then shift by sight-setting to right, or to left, as necessary, when he received corrections from the spotting aircraft. This elementary consideration must have been well known to any competent gunnery specialist, yet no tests or practices of battleships firing with aircraft spotting were carried out during the seventeen days between the arrival of the seaplane carrier *Ark Royal* at Tenedos on 17 February with six seaplanes and the time of the *Queen Elizabeth* firing over the peninsula on 5 March. Group-Captain Williamson stresses that the detachment of a battleship or two and a few gunnery officers to carry out essential spotting tests on a shore target, for which an unoccupied Aegean island could have been used, would not have impaired fleet efficiency or operations in any way. Such exercises were all the more necessary because the seaplanes were so few and could be used only in favourable weather. (They were generally unable to rise in any but smooth water.) The Aegean weather in March was a definite limitation, although, as it happens, four of the first five days of the month had perfect flying weather. 'The heavy and cumbersome floats over-taxed the low-powered engines, and we were constantly pre-occupied with keeping our machines in the air', writes Williamson. Also, the wireless gear was somewhat unreliable. But such disadvantages were largely counterbalanced by the enemy having no aircraft and no anti-aircraft guns, whereas usually the seaplanes were able to fly at

[6] Mitchell Report, p. 78.

sufficient height to be untroubled by rifle fire. In addition to tests it was equally important to conserve flying hours for the all-important bombardment of the Narrows forts, especially in view of the many warnings of the limitations of the seaplanes. Machines were not getting off, or were unable to reach a satisfactory altitude, or were being forced to return with engine trouble.

But, as noted, there were no spotting tests to see what the seaplanes could do for the ships, and to ensure that their spotting would be reliable by correcting any problems that might be uncovered.[7] And instead of expending flying hours in essential work and reaching top efficiency in spotting, there were reconnaissance flights which contributed nothing to the success of the campaign. This policy culminated on 4 March, when, on the Admiral's instructions, the *Ark Royal* (she had moved up to the Dardanelles entrance) had aircraft flying for seven hours of precious flying time over the demolition parties, supported by marines, which had been put ashore after the outer forts had been silenced. This resulted in most of the aircraft being temporarily out of action when most required. It was 'an unnecessary and useless job', Williamson claims. 'The whole affair was a waste of time and effort', and the result was fiasco on the crucial day.[8]

That very evening (4 March), the *Ark Royal* received orders that

[7] Why, if the spotting tests were so important, did not the CO, a sound and reliable naval officer, ask the Admiral for them? And why had he not pressed to have the *Ark Royal*'s aircraft conserved for use some better way on some other day than how they were used on 4 March (see below)? The answer is that it would have been unthinkable for the Captain of the *Ark Royal*, Squadron-Commander R. H. Clark-Hall, to go and tell the Admiral he was using the seaplanes in the wrong way. This was one of the gravest shortcomings in the Fleet of the 'Fisher Era'. As Williamson has pointed out: 'Clark-Hall and I, and our contemporaries, were brought up in the pre-war Navy tradition under which junior officers never thought of questioning the decisions made by admirals. This was especially the case with regard to the difference between providing, and using, the war machine. Very junior officers, such as we were, were wholly concerned with providing, and had little occasion to think of how the machine would be used by the admirals. Clark-Hall was no more than a very junior Commander. As he saw it, his job was to supply the aircraft, and the Admiral would say how they were to be used.' Letter to the author, 31 July 1968.

[8] It could be argued that for Vice-Admiral S. H. Carden, who commanded the squadron at the Dardanelles, the reconnaissance meant a great deal. It was required to safeguard the landing party from surprise attack, to know about ships like the old Turkish battleship *Barbarossa* (which, firing from Maidos, made the *Queen Elizabeth* move off on 6 March), and to know what the Turkish destroyers (always a possible menace to Allied ships) were doing. Were the demolition landings really necessary? It would have taken days if not weeks to bring any of the forts into action again, and at any time the battleships could have destroyed the gun emplacements at short range. But assuming that there was something to be gained by the action taken that day, its importance was as nothing compared with spotting for firing over the peninsula, which, we shall now see, could have been done on 4 and 5 March.

an aircraft would be required to spot for the *Queen Elizabeth* the next morning, when she was to fire over the peninsula at the forts defending the Narrows. Williamson regards the mismanagement of the spotting for the *Queen Elizabeth* on 5 March as a crucial point—that, had, say, four aircraft been prepared days before and held in constant readiness 'for the one job on which everything depended', anything would have been possible. The morning of the 5th was a disaster. The *Ark Royal* joined the *Queen Elizabeth* off Gaba Tepe. Lieutenant-Commander Williamson was to do the spotting, and his Captain told him to take any machine and any pilot he liked.[9] He took the best one available; his own special machine had been hit and damaged on the 'useless job' on the 4th. (Contrary to Admiralty regulations, on the way out from England he had altered this machine, exchanging the positions of pilot and observer to give the latter the best possible view for spotting.) Had they not 'wasted' those seven hours the day before, he would have had his own good aircraft. At the appointed time on the 5th the aircraft was hoisted out. Williamson has recorded:

It was a perfect day, with just the right amount of wind for taking off from the water, and we were soon in the air. It was an exhilarating moment. There below was the *Queen Elizabeth* with her eight 15-inch guns ready to fire and trained on the coast. The conditions were ideal; stationary ships and stationary target, only eight miles apart, and perfect visibility. I believed that there was every prospect of destroying the Forts, and that the Fleet would be able to go through the Straits and accomplish the object of the campaign by appearing off Constantinople. Few junior officers have ever been in a position so favourable and of such importance, and I was thrilled with confident expectation. We soon reached 3,000-ft. and were ready to cross the peninsula to the target . . . Then it happened. In a moment the machine was out of control and we were hurtling towards the sea.

The propeller had broken up (the cause remains a mystery); the machine hit the water and practically disintegrated. Williamson and his pilot miraculously survived and were picked up by a destroyer. Another machine was sent up, but the pilot, unable to gain much altitude, was wounded by a rifle bullet and had to return. A third machine was able to signal only one spotting correction.

The negligible assistance of the seaplanes in spotting fall of shots was the immediate cause of the failure of the *Queen Elizabeth*'s

[9] When Williamson went up to spot for the *Queen Elizabeth*, he received no instructions whatever. He was told nothing about the arrangement for a ship inside the Straits spotting for range, and so presumably was expected to give the necessary corrections for both range and direction, which he was quite prepared to do.

indirect fire at 14,000 yards range, since her gunlayers, unable to see the forts, were wholly dependent on aircraft for direction spotting. Seventeen shells out of thirty-three fired landed inside the forts and did some damage, but no guns were hit. (With only seventeen shells on target nobody could expect a gun to be hit, owing to the inevitable 'scatter' for range.) The fire had, however, taken the Turks by complete surprise and had, as a Turkish captain of artillery testified after the war, 'a very great moral effect on gun crews as the batteries were quite unprotected from this direction'.[10] This was not known to the fleet. On 6 March the indirect firing was continued, with the *Queen Elizabeth* having to move out to 20,000 yards from her objective and use full charges because of the fire from the *Barbarossa*. There was no seaplane spotting, only spotting by a battleship inside the Straits. It was ineffective and was abandoned on account of bad light. The difficulty of indirect-fire bombardment of the Narrows forts led to a resumption of a direct bombardment of the forts by battleships inside the Straits on 7 and 8 March. No damage of military importance was inflicted, although the forts were apparently silenced. There were no further daylight bombardments of any consequence until 18 March.

'Had aeroplane observation been possible,' the Mitchell Report judged (speaking of the indirect bombardments of 5 and 6 March), 'there is little doubt that great damage would have been done to the forts, and that, with sufficient expenditure of ammunition, every gun might have been smashed. The forts were quite unprotected from this direction and each gun and mounting presented a maximum target. . . . Without aeroplane observation, little except moral effect would be expected, and this moral effect could be discounted unless the attack were accompanied by a simultaneous break-through of the Fleet.'[11] The Report points out that it was not only on 5 and 6 March that the seaplanes 'entirely failed to meet the main requirement of the Fleet, which was accurate spotting'. Spotting results throughout had proved generally unsuccessful, and it was evident that *aeroplanes*, with trained observers for spotting, were a necessity. But these did not arrive until 24 March. (They had been ordered out several weeks earlier after complaints about the inefficiency of the seaplanes.) Not till then was the importance of the Dardanelles operation considered to be sufficient to justify the removal of aeroplanes from other areas. The Report draws this conclusion: 'The lack of aeroplane observation was throughout the [naval] operations found to be the heaviest

[10] Mitchell Report, p. 425.   [11] ibid., p. 49.

handicap.' Again, 'the importance of good aerial spotting for correction of ships' fire cannot be overestimated, and the lack of this . . . was one of the three main causes of the failure of the naval attacks on the Dardanelles'.[12] The other two were 'the lack and unsuitability of ammunition' ('The ammunition reserve available at this time and the necessity of preserving ammunition for operations in the Sea of Marmora made economy in expenditure essential') and the 'lack of adequate sweeping material and personnel', to the latter of which we will turn in a moment.

These comments on air spotting need qualification. A popular view concerning the opening phase of the campaign (enshrined in the Mitchell Report) attributes much of the failure to the unreliability of the *Ark Royal*'s aircraft. This is misleading. It stems from the fact that Admiral Carden was never questioned by the Dardanelles Commissioners or the Mitchell Committee on how many hours were actually flown by his aircraft and what he did with those flying hours. Between 17 February and 5 March, though not less than 50 hours were placed at his disposal, most, if not the whole, of the flying time had been expended in tasks none of which could have influenced the operation in any important way.

Even had things gone better, would the spotting of the *Ark Royal*'s pilots have been of much use, given their lack of experience? Group-Captain Williamson replies:

It was, of course, true that at that time neither I, nor anyone else, had ever spotted for ships firing at a shore target. (A good reason for doing a little practice before attacking the forts.) But it had never struck me that the spotting required would present any difficulty. With good visibility, no hurry, no interference by enemy aircraft or anti-aircraft guns, and a target which was stationary, in no wise camouflaged and very conspicuous, it would have interested me to know in what way it was thought that I would go wrong. This point is connected with an obsession which was strong in the Flagship. A conviction that they wanted aeroplanes and not seaplanes. I do not know whose idea this was, but it was so strong that within a few hours of the *Ark Royal* joining the Fleet a party from the Flagship, including the Flag Captain, came to us in a picket boat wanting an opinion on the suitability of a landing ground which they had chosen on Tenedos Island.[13]

I can almost visualize the sailors saying, 'those ruddy seaplanes, they are no damned good!' and can therefore understand their feeling that land aircraft were likely to prove a better bet. In certain respects indeed aeroplanes would have been more efficient than seaplanes for the work of the fleet. Their great advantages were

[12] ibid., pp. 31, 73.   [13] Williamson's letter to the author, 27 Dec. 1971.

that on several days they could fly from a land base when seaplanes were unable to rise from the sea, and they could fly higher and so out of rifle range. But it is not clear why aeroplanes should have been better for observing. It was not wheels versus floats that mattered, but the way the aircraft were used. In any case, aeroplanes were not available, and one wonders, therefore, why the Admiral's staff had not given a modicum of thought to using the seaplanes available efficiently, instead of grieving all the time at not having aeroplanes. The same attitude in an extreme form appears in the Mitchell Report.

At the root of the failure to make the most of the seaplanes, according to Williamson, was the fact that no one in the fleet at the Dardanelles had any real appreciation of what these aircraft could do in the way of spotting. 'But to be fair, there was no one [in the whole Navy] who had had any experience, and no doubt they would have learnt sooner, if we had not had such very bad luck.' He cites these instances of 'bad luck' which worked against the pilots in the *Ark Royal*, who understood the importance of air spotting, being given many chances to show what they could do: (1) In the first bombardment of the outer forts on 19 February, when he was up to spot for HMS *Cornwallis* and could have made a practical test of air spotting for battleship fire, the Admiral ordered her to stop firing as soon as Williamson's plane was at 2,000 feet and ready. (The *Cornwallis* was ordered to anchor in deep water, but could not owing to a defective capstan and so had to swop places with the *Vengeance*.) (2) When Keyes, who was COS to the Admiral, wanted a particular spotting job done, Williamson looked forward to showing what the seaplanes could do. 'While I was in the Flagship my pilot (I was doing the observing) had to get his aircraft ready and then come over to pick me up. He was a capable officer, but unfortunately in the excitement of his first day of actual war he forgot to fill up with petrol—result, fiasco!' (3) The wastage of no less than seven hours on 4 March in doing 'an unnecessary and useless job'. (4) Williamson's experience on 5 March. He concludes: 'This was a sorry record, and it is understandable that the senior officers, who knew nothing of our difficulties, formed a poor view of aircraft.'[14] One should mention the inexperience of ships' personnel as regards co-operation with aircraft. In these four cases, the air was definitely to blame for the second; but it was the least important. The first and third failures were directly due to the Admiral's orders. Had he used the full air-spotting capability at his disposal on the 4th and 5th, the fourth

[14] Williamson's letter to the author, 26 Nov. 1971.

failure might not have happened, and if it did, it would have been of minor importance.

To sum up, had Admiral Carden concentrated the air resources he had on what should have been the obviously vital job, instead of squandering them as he did, *and* had there been ample ammunition, it is at least arguable that naval gunnery would have destroyed the Narrows forts in the first days of March and have permitted the fleet to destroy the minefield batteries and go through into the Sea of Marmora before the fateful line of mines was laid on 8 March (see below). As matters developed, however, good aerial spotting was not the crucial consideration.

We have to remember that these were the very early days of military aviation. Nowhere in the Navy at this time had naval gunners contemplated, let alone tried out, air spotting to assist in the attack of ships on shore targets. All gunnery thinking was concentrated on ship-to-ship gunnery. The gunnery specialists in the fleet at the Dardanelles can therefore not be blamed for not foreseeing immediately the importance of air spotting when the *Ark Royal* arrived with her six low-performance seaplanes on 17 February. Furthermore, the fleet would not have been impressed with their capabilities or potential when they started co-operating with the ships. Would a fully developed and reasonably competent Naval Staff, before the outbreak of the war or in its first months, have made a thorough investigation of methods of aircraft spotting, as well as of minesweeping and of the ammunition required to attack shore defences successfully and have given the fleet special training in such matters? Perhaps this is too much to expect of a Staff which had only come into existence in 1912 and which shared the Navy's obsession with the big-gun duel between lines of dreadnoughts.

*   *   *

By themselves the Narrows forts, owing to their obsolete guns and fire-control system, could not have prevented the fleet rushing the Straits. The Turkish minefields had the most important function in the defence of the Dardanelles: 'to form an obstruction sufficiently formidable to prevent the rushing of the Straits'. Responsible for the efficiency of the minefields was the able German Admiral Merten, the chief technical adviser at the Straits. By the end of February 1915 there.were five lines of mines across the Narrows and five more across the Straits just below Kephez Point, the southernmost about 8,000 yards from the Narrows forts.[15] Seventy-four

---

[15] Lines 1 to 5 were known as the Narrows minefield. Then there was a gap in

guns, mostly 3-inch and 4-inch, and six 90-cm. searchlights protected the minefields. The minefield batteries were partly fixed, like Dardanos (no. 8), and partly mobile field artillery. Having no fire-control system, they were useless against fast-moving targets. NID had moderately accurate intelligence on these minefields.

But on 8 March, no. 11 line, 'those mines of destiny', was laid in Eren Keui Bay. On this date there were 344 mines in place in the eleven lines. They were all contact mines, mostly German Carbonit (Company) mines, and were reliable as regards holding their depth—13 to 15 feet. Though not of the most powerful type (the weight of explosive was 180–220 lb.), they proved effective against the older battleships in the 18 March assault. The mine-fields were of such density (generally, spaced 44–55 yards apart, except for no. 11, where the mines were 110–165 yards apart) that the mathematical chances against effecting the passage to Nagara, beyond the Narrows, past the ten lines of mines, were greater than 100 to 1; that is, not one of 100 ships could expect to reach Nagara. 'It is, therefore, clear that the minefields did in reality constitute a formidable barrier against the Fleet and the above facts effectively dispose of the contention that the Straits might have been forced without sweeping the minefields.'[16]

It was the original intention of the Admiralty that battleship fire should destroy the forts and silence the minefield batteries before an attempt to sweep the minefields. But this plan had been reversed when the battleship fire had proved ineffective. After the fleet bombardment of 25 February, which had reduced the outer defences, the minesweepers were given the task of clearing the minefields by night sweeping. If successful, this would have permitted the battleships to destroy the forts at close range.

The minesweepers were a failure. On 10 March, at the seventh attempt, they actually reached the Kephez minefield (above line 8), but after one trawler had hit a mine and blown up, the others abruptly turned back. The following night they withdrew as soon as the first shells exploded nearby. Keyes harshly criticizes the fishermen, whom he all but accuses of cowardice.

The less said about that night [11 March] the better. To put it briefly,

Sari Siglar Bay, followed by the rest (lines 6 to 10), which were lumped together as the Kephez minefield. (Kephez Bay is at the end of line 9.)

[16] Mitchell Report, p. 484. It is unfortunate that paravanes were not yet available. The first set was fitted to a destroyer for trials in May 1915, and by August it was evident that this ingenious device for cutting mine moorings gave ships effective protection against mines. Arthur J. Marder, *From the Dreadnought to Scapa Flow: the Royal Navy in the Fisher Era, 1904–1919* (5 vols., London, 1961–70), ii. 73–4.

the sweepers turned tail and fled directly they were fired upon. I was furious and told the officers in charge that they had had their opportunity, there were many others only too keen to try. It did not matter if we lost all seven sweepers, there were 28 more, and the mines had got to be swept up. How could they talk about being stopped by a heavy fire if they were not hit. The Admiralty were prepared for losses, but we had chucked our hand in and started squealing before we had any.[17]

The sweepers faced certain handicaps which explain their miserable failure to do the job. (1) The minefields and the associated gun and searchlight defences appeared formidable, although the fire of the minefield batteries, even at short range, was more bark than bite—even the slow trawlers escaped, except on 13 March; but they did have a psychological effect on the trawler crews. Cruiser and destroyer attacks on the minefield batteries and searchlights during sweeping operations had little success, particularly since they could do nothing when the sweepers were actually in the minefield without adding to the dangers of the sweepers, owing to the difficulties of laying, ranging, and spotting at night. 'The minefield batteries had shown themselves to be so strong that the life of a trawler in a minefield was most precarious, and it was most doubtful, however determined and persistent the attacks made, whether any effective sweeping could be carried out in this area unless the batteries were first dominated.'[18] And yet no trawler was ever sunk by gunfire. The one badly hit had her engines stopped. The casualties were trivial compared to one attack on an enemy trench by the Army later on. How do we explain the timidity of the trawlers' crews?

(2) The sweepers themselves were quite unsuitable for the task. These were 21 small North Sea fishing trawlers (17 or 18 were available on 18 March), but owing to repairs and rest leave to the personnel, the maximum operating at one time was 7. And their speed was a mere 5 knots when working in formation, less the 2-to-4-knot current of the Dardanelles down the Straits. The slow speed prevented the sweepers from making much progress against the current with sweeps out. This necessitated their getting above the minefield, joining sweeps under fire, and sweeping with the current. Moreover, the steel plating fitted to their bridges rendered the trawlers' compasses useless. There was no way of fixing position and, even, at times of steering a course.

(3) The human material left something to be desired: raw fishermen from the north-eastern ports, trained in minesweeping,

<hr>

[17] *The Naval Memoirs of Admiral of the Fleet Sir Roger Keyes* (2 vols., London, 1934–5), i. 212.   [18] Mitchell Report, p. 58.

manned the trawlers. They were 'Hostilities Only' ratings, mostly of poor physique and lacking in discipline. Their commander, moreover, was a retired officer without sweeping experience. Awareness that the draught of the trawlers was greater than the depths of the mines did not improve the morale of the crews.

(4) The basic cause of the minesweeping failure was that the system of sweeping developed in British coastal waters was never intended for use in narrow waters under fire; it was indeed impracticable in such conditions—unless the minefield batteries were first mastered. Pairs of trawlers, 500 yards apart, towed a 2½-inch sweep wire (kept at the desired depth by two kites) between and behind them. On catching a mooring wire, the trawlers towed the mine into shallow water for sinking by rifle fire. In the Dardanelles this procedure would have to be worked directly under Turkish guns, and for this the crews were not prepared. 'The fact that their contract of service only insured them against the danger of exploding mines,' Vice-Admiral K. G. B. Dewar has pointed out, 'shows that exposure to shell fire was not even contemplated by experienced officers.' De Robeck observed after the 18 March attack: 'In some cases their crews appear to have no objection to being blown up by mines, though they do not seem to like to work under gunfire, which is a new element in their calling.'[19] There is indeed no earthly reason why they should have been expected to clear the minefields in the face of constant gunfire at short range. Nothing in their experience had prepared them for such an ordeal.

Leadership could do something towards correcting this situation. On 12 March it was arranged that each trawler was to be given an officer, a petty officer, and a signalman from the fleet, all volunteers, to stiffen the morale of the trawler crews. We hear of one officer carrying a revolver and 'determined to threaten the trawler skipper with it if he showed any sign of running away!' On the night of the 13th–14th a really determined attempt was made. This time the trawlers, though under hot fire, did not turn until they were above the Kephez minefield. The first pair made a successful sweep, but this was all that was accomplished. All seven trawlers received hits, some of their sweeping gear was shot away, and they were forced to retire.

The upshot was that the minefields and their defences remained more or less intact. Churchill has summed up the obstacles this way: 'The minefields blocked the passage of the Straits and kept the Fleet beyond their limits. The minefield batteries prevented the

[19] De Robeck, 'Report of Operations, 18 March 1915', 26 Mar. 1915, de Robeck MSS., 4/4.

I Aboard HMS *Triad* at the Dardanelles, 17 October 1915.
Left to right: Commodore Roger Keyes (Chief of Staff to de Robeck),
Acting Vice-Admiral Sir John de Robeck (C-in-C, Eastern Mediter-
ranean Squadron), and General Sir Ian Hamilton (C-in-C, Mediterranean
Expeditionary Force).

IIb Admiral Sir William Fisher, C-in-C, Mediterranean
Fleet, 1932–36

IIa Admiral Sir Ernle Chatfield, C-in-C, Atlantic Fleet,
1929–30

sweeping of the minefields. The forts protected the minefield batteries by keeping battleships at a distance with their long guns. The
mobile howitzers kept the battleships on the move and increased
the difficulty of overcoming the forts. So long as all four factors
stood together, the defences constituted a formidable obstruction.'[20]
On 15 March Carden decided to revert to the original strategy of
first destroying the forts with the battleships, then dominating the
batteries, before attempting to sweep the minefields. But the next
day he gave up his command for reasons of health. It was time he
went. Carden was a charming man and an ideal peacetime admiral,
but he had none of the qualities needed for an admiral at war in
the technical age.

Carden was succeeded by his Second-in-Command, Vice-Admiral
J. M. de Robeck—a 'fighting leader', an officer on his staff called him.
A journalist on the spot described him as 'a most delightful man,
a perfect replica of the courteous type of the old English sportsman
and country gentleman of bygone days'. 'His character, personality
and zeal inspired confidence in all', Churchill has remarked. But
within a fortnight of de Robeck's appointment, Churchill was not
to be numbered among his admirers. The Admiral's plan of attack
called for a simultaneous 'silencing' of the Narrows forts and the
batteries protecting the Kephez minefield, so as to enable sweepers
to clear a passage through the minefields. 'It is not expected to
destroy the forts even at 8000 yards, but it is expected that ships
will dominate the forts to such an extent as to make it impossible
for them to interfere with the sweeping operations.'[21]

A telegram Carden had received from the First Lord on the 14th
boded well for the coming attack. They had

information that the Turkish forts are short of ammunition, that the German
officers have made despondent reports and have appealed to Germany for
more. Every conceivable effort is being made to supply ammunition, it is
being seriously considered to send a German or an Austrian submarine,
but apparently they have not started yet. . . . All this makes it clear that
the operation should now be pressed forward methodically and resolutely
at night and day. The unavoidable losses must be accepted. The enemy is
harassed and anxious now. The time is precious as the interference of submarines is a very serious complication.[22]

[20] Winston S. Churchill, *The World Crisis* (5 vols. in 6, London, 1923–31), ii. 256.
[21] De Robeck's memorandum, 'Attack on Minefield at Kephez Point', 17 Mar. 1915,
de Robeck MSS., 4/3.
[22] Keyes, *Naval Memoirs*, i. 217. This intelligence was derived from a 'most secret'
telegram from the Kaiser (via the Chief of the Naval Cabinet, Admiral Georg von
Müller) to Vice-Admiral von Usedom, Inspector-General of Coast Defences and Mines
at the Dardanelles. It was intercepted by NID on 12 March—not on the 19th, the
day following the big attack, as stated by Martin Gilbert in *Winston S. Churchill*,

B

There came the day of the attack, 18 March, which saw the heaviest and last naval bombardment of the forts. The results of the attack were: (1) 14 old battleships (10 English, 4 French) and the *Queen Elizabeth* and *Inflexible* attacked the Narrows forts with direct fire, putting out of action 4 of the 19 heavy guns, though only temporarily. De Robeck believed that 'although the principal forts remained silent for considerable intervals, only a portion of their armaments can be considered disabled'.[23] (2) Four battleships attacked the minefield batteries, and when the Turkish fire let up, six minesweepers were ordered up. They did not get within 2 miles of the Kephez minefield, still less commence to sweep it, before the gunfire sent them back, although none was hit. The minefields and their defences remained practically intact. (3) The loss through unswept mines of line 11 of two old British battleships (*Irresistible, Ocean*) and severe damage to the battle cruiser *Inflexible*, as well as the loss of the old French battleship *Bouvet*, which led to the abandonment of the attack. 'Though the Squadron had to retire without accomplishing its task it was by no means a defeated force, and the withdrawal was only necessitated owing to the mine menace, all ranks being anxious to renew the attack.'[24] The basic cause of the failure on the 18th was the old story: the battleships needed to close the forts to silence them, but they could not do this until the mines had been swept; the mines could not be swept until the minefield defences had been smashed—unless fast sweepers were used.

The particular spoiler on the 18th was line 11 of the minefields. Lieutenant-Colonel Gheel, a Turkish mining expert, had had an inspiration. Noting that the enemy's ships, when inside the Straits, sometimes manœuvred in the still water on the Asiatic side, off Eren Keui Bay, he thought it might be worth while to moor a line of mines there. Twenty were laid from the small minelayer *Nousret* in the night of 8 March in Eren Keui Bay, about $2\frac{1}{2}$ miles south of the permanent minefields and parallel to the Asiatic shore. Four of the twenty mines had been exploded in trawler sweeps of the bombarding area on the nights of the 15th and 16th; yet on the

---

iii (London, 1971), 357. See the testimony of the DNI (Captain W. R. Hall), *Proceedings of the Dardanelles Commission*, p. 282, ADM 116/1437B.

[23] De Robeck, 'Report of Operations, 18 March 1915'.

[24] ibid. 'If any man in the Navy Trade could have got through on the 18th we all know jolly well that John de Robeck would have.' This from Vice-Admiral A. H. Limpus, Admiral Superintendent at Malta, on 24 March. On the 30th Carden sent these words of comfort: 'The more one learns of the action on the 18th the more it shews how splendidly you & the squadron stuck to it—it was indeed bad luck to meet those sneaking mines.' De Robeck MSS., 4/36, 37.

morning of the 18th the commander of the minesweepers reported the area clear. It is a serious reflection on the competency of this officer that the sixteen other mines were not discovered and swept before the 18th.[25] Captain Boswell suggests that the cause of this failure might have been any one of these:

(*a*) No. 11 line, having been laid at right angles to all the other lines, the sweepers may have been looking for the rest of the mines in the wrong place. [Anyone, except perhaps a reliable augur, when dealing with mine-fields blocking a narrow strait would assume that the lines of mines would be at right angles to the strait.]

(*b*) The sweepers may have thought that the mines were strays dislodged from the Kephez lines which had drifted down with the current. This was in fact impossible as the area was out of the current.

(*c*) Inside the Dardanelles there were no lighthouses, beacons, or buoys by which a trawler could fix her position, and so it was impossible to return exactly to a suspicious area.

(*d*) The officer in charge and the trawler skippers were completely inexperienced in night sweeping of this type.[26]

[25] The trawlers had swept the area to be used by the bombarding ships during the night of the 17th–18th. Captain Boswell's trawler was one of the six on duty that night. 'All we did was go a couple of miles up inside the Straits, and then the leader turned round and we all returned to the depot ship at Tenedos, having done absolutely nix. We had been given no orders about the area to be swept, etc., and only told "Follow the leader". If the leader had been an early casualty, nobody would have known what to do. And, mind you, this came at the end of a fortnight's sweeping, when some kind of order should have been created.' Boswell's letter to the author, 16 Oct. 1972. This points up the fact that every battleship at the Dardanelles had a qualified torpedo officer kicking up his heels. These 'T' officers were the specialists in underwater weapons, including, of course, mines and minesweeping. If three of them had commanded the three trawler groups (that is, each commanding one 'leader' plus the three pairs sweeping) soon after 9 March, when it was obvious that the minesweeping was getting nowhere, I am sure it would have been under more intelligent and forceful control, hence more effective. (See below, p. 24 n., for what a T officer could do.) Had the trawlers been properly handled on the nights of 15 and 16 March, the *Nousret* mines would have been swept before the 18th.

On 14–16 March seaplanes had made a careful search for mines in the bombarding area and reported it clear of mines. De Robeck was fatally wrong in accepting their evidence at face value. Trials on 15 March had determined that seaplanes could locate a moored mine down to 18 feet when flying at 3,000 feet. But the experiment smacked of the bogus, the Mitchell Report observing wryly (p. 83), 'There is something misleading about this experiment, for no such satisfactory results would seem to have been since achieved . . .' Under certain limited conditions of sun angle, water clarity, colour of mine and bottom of sea, etc., mines *can* be seen. But it was a grave mistake to rely entirely on it under all conditions. It is possible that the trial was done on a mine moored on a *sandy* bottom: there was a lot near Tenedos, which is where the *Ark Royal* used to anchor. In clear water it is easy to see one's anchor and cable on the bottom in 30 feet of water on a *sandy* bottom. The Dardanelles with its current would have a rocky bottom, which looks brown or grey, and the mines would not have shown up.

[26] Boswell, 'The Naval Attack on the Dardanelles, 1915', *Royal United Service Institution Journal*, cx (May 1965), 146.

Two pairs of trawlers had exploded three of the *Nousret* mines at about 3 p.m. on the 18th before they turned tail and fled. This was reported to de Robeck the *next day*! If reported at once, it might well have saved the three British ships that were to be mined in the same area (the *Bouvet* had already been mined).

Though little damage was done to the Narrows forts on the 18th (what there was was quickly repaired), the shortage of ammunition was of concern to the Turks. Having fired nearly 2,000 shell, the Narrows forts were down to twenty-seven armour-piercing shell, the only kind effective against battleship armour. There was no shortage of ammunition for the medium and light guns. The morale of the defenders of the Straits, despite the ammunition shortage for the heavy guns, was high. There was confidence that their defences would hold, were another naval attack mounted, and that their fleet would deal with any ships that did pass the Narrows. The view of the officers, Turkish and German, was not so sanguine, a number of them believing that a second naval attack would force the Straits or stand a good chance of doing so. There is evidence that responsible Turks and their advisers regarded the situation as desperate. An Associated Press correspondent, who spent 18 March at the Dardanelles, was told that evening by Admiral Merten: 'We expect that the British will come back early to-morrow morning, and if they do we may be able to hold out for a few hours. I should advise you to get up at six o'clock to-morrow morning and take to the Anatolian Hills. That's what we are going to do.'[27] The official Turkish view (1919) was that a naval 'break through' was regarded as 'not beyond expectation', and that the Ottoman Government and public were in a state of excitement.[28]

Neither de Robeck nor the Admiralty was aware of the state of Turkish morale, though, as pointed out, they were aware of the

[27] Henry Morgenthau, *Secrets of the Bosphorus* (London, 1918), p. 148. (The U.S. edition has the title *Ambassador Morgenthau's Story*.) Morgenthau was the American Ambassador to Turkey, 1913–16. The German Ambassador, after writing about the 'great elation' in the capital 'following the splendid Dardanelles victory', was forced to admit that 'the lack of ammunition hangs like a dark cloud over the entire situation. The Dardanelles might be able to withstand perhaps one, but no more than two, such assaults. And that would be the end of it and the spectre of our enemy's appearance would become reality.' Baron von Wangenheim to the German Foreign Office, 23 Mar. 1915, German Foreign Office MSS. (Bonn).

[28] Mitchell Report, p. 71. The details on Turkish opinion are in ibid., pp. 71, 432–8, as gleaned from postwar information provided by the Turkish War Office and from interviews with German and Turkish officers. See further, Harry Stuermer, *Two Years in Constantinople* (New York, 1917), pp. 78–9. He was the correspondent of the *Kölnische Zeitung* in Constantinople, 1915–16.

ammunition factor. The War Council authorized the Admiralty on the 19th to instruct de Robeck to continue the assault 'if he thought fit'. This they did the next day, informing him that he would be reinforced by four old battleships and that ample supplies of 15-inch shell were now available for indirect fire across the peninsula by the *Queen Elizabeth*. It was the C-in-C's first intention to renew the attack as soon as practicable. His spirits were temporarily buoyed up by his staff, notably by Keyes and Major W. W. Godfrey, of the Royal Marines. The latter has been described as 'the hard core of the Admiral's staff . . . He was heart and soul for continuing the naval attack on the forts with the object of breaking through the narrows and demonstrating off Constantinople. He believed that the naval operation, given well trained fleet minesweepers, was feasible, and that the Turks would collapse if we appeared off Constantinople. He was a very determined, hard-working and persistent staff officer. He and Keyes never wavered . . .'[29]

'We are all getting ready for another "go",' de Robeck wrote to Sir Ian Hamilton (commanding the Mediterranean Expeditionary Force) on the 19th, 'and not in the least beaten or down-hearted.' The next day he informed Churchill that he hoped to be able 'to commence operations in three or four days . . . but delay is inevitable, as new crews and destroyers [being fitted as minesweepers] will need some preliminary practice'. On the 21st he telegraphed the Admiralty that he hoped to continue the *Queen Elizabeth*'s indirect fire from Gaba Tepe, with the assistance of a spotting seaplane, once the gales moderated.

De Robeck changed his mind on the 22nd. He had been brooding ever since the 18th on the loss of nearly a third of his capital ships, intensified by his remaining in the dark as to the precise cause. The only reasonable explanation of his losses seemed to be that the Turks were floating mines down with the current. Nobody seems to have realized that all the ships mined were out of the current. Had de Robeck shown more alertness, he would have had the positions of the mined ships plotted on his chart. The result (see Mitchell Report, plates 16 and 19) would have indicated a line of mines, and a searching sweep by two 'River'-class destroyers (six of them were being fitted with light 1½-inch sweeps as 'mineseekers') would have cleared up his gloomy broodings in half an hour. There was also his fear of possible minefields above the Narrows and about which they knew little, and of obstacles like large pontoons that might be sunk in the Narrows. There were no

---

[29] *Naval Memoirs of Admiral J. H. Godfrey* (8 vols. in 11, privately printed, 1964–6), ii. 2. Admiral Godfrey was at the Dardanelles from 12 April 1915.

mines above the Narrows, and as for the obstacles, Keyes has pointed out that such a blocking 'would have been a physical impossibility' in the over 40 fathoms of water in the Narrows.

The 'dominating consideration' in de Robeck's mind was his strong belief that if he got through into the Marmora without the destruction of the Narrows forts, that is, without the Army in control of the peninsula, his lines of communication would not be secure. This would place the fleet in a desperate position if its appearance off Constantinople did not quickly result in Turkish capitulation. And he did not expect that to happen. In his testimony to the Dardanelles Commission he maintained: 'I think it was obvious [from the Turkish resistance on the 18th] then that the Turk was not going to give in easily; he was going to fight the whole way; and what one had been led to suppose, namely, that if we issued with the Fleet or arrived at Constantinople with the Fleet, there would be a change of Turkish Government, went by the board. It appeared clear that we had to fight the whole way and if we went to Constantinople we should have to go there with troops as well as ships.' What he had in mind by security of communications was the fear that, with the forts still intact, not many colliers and ammunition ships would be able to get through the Narrows, so that he would not be able to operate and maintain the fleet in the Marmora. After three weeks at the most he would have to come down 'like Admiral Duckworth' (1807), and in coming down he would risk the loss of many ships.[30]

By the 22nd de Robeck was convinced that he could not hope to make a success of the purely naval operation. He came to the point swiftly at a conference in the *Queen Elizabeth* at Mudros on the morning of the 22nd: to get through he would need the help of the Army. Hamilton's assurance that the Army was prepared to land at the toe of the peninsula when it was ready (this would not be before 14 April), with the object of occupying the Kilid Bahr Plateau and thereby dominating the forts on both sides of

[30] *Proceedings of the Dardanelles Commission*, pp. 173–4. And see ADM 137/110 or, more conveniently, though with minor stylistic differences, Keyes, *Naval Memoirs*, i. 258–9, 266–9 (telegrams to the Admiralty of 22, 26, 27 Jan.) for de Robeck's reasons for not renewing the naval attack. The German General Liman von Sanders (he took command of the Turkish 5th Army at the Dardanelles on 24 March) supports de Robeck's judgement: 'Even in case the allied fleet forced a passage and won the naval battle in the Sea of Marmara, I judged that it would be in a nearly untenable position so long as the entire shores on the Dardanelles strait were not held by strong allied forces. Should the Turkish troops succeed in holding the shores of the straits or in regaining them, the regular supply of food and coal would become impossible.' Liman von Sanders, *Five Years in Turkey* (Annapolis, 1928), p. 48. But see below, p. 29, for de Robeck's prospects if he had to quit the Marmora.

the Straits, clinched the new strategy for de Robeck. Convinced that a combined operation would afford a better chance of success, the Admiral decided to drop the naval attack and to prepare the fleet for its venture with the Army. Keyes's estimate (22 March) that the destroyer sweepers would not be ready until 4 April strengthened de Robeck's resolve: it was only a case of waiting another ten days for military support. As it happens, the combined operation did not take place until 25 April.

The Admiral transmitted the vital decision to the First Lord after the conference in the flagship. Churchill read the telegram 'with consternation'. With the half-hearted concurrence of the First Sea Lord, Fisher, he sent de Robeck a prescient appreciation on the 24th:

It is clear that the army should at once prepare to attack the Kilid Bahr plateau at the earliest opportunity . . . But the question now to be decided by Admiralty is whether the time has come to abandon the naval plan of forcing the Dardanelles without the aid of a large army. It may be necessary to accept check of the 18th as decisive and to admit that the task is beyond our powers, and if you think this you should not fail to say so. But before deciding, certain facts must be weighed; first the delay and the consequent danger of submarines coming and ruining all; second the heavy losses at least 5,000 which the army would suffer; third the possibility of a check in the land operations far more serious than the loss of a few old surplus ships; fourth the fact that even when Kilid Bahr plateau has been taken by the army and the Kilid Bahr group of forts rendered untenable, the Asiatic forts will be still effective and most of the mine danger which is now your principal difficulty will menace you in the long reaches above the Narrows. . . .

What has happened since the 21st to make you alter your intention of renewing the attack as soon as the weather is favourable? We have never contemplated a reckless rush over minefields and past undamaged primary guns. But the original Admiralty instructions and telegram 109 [15 March] prescribed a careful and deliberate method of advance, and I should like to know what are the reasons which in your opinion render this no longer possible, in spite of your new aircraft and improved methods of mine-sweeping. We know the forts are short of ammunition. It is probable that they have not got many mines. You should be able to feel your way while at the same time pressing hard. . . .[31]

[31] ADM 137/110 and, with minor differences, Keyes, *Naval Memoirs*, i. 264–5. Earlier (6.05 p.m., 22 March) Churchill had telegraphed de Robeck: 'With regard to Turkish ammunition, we know that on the 12th instant the forts were short of ammunition and that efforts were being made to replenish them from Germany. We do not think these efforts have yet been successful.' ADM 137/110. De Robeck did not accept at face value Admiralty statements after the 18th about the Turkish ammunition position. His experience on the 18th had not confirmed any serious shortage. 'When a ship was mined they opened fire on her again and again and while we were bombarding, the guns' crews went into their dug-outs.' *Proceedings of the Dardanelles Commission*, pp. 172–3.

De Robeck wired a full appreciation to the Admiralty on the 27th. It concluded: 'With Gallipoli Peninsula held by our Army and Squadron through Dardanelles our success would be assured. The delay possibly of a fortnight will allow co-operation which would really prove factor that will reduce length of time necessary to complete the campaign in Sea of Marmora and occupy Constantinople.' A shocked and dismayed First Lord would have ordered de Robeck to make a fresh naval assault, but he was unable to carry the Admiralty War Staff Group, who would not overrule the decision taken by the naval and military commanders on the spot. He bowed to the decision of his professional advisers. 'But with regret and anxiety', as he says.

Churchill later blasted de Robeck for his pusillanimity: he looked upon his old ships as 'sacred'. 'The spectacle of this noble structure on which so many loyalties centred . . . foundering miserably beneath the waves, appeared as an event shocking and unnatural in its character.' Similarly, a quarter-century after the event: historical judgement would 'pronounce him inadequate to the supreme moral and mental trial to which he was subjected'.[32] Following this lead, Captain Boswell puts the blame for the failure to renew the naval attack squarely on de Robeck. 'The man who stopped the Navy achieving this great feat of arms was, I'm afraid, dear old Johnnie de Robeck, a splendid old type, but obsessed by secret fears of the unknown after March 18th—and who on March 22nd had forgotten that the mere arrival of the fleet off Constantinople would end the war and secure his line of communications through the Straits. It is a terrible example of what happens when the C-in-C loses sight of his true AIM.'[33] These and other critics of their persuasion are being unfair. De Robeck's decision required an extraordinary degree of moral courage. It was, moreover, based on the knowledge at his disposal. He was not aware of the shaky morale of the German and Turkish officers. He did not know what had brought on the losses of 18 March, which induced a more conservative strategy. Most importantly, as he had informed the Admiralty on 26 March, 'To attack the Narrows now would be a mistake, as it would jeopardise the execution of a better and bigger scheme', that is, the capture of the Gallipoli Peninsula, in order to safeguard the fleet's communications once it was in the Marmora. *He could not have foreseen the*

[32] Churchill, *The World Crisis*, ii. 254, Churchill to Vice-Admiral E. P. A. Guépratte (commander of the French naval force at the Dardanelles), 9 Oct. 1930, Keyes MSS., 15/5 (Churchill College).

[33] Boswell's letter to the author, 15 Sept. 1965.

failure of the Army, beginning with the disasters of V and W beaches on 25 April.

*   *   *

For Keyes, 'this time it must be an onslaught on the mine field—the forts we can always dominate—but the mine field is the devil—and I am making it my own!'[34] He had on 22 March, after the fateful decision in the *Queen Elizabeth*, pointed to the new sweeping force as the key to a successful fresh naval attack. He saw that the revamped minesweeper organization had the power to drive a broad channel through the minefields and permit the fleet to pass the Narrows and anchor off Constantinople, although, as will be seen, Lieutenant F. H. Sandford deserves a large share of the credit. 'I wish to place on record that I had no doubt then, and have none now—and nothing will ever shake my opinion—that from the 4th April, 1915, onwards, the Fleet could have forced the Straits, and . . . could have entered the Marmora with sufficient force to destroy the Turco-German fleet. This operation would have cut the communications—which were sea-borne—of any Turkish armies either in Gallipoli or on the Asiatic side, and would have led immediately to a victory decisive upon the whole course of the War.'[35] The significance of 4 April will be indicated below. The argument did not impress the Admiral. The new minesweeping organization would not be ready till 4 April, a mere ten days before the Army was prepared to land. There is also this hard-to-weigh factor. De Robeck, much as he liked and admired Keyes, doubted the soundness of his judgement. The Chief of Staff was, as Admiral Godfrey affirms, 'a very gallant and inspiring leader but an indifferent chief of staff'. He was never one to see beyond the immediate next step, and his judgement was clouded by his eagerness to get at the enemy. To sum up, there were good reasons, *in the context of the post-18 March period*, for de Robeck's preference for what appeared to be a surer and safer method of forcing the Straits. And yet . . . and yet . . .

The Mitchell Committee would not offer a definite opinion. 'Whether the Fleet alone could or could not, after 18 March, have forced the Straits and maintained the passage, or whether there was less risk involved in a combined operation at this time, is not within the province of this Committee to decide.' A careful study of the Report, however, points to the former as at least offering a 50–50 chance of success, *if attempted after 4 April*.

[34] Keyes to his wife, 21 Mar. 1915, Keyes MSS., 2/9.
[35] Keyes, *Naval Memoirs*, i. 186.

The key to the situation was without doubt the minefields. İt was obvious that the attacks on them had failed for three reasons: (1) the paucity of the sweepers; (2) the slow speed of the trawlers; (3) the inefficiency of the fishermen crews. Each shortcoming was remediable in fairly short order. As regards (1), in the sweeping operation of the night of 13–14 March the Turks had experienced great difficulty in controlling their guns on so many targets with so few searchlights. The minefield batteries lacked a proper fire-control system: theirs was barrage fire directed by telephone on a specified area. The logical deduction was that attacks by a large number of sweepers at one time might be successful. Concerning (2), the fact that the four to six destroyers which supported the trawlers in their sweeps were never hit by the batteries (their speed was their protection) pointed to the need for fast vessels, and of a draught less than the depth of the mines, able to sweep against the current, cutting the mine mooring wires as they proceeded. (3) was self-evident almost from the beginning and pointed to the need for a disciplined personnel.

Substantial progress was made in all three directions within weeks. Indeed, most of the measures had been ordered as early as 14–17 March. Most importantly, eight 'Beagle'-class destroyers were by 4 April fitted and trained as heavy minesweepers.[36] They were joined by eight other 'Beagles' on the 14th, and by eight fleet sweepers from the Grand Fleet (small steamers specially fitted as minesweepers) on the 16th. The last-named came out fully equipped and trained, and were manned with volunteers on arrival. This new sweeping force was put under Captain Algernon Heneage, of

[36] It was Sandford who first appreciated that the destroyers were the only way to 'tear a way through the mines' and get the fleet into the Marmora. He had as a volunteer commanded the leading pair of trawlers on the night of 13–14 March which had actually swept through the Kephez field. The next morning he realized that they could never sweep a passage for the fleet with trawlers only. He knew the small 'River'-class destroyers had the light sweep wire which could only detect the presence of mines, but he thought that if the big 'Beagles' used a wire four times as strong, they might part the mine moorings at high speed. He went over to the *Queen Elizabeth* on the 14th to report the results obtained during the night, and probably told Keyes about the 'Beagles'. He saw him again on the 19th, following the abortive sweep on the 18th. Keyes, who had been thinking more of fleet sweepers and fast trawlers, gave Sandford all the backing he needed. It was on Keyes's authority (he received a free hand from de Robeck on the 19th to reorganize the minesweeping force) that signals were sent on the 19th for 2½-inch wires and kites to be sent from Malta, and that the destroyers were detailed to take on the sweeping job. Sandford overcame all the difficulties in fitting and training the 'Beagles'. I am indebted to Captain Boswell (letter of 9 Feb. 1973) for this first-hand account of Sandford's role. Incidentally, Sandford, by then a commander, was a member of the Mitchell Committee. There is nothing in the records to suggest that either de Robeck or the Admiralty expected very much from the new sweeping force.

the *Albion*, a pleasant, unimpressive officer. By 18 April it was proven by trials to be capable of sweeping at 14 knots. At that speed the sweepers were probably immune from Turkish fire and at the same time were able with their heavy $2\frac{1}{2}$-inch clearing sweep to cut the mine moorings when sweeping *up* the Straits, thus avoiding having to tow the mines to a place of safety. The mines would now simply float away on the surface. And the draught of the destroyer minesweepers was only $10\frac{1}{2}$ feet, which was less than the depth of the mines. The fleet sweepers, too, had a safe draught to go over the minefields. Even if not all of the second batch of 'Beagles' were equipped and practised by 18 April, there were, in Captain Boswell's carefully considered opinion, more than enough trained and disciplined fast minesweepers by that date 'to sweep a channel half a mile wide in one determined thrust ahead of the fleet in line ahead'. With, say, ten 'Beagles', there would be no fear of the sweep being ruined by a lucky shot or two knocking out a destroyer. The four fleet sweepers were better equipped to manage the surface sweep against floating mines, while they had a deep sweep out as well. They would have gone between the destroyers and the leading battleship.

Any possible doubts that the mine mooring wires of a line of mines would have been cut appeared to have been met the first times the destroyer-minesweepers were used: on 18 April, when two 'Beagles' swept at 20 knots ahead of two battleships inside the Straits, 'at which speed the sweep behaved well' (the purpose of the operation, not achieved, was to destroy the remains of the submarine *E-15*, aground at Kephez Point, by gunfire), and in the combined operation of 25–27 April. For this operation, the orders read, 'the efforts of the Navy will primarily be directed to landing the Army and supporting it till its position is secure, after which the Navy will attack the fortifications at the Narrows assisted by the Army'.[37] In the first days of the operation the sweeping of the Dardanelles would be commenced by the destroyer-minesweepers. (The fleet sweepers were not needed as sweepers and were used as troop carriers between the transports and the tows of boats off the beaches.) This facet of the operation called for progressive attacks on the minefield defences from inside the Straits. These were to synchronize with the landing and capture of Achi Baba (first day), the advance of the Army on the Kilid Bahr Plateau (second day), and the occupation of the Kilid Bahr forts (third day). Phase I for the sweepers called for sweeping the lower areas of

[37] De Robeck's memorandum, 'Orders for Combined Operations', 12 Apr. 1915, de Robeck MSS., 4/3.

the Dardanelles as far as Domez Deresi (Chomak Dere), 14,000 yards from the Narrows forts; phase II: sweeping up to Suandere, 8,000 yards from the Narrows forts; phase III: the complete domination of the forts and batteries from a range of 8,000 yards, following which the battleships, preceded by all the fast sweepers, would force the passage of the Narrows.

The Army landed on the first day, but did not reach Achi Baba, then or later. Four pairs of destroyer-minesweepers swept an area 2 miles wide within 14,000 yards of the forts, including a line laid on 31 March (no. 13, off Chomak Dere). On the second day the destroyers continued sweeping to within 10,000 yards of the forts. On neither day were the destroyers hit by the Turkish guns, though under constant fire from forts 7 and 8. On the third day the sweeping was continued up to 8,000 yards, including a line laid on 28 March (no. 12, off Tenkir Dere), but this time one pair of destroyers suffered damage and casualties. (The two new lines were laid to catch ships when bombarding, so emulating, it was hoped, the exploits of line 11 on 18 March.) 'The sweepers were becoming more and more efficient and had by now demonstrated their ability to sweep minefields under fire. It was, however, considered that Phase II could be carried out in a shorter time and with fewer casualties when strongly supported by the Fleet. Sweeping operations in the Straits were, therefore, ordered to be abandoned until, by the advance of the Army, the Fleet could be freed to support the sweepers, which would also be reinforced by the remainder of the sweeping destroyers then supporting the Army.'[38] The idea, that is, was to give the Army a chance to advance and so free the fleet to support the sweepers. 'From the experience gained, however, there can be little doubt that the minefields up to 8,000 yards from the Narrows Forts could have been quickly cleared under the supporting fire of the Fleet, which thus opened up the area below Suandere for the manœuvring of the Fleet in the final attack on the forts and the batteries.'[39]

*　　*　　*

Supposing the fleet at the Dardanelles had been led by a Nelson— or even by a Keyes! One can envisage him saying to the Generals

[38] Mitchell Report, p. 179.

[39] ibid. Captain Boswell suggests that 'apart from a perfunctory signal [from Captain Heneage] reporting completion of the task assigned, de Robeck and his staff may have had no knowledge of what they had achieved. There is nothing in the official despatches on the subject, and only recent research has unearthed the full facts in the Annual Report of H.M.S. *Vernon* for 1915.' The 'full facts' are also in the Mitchell Report.

at the fateful meeting in the *Queen Elizabeth* on 22 March: 'As soon as my fast sweepers are ready, I am going through to Constantinople. If we don't then succeed in getting a peace settlement, it may be necessary for me to leave the Marmora and to land your army to occupy the peninsula, so that I can keep the fleet in the Marmora indefinitely.' Further, let us suppose that the War Council, taking a real decision for once, had given orders to the Admiral to do it, accepting, if necessary, the loss of half the old battleships in view of the tremendous political prize. Had the fleet tried again, on 4 April, or, better still, 18 April, would it have got through? The crucial point is the effectiveness of the new minesweeper organization. One cannot prognosticate complete success by the new sweeping force, had a fresh naval attack been made. The destroyers had swept a large area in the lower Straits with complete success against the two new lines, 12 and 13, and with no losses; but these were short lines with few mines and they had not tackled the Kephez minefield, to say nothing of the minefield in the Narrows. One cannot therefore be certain that the reorganized force had overcome all the inherent defects in the old system. On the other hand, nothing is certain in war, and the performance of the destroyer-sweepers was distinctly encouraging. Even had they failed on 18 April in the suggested operation, the purely naval attack could have been broken off without loss of face and the combined operation been permitted to proceed on the 25th.

Let us assume that the sweepers had preceded the battleships in a daytime attack (the fleet was not trained in night fighting, whereas the Turkish searchlights were quite well used) and had done their job, eliminating the minefield obstacle. The 'Beagles' did light sweeps on each of the first two days of the combined operation, and about four on the third day: twenty sweeps under fire before they had a single hit, so I think it fair to say that for one sudden thrust they were practically immune to Turkish fire. What of the battleships? Four British pre-dreadnoughts and one French had reinforced the fleet, making it stronger than on the eve of the 18 March attack (eighteen old battleships and the *Queen Elizabeth*, as compared with fourteen old battleships and the *Queen Elizabeth* and *Inflexible* on 18 March). Ample stocks of ammunition were on hand. It is exciting to think of the possibilities in the new sweeping force, and of the psychological and material effects of a determined sudden thrust by the fleet, steaming at full speed (15 knots) close behind the fast destroyer-minesweepers, straight at the Narrows (I do not think the Turkish gun crews would have stood up to the close-range rapid fire of the fleet's numerous light guns)[40]—and the *Queen Elizabeth* and her indirect fire in support achieving the *moral* effect needed. Aircraft and ship flank-spotting would have put her salvoes on to the forts.[41] Let us also bear in mind that the ammunition situation at the forts was unchanged and the supply of mines limited. It does not require too much imagination to assume that the fleet would have dominated the forts at close range and passed the Narrows. There was nothing above Point Nagara beyond a couple of ancient batteries and the Turkish Fleet to stop it from arriving at Constantinople. De Robeck's instructions called for the destruction of the enemy fleet as 'the first objective' after forcing the Dardanelles. This should not have posed any great difficulties.[42] When this had been achieved, the Turkish Army in Europe was to be cut off by the destruction of the Scutari–Ismid Railway and the Constantinople–Kuchuk Chekmeje road and railway. (Cf. Kitchener's statement below.) The next step would have been, with Russian naval co-operation, to force the Bosphorus. Finally, 'Constantinople was to be summoned [to surrender] as soon as possible without prejudice' to the three objectives above. 'Massacre and futile resistance it was suggested might be prevented by informing Turkish authorities that, if the city was peacefully surrendered, private property and religious buildings would be absolutely respected. Operations were to be concerted with the General-in-Command of the Army and movements of troops prevented on Bulair Peninsula [isthmus].'[43]

Supposing the fleet had anchored off the Turkish capital. Again,

---

[40] The Turkish gun crews had never experienced this, but only the slow and ponderous single shots from the big turret guns on 7, 8, and 18 March; close-range rapid fire would have been a very different cup of tea when serving a fort gun entirely out in the open.

[41] The air-spotting resources of the fleet were strengthened with the arrival of three aeroplane squadrons on 24 March with eighteen aircraft. Only five were any good, but each of these could do three sorties a day, so that, even without the use of seaplanes, the *Queen Elizabeth* would have had continuous aircraft spotting. An aerodrome was established on Tenedos. HMS *Monica*, the first kite-balloon ship, arrived at Mudros on 9 April. At about 1,500 feet, the maximum height attainable by the kite-balloon, observation was considered good. During April the balloon conducted 'some most successful spotting operations' with the *Queen Elizabeth* and other battleships. So successful was the balloon that, initially, 'its co-operation would seem to have been preferred to that of an aeroplane'. Mitchell Report, p. 509.

[42] The Turkish Fleet was organized into an Active Squadron (the ex-German battle cruiser *Goeben* and light cruiser *Breslau*, and three old cruisers) under the German Admiral Souchon, and a Reserve Squadron (an ancient battleship, vintage 1874, reconstructed in 1902, and two of 1891, an old cruiser, and ten torpedo boats) under a Turkish captain.

[43] Instructions dated 4 Mar. 1915, as summarized in the Mitchell Report, p. 29.

I believe there was at least a 50–50 chance of making the Turks ask for peace in April. The critics of another attempt to force the Narrows claim that there would have been no revolution at Constantinople, that the Turkish Government and military command would have moved out and declared Constantinople an open city —*and then what?* That the Turks would have gone on fighting was always a possibility, in which case the fleet would have withdrawn from the Marmora. Despite de Robeck's fears, it is far from certain that he would have suffered Duckworth's fate. The guns of the Narrows forts, mounted to give an arc of fire to the south and west, could have been taken in reverse by ships coming down from the north.[44] Churchill, Grey (the Foreign Secretary), Kitchener (the War Secretary), and the Admiralty, however, were confident that the arrival of the fleet off Constantinople in sufficient strength to defeat the Turco-German Fleet, if it had not yet been defeated, would produce decisive results by leading swiftly to a revolution against the Young Turks in power, withdrawal from the war by the new government, and the probable joining of the Balkan Powers in the war against the Central Powers.[45] Under the armistice terms a token force to occupy the dockyard, telegraph office, etc., in Constantinople and to occupy the Narrows forts might have been needed until a peace was signed. The Royal Naval Division could have done this.

The basis of the expectation that the arrival of the fleet would have produced a revolution in Constantinople was, to quote the DNI in 1916, the 'undoubted evidence from a number of good sources' of the panic in the capital as the attack on the forts developed. There was 'direct evidence that the Government was preparing to shift to Asia Minor, and the archives had already started to go over. . . . the better families were preparing to pack up

[44] Vice-Admiral Sir Reginald Bacon, commanding the Dover Patrol, 1915–17, and one of the Navy's foremost gunnery experts, flatly stated at the Dardanelles hearings that the Narrows forts were 'so constructed for protecting the shore against a fleet coming up that you can take nearly the whole lot of them absolutely in reverse or in flank'. *Proceedings of the Dardanelles Commission*, p. 288. I might add here that the Turkish guns on both sides of the Bosphorus would have posed no threat to an Allied fleet anchored off Constantinople. The forts were sited and their guns mounted to give arcs of fire to engage ships approaching from the Black Sea. They could not even see the Marmora.

[45] Churchill at an early date knew what they wanted of a defeated Turkey: 'the surrender of everything Turkish in Europe'. The terms of the Armistice might well include 'the surrender of fortress of Adrianople and military positions affecting the control of the Bosphorus, Dardanelles & Constantinople', Allied occupation of Turkey in Europe, and Bulgarian occupation of the Enos–Midia line. 'Remember Cple is only a means to an end—& the only end is the march of the Balkan states against the Central Powers.' Churchill to Grey, 28 Feb. 1915, FO 800/88 (Public Record Office).

and to go over into Asia Minor rather than stay there.' Moreover, the state of mind revealed in the secret negotiations with 'the highest Turkish authorities' from 29 January (they peaked on 15 February and then dragged on) revealed the anxiety with which the Turks contemplated the prosecution of the operations.[46] On the basis of such evidence Hall thought they 'had every reason to expect that if we got to Constantinople we should have pulled the Turks out of the war'. Kitchener told Ian Hamilton that 'if the fleet got through, the Turks would make terms. He explained to me that the fleet would command the railways which feed Constantinople, and that although he hoped it would not happen so, they could blow a large part of the city to bits.'[47]

Wishful thinking? Possibly. But the American Ambassador in Constantinople at the time, who had no axe to grind at all, offers solid first-hand evidence that the expectation of decisive results was well grounded. 'Had the Allied fleets once passed the defences at the Strait, the administration of the Young Turks would have come to a bloody end.' Morgenthau claimed that the Ottoman State, which had 'no solidly-established Government', was 'on the brink of dissolution' on 18 March. 'As for Constantinople, the populace there and the best elements among the Turks, far from opposing the arrival of the Allied fleet, would have welcomed it with joy. The Turks themselves were praying that the British and French would take their city, for this would relieve them of the controlling gang, emancipate them from the hated Germans, bring about peace, and end their miseries.'[48] Morale in the capital had not improved noticeably by mid-April.

But how did the Turks and Germans visualize the scenario? In the postwar judgement of the Turkish War Office, 'It was impossible to estimate the situation which would have arisen if the Allied Fleet had forced their way past the forts, past the minefields, and entered the Sea of Marmara. However, if the British Fleet had attacked land transport from the direction of Bulair, and at the same time from the Gulf of Xeros [Saros], a very difficult situation would have undoubtedly arisen. It would have increased enormously the difficulty of transport between the Asiatic and European coasts and also in the Bosphorus and Marmara.' If this attack by the fleet on Turkish communications from both sides of the peninsula continued, it was but a question of time before the Turkish Army

[46] On these negotiations see *From the Dreadnought to Scapa Flow*, ii. 217 n., and in more detail, Robert Rhodes James, *Gallipoli* (London, 1965), pp. 48–9.

[47] Hall's and Hamilton's testimony, *Proceedings of the Dardanelles Commission*, pp. 281–3, 251, respectively.

[48] Morgenthau, *Secrets of the Bosphorus*, pp. 128, 149–50.

would have had to capitulate.[49] Enver Bey (not to be confused with Enver Pasha, the Turkish strong man and War Minister), COS to Admiral von Souchon, did not think the Allied fleet could get through the Dardanelles because of the minefields (Souchon thought it would), but if it did, he believed that the arrival of the Allied fleet off Constantinople would have precipitated a revolution against Enver Pasha. According to Enver Bey,

If the Fleet had got through at any time before the evacuation, it would have been able to control the communications of the Turkish Army on the Peninsula and it would have been necessary to make peace for that reason alone.

The Turkish Fleet could not successfully have fought the Allied Fleet if it had passed into the Marmara, as it was not sufficiently homogeneous to act as a fleet. An attempt would have been made to attack with torpedoes and by gunfire from *Goeben*, etc. . . . The hope was that ships would come in single file, and so be attacked singly. They would have been met at Nagara, and attacked by torpedoes, gunfire, and everything possible.

Lieutenant-Commander Baltzer, of the German Navy, who saw all naval reports in 1917 when attached to the Turkish Ministry of Marine, had 'no doubt whatever that Turkey would have made peace. There would have been a revolution. The appearance of ships before Constantinople would have been sufficient. Constantinople is Turkey.' On the other hand, the General in command at the Dardanelles in 1914–15, Djevad Pasha, claimed that the fleet, had it broken through to Constantinople, would not have done any good. There was an army at Constantinople (three corps until 27 March, but three of the nine divisions were sent to the Gallipoli front by the end of April) and the Straits would have closed behind the fleet.[50] Finally, we should bear in mind that the great boost to

---

[49] Mitchell Report, p. 433, and, similarly, pp. 71, 72.

[50] ibid., pp. 71–2, 382, 433–5. The German Ambassador was 'of the opinion that when the Straits are in the hands of the enemy, Turkey sooner or later is lost so far as we are concerned. The Turks will certainly continue to fight on our side for a time in Asia Minor, but it would be the end of any expedition against Egypt and to our plans concerning Persia, Afghanistan, and India. The Turkish forces fighting in Asia Minor would not draw off any enemy strength worth mentioning. *Goeben* and *Breslau* would have met an heroic end, so that further action in the Black Sea would no longer be possible. I believe that we would then have to draw a thick line under our Turkish policy.' Wangenheim's dispatch of 23 Mar. 1915. Enver Pasha, a notoriously unreliable authority, declared in January 1916 that 'even had the British ships got to Constantinople, it would not have availed them much. Our plan was to retire our army to the surrounding hills and to Asia Minor and to leave the town at their mercy. They would not have destroyed it [but cf. Kitchener's statement, above], and the result would have been simply an *impasse*.' Report of an interview with Enver Pasha by a 'Special Correspondent', *Daily Mail*, 27 Jan. 1916. Assuming that one can believe Enver Pasha, retirement from Constantinople would have

Turkish morale came when they realized that besides beating the fleet they had beaten the landings although greatly outnumbered. After that they were tough nuts to crack.

The political stakes were tremendous and well worth a fresh naval attack in April, even though half a dozen old battleships were lost. The object, we must remember, was to get Turkey out of the war and open the Dardanelles and Bosphorus to commerce with Russia. There was, of course, no certainty of success, but the stakes and the not impossible odds would have justified a shot at it. There was none. Captain Boswell mourns the 'glorious opportunity' that was missed. 'Once the Army landed, every effort the Navy could make was devoted to helping their brothers-in-arms, and history has so far failed to record what the Navy could have achieved by itself.' Therein lies perhaps the greatest tragedy associated with the Dardanelles campaign: the lost opportunity of April, one of the most poignant might-have-beens of the First World War.

availed the Turks nothing. As the British Official Historian remarks, 'It is important to realize that had Constantinople been abandoned, the Turks would have been unable to continue the war. Their only arms and munition factories were at the capital and would have been destroyed by the fleet, and the supply of material from Germany would have been impossible.' Brigadier C. F. Aspinall-Oglander, *Military Operations. Gallipoli* (2 vols., London, 1929–32), i. 105 n.

Chapter Two

The Influence of History on Sea Power

The Royal Navy and the Lessons of 1914–1918[1]

IT is an axiom among historians that a knowledge of history can serve as a guide to the present. This is not to say that the present ought simply to imitate the past, for every human situation is indeed unique, but rather that individuals and groups should act to meet new situations partly on the basis of past experience. Armed forces have a particularly bad reputation for not taking this axiom seriously. Let us examine in some detail one case history, the Royal Navy after the First War, with a view to understanding how much that Service profited from 1914–18 and why it did not learn as much as it might have from its war experience.

The gruelling test of battle in the war naturally had brought to the fore a host of defects in the Royal Navy—in *matériel*, tactical

---

[1] Or: the extent to which British failure to apply the lessons of World War I influenced the conduct of World War II. I am not concerned with failures of other kinds, as, for example, the lamentable anti-aircraft control, which is a reflection on the Navy's failure to keep up to date with scientific and engineering progress. I must begin by making clear that this is a tricky subject, about which there are a good many differences of opinion. I would also stress that I could have used the interwar experience of the U.S. Navy with equal validity to support my thesis! The information and constructive criticism offered by the following officers, who read an early version of the chapter, have been extremely helpful in permitting me to get at a measure of the truth: Admirals of the Fleet Sir George Creasy, Sir Caspar John, and Sir Algernon Willis, Admirals Sir Desmond Dreyer, Sir Guy Grantham, Sir Derek Holland-Martin, Sir Charles Madden, Sir Henry Moore, and Sir Manley Power, Vice-Admirals Sir Ronald Brockman, Sir Peter Cazalet, Sir Norman Denning, Sir Aubrey Mansergh, R. D. Oliver, and B. B. Schofield, Rear-Admirals R. M. Dick and G. A. Thring, Captains G. R. G. Allen, L. A. K. Boswell, R. H. Johnson, J. S. S. Litchfield, Donald Macintyre, H. C. B. Pipon, and Andrew Yates, and Commanders R. C. Burton and G. A. Titterton. Marshal of the Royal Air Force Sir John Slessor, Admirals Sir Angus Cunninghame Graham and the late Sir William James, Vice-Admiral Sir Hector MacLean, Captains Geoffrey Bennett, J. E. ('Jack') Broome, and J. S. Cowie, Commander W. M. Phipps Hornby, and Lieutenant-Commander D. W. Waters provided useful information on particular points.

doctrine, and system of command. What would the postwar Navy do about these shortcomings—that was the question. During the hostilities, the 'Young Turks', led by Captain H. W. Richmond, partly to assuage their bitter criticisms of the inefficiency of the Navy, looked forward to a postwar British version of '*J'accuse*', to be followed by an era of reform which would capitalize on the lessons of the war. They were confident that the war would provide the will for, and create an atmosphere favourable to, reform. 'The English won't learn in peace,' declared one of Richmond's disciples, 'but they *can't* fail to learn from war. It may be 5 years, or 10 . . . but sooner or later the truth *must* come to light and a renaissance will result, followed by a sound system of education.'[2]

Early postwar prospects were good. Before leaving the Admiralty at the beginning of 1919, the First Lord, Sir Eric Geddes, recommended to the Board of Admiralty the appointment of 'a strong, critical, and as far as possible independently-minded Committee' to examine 'the naval position on the outbreak of war and the steps taken during the war to remedy defects and meet new requirements'. Captain Stephen Roskill says that this suggestion, 'with its implied criticism of the Admiralty's conduct of the war', was not implemented.[3] Early in 1919 the Admiralty took steps 'to appoint Committees of Sea Officers to summarise the more urgent lessons of the War and to make recommendations as to future policy, whilst the experience of the War is fresh in their minds. . . .'[4] Here again there was no immediate follow-up. The only two committees formed were the 'Mitchell Committee', appointed on 21 March 1919 to make a thorough investigation of what had gone wrong at the Dardanelles and on Gallipoli in 1915, and a Post-War Questions Committee in August 1919 (Rear-Admiral R. F. Phillimore, chairman) with narrow terms of reference. It was to 'consider in the light of the experience of the war the military uses and values of the different types of war vessel' and 'consider and advise the Board of Admiralty on the part likely to be taken by aircraft, both in attack and defence'. A Government directive struck the examination of the naval air situation from the terms of reference. As regards the first charge, no doubt because of Admiralty sensitivity to what might emerge from a searching study, the Committee made a superficial examination of the pertinent experience of the

[2] Captain Reginald Drax to Richmond, 28 Sept. 1917, Richmond MSS., 7/4 (National Maritime Museum, Greenwich).

[3] Roskill, *Naval Policy between the Wars*, vol. i, *The Period of Anglo-American Antagonism, 1919–1929* (London, 1968), p. 113.

[4] An undated, untitled memorandum by Sir Rosslyn Wemyss (First Sea Lord) of early 1919, Wemyss MSS. (Hon. Mrs. Francis Cunnack).

war and put its imprimatur on the continuing predominance of the battleship (March 1920).

More promising was the work of the Naval Staff College, which was started at Greenwich in June 1919 on Sir Rosslyn Wemyss's initiative to train officers for Naval Staff duties. Its very establishment proved that one all-important lesson of the war had not gone unheeded. As Lord Beatty, who succeeded Wemyss at the end of 1919, put it: 'Such naval disasters as occurred during the war were the direct result of the lack of sufficient and efficient staff. . . . We paid very dearly for the experience which led to its formation and nothing should interfere with its development.'[5] The main object of the staff course training (the course was approximately nine months) was (and remains), in Admiral J. H. Godfrey's words, 'to broaden the mind to study war and to make officers think'. By 1939 the list of officers who had completed the course, or had served on the staff of the College, filled two pages of the closely printed *Navy List*. During the 1920s the Navy, generally, regarded staff officers with a good deal of suspicion, particularly those with really independent thoughts and ideas. This attitude had changed by the beginning of its second decade, and 'it seemed to be universally accepted that the staff course should form part and parcel of a promising naval officer's career, and that the qualifications for selection to the course were the same as those for promotion. Of the fifty-one executive officers who did the course during 1929 and 1930, eighteen have become Flag Officers.'[6] As part of its work, the Staff College did its best to study and absorb the lessons of 1914–18, and the evidence is that it made as good a job of it as could be expected. The battles of the First War were studied, Jutland above all, with personal talks by the leading admirals of that time—J. R. Jellicoe, W. E. Goodenough, and others—adding a realistic element. In 1936 Admiral Sir Reginald ('Blinker') Hall, the great wartime Director of Naval Intelligence, delivered a 'magnificent' talk on intelligence and on ways of communicating with those at sea. He also discussed trade protection, drawing on the experience of 1914–18.

The Tactical School was founded at Portsmouth Dockyard in 1924 (it was the proposal of Admiral Sir Frederic Dreyer, Jellicoe's Flag-Captain at Jutland) to promote a more scientific study of naval tactics.[7] It expounded the *Battle Instructions* (title changed in the

---

[5] Quoted in Godfrey, *Naval Memoirs*, iii. 33. Godfrey was on the directing staff of the Royal Naval Staff College, 1923–5, and Deputy-Director, 1929–31.

[6] ibid., pp. 36–7.

[7] There is a rather ludicrous, though reliable, story of the start of the School. For

summer of 1939 to *Fighting Instructions*), with a well-organized demonstration of Jutland on the big tactical board as the high spot. This was laid on to bring out the lessons to be learned. For the rest the officers did convoy exercises and staged imaginary fleet actions. Admiral of the Fleet Sir Algernon Willis has 'always thought that the Tactical School did a good job and I believe this was the general opinion in the Service. The fact that the Navy never put a foot wrong "tactically" in World War II is generally attributed largely to the work of the Tactical School.' I would not dispute this expert judgement, except to note that there was perhaps too much emphasis on fleet action as being the ultimate test of war. One must add that a lot of tactical experiment and investigation went on at sea, where it should, and was carefully analysed. All the same, as will be indicated below, not all the tactical lessons of the First War were learned.

The accepted doctrine of the Navy's strategical ideas was supposed to have been enshrined in the *Naval War Manual*, first issued in September 1921 and revised in October 1925. There was little in it beyond a few catchwords pertaining to the 'principles of war' and generalities on 'naval policy', the 'functions of the Navy', 'war plans', and so on. A much fuller statement, completed in October 1938 by Commander John Creswell at the R.N. College, Greenwich, at the direction of the Admiralty, had not been issued when the war came.

In short, there was in the interwar years a fairly close study of the lessons—*some* of the lessons, at any rate—of the war, and certain principles were evolved and reforms instituted. It may rightly be claimed that British naval successes in the Second War can be attributed in part to these studies and exercises. Apart from the establishment of the Staff College, there were various ways in which the lessons of the First War had obviously been learned and were well applied. Thus, enemy reporting was much improved and the Navy had good success in solving the problem of a massed torpedo attack by destroyers on a battle fleet, which had hobbled Grand Fleet tactics.[8] The Grand Fleet doctrine of not committing a fleet

some years there had been courses at Portsmouth to keep senior officers up to date in technical matters, mostly at the gunnery and torpedo schools. To avoid the danger of any enemy suspecting that they were studying tactics, and finding out what their intentions were, the new establishment was initially dubbed the 'Senior Officers' Technical Course, Part II'. In 1930, after someone said, 'This is too silly: let's call it the Tactical School', it was so re-named!

[8] Many postwar experiments tested the three methods of resisting such an attack: (1) turning towards the torpedoes, (2) remaining in line of battle without turning, and (3) turning away, as carried out at Jutland. The results proved that the third

to night action was rejected, and improvements were introduced in night fighting (as through the introduction of star shell and improved searchlight control), with the reward of Matapan. Ernle Chatfield and W. W. Fisher in the Mediterranean in the early thirties placed great emphasis on night-action training. In the last prewar months the new DNI, Rear-Admiral J. H. Godfrey, was able to apply an important lesson of the First War—that Operations and Intelligence must work together, avoiding any semblance of secrecy. The neglect of this common-sense principle had had disastrous results at Jutland. There was a big improvement on the First War as regards initiative and leadership. Those in command of operations, even small ones involving perhaps only a few units, showed a high degree of initiative, in no small way regaining the confidence in, and capacity for, independent judgement of those captains of the old sailing days who usually had to rely on themselves. Staff work generally, ashore and afloat, was improved. 'There was', writes Admiral Sir Manley Power, 'a tremendous change in the behaviour of Senior Officers in the period between the wars, particularly in their attitudes towards their staffs. Early ones resented having staffs thrust upon them at all. Chatfield, as C-in-C [Mediterranean, 1930–2], used his staff to the full, but officers venturing opinions uninvited were severely choked off. [A. B.] Cunningham, whom I served [1939–43], professed to despise Staff training, but thrived on controversy and encouraged it. One of his earliest remarks to me after I joined him was: "I *hate* Staff Officers who agree with me." This made me a No man for the duration!' 'A.B.C.' was typical of the new breed of senior officer—men like John D. Cunningham, B. H. ('Bertie') Ramsay, and James Somerville—who encouraged controversy.

There was after the First War tremendous room for improvement in inter-Service understanding and co-operation. 'To appreciate the atmosphere in which the Dardanelles assault was hatched, one must accept the fact that Admiral [Sir A. K.] Wilson, Lord Fisher, and Lord Kitchener were incapable of co-operation and would have been deeply shocked at the idea of revealing a naval plan to a soldier, or a military project to a sailor.'[9] The lesson was learned. After the war the three staff colleges held a joint exercise every year (the one in 1935 was 'The Recapture of Singapore'!), which welded

was the only safe method. The Navy had a change of view by the 1930s: it was now believed that, in certain circumstances, the attraction of coming to grips with the enemy quickly justified the extra risk. During World War II it was generally accepted that the best counter-measure was to turn *towards* the torpedoes.

[9] Godfrey, *Naval Memoirs*, iii. 25.

together Royal Air Force, Army, and Navy officers from the staff and personal points of view. The creation of the Chiefs of Staff Sub-Committee of the Committee of Imperial Defence in 1923, a body where the three Service Chiefs met as a team to work out a common strategy and advise the Government on defence, was another encouraging development in the same direction, as was the companion Joint Planning Committee. I should mention, too, the establishment in 1927 of the Imperial Defence College to 'train a body of officers [from all three Services] and civilian officials in the broadest aspects of Imperial Strategy'. As a result, despite the fact that differences of opinion continued and good relations were bedevilled by the Navy–RAF feud over control of Naval Air, inter-Service co-operation in the last war in the strategic field, though far from perfect, particularly at the very top, was highly effectual.

But all this gives a false impression of what actually was achieved in the twenty years between wars in the way of profiting from the lessons of 1914–18. Much was done at Staff and War colleges and at the Tactical School, but it was not based on a really critical study of the past. Moreover, investigation focused on *matériel* problems. Ship design, questions of gunfire (success was achieved in the control and concentration of gunfire), the development of smoke screens, and the like absorbed the energies of Admiralty committees. Apart, however, from the Mitchell Committee on the Dardanelles in 1919, there was little attempt by these committees to study the larger problems and lessons of the war. The results of this neglect were most serious in the field of trade defence.

*   *   *

There is substance in Lieutenant-Commander D. W. Waters's assertion that 'virtually every surface and air anti-submarine lesson of the first submarine war had to be, and ultimately was, re-learnt in the second at immense cost in blood, tears and treasure'. One would have thought that the entire Service knew that the most important lesson of the First War was that the U-boat attack on the merchant fleet was Britain's most serious danger, and that it was only the introduction of convoy in 1917 that had saved the day. But the anti-submarine lessons of the war, which had never been fully understood anyway,[10] were quickly forgotten after the war because there was no serious attempt to study the larger meaning of the U-boat campaign of 1917–18. During the interwar years, consequently, the convoy system was understood imperfectly at best. Although Captain Roskill was off the mark in stating that

[10] See Marder, *From the Dreadnought to Scapa Flow*, v. 97–105.

in 1919–39 there was not a single exercise in the protection of a mercantile convoy against air or submarine attack, the fact is that the Navy paid all too little attention to convoy work between the wars.[11]

Ignorance was doubtless the chief explanation of the indifferent attitude towards convoy during much of the interwar period. The Admiralty's German Navy expert, who was in charge of the captured German naval archives, has written:

A point that has emerged with startling clarity from all our researches

[11] Roskill, *Naval Policy between the Wars*, i. 536. Apparently he could not find a report of a convoy exercise in the Admiralty records. Admiral Brockman remembers no convoy exercises in the Fleet exercises of the 1920s and 1930s. Admiral of the Fleet Willis and Captain L. A. K. Boswell, however, remember fleet exercises involving convoys and anti-submarine forces, although Rear-Admiral R. M. Dick says the convoy exercises were often a matter of fighting a convoy through against threatened surface and air attack quite as much as against the submarine. Vice-Admiral B. B. Schofield 'personally took part in a convoy exercise when serving in H.M.S. *Malaya* in March 1930 on passage from Gibraltar to Plymouth. Also the Combined Fleet Exercises of (I think) 1935 [1934?] were based on trade protection in the Azores area. *This is not to say that such exercises were of frequent occurrence, and they were chiefly designed to give destroyers practice in using their Asdic equipment*' (italics mine). Admiral Sir Hector MacLean, who served with the fleet destroyers in the Mediterranean in 1938–9 (prewar)—these were destroyers with the speed and endurance to screen the battle fleet—testifies that, though they did a lot of screening exercises of battleships and cruisers, there never had been any proper convoy exercises that he remembered. This can be explained by the acute and chronic shortage of destroyers, which left no alternative but to concentrate on using them with the fleet. That is, the fleet destroyers in the Mediterranean could never be spared to learn about convoy work. There is evidence that the convoy system worked better initially than could have been expected from the prewar neglect of convoy exercises. Admiral of the Fleet Sir Caspar John, who was Second-in-Command of the cruiser *York* at the outbreak of war, says: 'We were detailed as ocean escort for the first West–East convoy from Halifax, Nova Scotia, HX1. The assembly of the convoy in Bedford Basin, the pre-sailing briefing conference, the conduct of the convoy in forming up and on passage were first-class performances, as though all concerned had been practising for years. One is tempted to ask, "So what were we all beefing about? It worked on the day!" I don't say every convoy ran as smoothly as HX1—but it was a good start. The explanation may be that although convoy exercises at sea were conspicuous by their absence, there were plenty of convoy exercises on tactical tables ashore, the convoy instructions were up-to-date, and distributed, and certainly must have been studied and understood if HX1's performance is anything to go by.' The 'convoy instructions' were the Mercantile Convoy Instructions, which at the outbreak of war were still the 1918 ones, which needed no change. There were, of course, revisions as regards the disposition of escorts, but that did not affect the conduct and organization of the convoy. To judge from Vice-Admiral Sir Peter Gretton's recollection, the MCIs were not as influential as they might have been. He remembers that when he left the Home Fleet early in 1941 to assume a command in a convoy escort group in the Western Approaches, he 'read the MCIs in the train and found nothing of any help to me in it. When I got to Londonderry, my base, and mentioned this, no one whom I spoke to had ever heard of the MCIs, from Captain D[estroyers] down.'

into British and German records since the end of the Second World War is that no historian writing between the two wars (either British or German) drew the full and accurate conclusions from U-boat operations of 1917–18. The principal reason for this omission was that in those between-war years the full records of both sides were never available to any one historian, as they are available today. In this country the fact that we had eventually defeated the U-boats, and the advent of asdics shortly after the end of the First World War combined to produce in many officers an attitude of over-confidence in regard to any resurgence of the U-boat menace. In Germany, on the other hand, the researches of Admiral Spindler (the historian of the 1914–18 U-boat operations) were never completed. His work only went as far as 1917, and therefore did not include many of the lessons of U-boat operations against convoys.[12]

Contributory causes of the failure to profit fully from war experience were (1) the old obsession with the battleship and fleet actions, which will be dealt with below; (2) an over-confidence, particularly in the 1930s, in asdic, the device that had been developed since 1917 as the answer to the problem of locating submarines;[13] (3) the

[12] Commander M. G. Saunders's memorandum, appended to Rear-Admiral Roger M. Bellairs's letter to Captain John Creswell, 2 Nov. 1954, Creswell MSS., 2/1 (Churchill College). Volumes iv (Feb.–Dec. 1917) and v (1918) of Spindler's *Der Krieg zur See: Der Handelskrieg mit U-Booten* were not published until 1941 and 1966.

[13] One must give credit to the Navy for having invented what is, albeit with improvements, still the principal instrument for detecting submerged submarines. There was, unfortunately, a widespread exaggerated confidence in asdic (the term was replaced by 'sonar' in 1943). This may have been due to extrapolating the results obtained by a small band of dedicated experts in the limited conditions off Portland, where nearly all the anti-submarine training was carried out. It was encouraged by some of the results of fleet exercises, in which the destroyer screens were very strong and all units were moving at comparatively high speed. Those who served in submarines between the wars were aware of the ineffectiveness of asdic. They knew how to escape detection and penetrate a destroyer screen nine times out of ten, though they were not always successful in their attack. Captain Jack Broome, who spent several of the interwar years in the submarine flotilla at Portland, maintains that 'asdic was never the infallible weapon we cracked it up to be . . . In various set-piece exercises, we dived and asdic-fitted ships hunted us. To facilitate their training and strengthen their confidence, our movements were generally restricted; seldom were we allowed to evade. When evasion was allowed, we generally succeeded. . . . On other occasions, in Fleet exercises, we submarines carried out many dummy attacks on battleships steaming at 18 knots, zig-zagging, with anti-submarine destroyer screens. Our movements were, of course, unrestricted, but even then everyone above the surface knew that a succession of submarines would be attacking between certain times in a particular area. But *still*, an average submariner stood an odds-on chance of getting in close enough to fire torpedoes undetected.' Broome, *Convoy Is To Scatter* (London, 1972), pp. 79–80. Admiral Sir Manley Power is another who believes that this confidence in asdic was nourished in spite of evidence to the contrary. 'Memory is notoriously unreliable, but I think I used to achieve about 50% undetected attacks, though this was in the Med, where Asdic conditions were bad. The sad truth is that much of the Navy disliked and feared submarines and was all too inclined to think that if they shut their eyes, the bogeyman would go away. Lack of training was used as the excuse for failure to detect, and that it would be

antipathy of many senior officers to what was falsely regarded as a defensive, to say nothing of a generally dull and monotonous, measure. Concerning the last, Admiral of the Fleet Sir Caspar John (among many others) bears out my contention: 'You are very correct in writing that Convoy protection was regarded with martial antipathy by the Navy—it was too defensive in outlook for peace-time training—and, anyway, unlike battleships, there was never a visible convoy to "protect".'[14] This attitude is borne out by the fact that in general the commands of fleet destroyers rather than of convoy escorts were regarded as the plums. Consequently, although, of course, there were some brilliant exceptions, the best officers were with the Fleet and the second team with the convoy escorts. Nor did it help that until the last prewar years it was the assumption that Japan would be Britain's principal enemy in a war, not Germany, and the problem here was how to get at Japan across the world, not how to escort merchant ships across the Atlantic.

I do not want to leave the impression that progressive thought on convoy was entirely absent. The President of the Naval War College at Greenwich during 1934–7, when over a hundred officers went through the war course, recalled that 'neither staff nor courses

"all right on the night". It is true that highly trained A/S ships were difficult to evade. However, these failures under fairly easy conditions should have been clear warning of what to expect in a slow-moving thinly screened convoy.' Admiral of the Fleet Sir George Creasy says that in the last Combined Fleet Exercises before the war (March 1939), in an attack by a combined flotilla of submarines on the fleet, only one was detected, and he asserts that the overrating of asdic was the worst of the Navy's failures to foresee problems before the Second War. Record of Donald McLachlan's interview with Creasy, 14–15 Mar. [1967?], McLachlan MSS. Creasy was Assistant Director of Plans, 1936–8. See further on these exercises ADM 116/3873 (Combined Fleet Exercise 'XZQ') and Rear-Admiral G. W. G. Simpson, *Periscope View: a Professional Biography* (London, 1972), pp. 73–6, which bear Creasy out. The submarines, according to Simpson, obtained 22 per cent of hits. On the other hand, Vice-Admiral Sir Peter Cazalet, who had twenty years' connection with the A/S Branch, has an exactly opposite recollection as regards asdic. 'The difficulty between the wars was to get anyone to take any interest at all in A/S matters. A/S exercises were admittedly very dull and were generally regarded as time-wasters and an un-mitigated bore. Both before and during the war I cannot recall a single example of over-optimism.'

14 The Admiral points out that 'peace-time training and thought depend as much on the Merchant Navy as they do on the Royal Navy. In a "No war for 10 years" atmosphere how does one persuade a shipping Chamber of Commerce, or whatever is the appropriate body, to persuade its members to take their ships out of trade (profitable) for a month—or for a voyage—to be guinea pigs (*un*profitable) for an up-dating of methods to keep them buoyant?' It was impossible to collect together ten or twenty ships for such an exercise, and the convoy was generally represented by three or four ships only—a repair ship, one or two depot ships, and perhaps a Royal Fleet Auxiliary.

had any doubt on this subject. It was in fact Common Doctrine that convoy had rescued us in the first war and that it would be necessary in the future. So I cannot understand the Financial Secretary's speech [see below]. It certainly had no effect on our teaching and as we were in close touch with the Admiralty we should have known if they thought differently.'[15] All that I maintain is that there was always a body of naval opinion which, through a failure to analyse the U-boat war of 1914–18, or for one or more of the other reasons mentioned above, preserved an anti-convoy outlook. The remarks of the Parliamentary and Financial Secretary of the Admiralty, Lord Stanley, speaking in the House of Commons on 14 March 1935, sum up the views of the Board and the Naval Staff at that date and are a reiteration of all the standard objections of the anti-convoy school of thought (or prejudice):

I can assure the House that the convoy system would not be introduced at once on the outbreak of war. Even the right hon. member for Swindon [Dr. Addison] would admit that the convoy system has very great disadvantages, and it certainly would not be welcomed by the trading community until conditions had become so intolerable that they were prepared to make the necessary sacrifices. In the first place, you would get delay at each end. You would get delay while the ships assembled at the starting point to be taken up by their convoy. You would get delay by the ships arriving at the same port at the same time. You would also have the difficulty of the faster ship having to go at the same pace as the slower one. Therefore, the convoy system will only be introduced when the balance of advantage is in its favour and when sinkings are so great that the country no longer feels justified in allowing ships to sail by themselves but feels that for the protection of their crews the convoy system is necessary.

(Dr. Addison:) Am I to understand the Noble Lord to suggest that the Admiralty would wait before instituting the convoy system until so many ships had been sunk that the country would not stand it any longer? Surely, they are not going to wait until such conditions arise as occurred on 17th April, 1917, when 34 ships were sunk one night. Are they going to let us get to that pitch before they start the convoy system?

(Lord Stanley:) Certainly not, but it will not be introduced in the first place. You will not know in the first place whether the ships are going to be in any great danger. It may be that it will be safer for them to sail by themselves. They will be a smaller target. The enemy ships would not know where they were to be found. If raiders were about we should have to institute the convoy system at once. It is simply a matter of expediency. We should be ready to put the scheme into operation but we should wait

[15] Admiral Sir Ragnar Colvin to Vice-Admiral K. G. B. Dewar, 7 Mar. 1952, Dewar MSS., 4 (National Maritime Museum). Colvin's impression is also that of Admiral Sir Desmond Dreyer ('The understanding in the Fleet was certainly as indicated by Admiral Colvin') and Captain John Creswell, who in 1934–5 was doing the tactical course at Portsmouth and then running junior officers' tactical courses at Malta.

until we thought that the proper moment had arrived. Having got to the point when it is considered that the ships ought not to sail by themselves but should be protected by an escort, we have to decide what is the best form of protection for the convoys, and I think it is agreed by everybody that what is known as the general convoy is the best system. That is the convoy which has an escort ready to protect its ships from surface attack, from submarines and possibly from the air. . . .

Therefore, we must put the provision of sloops into its proper order of priority. In doing that, I would ask the House to remember two things, first, that our anti-submarine defences and devices for finding out exactly where submarines are are so very much better than they were during the War that we should want fewer protective vessels in the convoy. Secondly, that as convoys will not be needed immediately on the outbreak of war it will give us time to improvise protection by destroyers and trawlers whilst orders are given to build the sloops which we shall eventually require.[16]

The Naval Staff did not realize that, due to the closure of dangerous routes for days at a time, independent sailings had entailed even longer delays in 1917–18, while convoys guarded by escorts steamed directly to their destinations. Although it is true that Naval Staff officers had by 1935 come to favour convoy in principle, they did not think that it would be needed, at first, anyway, since the enemy, afraid to alienate neutral opinion as in 1917, would not launch unrestricted air or U-boat attacks on shipping.[17] I should also mention that Germany was a signatory to the Submarine Agreement of 1936, which prohibited unrestricted submarine attack. Of course, we now know that Hitler's word was worth nothing, but that could not be assumed at the time, at least openly. To proclaim a convoy system would have been to imply that the treaty was being, or would be, deliberately broken! The Air Staff, on the other hand, opposed convoy, using the discredited argument of 1917 that the massing of ships in convoy would only invite air attack and heavy losses. Criticism forced a modification of policy. In 1937 the Naval and Air staffs came to an agreement that convoy should be instituted at the outbreak of war. In March 1938,

[16] Hansard, *Parliamentary Debates* (House of Commons), 5th series, ccic, cols. 674–7.

[17] It may seem absurd now how many naval officers were lulled into a sense of security by the thought that unrestricted submarine warfare by the Kaiser's Navy had brought the United States into the First War, and so had lost it for the Kaiser, and nobody would be stupid enough to try *that* again! For this, and a variety of other reasons, we should not be surprised to learn that there was no Anti-Submarine Division of the Naval Staff when the war began. Actually, the A/S representation at the Admiralty was *doubled*, from one commander to two, the day before war was declared! These two officers constituted the A/S section of the Local Defence Division of the Naval Staff. It soon became obvious that anti-submarine warfare was much too large a subject to be dealt with in this way. A separate A/SW Division of the Naval Staff was created on 2 October 1939.

to satisfy naval opinion, the Admiralty undertook to make all preparations for convoy (for instance, Naval Control Service Officers were dispatched to all shipping ports),[18] but not necessarily to institute it in the event of restricted submarine warfare. As the Deputy Director of Plans observed early in the war: 'Our pre-war A/S plan was to attack U-boats with hunting groups until it became necessary to go into convoy . . .'[19] Ships were to continue to sail independently, if the enemy confined himself to restricted warfare —that is, stopping prospective victims and giving them time to evacuate passengers and crew. Having made this decision, the Admiralty neglected to provide the necessary convoy escorts for unrestricted warfare, under which ships were sunk without warning. All doubts were cleared up almost immediately upon the outbreak of war: *Athenia* torpedoed (against Hitler's orders) on the first day, 3 September 1939; first convoy sailing, 6 September.

However, despite Britain's stronger navy, assisted by Canada and the United States, it took nearly four years (i.e. not until May 1943) to overcome the German submarine menace. There was an insufficiency of escorts, unsuitable types, and inadequately trained groups, a diversion of anti-submarine vessels in the early part of the war from escorting convoys to futile offensive action by 'hunting groups', and a lack of air power on the convoy routes, particularly very long-range aircraft and escort carriers. (It was $3\frac{1}{2}$ years after the outbreak of war before there was a single true escort carrier on the North Atlantic convoy route.) All this was in part a reflection of the low esteem in which convoy was generally held between the wars and indeed into the early stages of the Second War. It should be pointed out that Western Approaches Command did a great job with the *matériel* and personnel available, and that its C-in-C (1941–2), Sir Percy Noble, was against the 'hunting group' concept.

As regards air power, forgotten in the interwar years was the highly successful role of naval aircraft as a convoy escort in 1917–18, when a mere five ships were sunk in convoys with a surface and air escort.[20] *There were virtually no aircraft available for convoy*

[18] These NCSOs, one at each port, implemented the Admiralty control of merchant ships—routing, information, and so forth—and when convoying was started, they organized the convoys. For about a year before the war started there were courses at Greenwich for NCSOs, as also for prospective commodores of convoys, who had entire responsibility for the movements of convoys, based on Admiralty orders, in time of war.

[19] Captain J. H. Edelsten's minute, 26 Nov. 1939, ADM 1/10084.

[20] But its capability as a U-boat sinker was exaggerated by the air-power school, which was one of the reasons the U-boat menace was discounted by the Navy. A gross exaggeration of the performance of bombs in attacks on U-boats must no doubt be blamed for the failure to produce an airborne depth charge before 1941.

when war came, since the responsibilities of naval aircraft did not include the protection of merchant shipping. One cause of this deplorable state of affairs was the fact that the last volume of the official history of British airpower in World War I (*The War in the Air*), which clearly showed the importance of aircraft in commerce protection, only came out in 1937, much too late to influence policy. Similar results to the First War were obtained in the Second War once suitable aircraft were made available for use as convoy escorts and supports, but this was not until *1943*. It can be argued, and has indeed been vociferously argued by the Navy ever since, that the RAF's obsession with the 'wasteful and largely discredited' policy of bombing Germany indiscriminately deprived the Fleet of the aircraft required for convoy and other sea work, while achieving no significant reduction in Germany's war potential. The issue is not of a black-and-white sort, however. The bomber offensive, the airmen have replied, was not always what it should have been (this was the first real air war and much had to be learned), yet, in the words of the Official Air Historians, 'both cumulatively in largely indirect ways and eventually in a more immediate and direct manner, strategic bombing and, also in other roles strategic bombers, made a contribution to victory which was decisive'.[21]

Valuable experience of 1914–18 was disregarded in other respects as concerns convoy. Until 1943, when Professor P. M. S. Blackett produced some interesting statistics about ocean convoys and changed the staff view on convoy escort, it was Admiralty gospel that 'the larger the convoy the greater the risk'. Had the convoy statistics of 1917–18 been analysed after the war, and the printed results of the mathematical research on comparative escort strength

[21] Sir Charles Webster and Noble Frankland, *The Strategic Air Offensive against Germany, 1939–1945* (4 vols., London, 1961), iii. 310. The airmen would add these specifics: that the bombing of Germany was the primary agent in bringing about that extraordinary degree of air superiority which alone made the victories of the Army possible and, by protecting Britain against the same sort of scale of attack, had an equally decisive effect on the war at sea by securing British ports, naval bases, and Coastal Command bases. ('If Liverpool and Glasgow had suffered the fate of Hamburg, how do you think the North Atlantic convoys would have got on?' a distinguished airman has asked.) Finally, the bomber offensive destroyed 63 commissioned U-boats in port and well over 100 under construction (the Official Air Historians put it at 153), and the air forces of the Western Allies (largely by their bombers) accounted for something like 30 per cent of the enemy merchant shipping losses in Home waters. ibid. iv. 524, Marshal of the Royal Air Force Sir John Slessor, *The Central Blue* (London, 1956), pp. 469–71, Slessor's letter to the author, 23 May 1973, and Roskill, *The War at Sea*, iii, Pt. 2, p. 473. As regards the U-boats, however, it should be noted that most of those referred to in these figures were destroyed in April/May 1945, after the capture of fighter airfields in the Low Countries, and the total breakdown of German air defence.

by an acting commander, RNVR (Rollo Appleyard) early in 1918 been studied, the Admiralty would have been aware of 'the law of convoy size': 'The escort strength requires to be measured, not in terms of the number of vessels in convoy, but in terms of the total area comprised within the boundary formed by lines connecting all outer vessels.' Appleyard went on to prove mathematically that the ratio of the torpedo attack area around the convoy perimeter to the number of escorts directly watching it is 'a more correct numerical measure of the escort strength of a convoy than is the ratio of the number of ships in convoy to the number of close escorts'.[22] It is sad that operational research was not understood in the interwar years; it needed someone of the standing of Blackett to show what could be done in this field.

Another instance of how the postwar failure to study with care the U-boat campaign of 1917–18 exacted a heavy penalty was the refusal of the Admiralty in the interwar period to believe the U-boats would make surface night attacks. Although by the end of the First War nearly two-thirds of all submarine attacks were being made at night and on the surface—to be sure, they proved un-rewarding—the Second War found the Navy unprepared for a repetition of these tactics, this time successfully.[23] The evidence was available, but it took the Admiralty a year (August 1940) to realize that the majority of the ships sunk by U-boats since the start of the war had been sunk at night—by, of course, surfaced U-boats. When, in 1940, the U-boats in the Atlantic, organized in

---

[22] Commander D. W. Waters, who rescued Appleyard's work from oblivion, sums up the essence of the matter: '. . . as the escorts of a convoy protect the perimeter of that convoy and not the individual ships in the convoy, for the purpose of assessing comparative escort strength the number of ships within the perimeter of the convoy is irrelevant. . . . The investigator had almost, but not quite, formulated the explanation of why the larger convoys sailed in 1918 did not incur heavy losses, or why their escorts proved as intimidating as a like number escorting numerically smaller convoys, that is to say, that the perimeter of a large convoy is only slightly larger than that of a small convoy, because the area occupied by the ships increases as the square, while the perimeter is directly proportional to the length of the radius.' Waters, 'Notes on the Convoy System of Naval Warfare, Thirteenth to Twentieth Centuries', Part 2, 'First World War, 1914–18', Historical Section, Admiralty, 1960 (Naval Historical Library).

[23] A contributory cause was the ban imposed, for safety reasons, on submarine operations at night in exercises. This continued absolutely until 1936–7, when this ban was relaxed in the Mediterranean. 'The effect was immediate', writes Admiral Power, who was then Operations Officer in the Mediterranean Submarine Flotilla. 'I well remember the C-in-C [Dudley Pound] commenting on the wash-ups [post-exercise conferences] of two successive Fleet exercises on the success achieved by S/Ms operating on the surface at night. We did of course operate singly and not in wolf-packs, but the message was clear enough and widely recognized in the Med[n] Fleet—*and by the First Sea Lord in the earlier part of the war.*' That is, from August 1940!

III Winston Churchill, First Lord of the Admiralty, with King George VI and Queen Elizabeth, and Neville Chamberlain, meeting relatives of men of HMS *Exeter* who were killed in the River Plate action, when men of the *Exeter* and *Ajax* marched through London, *en route* to the Guildhall, 23 February 1940

IV Admiral of the Fleet Sir Dudley Pound, First Sea Lord and Chief of Naval Staff, between (*left to right*) Air Chief Marshal Sir Cyril Newall (Chief of Air Staff) and General Sir Edmund Ironside (Chief of Imperial General Staff), arriving for a War Cabinet meeting at No. 10 Downing Street, 27 September 1939

'wolf packs', attacked convoys at night while on the surface, the Admiralty had no immediate answer. It was, as a joint Admiralty–Air Ministry statement of 1946 misleadingly claimed, 'a new and unheard of German tactic'. The problem was not mastered until 10-centimetre radar was fitted generally to convoy escorts. The turning of night into day with 'snowflake' flares and other pyrotechnics also played an important role in the defeat of surface attacks. There is no excuse for the Admiralty not having learned by 1939 that U-boats might attack on the surface at night. Whether the use of 'wolf packs' could have been foreseen from a study of the First War is another matter.[24]

Finally, before the end of the First War the question of convoy escort dispositions was being most carefully studied in the Mediterranean. Some sensible plans were produced initially and were amended from time to time in the light of experience. In Home waters and the Atlantic, where there were many authorities involved and many different routes, there seems to have been little or no direction, or even guidance, from the Admiralty until late in 1918. Each authority had its own ideas and there was no standard doctrine. By October 1918, however, a mass of experience had been built up. This was analysed by the Anti-Submarine Division of the Naval Staff and its lessons passed on to the operating authorities. This information was published soon after the war in the Technical History series, but does not appear to have had much impact. The technical histories were confidential and therefore in practice virtually inaccessible, and, in 1939, they were declared obsolete and all copies were ordered to be destroyed. (I know of only two complete sets: in the Naval Historical Library and the Naval Historical Branch, Ministry of Defence.) Vice-Admiral Sir Peter Gretton, a distinguished convoy escort commander in the Second War, writes: 'It seems certain, though I have no proof, that this invaluable information was not studied by those planners responsible for convoy defence in World War II. In 1939 no guidance was available to escort commanders, and until the middle of 1940 each escort commander had his own private plans and schemes.'

*   *   *

One of the chief failings of naval training between the wars was in relating a key 'lesson learned' to the setting of the 1914 war,

[24] See Marder, *From the Dreadnought to Scapa Flow*, v. 94–5 n. But what made the wolf packs effective was the conquest of France, which the Navy would have been loath to base its plans on before war, and the ineffectiveness of asdic against submarines on the surface, which perhaps it ought to have thought about, but not as a lesson of history.

C

instead of to the changed circumstances of an entirely new situation
–that is, a situation in which the Navy was unlikely to have to
fight an enemy battle fleet of anything like the size of Germany's
High Seas Fleet. Naval strategy and tactics were largely conditioned
by a determination to make the next Jutland a Trafalgar–when
a second Jutland was highly improbable. A reconstruction of Jutland was the *pièce de résistance* of the work of the Staff College during
most of the interwar period. Thus, during 1934 there was a three-
day study of the battle. (Contrast this with the hour devoted to
submarines and no time at all to the U-boat crisis of 1917 and the
A/S campaign of 1917–18!) And throughout that time the main
exercise at sea every year was the Combined (Atlantic and Mediterranean) Fleet Exercises off Gibraltar (the Atlantic Fleet became the
Home Fleet in 1932): endless battle-fleet tactical manœuvres and
usually a grand fleet action. This excessive emphasis in prewar
training on a fleet action had considerable value for captains and
other officers on the bridge in handling ships in close company;
but it bore little relation to what was to come in 1939. There is
only the one extenuating factor that the major planning effort
envisaged, right up to 1937, the passage of the fleet to the Far
East resulting in a fleet action against the Japanese Navy. I turn
to Admiral of the Fleet Sir Caspar John, who has this to say about
the interwar obsession with a fleet action and some of its consequences:

The obsession with Jutland ran through the Navy as a deadening virus.
As a Lieutenant in 1930 I attended the Tactical School in Portsmouth
Dockyard. The rigid doctrine of the A–K line,[25] the stately progress of
the Battle Ships (with nothing to battle with or against!) left a scar on the
Naval side of me which remains to this day. I recall a member of the
Board of Admiralty lecturing to us one forenoon, his subject: 'Naval
Tactics'–a very appropriate title–but in the event, we endured an hour's
talk on the rival merits of in-turning and out-turning screws in the context of manoeuvring battle ships in close order! To give the Tactical
School its due we *did* have one convoy exercise, in the wash-up of which
I was severely censured for *not* ordering the convoy to scatter! Needless
to say, flying machines had no seats in the stalls. One has only to study
the Combined Fleet exercises of those years to produce practical proof
of the persisting Jutland myth (i.e. that *that* kind of scrap would recur)
–and when the two great fleets berthed at Gibraltar the aircraft carriers
were ostracized to the Algeciras side of the bay, lest their heresies should
infect the *real* Navy (battleships, battle cruisers, cruisers, destroyers),
which were awarded the plum berths closest to the Rock.

[25] The 'A–K line' was the scouting line of light cruisers ahead of the battle fleet
in which the individual stations were lettered, though they could never have needed
that many letters.

We shall return to the Jutland syndrome.

In other respects the interwar period offered proof that new wars usually begin where the last one left off. The First War had demonstrated that Q-ships (armed craft disguised as merchant ships) were not an effective A/S weapon once unrestricted warfare commenced (from the spring of 1917 only six U-boats were destroyed at a cost of twenty-seven Q-ships), and all Staff College teaching had made this clear. But it was a case of 'the importunate widow'—in this instance, Captain Gordon Campbell, V.C., the Q-ship hero of 1917, who pestered the Admiralty till it gave way, so as to keep him quiet. In 1939–40 eight Q-ships were commissioned for work in the North Atlantic. They accomplished nothing at the cost of two of their number which were torpedoed and sunk—they did not even sight a U-boat—and were paid off in March 1941. A wasted effort and an inexcusable episode.

It has often been said that the lessons of the mining and minesweeping experience of 1914–18 had to be re-learned in the Second War: for example, that the development of counters to magnetic mines was sluggish (minesweepers were designed to deal with *moored* mines). Not surprisingly, so goes the criticism, the German magnetic mine caught the British impotent in 1939. But this is not the whole story. The British, as well as the Germans, had developed a magnetic mine—it exploded without contact—in the latter part of the war and had laid a few in 1918.

> From 1919 onwards [we read in the standard work on mines and minesweeping], extensive investigations were made with a view to classifying the magnetic properties of ships. . . . By 1935 it had become obvious that progress had reached a stage at which the consideration of a counter to these devices was due, if not overdue. . . . An Admiralty Anti-non-contact Committee was set up in 1936 to examine the whole question. . . . The position may be summed up by saying that when World War II broke out we *knew* a lot, but we could not *do* a lot until we discovered what type of non-contact mechanism the enemy was employing . . . but the expenditure in peacetime of large sums of money based on a pure guess as to the type of mine to be used by a potential enemy was out of the question. Even if such expenditure had been acceptable, *and* the guess had been correct, it would have been impossible to make the necessary bulk preparations without the fact becoming known. It would then have been a simple matter for the effectiveness of those preparations to have been offset [by the enemy] by a modification to the design of the mines.[26]

It was not until Lieutenant-Commanders J. G. D. Ouvry and R. C. Lewis managed to dismantle the firing gear of a German magnetic

---

[26] Captain J. S. Cowie, *Mines, Minelayers, and Minelaying* (London, 1949), pp. 106–7, 124.

mine that had landed in the mud of the Thames Estuary off Shoe-buryness (November 1939) that information on the mode of actuation was obtained.[27] It turned out to be an improved version of the British magnetic mine of the end of the First War.

The experience of the First War had amply proven the efficacy of the paravane in neutralizing the danger from mines. Yet, when the Second War broke out, British destroyers were not fitted with paravanes to enable them to pass through the enemy minefields when laying mines in the Heligoland Bight.

The Northern Mine Barrage between the Faroes and Iceland that was started in July 1940 was an unforgivably wasteful business. The original planning was not quite so bad as it seems, because it was the 1918 type Orkneys–Norway line in about 40 fathoms that was intended, but of course that was cancelled by the Norwegian invasion. Only by a lot of ill-judged enthusiasm could it be imagined that a field could be efficient in the 200 fathoms of the Faroes–Iceland line, for the dip caused by the tidal streams would have been so much greater. Even worse was the failure to realize that the antenna mines used were, like their counterparts in the Northern Barrage of 1918, shockingly inefficient and unreliable. The results were predictably dismal: one U-boat was sunk by northern barrage mines, and there is no evidence to show that the barrage influenced enemy surface or U-boat operations or movements to any noticeable degree. Indeed, the Germans jocularly spoke of the minefield as the '*Rosegarten*'. One of the arguments for the barrage was that its predecessor, the Northern Barrage, had been a success against the U-boats—that six had been destroyed on the barrage within six weeks and others damaged. This was a misreading of the experience of 1918, when a mere three U-boats had been sunk for certain, an insignificant return for the vast expenditure of *matériel*.

The official *History of British Minesweeping in the War* (1920) stated: 'The use of aircraft . . . in connection with minesweeping is yet in its infancy, but it undoubtedly has a future. . . . *Given clear water*, aircraft could define and mark a large surface-laid field.' (Italics mine, for water of mineable depth that is clear is a rare commodity.) This lesson was allowed to be forgotten. Aircraft were not used for systematic mine searches until 1944.[28]

[27] The two officers arrived at the Admiralty to tell the First Lord and First Sea Lord what they had done. At the end of their story, Churchill asked, 'And were you frightened?' Before they could say 'Yes', Dudley Pound, the First Sea Lord, turned on Churchill and said, 'Of course they were not frightened.' That ended it!

[28] Aircraft were, however, employed in the Sicilian Narrows early in 1943 to observe the extension of the westernmost Axis minefield, round the northern end

In a repeat performance of 1914 and in disregard of the lessons of 1914–18, Scapa Flow was poorly defended in 1939. The defences had been allowed to rot, which was bad, but not nearly so deplorable as the failure to get them repaired on the first signs of another war. Admiral Sir Charles Forbes, C-in-C, Home Fleet, had battled in vain to remedy the deficiencies of Scapa Flow between the time of the Munich crisis and the outbreak of the war. In the same period the Flag Officer, Rosyth ('Rear-Admiral and Commanding Officer, Coast of Scotland'), E. C. O. Thomson, moved heaven and earth, primarily through his brilliant Staff Officer Operations, Commander E. S. Brand, to get the Scapa defences improved. Time after time Brand went down to the Admiralty about it. Everyone agreed in principle, but 'Where was the money to come from?', 'What are the priorities?', and similar obstacles nullified these efforts. When the war broke out, the anti-submarine defences consisted only of a line of nets across the three main entrances of Hoxa, Switha, and Hoy; the eastern entrances were partially protected by the remains of the blockships of the First War. The consequences of these grossly inadequate defences were, first, in the words of Churchill, 'We were driven out of Scapa [to the west Scottish coast anchorage of Loch Ewe very early in the war] through pre-war neglect of its defences against air and U-boat attack'; and, second, to quote Captain Roskill, 'The failure to defend Scapa Flow adequately against either air or submarine attack not only caused the loss of one battleship [*Royal Oak*, torpedoed and sunk by *U-47* on 14 October 1939], damage to another [Home Fleet flagship *Nelson*, mined in Loch Ewe on 4 December 1939] and to a valuable new cruiser [*Belfast*, mined off the entrance to the Firth of Forth on 21 November 1939] but vitiated the ability of the fleet to perform its proper functions.'[29]

of which the fast minelayer *Abdiel* passed in order to lay several fields in the centre of the funnel.

[29] Stephen Roskill, *The War at Sea, 1939–1945* (3 vols. in 4, London, 1954–61), i. 80. The low priority given to Scapa Flow before the war was in part political; it would have implied, had its defences been put into proper shape, that they were preparing for war against Germany. The Admiralty war plan did not envisage the use of Scapa as the Main Fleet Base until late in the day. In the War Memorandum (Germany) of May 1937, Rosyth was designated as the Main Fleet Base, Scapa Flow a subsidiary one; but a supplement issued in September 1938, just before the Munich crisis, left the choice to the C-in-C, Home Fleet. He selected Scapa Flow, which decision was confirmed by the Naval War Memorandum (European) of January 1939. The cumbersome machinery of the Admiralty was incapable of a sudden alteration of course, such as the change from the Forth to Scapa entailed. One of the arguments against Scapa was the tremendous hurry to develop a radar chain which would cover the East coast against air attack. This must obviously include Edinburgh

The failure to learn the lessons about combined operations from Gallipoli was lamentable. Despite the successful seaborne landings on the Gallipoli Peninsula in 1915, to say nothing of the whole British maritime tradition (Wellington's Peninsular Campaign of 1812–14 and other examples), the Gallipoli disaster had discredited amphibious warfare. Brigadier Fergusson sums up the results:

> In the twenty years between the wars, Combined Ops took a back seat. The Dardanelles were fought all over again, in printer's ink and at the Staff Colleges, in Britain, the United States and Australia. Churchill and Keyes remained unrepentant and defiant apologists for the attempt; but on the whole people remembered the carnage on the beaches to the exclusion of all else. . . . Most people, even the sanguine Keyes, reckoned that daylight assaults against a defended shore were suicide and folly. Everybody was looking at the past rather than the future; money was tight, and what there was had to be spent on needs more obviously urgent than experiments in Combined Operations.[30]

Part of the blame must lie in the fact that the Mitchell Report seems to have been little known in the Services. The doctrine between wars was that such operations were unlikely, at least in the early part of a war. A senior officer at the Admiralty informed an inter-Service meeting shortly after the Second War got under way: 'We do not see any likelihood of Combined Operations in *this* war, except possibly a landing at Petsamo.' The development of suitable landing craft and training for joint operations languished. The total number of landing craft built before the Second War was nine slow motor landing craft (MLCs: 20 tons, 5–6 knots, and drawing 4 feet 6 inches), and Captain Roskill claims that 'such exercises in combined operations as were carried out were so primitive as to be laughable'. No command responsible for such operations existed until Combined Headquarters were established after the Norwegian débâcle in 1940.

This is not to suggest that the study of combined operations was entirely neglected. The staff colleges did an annual 'joint theoretical combined exercise, used much ink and consumed much gin, and built up a voluminous typewritten dossier which in the event proved surprisingly useful'. A joint *Manual of Combined Operations* was produced in 1925; revised editions were prepared in 1931 and 1938. In May 1938 the Chiefs of Staff established the

and Glasgow, but to carry it on to Scapa seemed impossible, with the result that the latter would have to depend on a single station.

[30] Bernard Fergusson, *The Watery Maze: the Story of Combined Operations* (London, 1961), pp. 35–6. The quotations that follow in the next two paragraphs, but for the Roskill one, are from ibid., pp. 36, 38, 40–3.

Inter-Services Training and Development Centre (ISTDC) at Fort Cumberland, near Portsmouth, and endowed it with 'a small clerical staff, a free hand, much encouragement, direct access to the Deputy Chiefs of Staff, and thirty thousand pounds'. Solid work was done before the war by the ISTDC and its small group of dedicated officers—Captain L. E. H. Maund, RN, assisted by Major M. W.-M. MacLeod, RA, Wing Commander Guy Knocker, RAF, and Captain Peter Picton-Phillips, RM. Without much money, however, they could produce little more than a doctrine and the design of the LCA 1, the backbone of British assault craft through the war. By the end of 1938 they had 'hammered out a broad policy for landings, and defended it at Staff College discussions. With variations won by experience, it was broadly the policy that was used in the North African and Sicilian landings, that lay, had they but known it, only four years ahead. . . . Throughout the summer of 1939, the I.S.T.D.C. worked away. Training cruises and experiments went on, many and various parlour tricks were practised (including the use of infra-red beacons to guide craft on to beaches at the right point), and a landing exercise was mounted in Malta.' Much had yet to be done when war began. Naturally, amphibious warfare got off to a slow start. The amphibious aspects of the first expedition sent to Norway in April 1940 were a mess. 'It was as unhappy as a campaign could be: unplanned, unprepared, divergent instructions, non-tactical loading of ships [repeating the mistake of March 1915], inadequate equipment and intelligence—all the familiar trappings of a real hurrah's nest.'

In tactics as well the lessons of the First War were not completely absorbed. The *Fighting Instructions* (FIs) of 1939 were not as verbose as the *Grand Fleet Battle Orders* (GFBOs) and *Fighting Instructions* (GFFIs) of 1914–18, but they possessed in some respects, notably in the tactical handling of fleets and squadrons, as great a rigidity. (The FIs, like their predecessor, were a Fleet publication and not an Admiralty issue. Amendments were agreed upon between the Commanders-in-Chief, Home and Mediterranean Fleets.) Indeed, several of the articles of the FIs issued between the wars were merely a *réchauffé* of the old GFBOs and GFFIs. It was not generally appreciated that the need for detailed *Fighting Instructions* disappears when the number of ships in company is reduced and what was once a great fleet becomes a 'task' force or group. Yet to the outbreak of war the FIs retained the sections about large battle-fleet actions. An important reason for this was the feeling of Dudley Pound, the C-in-C, Mediterranean Fleet (1936–9), that there might be a fleet action against the Japanese. And so the FIs dealt with 'forms of battle' A, B, C, and D–respectively, two lines of battleships engaged on similar and parallel courses, two lines on parallel and opposite courses, one battle fleet retiring with the other in chase, and one battle fleet fighting a retiring rearguard action. (The C-in-C, Home Fleet, Forbes, thought all this was nonsense but accepted it in the end in order to get agreement.) The saving feature, however, was that the *Fighting Instructions* lacked the sanctity of the GFBOs and GFFIs. As an officer who helped to draft the final prewar revisions (1938–9, issued in the summer of 1939) remarks: 'Rather naturally, anyone I met who had read our smart new book printed on good paper with red hard covers usually said it was all rubbish.' It was the section concerning the 'Forms of Battle' which was so much criticized, especially by young captains and officers commanding destroyers and sloops, who felt certain there would not be a Jutland type of action. There were no longer large battle fleets as there had been in 1914–18 and they did not envisage all the battle fleet strength of any one nation operating as a single force. The *Fighting Instructions* were often ignored by commanding officers during the war.[31]

Nor had the lesson of the First War as regards an over-centralized administration at the Admiralty, which made it extremely difficult for the directing authorities to concentrate on the larger questions of policy, been learned. Thus, when Cunningham came to the Admiralty as First Sea Lord in October 1943, he was 'rather appalled by the number of departments and people who had to be consulted before action took place'.[32] The lesson has not been

[31] However, a number of senior Admirals, who appreciated that the FIs contained the accumulated thought of the two most important Commanders-in-Chief, took them more seriously. Thus, during the action with the Italian Fleet off Calabria on 8 July 1940, the C-in-C, A. B. Cunningham, remarked to his Chief of Staff (Algernon Willis) how closely the movements of the various units of the fleet had followed the *Fighting Instructions*. There are other instances, as when Admiral Willis, commanding the 3rd Battle Squadron in the newly formed Eastern Fleet in 1942, urged his captains to study the *Fighting Instructions*. And in Force H in 1943, when they had to be prepared, unlikely though it was, for an action with the Italian main fleet when Sicily was invaded, Willis based his instructions to the force on the *Fighting Instructions*. The *Fighting Instructions* contained at least one invaluable contribution in Chapter I, paragraph 6, which was rubbed in at the Tactical School before the war: 'Consideration should be given to the possibility that orders received were originated without knowledge of the circumstances prevailing at the time of receipt. Above all, very good reason should exist before touch with the enemy should be relinquished.' (This is an approximation of the original, according to my informant. I have not been able to lay my hands on a copy of the prewar FIs, but the edition of June 1947 has a Chapter I, paragraph 6, in the same spirit.) We hear of one commanding officer who was able to quote this paragraph as an excuse for disregarding orders. It was of great help to many.

[32] *A Sailor's Odyssey: the Autobiography of Admiral of the Fleet Viscount Cunningham*

learned to this day, or to recent years at any rate, to judge from this statement made by an officer in 1965: 'I believe that the major problem facing the Service today is over-centralisation. . . . The Admiralty Board retains the right to be the authority for all decisions and the clearing house for all information. Regrettably, due to the failure to separate policy from management, the machine is so clogged with paper that it is not possible to sift the often conflicting recommendations from numerous authorities.' Nor had the lesson of 1914–18 concerning excessive centralization of operational control at the Admiralty been learned by the time of the Second War.[33] This criticism can be sustained by reference to some of the Home Fleet operations in the Second War, particularly at the time of the Norwegian campaign and on 20 April 1941, when the Mediterranean Fleet was ordered to bombard Tripoli, despite Admiral Cunningham's strong protests. However, the extent to which the Admiralty (in practice, the First Sea Lord) should exercise direct control over operations, instead of leaving them to the C-in-C, is a complex question. Indeed, there are two sides to the coin, and only the wrong one gets remembered. For instance, the *Bismarck* was destroyed because the Admiralty took a very energetic hand in the business, as was handsomely acknowledged by Admiral Tovey in his dispatch. The real solution lies in knowing *when* to exercise direct control and *when* not to.[34]

Finally, there was a sad failure to develop naval aviation, though this stemmed as much from special circumstances as from a misreading of one of the lessons of the war. When the war ended, the Royal Navy, in quantity and quality of planes and carriers, in commission and building, had a substantial lead over all other navies. This long start was thrown away. British naval aviation soon went into a tailspin from which it did not begin to recover until the eve

of Hyndhope (London, 1951), p. 577. On the situation in the First War, see Marder, *From the Dreadnought to Scapa Flow*, v. 327–8.

[33] On the First War, see ibid., pp. 328–9.

[34] The crux of this terribly difficult problem is that the admiral at sea, remote from his sources of intelligence, cannot react quickly enough in a widely dispersed and fast-changing situation. Some shore authority *must* intervene. If the Admiralty have vital information that they cannot explain to the C-in-C, or cannot explain it in time to be effective, then the C-in-C must do what he is told. In 1914–18 there seemed to be a vital need to keep Room 40, the Navy's special intelligence organization (established in November 1914), secret from everyone except the DNI and a few others at the very top, and that resulted in the C-in-C being given strict orders for movements which ought to have been left to him, e.g. the Scarborough Raid in December 1914. Another occasion when the Admiralty could, with advantage, have told the C-in-C what was known about German intentions and movements and left it to him to make his own dispositions was in the Dogger Bank action of January 1915, when Jellicoe was withheld from close support of Beatty.

of the Second War. When that war came, the Fleet Air Arm was at least ten years behind the developments in the American and Japanese fleets. The explanation is partly the financial stringency of those years. More important was the divided control of the Fleet Air Arm following the amalgamation of the Royal Naval Air Service and the Royal Flying Corps to form the RAF on 1 April 1918, under the Air Ministry. This was the result of the Air Ministry's adoption of the Trenchard doctrine of the 'indivisibility' of the air. Its results included the Navy's loss of virtually all its air expertise: only a handful of officers with practical air experience remained. As another consequence, naval aviators were not valued high in the promotion stakes in either Service. Moreover, the Air Ministry supplied very low-performance aircraft to the Fleet Air Arm of the RAF and many low-quality officers to Coastal Command and the Fleet Air Arm. This confirmed senior naval officers (none of whom had any aviation experience or knowledge) in their low opinion of the capabilities of aircraft. An example is Admiral Chatfield's remark in 1931: 'My own recent experience of the Air Arm makes me hesitate to subscribe to any policy that increases the strength of the Air Arm at direct expense of other more reliable, if less ambitious weapons.'[35] It took the Navy nineteen years of agitation and deplorable inter-Service wrangling to secure a partial reversal of the decision of 1918—*partial*, because under the 1937 reorganization the RAF retained control of all aircraft production (this resulted in a failure to develop types of aircraft that would be invaluable in a fleet action or in trade protection) and because the Navy regained operational control only of ship-borne aircraft when embarked, and not of the shore-based aircraft needed for co-operation with the Fleet.

But I attribute the lamentable failure to develop the Fleet Air Arm in the interwar years as much to the battleship complex from which the Navy suffered, for within the Navy itself there was by no means wholehearted support for the fight to regain and develop its own tactical air component. The pro-battleship faction, misreading the lessons of the First War, was very powerful and regarded the onset of the Fleet Air Arm with profound distaste—not only from the point of view of a potential challenge to the supremacy of the battleship, but also from the point of view of draining resources away from the Big Gun.

You will know [writes Admiral of the Fleet Sir Caspar John, himself a

[35] Naval Historical Branch (Ministry of Defence) records. Chatfield was then C-in-C, Mediterranean. His previous appointments were C-in-C, Atlantic Fleet, 1929–30, and Third Sea Lord and Controller, 1925–8.

naval aviator in his younger days and the first naval flyer to become First Sea Lord, in 1960] that the Gunnery specialist was of the elite among officers and ratings, and collared the best promotion prospects. I recall that as a sub-lieutenant I achieved a First Class in my Gunnery Course at Whale Island in 1924. I was sent for by the Captain to be congratulated; he ended his pat-on-the-back by saying, 'By the way, I assume that in due course you will specialise in Gunnery.' I gulped, as I had that morning forwarded to him my request to be considered for training as a pilot. I had to confess my crime. The Captain shuddered and visibly blanched—rang for his secretary and asked to see my request. He read it, tore it into many pieces and dropped it into his wastepaper basket, remarking to his secretary, 'Another soul saved.' I had better luck when I repeated my request to a wider-minded skipper at Greenwich. That incident was very typical of a considerable body of influential Naval opinion.

As the Admiral says, with that combination of forces antipathetic to naval air development, it is something of a miracle that the Navy ever got off square one! It was a surprising and considerable achievement to arrive at September 1939 with even the kernel of naval air power on which to base a large wartime expansion.

*   *   *

When the Navy went into war in 1939, 'what was lacking was not foresight but hardware', Captain John Creswell maintains. I would not dispute that the degree of lack of foresight has sometimes been exaggerated. Nevertheless, I think it fair to say that many of the lessons of 1914–18 were forgotten, neglected, not thoroughly absorbed, or were misread in the interwar years. Why was this the case? The simple explanation is that armies and navies rarely learn from success, and the Royal Navy had been successful in its main objective. Also, there was a school of thought that said: 'We did it in the last war, *therefore* we must do it in the next war', irrespective of *why* they had done it, or what the results were. (Rear-Admiral Tom Phillips, who was DCNS at the outbreak of the Second War, has been called 'the High Priest' of this cult.) Again, in the immediate postwar period, the ideal time to have launched an intensive investigation, both the Navy and the politicians were not keen on investigating the mistakes of the war. The Admiralty instituted a censorship (until 1926) of the *Naval Review*, the organ of the reform-minded officers who wanted to study and to profit from the lessons (or 'blunders', as they would have it) of the war. Bonar Law, the Lord Privy Seal, was reported to have talked about avoiding 'washing dirty linen in public'.[36] Also, it was difficult to

[36] Captain H. W. Richmond to Commander Carlyon Bellairs, 12 Mar. 1919, Arthur J. Marder, *Portrait of an Admiral: the Life and Papers of Sir Herbert Richmond*

get many officers, to say nothing of the country, to take an interest in naval reform while peace conferences and industrial unrest were filling men's minds. The feeling of relief that the war was over and won prevailed over any desire to criticize the naval conduct or failures of the war. The many officers with whom I have discussed this do not remember much discussion about these things immediately after the war. Everything conspired against it. The squadrons on foreign stations were revived, as the Navy in peacetime had a worldwide job to do, especially while Britain still had an empire. The Navy was soon dispersed all over the world—a China Fleet, an East Indies squadron, a North American squadron, a South American squadron, and a large Mediterranean Fleet. It was a new and exciting life for the officers, very different to the years in Scapa or the Firth of Forth, and officers and ships' companies were all absorbed in peacetime activities—regattas, sports, armament practices, and visiting interesting places and people, and were not thinking about where and why the Navy had failed in the war and how to put it right.

There are other causes. The war offered a gold mine of information, yet few officers displayed interest in working that kind of mine. 'It necessitated', Vice-Admiral K. G. B. Dewar has pointed out, 'a keen interest in these subjects and their bearing on strategy, tactics, command, and so on. It involved continuous and regular research and required constant encouragement from superiors, with a reasonable prospect of the lessons being put to practical use. But these incentives were completely lacking. Officers who expressed independent or unorthodox opinions were viewed with suspicion, and it was dangerous to write anything which might question the infallibility of the higher ranks. This repressive attitude killed honest research by officers on the active list. It created a spirit of apprehension and caution. . . .'[37] The case, coloured by Dewar's anti-establishment bias, is overstated, yet I believe there is more than a soupçon of truth in his indictment. It is unfortunate that the officers who understood the lessons of the war and worked hard to translate the lessons into practical reforms and innovations were led by a couple of very difficult men—Richmond and his leading disciple, Dewar, who did not realize that tact was essential if they were to achieve their aims. They contrived to put people's

(London, 1952), p. 340. Richmond was repeating what Bellairs had told him. 'The answer,' Richmond replied, 'if he can be induced to say it in public, is that if the linen is not washed at all, it creates a pestilence. And it is *not* being washed.'

[37] Dewar, 'The Problem of Naval Command', n.d. (post-World War II), Dewar MSS., 13.

backs up by their conviction of the absolute correctness of the positions they espoused and their ill-concealed contempt of their intellectual inferiors. Dewar, in particular, who never had a good word to say of anyone in authority and always seemed to have a chip on his shoulder, was the last person to succeed in selling his ideas in high places. But the fact that these intellectuals were their own worst enemies and were distrusted by the Navy as a whole does not appreciably weaken my argument, which is accepted by many distinguished senior officers, that bold thinking and forthright criticism were not welcome *at the Admiralty*. It was a different matter beyond Whitehall. The R.N. Staff College encouraged individual thinking, and many senior officers afloat welcomed sensible criticism. In this respect there had been a marked improvement on the situation in the 'Fisher Era'. Again I summon Admiral of the Fleet John as an authoritative witness:

Promotion of officers depended more on deportment, practical seamanship and leadership than on intellectual power of thought and expression. Sea-going officers, high and low, were not encouraged to think and express their thoughts, as they now are. The officers of a clean and 'efficient' ship (in the sense of being first in General Drill every Monday morning) were more likely to get promoted than those who took time off to ponder the shape and size of a Navy tailored to the developments of 10 years ahead. By luck, I sense, rather than by design, there were just enough of the latter who made the grade and saved something significant from what could well have been a total wreck.

Among the forward thinkers were senior officers like Geoffrey Blake, W. W. Fisher, Reginald Henderson, G. M. B. ('Max') Langley, Alexander Ramsay, and James Somerville.

Another facet of this anti-intellectualism was the not uncommon Service view that history does not repeat itself—'it's all so different now!'—and therefore nothing of great value could be learned from a study of the First War.

The obverse and complementary side of anti-intellectualism is conservatism, not as pronounced as in the preceding generation, but visible and effective enough all the same in Whitehall. Admiral Power goes so far as to say that

the conservatism, dilatoriness and inertia of the Admiralty had to be endured to be believed. They said that the Admiralty was kept up to date by the constant importation of talent from sea; but you could arrive in there with salt water dripping off your finger nails and put up ideas which were then bumbled around on dockets for some months and then referred to the Fleets for sea-opinion! If a device did finally win through and get sent to sea for trial, it might meet approbation but come back with suggestions for improvement. Instead of getting on with it straight away for issue it would be side-tracked for further sea trial and so on *ad infinitum*. Caution and, above all, money ruled the day. It must be said, in fairness, that under the pressure of war the Admiralty was capable of astonishingly rapid and efficient action: though it reverted happily and eagerly to its old snail-like habit the moment peace broke out. Only emergencies could break the spell.[38]

A practical consequence of anti-intellectualism, as well as of the economizing policy of postwar Governments, is the saga of the Historical Section of the Naval Staff.[39] When First Lord, in April 1914, Churchill had put forward the idea of such a section with the duty of 'sifting, developing, and applying the results of history and experience and of preserving them as a general stock of reasoned opinion available as an aid and a guide for all who were called upon to determine, in peace and in war, the naval policy of the country'. The Historical Section came into being on 4 August 1914, but there was no interest in nurturing it with a great war on. It soon became part of the Historical Section of the Committee of Imperial Defence, whose function was the collection of the raw material for the official naval history of the war. On 23 November 1918 Captain A. C. Dewar, of the Admiralty's Training and Staff Duties Division, proposed the formation of an Admiralty Historical Section to 'pre-pare monographs and historical papers on the war and provide a training ground for naval officers in research work'. He suggested that 'these monographs should deal with operations more inten-

---

[38] A factor in the situation was the numbing effect that the Admiralty had on most officers. Some liked it, and went there readily, becoming adept 'Whitehall warriors'. They, by acquiring the technique, could occasionally achieve effective results. But for the average officer it took some months to get on to the right fre-quency at all, by which time enthusiasm had waned and a feeling of the hopelessness of changing the rhythm of this ponderous machine supervened. 'Initiative became stifled by the sheer cotton-woolliness of the whole setup', as one officer who should know has told me. It must be remembered, too, that naval officers usually did only two years at a time in the Admiralty (some very senior officers did far more time), so the continuity lay too often in civilian hands, which in their turn were much too close to the politicians and the Treasury. This is, I suppose, inevitable in peacetime.

I think this yarn belongs here. Quoting Brigadier Fergusson (*The Watery Maze*, p. 37): 'One tends in the British Services to become cynical about submitting papers to higher authority. Many an officer has sweated his heart out putting on paper some project about which he feels deeply; in draft after draft he tries to ensure that the emphasis is right, and that he has anticipated and dealt with all possible objec-tions. He then entrusts it fearfully to the machine, and never hears of it again—unless by chance, months later, he recognises bits of it in some wholly different document in tatters and the wrong context. General Sir John Burnett-Stuart, as noted a wit as a soldier, once said of this system: "If you will insist on feeding a bird at the wrong end, what can you expect but bad breath?"'

[39] Many of the details are in Lieutenant-Commander P. K. Kemp, 'War Studies in the Royal Navy', *Royal United Service Institution Journal*, cxi (May 1966), 151–5.

sively than Corbett's History [Sir Julian Corbett and Sir Henry Newbolt's official *Naval Operations*], providing an account of what actually happened, without criticism, but giving the text of telegrams and references to the actual papers, sources, etc., so as to enable officers at the Staff College to study doubtful points for themselves.' He also pointed out that in time these monographs would provide the material for a staff history, one of whose purposes would be to examine the lessons of the war and deduce facts and principles for future guidance. Wemyss approved Dewar's idea on 6 December 1918, and work commenced in March 1919 under A. C. Dewar's direction, with the Section attached to the Training and Staff Duties Division of the Naval Staff. Between wars the Historical Section, which had been reduced on grounds of economy from the original five officers to two by 1923 (it was saved from total extinction only by direct personal appeal to the First Sea Lord, Beatty), operated on a hand-to-mouth basis. This skeleton Section managed to produce by 1939 thirty-seven monographs on the naval side of the war. Much remained to be done when war broke out. The 'Home Waters' volumes had only reached July 1917. 'Overseas' had not been completed, and the Dardanelles had not been started. The work would have been finished by 1932, had the staff remained at its original strength. As matters stood, when World War II came, the crucial part of the First War at sea, the convoy period, had not been analysed. Moreover, the worth of the histories was vitiated by the fact that criticism of the Admiralty or of admirals was not permitted in them—a reflection of the anti-historical attitude of the Permanent Secretary of the Admiralty as well as of senior naval officers generally at that time. 'It would', in Vice-Admiral Sir Aubrey Mansergh's opinion, 'have needed men of intellectual stature far beyond that of Beatty, Madden, etc., to hoist in the fact that, from the point of view of value for money, we would have done better to pay off a couple of battleships in the 1920s to ensure that those 1914–1918 histories were truthfully written and properly digested.'

The last factor points to this important consideration that underlay much of the inability to profit from the lessons of 1914–18: the financial stringencies of most of the interwar period. And so it helps to explain the shortage of war *matériel* when war broke out —mines and torpedoes, for example, as well as an alarming weakness in escorts. Again, the 1931 cuts on ammunition and fuel were a serious handicap to training. If the Navy (in common with the other Services) entered the war unprepared intellectually, it had itself to thank for this; but for the utterly inadequate hardware and manpower of all kinds, the politicians were responsible.

Consideration of the interwar years should take into account the 'Ten-Years-No-Major-War Rule' of 1919–33. Whatever its strategic justification, it served as a 'wet blanket' which inhibited fresh thinking to a large degree and was a godsend to the Treasury's parsimony. 'Why worry? What are you bellyaching about?' 'The results of the Ten-Year Rule', a scholar has recently pointed out, 'reverberated far beyond the immediate impact upon the Services. Funds for research and development were curtailed, new ideas and new weapons were sadly lacking. Training–a large consumer of material, especially fuel and ammunition–was cut back so that the Services were not trained for war.'[40]

There is the related factor that the British people tend to develop complacency and a pacific complex after a war: the more successful the war, the greater the demand to put it all behind them and to cut armaments to the bone. This old British tradition has frequently become articulate, as after the highly successful Seven Years War of 1756–63, which led to the Navy being in poor shape in the War of American Independence, and not least after World War I and the scuttling of the Kaiser's Fleet at Scapa Flow. Peacetime apathy in defence matters, and resentment against money spent on defence, is, of course, endemic in all nations, except perhaps those under totalitarian governments. It is an old practice, *vide* that great seventeenth-century Dutch statesman, Jan de Witt: 'Never in time of peace and from fear of rupture will they [the people] take resolution strong enough to lead them to pecuniary sacrifice beforehand. The character of the Dutch is such that, *unless danger stares them in the face*, they are indisposed to lay out money for their own defence.'

One of the reasons which lay behind the lack of drive in naval affairs during the first ten or so years of peace was the universal revulsion against the type of war which had been fought in Europe. The true dimensions of the slaughter really began to penetrate the public mind, and there was the suspicion that all the time the answers were there but the admirals and generals had failed to recognize them–convoy at sea and the tank on land. In the general temper of the country, war, weapons, and the study of war were *out*. It took at least ten years to get over this utter revulsion.

Finally, there is a factor in the pre-Hitler period to which Professor Max Beloff has called attention: 'The temptation to rely upon

[40] Peter Silverman, 'The Ten Year Rule', *Royal United Service Institution Journal*, cxvi (Mar. 1971), 45.

the League of Nations as a method of avoiding effort and expense was an ever-present one. . . . Indeed much that has rightly been criticized in post-war Britain—the intense conservatism of the restored peacetime regular army [I would add 'navy' here], and its [their] apparent unwillingness to take account of the lessons of the war itself, must in part be ascribed to the very modest role that armed force was now allotted in the eyes of the country's leadership.'[41]

The Royal Navy's inability to profit fully from the lessons of 1914–18 was, then, due to a complex of causes. But what I have tried to show is how failure can, and did, result from insufficient study of the lessons of history, and, equally (though this has intentionally not been my thrust), how success may follow from reading these lessons correctly and applying them. I am not for a moment suggesting that all disasters in war are the result of neglecting the past. In the 1939–45 war there were two notable disasters, the sinking of the *Prince of Wales* and *Repulse* and the tragedy of Convoy PQ 17, neither of which is traceable to neglect of the experience of 1914–18.

In conclusion, one can only agree, albeit sadly, with the substance of A. L. Rowse's observation: 'It is very disheartening how human affairs always follow the same patterns—as against Herbert Fisher's view that he could detect no pattern in history; nobody ever learns anything, nobody ever profits by the mistakes that have been made before, but lets himself (and others, more intelligent, who would emancipate themselves if they could) in for the same mess of blood and misery as before.'[42] But I would not leave it there. Naval historians (indeed, all historians) have an obligation to Clio to continue with their task, however thankless it often seems, of stating the rights and the wrongs of events and policies— where a navy did well and where it might have done better. And from such studies much good can be distilled for the progressive officers who, one would hope, will be the leaders of their Service —and for their political masters.

[41] Beloff, *Imperial Sunset: Britain's Liberal Empire, 1897–1921* (London, 1969), p. 355.
[42] Rowse, *A Cornish Childhood* (London, 1942), p. 16.

Chapter Three

The Royal Navy and the Ethiopian Crisis of 1935–1936[1]

(Chart 2)

EVER since its unhappy denouement, the Ethiopian Crisis has been turned into a kind of morality play. As an example, a review of a recent work on the crisis concluded that 'the verdict of history is likely to confirm [Haile Selassie's] view that the invasion of Ethiopia was a crime and the policy of Britain and France a foolish and in the end pointless betrayal of principles'.[2] Without attempting an analysis of the pros and cons of the policy of appeasement, which is quite another matter, this chapter will try to demonstrate that the orthodox judgement on British policy is far too simplistic, ignoring as it does powerful military considerations.

The clash of Italian and Ethiopian troops at Walwal on the undefined frontier between Italian Somaliland and Ethiopia on 5 December 1934 had been seized upon by Mussolini as the point of departure for the conquest of Ethiopia. Italian intentions were clear as early as February 1935, when large forces were dispatched

---

[1] My principal unpublished sources have been the Chatfield MSS., through the courtesy of the second Lord Chatfield (the papers are now in the National Maritime Museum, Greenwich), and the Admiralty and Foreign Office records, the Cabinet minutes (CAB 23/82–84), the minutes and papers of the Committee of Imperial Defence (CAB 2/6, CAB 4/24) and of the Defence Policy and Requirements Sub-Committee of the CID (CAB 16/136, CAB 16/138–40) and the Chiefs of Staff Sub-Committee of the CID (CAB 53/5–6, CAB 53/25–28), all in the Public Record Office. The DPR papers include many of the COS papers, which are also given a 'DPR' number. I am grateful to the Earl of Avon, the late Viscount Monsell, Admiral of the Fleet Sir Algernon Willis, Admirals Sir Guy Grantham and the late Sir William James, and the late Sir Basil Liddell Hart for providing a number of insights and sidelights of value.

[2] *Times Literary Supplement*, 20 Feb. 1969, in a review of A. J. Barker, *The Civilizing Mission: the Italo-Ethiopian War of 1935–6* (London, 1968).

to Eritrea. The British Services came into the Ethiopian picture for the first time in an important way on 5 July 1935. On this day the Italo-Ethiopian arbitration commission, meeting at Scheveningen in the Netherlands, reached an impasse; it adjourned on the 9th *sine die*. On the 5th Sir Maurice Hankey, the indispensable Secretary of the Cabinet (as well as of the Chiefs of Staff and Defence Policy and Requirements Sub-Committees), informed the Service Chiefs that the Prime Minister, Stanley Baldwin, wished them to bear in mind the military implications of Britain's carrying out the requirements of Article 16, the sanctions article, of the League of Nations Covenant. On 30 July the Chiefs of Staff stated their position: the exercise of economic pressure 'would almost inevitably lead to war' with Italy, as would 'any steps taken to interrupt Italy's communications with Abyssinia'. The possibility of war necessitated the active co-operation of the other naval participatory powers (they had in mind France in particular) and preconcerted arrangements with them.[3] These conditions became leitmotivs in the months that followed.

On 31 July, the day the League Council convened in Geneva, Mussolini trumpeted his defiance of world opinion in *Il Popolo d'Italia*: 'Put in military terms, the problem admits of only one solution—with Geneva, without Geneva, against Geneva.' Italy's war preparations were far advanced by this date. The British Government were deeply concerned over the deteriorating situation. Especially were they afraid of an extreme Italian reaction to a possible decision in the coming Anglo-French conversations to uphold the League Covenant even to the extent of applying sanctions. On 6 August the Cabinet instructed the Chiefs of Staff to examine at once what the position would be if Italy 'took the bit between her teeth', and what steps should be taken to provide against this contingency.

The Chiefs were alive to the ever-present possibility of a war brought on by some Italian folly. The First Sea Lord, Chatfield, afterwards wrote that when the alarm occurred in August, 'we were expecting the possibility of hostilities at a moment's notice'. But the Services were not ready, and in the negotiations by Britain and France with Italy in Paris beginning on 16 August 'care should be taken', in Chatfield's words, 'not to precipitate the possibility of hostilities, but on the other hand every endeavour should be made to delay this possibility as long as possible. It should also be emphasised that the enforcement of sanctions could not be undertaken at the moment which was necessarily diplomatically

[3] COS (35) 147th meeting, 30 July 1935, CAB 53/5.

convenient, but only when the Services were in a position to back the enforcement.'

So far as the Mediterranean Fleet was concerned, it was much below the required strength, especially in cruisers and anti-submarine fitted destroyers.[4] Some two months were needed to make defence preparations, meaning, essentially, the movement of reinforcements and supplies to the Mediterranean. 'It therefore seemed of some importance,' declared the Deputy Chief of the Air Staff, Air Vice-Marshal C. L. Courtney, 'that the Conversations with Italy should endeavour to "keep the pot simmering" until that period of two months was up.' The Chiefs reminded the Government of the importance of the assured military support of France; her moral and political co-operation would not suffice. Britain must not find herself carrying the risks alone; that is, there must be no unilateral action in support of the Covenant.[5] To make certain that the Foreign Office got the message, Chatfield repeated the essence of the recommendations and reasoning of the Chiefs in a personal letter to Sir Robert Vansittart, the Permanent Under-Secretary of State for Foreign Affairs, concluding: 'War is not a light measure which we can go into blindfold trusting to luck. I only want to be sure that the Foreign Office are fully apprised of the military situation and they do all they can to delay the danger of hostilities, meanwhile authorising us to prepare.'[6]

Sir Samuel Hoare, the Foreign Secretary, and Vansittart agreed that the admonitions of the Service Chiefs, and all that lay behind them, must guide their actions in Paris. 'We shall have to be exceedingly cautious in Paris and for long after, if there is any prospect whatever of a stiff or drastic line being taken', wrote Vansittart. 'What [Chatfield's letter] comes to is this. This country has been so weakened of recent years that we are in no position to take a strong line in the Mediterranean . . . we should be very cautious as to how far and in what manner we force

---

[4] Ammunition was a bit of a problem, too. The Second-in-Command of the Mediterranean Fleet, Vice-Admiral Sir Charles Forbes, confided to the British Ambassador in Cairo at about this time that his ships had enough ammunition to shoot for fifteen minutes! Lord Vansittart, *The Mist Procession* (London, 1958), p. 544. Colonel H. R. Pownall, Military Assistant Secretary of the CID, stated that 'the A.A. ammunition of the Fleet is only sufficient for *one* week! That being because it has been based on the assumption of Fleet actions—not to defend a fleet sitting, much of its time, in an anchorage within air range of an enemy. The fact is we are properly caught with our trousers down. The Service deficiencies are very great . . .' Diary, 2 Sept. 1935, Brian Bond (ed.), *Chief of Staff: the Diaries of Lieutenant-General Sir Henry Pownall*, vol. i, 1933–1940 (London, 1972), p. 78.

[5] COS (35) 148th meeting, 8 Aug. 1935, CAB 53/5.

[6] Chatfield to Vansittart, 8 Aug. 1935, Chatfield MSS.

the pace in Paris, with an unreliable France and an unready England.'[7]

When Anthony Eden, the Minister for League of Nations Affairs, met with Laval, the French Premier, on 13 August and again (with Vansittart) on 14 August, in an attempt to establish a common front, Laval then, as throughout the crisis, was not prepared to adopt a strong stance at Geneva. He would do nothing that might antagonize Mussolini and deprive France of his support against Hitler. In the tripartite discussions on 16 August the British and French offered to support Italian economic and political preponderance in Ethiopia but would go no further. This was not good enough for the Duce, who was bent on annexing the non-Amharic territories of Ethiopia and establishing a protectorate over the rest, and he torpedoed the conference on the 18th.

With the possibility of a negotiated settlement increasingly remote, on Eden's initiative the holidaying Prime Minister was persuaded to summon an emergency Cabinet for 22 August to consider precautionary military measures. Chatfield, who was snatching a holiday in Austria, was among those recalled to London. He met Baldwin in the cross-Channel steamer and was told: 'We shall have a Cabinet to-morrow and then I shall, I hope, go back to Aix.'[8] There was to be no going back.

The Cabinet had before it on the 22nd the defence measures recommended by the Chiefs of Staff pursuant to the Cabinet directive of 6 August. The immediate problem concerned the programme of the Home Fleet. As had been announced in the press, the fleet was supposed to leave Home ports on 8 September for a cruise in Home waters. The Cabinet accepted the recommendation of the Chiefs that this be scrapped and that the fleet concentrate at Portland on 29 August, ready to sail for Gibraltar, with certain units to part company unobtrusively and sail to join the Mediterranean Fleet. The press was in due course informed that these ships were not reinforcing the Mediterranean Fleet, but that the movement was in accordance with the routine work of the Service. A second major decision was to authorize the Admiralty to keep the Mediterranean Fleet at Malta until 29 August and then to send it to the eastern Mediterranean. Finally, the Cabinet turned down the Admiralty's bid for mobilization of naval reserves, necessary to complete the Home and Mediterranean Fleets to full complement,

---

[7] Vansittart to Hoare, 9 Aug. 1935, and Hoare's note on the letter, 9 Aug., FO 371/19123.

[8] Admiral of the Fleet Lord Chatfield, *It Might Happen Again* (London, 1947), p. 88.

'owing to the resounding effect it would have on public opinion both at home and abroad'.[9]

Further preparatory steps were approved the next day by the recently constituted Sub-Committee on Defence Policy and Requirements of the Committee of Imperial Defence[10]—the maximum reinforcements in the Mediterranean that would not be considered likely to provoke hostilities on the eve of the 4 September meeting of the League of Nations Council: the aircraft carrier *Courageous*, the 5th and 6th Destroyer Flotillas, and the 2nd Submarine Flotilla. They left Home waters on 30 August.

The naval Commander-in-Chief in the Mediterranean, W. W. Fisher, not only wanted all the reinforcements he could get, but he also pressed for the Home Fleet to proceed to Malta, where he apparently expected it would come under his command. 'Any hostile act by Italy', he telegraphed the Admiralty, 'should in my opinion be met by strongest possible counter offensives within 24 hours if possible. Delay adds to difficulty. If Mediterranean Fleet is in Eastern [?bases] and Home Fleet at Malta the latter would be available for immediate counter offensive but major offensive would have to await junction of the two Fleets.'[11] Chatfield preferred that not all the projected reinforcements go out immediately and that the Home Fleet remain concentrated at Portland, though at short notice. This was the line taken by the Sub-Committee on Defence Policy and Requirements on 23 August. The First Sea Lord explained the situation to a frustrated Commander-in-Chief:

The Cabinet [22 August] wanted to send you at once *all* the reinforcements I had envisaged. So did I, but *only* if they made France also take military measures such as concentrating aircraft on the Italian frontier. It was their view that to send out everything and the Home Fleet to Gibraltar would act as a *deterrent* to Mussolini but I had to point out the danger if they proved incorrect as the Foreign Office so often are. They would not approach the French however, as they feel the latter would refuse to cooperate in military measures at this time—whatever they *may* be willing to do later on.

Now if the sending of the Battle Cruisers to you and the Home Fleet to

⁹ Cab. 42 (35), 22 Aug. 1935, CAB 23/82.

¹⁰ DPR (35) 5th meeting, 23 Aug. 1935, CAB 16/136. The Cabinet had invited it on 22 August 'to consider any matter that might arise in connection with the Italo-Abyssinian Dispute'. The membership of the Sub-Committee consisted of eleven cabinet ministers, including the Prime Minister, who served as chairman, the Foreign Secretary, the Minister for League of Nations Affairs, and the Service heads, with the Chiefs of Staff of the three defence Services acting as expert advisers. The COS Sub-Committee and the Chiefs of Staff individually prepared papers for the Committee. Its broad mandate was the co-ordination of defence and foreign policy.

¹¹ Telegram no. 426, 20 Aug. 1935, ADM 116/3038.

Gibraltar had the effect of touching off the excitable Iti we should be plunged into War under the most unfavourable conditions possible, i.e., unready, no French support, no French dockyards for repair of ships, no Greek harbour, the M.N.B. [Mobile Naval Base] organisation not available. For this reason I advised holding up the Battle Cruisers for the present, badly as I wish them to be with you with your weakness in cruisers.[12]

In short, unless the French also took military measures, the First Sea Lord would not risk a too heavy naval concentration in the Mediterranean.

Fisher was also overriden in his desire to keep Malta as his main base. The Admiralty were seriously concerned about the vulnerability of Malta to air attack from Italy. It was within 60 miles of Sicilian air bases and its defences against such attack (a War Office responsibility) were slight, owing to the financial stringency of preceding years. (Malta apparently had no AA guns in the beginning!) Fisher's answer to Admiralty arguments about the untenability of Malta was that he would use the fleet aircraft to defend Malta. Chatfield pointed out on 25 August that he had '*only* the exact number required for the 3 carriers, no reserve pilots other than those with the Fleet doing sea-time. If the aircraft at Malta were lost the Carrier is immobilised.' On 28 August the Admiralty overrode Fisher's intention to use Malta as a base and, carrying out the Cabinet decision of the 22nd, sent the Mediterranean Fleet to Alexandria. It left Malta in dribs and drabs starting on 29 August, with the last unit, the flagship HMS *Resolution*, not arriving in Alexandria until 24 September.

The First Sea Lord was clear in his mind that 'Malta is a minor matter in the long run . . . if Italy is mad enough to challenge us, it is at the ends of the Mediterranean she will be defeated and, knowing that her communications with Abyssinia are cut, you yourself will have a freer hand in the Central Mediterranean and Malta, even if it is demolished, will come back again.'[13] This, too, was the position taken by the Chiefs of Staff, who declared that Malta's defence would probably have no adverse effects on the result of the war—indeed, enemy air attacks on Malta would be a diversion favourable to the operations of the fleet. However, 'emphasis should be laid on the probable results to Italy of the

---

[12] Chatfield to Fisher, 25 Aug. 1935, Chatfield MSS. Pownall called Chatfield's successful opposition to the Cabinet decision to send the whole Home Fleet to Gibraltar 'a very interesting example of the "military" people holding back the Statesmen—for the former are always being accused of being pugilistic and demanding measures on military grounds which are politically dangerous.' Diary, 22 Aug. 1935 (unpublished).

[13] Chatfield to Fisher, 25 Aug. 1935.

cutting of her communications with her forces in Abyssinia and this was likely to be the main cause of bringing Italy to her knees . . .'[14]

Alexandria had important advantages. It controlled the Suez Canal, lay on the Italian line of communications to Ethiopia, and was an easily defended harbour. It had one grave shortcoming: it lacked repair facilities for the fleet, and Malta, the nearest dockyard and naval base, was 815 nautical miles away. Recreational facilities were few, and its narrow-mouthed harbour, if blocked, would trap the warships inside. Alexandria had a further disadvantage. The submarine-detecting apparatus (asdic) of the anti-submarine forces was rendered ineffective by the varying densities of the sea water in different layers, a condition caused by the outpouring of fresh water from the mouths of the Nile.

Among other elementary precautions taken at this time on Admiralty initiative, the Home and Mediterranean Fleets were ordered to complete to full capacity of naval and victualling stores to make them self-contained for four months, the charts that might be required were printed and distributed, and there was an acceleration of the provision of anti-submarine apparatus for small craft.

Meanwhile, in September, the one achievement of the League Council that had convened in Geneva on the 4th was the appointment on the 6th of a conciliation committee of five (Britain, France,

[14] COS (35) 150th meeting, 13 Sept. 1935, CAB 53/5. Throughout the crisis the Chiefs of Staff were concerned about the vulnerability of Malta to air attack, but they believed that the best method of relieving this pressure would be by air counter-attacks from southern France on northern Italy. To maintain adequate naval control in the central Mediterranean after the abandonment of Malta by the fleet, the Chiefs, led by Chatfield, held that it would be necessary from the start of the war to make use of an advanced base of operations. For security reasons this base was referred to as Port 'X'. Actually, it was Navarino, a large fleet anchorage on the west coast of Greece that the Mediterranean Fleet had frequently used for such events as regattas. The assumption was that the Greeks would co-operate. Greek permission or no, the fleet must have Port X. 'I do not know if Greece will give us Port "X",' Chatfield assured Fisher on 25 August, 'but if not I shall not hesitate (nor will the Cabinet) to seize it. I have told them so. So you can rely on that.' In mid-December, however, this item in the war plan was scrapped, temporarily at any rate, after Fisher had convinced the Admiralty that the advantages of Port X did not justify the risk of trying to establish and maintain a base there in the face of the Italian air threat. Thereafter Alexandria was considered the main fleet base in the event of war. From it the fleet would attempt to exert at least an intermittent control of the central Mediterranean. Chatfield anticipated that the fleet might have to be established at Port X so that it could 'advance closer to Italy in order to force things to a conclusion'. This time might arrive when the French were prepared for full military co-operation and were to put pressure on Italy by air attacks on northern Italy. COS (35), 159th meeting, 13 Dec. 1935, CAB 53/5, Chatfield to Fisher, 19 Dec. 1935, Chatfield MSS.

Spain, Poland, and Turkey) 'to make a general examination of Italo-Ethiopian relations and to seek for a pacific settlement'. Italy ignored it. On the 9th the sixteenth session of the Assembly of the League opened. On the 11th Hoare delivered his now celebrated speech. He made a ringing affirmation of Britain's support of 'the League and its ideals as the most effective way of ensuring peace', and in emphatic tones, with raps on the desk of the rostrum for additional emphasis, he electrified the Assembly with these words: 'In conformity with its precise and explicit obligations, the League stands, and my country stands with it, for collective maintenance of the Covenant in its entirety, and particularly for steady and collective resistance to all acts of unprovoked aggression.' We know that what struck his listeners as a British pledge to go to war if necessary to stop Italian aggression was only a bluff to scare Mussolini into a more moderate policy. In secret talks on 10–11 September Hoare and Laval had ruled out the adoption of military sanctions and had decided that any economic sanctions imposed by the League must be applied cautiously. The conciliation committee reported back on 18 September, calling for administrative reforms in Ethiopia under European supervision and the recognition of Italy's paramount economic interests in that country. Italy found the scheme unacceptable.

British naval preparations were intensified as the crisis deepened during September. Chatfield 'felt that all efforts must be sacrificed in the interests of the Mediterranean. So far as he was concerned he had already burnt his boats in the East. He did not consider that anything should stand in the way of improving our position in the Mediterranean.'[15] The 4th Cruiser Squadron, under the Commander-in-Chief, East Indies, concentrated at Aden to seal off the southern entrance to the Red Sea.[16] Reinforcements from Home waters and the China, Pacific, and America and West Indies stations arrived to join the Mediterranean Fleet, and a Home Fleet detachment consisting of the battle cruisers *Hood* and *Renown*, three 6-inch cruisers, and six destroyers arrived at Gibraltar on 17 September.[17] The Mediterranean and Home Fleets were completed with

---

[15] COS (35) 149th meeting, 6 Sept. 1935, CAB 53/5.

[16] The naval concentration at Aden during the crisis gave the Germans the key to the British naval cipher. The ships used their wartime codes and ciphers, 'offering a cryptanalyst's feast. Call-signs were easily identified; key words and phrases regularly repeated.' Donald McLachlan, *Room 39: Naval Intelligence in Action, 1939–45* (London, 1968), p. 77.

[17] During the crisis the China Station was so drained of ships for the Mediterranean (by the end of 1935, ten of its units—1 cruiser, 1 minelayer, 4 destroyers, and 4 submarines) that, to give the Japanese the impression that it had not been

ammunition, torpedoes, depth charges, and the like (although the former fleet continued to lack reserve ammunition). They were completed to full complements without mobilizing by denuding all the training schools and, without publicity, by calling up 3,000 volunteers. The ships, equipment, and personnel constituting the Mobile Naval Base Defence Organization (MNBDO), consisting of boom nets, controlled mines, 22 AA guns, 33 searchlights, moorings, communications, and base staff (largely Royal Marines), also four 6-inch coast-defence guns, were sent to Alexandria. The intention was to use them in the defence of Port X and other eastern Mediterranean bases. Two flying-boat squadrons from home were sent to Alexandria for eventual co-operation with the fleet, another was dispatched to Gibraltar, and the air squadrons in the Middle East were increased by 30 aircraft. Three battalions were sent to Malta. To intercept contraband destined for Eritrea or Italy, wartime contraband control staffs were established at Aden, Port Said, and Gibraltar. The Admiralty took preliminary steps to enable the control and routing of British shipping to be instituted should an emergency necessitate diversion of through Mediterranean trade to the Cape route.

It certainly looked as though the British meant business. Their Ambassador in Rome, however, assured Mussolini on 20 September that the build-up in the inland sea was 'not intended to imply any aggressive intention', but was rather a 'natural consequence' of the violent Anglophobe tone of the Italian press.[18] The latest study of the Italo-Ethiopian War holds:

> The most generous interpretation of the reasons for the concentration of a British naval force in the Eastern Mediterranean during September 1935 was that the British Government considered there was the possibility of Mussolini taking a swipe at Britain if there was any interference at Suez. Yet this explanation seems far-fetched when one considers that with a quarter of a million men on the far side of the Canal in an area where they could hardly get enough drinking-water and certainly not enough food, Mussolini had provided a hostage for any maritime power that chose to attack her. More likely the comings and goings of the British fleet, its concentration at Alexandria and the reinforcements sent to Egypt, were deceptive measures designed to provide the necessary atmosphere at home where the Conservatives had to be kept quiet, at Geneva where Britain could pose as a weary Titan with the world's troubles on her shoulders,

weakened appreciably, one old cruiser and four destroyers 'rushed madly about and pretended they were the China Station Fleet!' Vice-Admiral Sir Geoffrey Barnard's letter to the author, 15 Sept. 1970. He was a destroyer commander on the station during the crisis.

[18] Sir Eric Drummond to Hoare, 20 Sept. 1935, FO 401/35.

and in Rome where there was still hope that a show of strength from the Royal Navy could call the Duce's bluff.[19]

In this case 'the most generous interpretation' is the correct one. The naval measures were, in fact, precautionary. 'There has been so much wild and threatening talk in Italy of late', Hoare informed Eden, 'that we have found it necessary to be on the safe side and to take some precautionary measures.'[20] Should the League impose non-military sanctions, the Admiralty believed it was 'possible but not probable that Italy would take some action which would bring about a state of war. We must therefore be prepared for war to follow the imposition of any form of sanctions.'[21] So little were the British interested in pressuring the Italians with a display of force that they took the various naval measures with as little publicity as possible. So far as was practicable the Government and Admiralty were anxious to avoid giving Mussolini an excuse for breaking off the negotiations at Geneva.

On the Italian side, a scholar has pointed out, 'Mussolini did not want a war with Britain: at this time he had everything to lose and nothing to gain, despite his belief that the Italian air force was capable of inflicting great damage on the British Fleet. But he was irrevocably committed to the success of the Ethiopian campaign and it is not impossible that, had the threat from Britain become critical, out of desperation he might have retaliated.'[22]

Their preparations for war completed, on 3 October the Italians began the invasion of Ethiopia. On the 7th the Council of the League condemned Italy's resort to war as being 'in disregard of her obligations under Article 12' (the compulsory arbitration article) of the Covenant. This brought into use Article 16, which called for the application of sanctions in such a case. On the 11th representatives of fifty nations in the Assembly endorsed this decision; only four

[19] Barker, *The Civilizing Mission*, p. 117.

[20] Hoare to Consul, Geneva, for Eden, 16 Sept. 1935, FO 401/35.

[21] Admiralty to Cs-in-C, Mediterranean, East Indies, Africa, 11 Sept. 1935, ADM 116/3038. Hoare believed that 'the greatest risk . . . was liable to arise out of the probable lifting of the embargo on the export of arms to Abyssinia by the various nations whenever Italy was declared in the wrong. In that contingency it was quite conceivable that a serious incident might arise if Italy should claim belligerent rights and seize a ship carrying munitions.' DPR (35) 8th meeting, 17 Sept. 1935, CAB 16/136. Various European nations, among them France and Britain, had imposed an arms embargo on Ethiopia early in the summer. It was raised on 11 October.

[22] George W. Baer, *The Coming of the Italo-Ethiopian War* (Cambridge, Mass., 1967), p. 355. That the Italians were not looking for war with Britain is borne out by the fact that as late as February 1936 no war orders had been sent to the Italian naval commander. Ibid., pp. 352–3 n.

were opposed. It was not until 18 November that sanctions were imposed. Although Article 16 provided for military action as well, the only sanctions invoked were economic: the prohibition of Italian imports, of export of certain raw materials to Italy, and of loans and credits to Italians, and the imposition of an arms embargo. The League Assembly's Committee of Eighteen unanimously agreed in principle to oil sanctions on 15 November, subject to further inquiries about the attitude of the United States.

The most critical phase of the crisis, for Britain above all, began with the adoption of sanctions, as it was obvious that the main burden of enforcing them, should the Italians make trouble, would fall on the Royal Navy. Late in October the British Government expressed interest in an Italian overture, conveyed through Laval, to effect a military détente in the Mediterranean by the withdrawal of the two British battle cruisers at Gibraltar in exchange for the withdrawal of one Italian division from Libya (in addition to the one pulled out recently). The existing situation: 56,000 Italian troops in Libya and 15,500 British in Egypt, compared with the normal figures, 20,000 and 11,000, respectively. The Cabinet was ready to withdraw the battle cruisers if they had French assurance of naval support on the outbreak of war and if the Italians were willing to 'effect a change in the attitude of the Press towards this country' and to scale their forces in Libya down to a 'reasonable figure'. By early November, however, the British had softened their terms considerably, so anxious were they to ease the crisis. French assurance of instant naval support was no longer required: 'the proposal of the French Naval Staff that, in the event of an Italian aggression against British interests in the Mediterranean, France should delay going to war until her state of preparedness was improved, is the best we can hope for and should be accepted with good will'. Gone, too, was the provision about the Italian press. The withdrawal of one Italian division would be sufficient to order the withdrawal of the two battle cruisers from the Mediterranean—this despite Chatfield's unwillingness to approve any weakening of the fleet in the Mediterranean.[23] Nothing was achieved, since Mussolini, who was now, Hoare reported, in an 'intransigent mood', would not consider the British proposal except as part of a wider agreement covering the future, and this was unacceptable to London. By mid-November the détente was a dead issue.

[23] See especially DPR (35) 12th and 13th meetings, 21 Oct., 5 Nov. 1935, CAB 16/136.

The situation deteriorated further in the latter part of November and into December, a period when the British regarded an Italian 'mad-dog act' as a distinct possibility. The Foreign Office picked up many rumours that Italy might well attack Britain 'if sanctions were imposed such as to humiliate Italy or to threaten her national life'. Hoare believed they could not ignore this threat, nor should they overrate it, since there was without doubt an element of propaganda in this rumour-mongering. Some of it, at least, was being used to frighten them.[24] The Cabinet of 2 December had before it secret information that indicated the Italians were making military preparations to back up their threats of active retaliation if oil sanctions were adopted. The Admiralty did not dismiss the possibility of an attack under the stimulus of oil sanctions. 'Should they be imposed it is considered that the possibility of an attack on this country will be greater than at any previous period, since, faced by eventual defeat, Italy may prefer to go down with her colours flying fighting this country rather than be ignominiously defeated by League action.'[25]

* * *

The pattern of British policy had been set by October and was to undergo no significant change while the crisis lasted. The opposition to military sanctions, the half-hearted espousal of an oil embargo—the only kind of economic sanction that really would have hurt Mussolini—and that futile early exercise in appeasement, the Hoare–Laval Pact of 8 December 1935, under which the League would have asked Ethiopia to sacrifice about half her territory in return for receiving a Red Sea port with a connecting corridor to it—these, as well as the ultimate decision to liquidate sanctions —all were in large measure determined by the weakness of the British naval position. Not that this position *vis-à-vis* the Italian Fleet was in much doubt, and therein lies an important facet of this study.

Admiral of the Fleet Sir Ernle Chatfield, the First Sea Lord and Chief of Naval Staff (1933–8), was the finest officer the Royal Navy produced between the wars. He had character, charm (even if he

[24] DPR (35) 14th meeting, 26 Nov. 1935, CAB 16/136, Cab 50 (35), 2 Dec. 1935, CAB 23/82. These rumours were what Chatfield may have been thinking of when he remarked long after the crisis: 'If I believed all the stories I heard at the time of the Abyssinian crisis and my nerves were less strong I should now be in a lunatic asylum.' Chatfield to Vansittart, 21 Jan. 1938, Chatfield MSS.

[25] Plans Division, Admiralty, 'Summary of Present Situation in Regard to Italo/ Abyssinian Crisis', 11 Dec. 1935, ADM 116/3049.

always looked rather severe and lacked a sense of humour), administrative ability, professional knowledge—the lot. Admiral Sir William James, who had been Chatfield's Chief of Staff in the Home and Mediterranean Fleets and became his Deputy Chief of Naval Staff on 30 October 1935, tells us:

With his unique experience afloat, in peace and war, and of the Admiralty, as Fourth Sea Lord, A.C.N.S. and Controller, he could very quickly master the contents of a docket or disentangle a problem and make his decision. Unlike some of his contemporaries he never wasted time on unimportant matters and so always found time to enjoy the sports and games, at which he was so proficient. . . . He was the best 'all-rounder' of his day and age. With his quiet manner, his charm, and friendliness he won the hearts of all who had the good fortune to be on his staff and so in daily contact with him.[26]

Chatfield completely dominated the Board of Admiralty, and it was he who conducted all the more important business arising from the crisis. Admiral James does not remember any Board meetings on it. The First Lord of the Admiralty during the Ethiopian Crisis was the tall, very handsome, and charming Sir Bolton Eyres-Monsell (soon afterwards first Viscount Monsell), a one-time naval commander. 'The great thing about him,' one officer recalls, 'was that he was a gentleman, ready to take the advice of the experts.' There is a revealing passage in the first volume of Chatfield's autobiography. 'Anyhow, I knew I should have a pleasant political chief who would "give me my head,"'[27] and that is exactly what he did. Chatfield also dominated the Chiefs of Staff Sub-Committee. There is no mystery here. The Chief of the Air Staff (1933–7) was Marshal of the Royal Air Force Sir Edward Ellington, in every way inferior to Chatfield. The same is true of the Chief of the Imperial General Staff (1933–6), Sir Archibald Montgomery-Massingberd. (His original family name was Montgomery, but he tacked on the surname of Massingberd on inheriting a property in Lincolnshire.) The War Secretary at this time, Duff Cooper, found him 'very inadequate and out of date' as CIGS.[28] Sir Basil Liddell Hart said that 'when his name comes up, Monty (Bernard Montgomery) is always quick to emphasize that they were in no way related!'[29] What it boils down to is that Chatfield's views on strategic matters carried exceptional weight with the Government.

---

[26] Admiral James's letter in *The Times*, 20 Nov. 1967.
[27] *The Navy and Defence* (London, 1942), p. 247.
[28] *The Memoirs of Captain Liddell Hart* (2 vols., London, 1968), i. 300.
[29] Liddell Hart's letter to the author, 29 Jan. 1968.

The Admiral was fully aware of Italy's 'disadvantageous general strategical position', the result of her dependence on seaborne trade for 76 per cent of her total imports. Sixty-two per cent of her imports came through Gibraltar, 3 per cent via Suez, and the remaining 11 per cent from the Mediterranean and Black Sea countries.

> With our forces based at Gibraltar and in Egypt, her main communications can be cut with comparatively little effort to ourselves, whereas to take any steps (excepting by submarine) to counter our action she would have to send her forces far from their bases where they would be brought to action. This strategical advantage is so great that it is unlikely that Italy could make any serious attempt with Naval forces to interfere with our control of the two exits to the Mediterranean except by the action of her submarines, which could not prove decisive. Further, Italy's object is the prosecution of her Abyssinian war, and the mere closing of the Canal to her by the presence of our Naval forces (whether closing is done in [the] Canal itself or by action outside it) might be decisive within a measurable period.[30]

On the other hand, he pointed out, 'the problem of putting warlike pressure on her is not so simple as might appear above', even if Britain had the support of the principal naval members of the League, because of certain Italian advantages. While Britain was doing nothing, Italy had long been preparing for war, and she occupied an excellent strategic position for operations in the central Mediterranean, since her Fleet could operate on interior lines as against the British and French fleets.

These advantages did not signify too much to Chatfield, for he had contempt for the Italians as fighters and did not rate their Navy highly. 'The modern Italian is an unknown quantity but I cannot believe he is a greatly different fighter than in the past. But Mussolini (like Napoleon to Villeneuve!) may say "Go to sea and don't return till you have damaged the British Fleet." '[31] He 'thought it improbable that the Italian Navy would ever prove really efficient at sea'.[32] On paper the naval position was fairly satisfactory. Admiralty figures on the relative strength of the two

[30] DPR 15, Chatfield's memorandum, 'Italo-Abyssinian Dispute. The Naval Strategical Position in the Mediterranean', 3 Sept. 1935, CAB 16/138.

[31] Chatfield to Fisher, 25 Aug. 1935, Chatfield MSS.

[32] COS (35) 150th meeting, 13 Sept. 1935, CAB 53/5. The other Chiefs held similar opinions as regards their own Service. The Director of Military Operations and Intelligence, Major-General J. G. Dill, representing the Chief of the Imperial General Staff, asserted that 'the Italian Army was technically highly developed and the officers were keen and efficient but they still remained Italians, and . . . there was considerable doubt as to how long that efficiency would last under active service conditions'. The Chief of the Air Staff agreed. 'The Italian airman might start full of confidence, but a few knocks would soon reduce his enthusiasm.' Ibid.

fleets in the Mediterranean late in September (including British ships *en route*) showed:

	British Empire	Italy
Battleships	5	2 (excluding 2 undergoing long refit and modernization)
Battle cruisers	2 (at Gibraltar)	..
Aircraft carriers	2	1
8-inch cruisers	5	7
6-inch cruisers	10 (including 3 at Gibraltar)	10
Flotilla leaders	..	18
Destroyers	54	65
Submarines	11	62

Comparative figures for the two fleets in the Red Sea showed:

	British Empire	Italy
8-inch cruisers	1	..
6-inch cruisers	2	2 (5·9-inch)
Flotilla leaders	..	2
Destroyers	5	3
Submarines	..	4
Sloops	5	2

The battle cruisers were regarded as 'a tremendous asset'. The destroyer situation could stand improvement, but no more could be sent without mobilization. The most serious limitations were seen as, first, docking accommodation in the Mediterranean unless they had the use of French ports; second, 'in the narrow waters of the Mediterranean aircraft attack was a serious preoccupation, especially as the anti-aircraft armaments of the Fleet were not as much as could be wished'.[33] The French naval factor, which was

[33] Figures presented by, and statement of, the First Lord, 24 Sept. 1935, Cab. 43 (35), CAB 23/82. On 25 August Chatfield warned Fisher of the Italian coastal motor-boats that might initially be an anxiety to him when he moved to the central Mediterranean. Admiralty figures at the end of October showed there were 544,000 tons of British warships in the Mediterranean and 49,000 tons in the Red Sea (compared with 208,000 and 2,000, respectively, on 5 August) and 382,000 tons of Italian warships in the Mediterranean and 23,000 in the Red Sea (370,000 and 9,100, respectively, on 5 August). Figures (prepared at Foreign Office request) attached to Sir E. Drummond's telegram no. 672, 30 Oct. 1935, ADM 116/3038. Early in October nine submarines and a depot ship were sent out to increase the 'very limited' submarine strength in the Mediterranean.

central to the entire Admiralty outlook, will be discussed elsewhere, as will the air threat. Here it is sufficient to note that neither seriously affected the supreme confidence of the Admiralty in the ability of the fleet to handle the Italians in the Mediterranean, even in a single-handed war. Chatfield early in the crisis asserted that 'the final outcome of a conflict with Italy cannot be a matter of doubt', and when the crisis was nearly over, he 'had no doubts as to the ability of the Royal Navy to carry out its tasks'.[34]

The Mediterranean Fleet shared this confidence. An officer who served in that fleet during the crisis is positive on this point: 'I am quite sure everyone in the Fleet felt more than ready to take on the Italian Fleet and was confident that the Fleet would be successful in any sea operation that took place. Morale was high. Little was then known about the efficiency of anti-aircraft defence, the Italian bombers were based a great distance to the west and they were not considered much of a menace.'[35] The Commander-in-Chief had not the slightest doubts about the outcome of a war. Shortly before the fleet sailed to Alexandria, Fisher received from the Chiefs of Staff 'a very pessimistic, not to say, defeatist, view of the Mediterranean Fleet's capacity to deal with the Italians'. (This mood in London vanished quickly.) An angry Commander-in-Chief told one of his flag officers that he had signalled 'their Lordships telling them I disagree with every word of this pusillanimous document. The Mediterranean Fleet is by no means so powerless as is here set out.'[36]

Fisher's confidence was based on the efficiency of the fleet, for which he was himself in large part responsible. Admiral Sir William Wordsworth Fisher, Commander-in-Chief in the Mediterranean since 1932, was an officer of magnificent, if somewhat aloof, presence, known to his contemporaries as 'W.W.' and 'the tall Agrippa'. (The latter from Heinrich Hoffman's children's classic, *Struwwelpeter*: 'Now tall Agrippa lived close by–/So tall, he almost touch'd the sky . . .'). Among his diversified interests was tennis, which he played every possible afternoon, three or four sets at a

[34] Chatfield's memorandum, 'The Naval Strategical Position in the Mediterranean', COS (36) 174th meeting, 13 May 1936, CAB 53/6.

[35] Admiral Sir Guy Grantham's letter to the author, 21 Aug. 1968. Grantham was in the Mediterranean from the end of 1935 and joined the staff of Fisher's successor in March 1936.

[36] Cunningham of Hyndhope, *A Sailor's Odyssey*, pp. 173–4. Cunningham was then Rear-Admiral, Destroyer Flotillas, Mediterranean. A few weeks earlier, on 14 August, the Duce had received the opinion of his Chiefs of Staff that a war with Great Britain would prove disastrous to Italy: the British Fleet was far superior to Italy's; the Italian air force, though larger, consisted mostly of obsolete planes; Italian cities, ports, and industrial centres would be heavily damaged. Baer, *The Coming of the Italo-Ethiopian War*, pp. 253–4.

D

time, even in the intense heat of the Alexandrian sun. More to the point, Fisher had a most attractive personality, immense energy, and a first-class brain, and he was an inspiring and understanding leader who possessed the confidence and affection of all who served under him. By continually exercising his fleet at sea, he kept it at peak efficiency, ready for any emergency. When he left for home in the *Queen Elizabeth* on 20 March 1936, his departure was an unforgettable experience for the officers and men. Cunningham had 'never heard cheers more hearty nor heart-felt. We were losing a friend, and a great commander.'

Fisher's successor, Admiral Sir Dudley Pound, who had been Commander-in-Chief designate, had been serving as Fisher's Chief of Staff since October 1935 – a most extraordinary arrangement. Pound was, in Cunningham's judgement, 'a master of detail, which at times led him into trying to do too much himself. He was not, perhaps, a man of great imagination or insight.'[37] But, as Cunningham admits, Pound succeeded in keeping the Mediterranean Fleet in the same high state of efficiency in which Fisher had left it. The forceful and tireless Pound (he never went to bed until 1 or 2 a.m. and normally would be up fully dressed and working by 6.30 a.m.) continued the routine in the fleet as before. Ships were ordered to be ready to sail in not more than two and a half hours, leave was very restricted, and all shore leave ended at 10 p.m., there being no night leave at all. 'There was a great deal of exercising at sea,' writes an officer on his staff, 'firings of all kinds, and a general atmosphere of tension, perhaps due to Dudley's eagle eye which resulted in "bottles" being flashed to ships the moment he spotted anything amiss. Ships' companies were driven hard all the time and a sense of tension was maintained.'[38]

The naval war plan that emerged during the autumn as a result of Admiralty guidelines and Fisher's definite ideas assumed that Britain must be ready to act single-handed, at least in the early stages of a war. The plan gave the main role to Fisher's fleet, which had the principal concentration of force. It called for an aggressive offensive against the Italians with the object of securing and maintaining naval control in the central Mediterranean to bring 'every means of pressure to bear upon Italy'. Economic pressure and naval action alone were not counted on to defeat Italy; but severing

[37] *A Sailor's Odyssey*, pp. 583–4.
[38] Admiral Grantham's letter to the author, 21 Aug. 1968. To give an officer a 'bottle' (a 'bottle of acid' is the full term) means to rap him on the knuckles. The origin of the expression is obscure. Perhaps the full meaning is that when an admiral is displeased, his comments tend to be pretty acid!

communications with her armed forces in East Africa and Libya would force their surrender before long, and this would probably cause her to sue for peace.[39]

Fisher saw no need to wait for the outbreak of a war provoked by Italy. He was confident that if told to do so, he could stop Italian ships carrying troops and war *matériel* through the Canal and put an end to Italian aggression in Ethiopia. He was prepared to deal with the Italians even if he had to go it alone. As he telegraphed the Admiralty: 'Without underrating characteristics of enemy vessels or morale of Italian Navy I feel content that on receiving suitable reinforcements from Home Fleet any situation at sea could be dealt with without active assistance of other Powers–provided that France was friendly.'[40] Nor did Cunningham have any doubts. 'To us in the Mediterranean Fleet it seemed a very simple task to stop [Mussolini]. The mere closing of the Suez Canal to his transports which were then streaming through with troops and stores would effectively have cut off his armies concentrating in Eritrea and elsewhere. It is true that such a drastic measure might have led to war with Italy; but the Mediterranean Fleet was in a state of high morale and efficiency, and had no fear whatever of the result of an encounter with the Italian Navy.' But the order was never given. Cunningham continues: 'Had we stopped the passage of Italian transports through the Suez Canal, and the import of fuel oil into Italy, the whole subsequent history of the world might have been altered.' 'No one was in doubt about the outcome,' Admiral Grantham writes, 'if H.M. Government was prepared to grasp the nettle and declare war regardless of world opinion.' Meanwhile, the fleet took out its frustrations by showing contempt for the Italians when it had the opportunity. On one occasion, when a transport passed across the bows of two British warships and the troops cheered defiantly and sang the Fascist anthem, the hundreds of British sailors shouted at them. 'It is impossible to describe the withering contempt the British bluejacket can put into his applause if he dislikes the entertainment or entertainer, and on this occasion their sarcastic shouts penetrated even the thick hides of the Italians.'[41] Fisher and his fleet must have found a *Punch* cartoon of

[39] DCNS (Vice-Admiral Sir Charles Little) to C-in-C, Mediterranean, 18 Sept. 1935, ADM 116/3038. A convenient résumé of the evolution of the naval war plan will be found in an Admiralty paper, 'History of the Italian-Abyssinian Emergency, August 1935 to July 1936', Pt. A, 'Commander-in-Chief's Narrative', 20 Dec. 1937, ADM 116/3476 (hereafter 'History of the Emergency'). See the Note at the end of the chapter for some of the details of the war plan.
[40] No. 426, 20 Aug. 1935, ADM 116/3038.
[41] Cunningham of Hyndhope, *A Sailor's Odyssey*, pp. 173, 177; Admiral

this period highly apropos; it showed Baldwin sitting at his desk—on the wall, a model of a battleship in a glass case labelled HMS *Unriskable.*

The order to Fisher to intercept the Italian transports and supply ships as they approached Port Said was never sent because it was, Hoare has written, 'our fixed resolve to avoid unilateral action against a potential ally in a war with Germany. The naval staff, considering the crisis from a wider angle, could not have been more insistent with their warnings against diminishing or dissipating our limited strength.'[42] Indeed, the Chiefs of Staff at no time so much as contemplated any forcible measures 'short of war', whether by enforcement of an oil embargo or denial of the Suez Canal to the Italians. Their energies were focused on the strategy to be employed against Italy in the event of the war that they and the Government were determined to avoid. We have come here to the crux of the matter so far as the Navy was concerned.

*   *   *

To begin with, Chatfield, in common with the other Service Chiefs, had little use for the League and none for the policy of sanctions, even if, as he admits, the nation 'stood solidly behind sanctions. The principle of the League and so-called Collective Security had been well planted in the public mind, and watered by every national leader continuously for fifteen years.' The First Sea Lord considered this 'a dangerous attitude': the armed forces of the League powers were not 'so strong as to enable them to fight for a common cause, *as well as to safeguard their own vital interests'.*[43] By 'vital interests' he meant the vast responsibilities of imperial defence with special reference to a restless and potentially hostile Japan. These responsibilities had to be met with a Navy that was up to a one-power standard only—the consequence of the 'Ten-Year Rule', which had lapsed in 1933, the building restrictions imposed by postwar naval conferences, and the policy of economy-minded governments. It had been planned that in a Far Eastern

Grantham's letter to the author, 21 Aug. 1968. This raw bit of history points up the attitude of the British sailors towards the 'Ities', and vice versa. In the words of one who was there: 'We were guard ship at Port Said for many weeks and used to see the troopships passing. In one of them an Italian sailor peed over the stern to show his feelings for the British. A sailor shouted, "Do it while you can!" which brought the house down, because the Ethiopians were well known for their trick of castrating their prisoners!'

[42] Viscount Templewood (Sir Samuel Hoare), *Nine Troubled Years* (London, 1954), p. 191.

[43] Chatfield, *It Might Happen Again*, p. 87.

emergency most of the Fleet would be sent out, leaving in Home waters a 'nucleus' of ships; the hope was that there would be no complications until the other ships returned. Chatfield could not appreciate the wisdom of creating a danger on their main line of communications to the Far East 'for a moral motive'. 'Personally,' he confided to Fisher on 25 August, 'I have mixed feelings about a war. The bumptiousness of Italy is so great that it may be worth fighting her now to re-assert our dominance over an inferior race. But against that a hostile Italy is a real menace to our Imperial communications and defence system. We have relied on practically abandoning the Mediterranean if we send the Fleet east. For that reason I do not want to go to extreme measures and hope the Geneva Pacifists will fail to get unanimity and the League will break up.' The First Lord shared the Admiral's feelings about the strategic unwisdom of going to war with Italy or, what was almost as bad, making an enemy of her. 'I was', he says, 'strongly against sanctions for the following reasons. (1) It was most important for the Navy to have a non-hostile Mediterranean and all war time arrangements for reinforcing places like Singapore were based on using the Suez Canal. (2) At the time Italy was opposed to Germany and I feared that sanctions might well unite the two dictators. Unfortunately, as I think, only one other member of the Cabinet supported me.'[44]

There were three ways in which a strong sanctions policy could hurt British imperial interests: (1) Creating hostility in Italy, a power of growing naval and air strength, would stretch British naval resources too thin in the event of a war in Europe and the Far East simultaneously. (2) A war with Italy would make it practically impossible to protect British interests against a hostile Japan. 'Our strategic plans in the Far East', declared the Chiefs of Staff, 'are based upon the possibilities of conflict with an increasingly powerful Japan. . . . Our problem in the Far East is now further complicated by the apparent possibility of our becoming involved in additional commitments in support of the League of Nations, and the prospect of being faced with a war in the Far East at a time when complications in Europe necessitated the retention of part or the whole of our Fleet, is one of the gravest significance.'[45] (3) A war

[44] Lord Monsell's letter to the author, 1 Dec. 1968. The 'other member of the Cabinet' was Ramsay MacDonald, Lord President of the Council.

[45] COS 405, 'Strategical Situation in the Far East, with Particular Reference to Hong Kong', 10 Oct. 1935, CAB 53/25. The Service Chiefs never lost sight of the possibility that Japan might be tempted to use the occasion of a British embroilment in Europe to take action contrary to British interests. As the CIGS remarked, 'It cannot be too strongly emphasised that it would be beyond our powers to secure

with Italy would leave the Fleet weakened, since it was bound to suffer losses and damage. This was too high a price to pay even in a victorious war, given the possibility of trouble with Japan or Germany.

The third consideration bulked very prominently in the strategic thinking of the Admiralty. Ships could not be built overnight; it took some four years to construct capital ships and aircraft carriers. The First Lord informed his colleagues that there could be no doubt that the Fleet had the capacity to win command of the Mediterranean. The difficulty was that they 'might sustain serious losses,

our communications in the Far East, and still more to bring a war with Japan to a successful conclusion, if at the same time we were involved in a war in Europe.' The British strategic position in such an eventuality would be desperate. Singapore could be defended but was 'dangerously weak'; Hong Kong could not withstand a 'determined attack'. Montgomery-Massingberd's memorandum, 16 Sept. 1935, and letter to Hankey, 25 Sept., COS 403, 398, respectively, CAB 53/25. Hankey was himself dismayed by the prospect. 'Owing to our weakness, combined with the concentration in the Mediterranean of a large proportion of what strength we still have, both we and the League are as powerless in the Far East as we were in 1932 and 1933.' Hankey to Vansittart, 20 Nov. 1935, CAB 63/50. Looking back when the peak of the crisis had passed, Chatfield outlined how shaky the Far Eastern situation would have become had war broken out with Italy. 'When the Italian situation arose, we had been forced to pay off a considerable proportion of the battlefleet [four battleships] to man the light craft required in the Mediterranean. Further, on the termination of the Ten-Year Rule in 1932 [1933] the Admiralty had started a system of laying up battleships in rotation for extensive modernisation, and this programme would not be completed till about 1941. The consequent weakness in battleships had been accepted in order that we should be at maximum strength at the critical time (then estimated at 1942). If war were to be declared to-day against Japan, we should have only seven battleships available for operations in the Far East. This position was a dangerous one.' COS (36) 174th meeting, 13 May 1936, CAB 53/6. (Repeated by Chatfield at a meeting of the Cabinet Committee on the Position of the Fleet in the Mediterranean, MF (36) 1st meeting, 19 May 1936, CAB 27/606.) Or, as Chatfield told a friend of Baldwin's, 'the cable of Imperial Defence was stretched bar taut. Italy was the gnat whose weight could snap it.' Keith Middlemas and John Barnes, *Baldwin: a Biography* (London, 1969), p. 876.

At the time of the crisis 'at least one-half of Japan's battle fleet of ten ships and one of her two big carriers were commencing [or already undergoing] drastic modernization, and her two latest cruisers [*Mogami, Mikuma*] were proving unstable. But the Admiralty did not appear to know this . . .' Anthony Clayton and H. P. Willmott's letter in the *American Historical Review*, lxxvi (Oct. 1971), 1257–8. The facts are true enough, and I think it very probable indeed that the Admiralty did not know them. Nor were the Admiralty aware that the so-called aircraft carrier credited to Italy (above, p. 78) was not a true carrier: the 4,882-ton *Miraglia*, an ex-merchant ship taken over when building and completed in 1927. She had a speed of 21½ knots and carried four 4-inch AA guns and fifteen planes. Faulty naval intelligence is the explanation. Donald McLachlan reminds us of an important extenuating factor: 'While Chatfield was toiling to build up the Navy with inadequate funds, it was not to be expected that NID would be treated as anything but the Cinderella of the Naval Staff.' *Room 39*, p. 54. In the case of Japan, moreover, it was exceedingly hard to get intelligence in the country itself.

since our forces were not in a proper state of readiness for war in a land-locked sea'. The Air Secretary, Cunliffe-Lister, uttered a similar warning:

From the Naval and Air point of view [the Cabinet minutes record], it was represented that our defence forces and defences in the Mediterranean were not in a proper condition for war, and from this point of view it was urged that an effort should be made to obtain peace, holding the threat of the oil sanction over Italy, and that the fixing of the date should not be decided until after a failure of peace discussions. . . . The Cabinet ought to give the greatest consideration to the grave observations of the First Lord of the Admiralty and the Secretary of State for Air and their warning of the possibility of serious losses, for if we proceeded with the oil sanction and it brought about a serious reverse, the public would not easily forgive the Government, especially when the serious warnings of the Defence Departments become known.[46]

So seriously did the Admiralty take the possibility of losses and damage in a Mediterranean war that a Naval Staff appreciation, endorsed by the Chiefs of Staff, emphasized the need to start a large construction programme immediately if a single-handed war were forced on Britain, so that the Navy would be able to fulfil its commitments in the Far East when the war ended.[47]

The Government were in sympathy with the strategic views of the Admiralty. A Cabinet Minister of those days has stated in a private letter to the author that it would 'probably be true to say that the naval aspect weighed with the Government in relation to the Far East. To that extent, any losses in the Mediterranean, even minor ones, could have had significance, for we had also to be able to meet our responsibilities in the Far Eastern Seas.'

The Admiralty's fear of ship losses and damage in a war with Italy brings us to a consideration of the air threat. Chatfield had a reputation for underestimating the air danger in a future war. At a dinner party in 1933 Liddell Hart overheard him dismissing that threat with the remark that it was 'All rubbish. What we want are battleships.' This attitude to air power was not peculiar to him. Liddell Hart continues, 'I also came to realise that to most admirals the respective value of battleships and aircraft was not basically a technological issue, but more in the nature of a spiritual issue.

---

[46] Cab. 50 (35), 2 Dec. 1935, CAB 23/82. The Admiralty, keen on not provoking Mussolini, continued to oppose oil sanctions vigorously, as through the First Lord at the Cabinet of 26 February 1936 (Cab. 11 (36)), which examined all the pro and con arguments. The Cabinet on this occasion, while expressing their concern for the naval difficulties in the Mediterranean, instructed Eden, who had succeeded Hoare as Foreign Secretary on 18 December, to vote for oil sanctions at the Committee of Eighteen meeting fixed for 2 March. Nothing came of this halfhearted venture.   [47] COS (35) 150th meeting, 13 Sept. 1935, CAB 53/5.

They cherished the battle-fleet with a religious fervour, as an article of belief defying all scientific examination. . . . A battleship had long been to an admiral what a cathedral is to a bishop.'[48] This is not the whole story. The Commander-in-Chief, India, Sir Philip Chetwode, wrote in August 1935 that 'the Navy laughs at the Air now. They have got protected decks, and with their "blisters" and multiple machine-guns and multiple anti-aircraft guns, they don't fear them in the slightest.'[49] There is another facet in the naval thought of the time, the valour of ignorance. The air threat was still pretty much of an unknown quantity and therefore regarded as one that need not alarm the Service. 'No doubt', Chatfield maintained, 'under certain circumstances attacks from the air will be a very serious menace to warships, but it is at present pure conjecture as to what those circumstances will be, and what the degree of the vulnerability of the ships will be.'[50] Cunningham says that 'the Regia Aeronautica was of course an unknown quantity; but we were not disposed to attach too much weight to its ability to affect the issue. As the war was to prove we were right.'[51] The Admiralty expected that, at least at the start of a war with Italy, it was unlikely that the air menace would interfere seriously with the operations of the fleet.

Despite the confident, even supercilious, attitude to the threat from the air, in practice the Admiralty and Fisher did not take it lightly. A statement by the three Commanders-in-Chief in the Mediterranean reflects Fisher's position: 'The effect of air attack on a fleet in harbour is an unknown quantity and one to which a fleet should not be subjected without the strongest reasons.'[52] Admiralty and Fleet concern over air attacks was shown by the Mediterranean Fleet's quick abandonment of Malta and by the decision on 27 September to rearm the cruiser *Coventry* with anti-aircraft guns and send her to the Mediterranean Fleet. (She did not arrive until January 1936.) A similar decision was announced for the cruiser *Curlew* on 8 November. Since the Navy had no surplus

[48] Liddell Hart, *Memoirs*, i. 325, 326.
[49] ibid., p. 329.
[50] Chatfield's letter, signed 'Sailor', in *The Times*, 19 Mar. 1935.
[51] *A Sailor's Odyssey*, p. 173. The total British air force in the Middle East, including the Fleet Air Arm, was numerically equal to the Italian Air Force. The Italian machines, especially the long-range bombers and possibly the fighters, had a better performance, but the British personnel were superior. Cab. 50 (35), 2 Dec. 1935. In fleet aircraft the Mediterranean Fleet outnumbered the Italian Fleet.
[52] COS 419, 'Combined Naval, Military and Air Force Appreciation of the Situation which Would Arise in the Middle East in the Event of War with Italy', 6 Dec. 1935, CAB 53/26. The Chiefs of Staff took the same line. COS 426, 'Defence in the Eastern Mediterranean and the Middle East', 22 Jan. 1936, CAB 53/27.

personnel, the Commander-in-Chief sent home the battleship *Revenge* in December to provide the crews for these specially fitted anti-aircraft vessels. A particular reason for the concern over what Italian air power might achieve was the anti-aircraft ammunition position, which Chatfield on 3 September described as 'serious'. The War Secretary designate, Duff Cooper, and the First Lord gave particulars at a meeting of the Sub-Committee on Defence Policy and Requirements on 26 November. They were anything but re-assuring. The stocks of anti-aircraft ammunition available in Malta, Egypt, and Aden were not sufficient for extended operations, and it would be some months before a reasonably satisfactory position could be reached. Monsell's estimate was that the fleet had only enough anti-aircraft ammunition for each long-range gun to permit 22 minutes continuous fire; the corresponding figure for each short-range gun was 13 minutes. By January 1936 the latter figure could be raised to 16 minutes, and by the end of the financial year, to 25.[53]

Another factor that contributed heavily to the Navy's opposition to the introduction of oil sanctions was that the prolongation of the emergency would seriously affect the efficiency of the Fleet. Almost from the commencement of the crisis we find the Admiralty making representations to the Government on the decreasing efficiency of the Fleet, in both the Mediterranean and Home waters. The longer the emergency continued and the Fleet was kept in a state of war readiness, the more intolerable the position of the fleet in the Mediterranean and the more dismal the prospect for the whole Fleet when the crisis was over. The First Sea Lord put the problem in a nutshell when he said that 'the longer the resumption of the refit programmes and reliefs of personnel were postponed, the more congested would this action become ultimately . . . the present situation could not be continued. . . . At the same time if steps were now taken to bring back personnel and ships from the Mediterranean, there would be a weakening in both the political and military position. It was a question for the Government whether they were prepared to take that risk.'[54]

The situation worsened progressively as there was no relaxation in the crisis. The Home Fleet ships that were not in the Mediterranean were denied their usual autumn cruise to Scottish waters

---

[53] DPR (35) 14th meeting, CAB 16/136. Duff Cooper afterwards 'thought that it was easy to exaggerate the importance of the shortage of anti-aircraft ammunition, as the effectiveness of anti-aircraft guns was doubtful, and there were occasions when clouds, and so forth, rendered them of little value'. Cab. 50 (35), 2 Dec. 1935, CAB 23/82.

[54] COS (35) 155th meeting, 19 Nov. 1935, CAB 53/5.

and were kept at Portland for months in 'execrable weather' that was depressing to the men and militated against efficiency. The normal procedure was to send the Home Fleet on a spring cruise to the Gibraltar area. All they were able to do to avoid inflaming Italian susceptibilities was, in January, to send four ships and a destroyer flotilla to Gibraltar, where they relieved four units of the Home Fleet. In August the Admiralty had brought the Mediterranean Fleet up to war strength without mobilization. The result by the New Year was that the leave of many of the personnel was long overdue. The situation had reached the point where, if a ship needed docking, she steamed to Malta at high speed; twenty-four hours was the maximum allowed there, 'and then she rushed back to join the fleet as if the Italians were chasing her'.

The Admiralty would have played a different tune had they been able to count on wholehearted French co-operation in the air and at sea. It was Chatfield's constant refrain that the political discussions should not get ahead of military arrangements, that is, sanctions should not be carried as far as an oil embargo before the solution of the question of military co-operation with the Mediterranean powers in the League, France above all. The Sub-Committee on Defence Policy and Requirements had early laid down as the condition for the adoption of sanctions that there must be 'a clear understanding that if Italy, as a consequence, should attack any of the nations concerned, all the participating nations will declare war on Italy'. Yugoslavia, Greece, and France 'in particular' were mentioned specifically.[55] Had this become a reality, the Government, with the backing of the Services, in all probability would have responded fully to the moral fervour of the country and have gone in for oil sanctions and very likely a blockade of the Suez Canal as well.

It must be stressed that, although the Chiefs of Staff and the Government were from the start keenly interested in obtaining naval, military, and air assurances from all those Mediterranean powers who were members of the League, in the event of aggression by Italy, it was French co-operation that constituted the key element and missing link in British policy. This was so for three principal reasons: (1) With Malta not to be used as a fleet base if it came to war, docking and repair facilities would be practically non-existent for Fisher's capital ships, and indifferent for other units of his fleet, in a single-handed war fought in the narrow

---

[55] DPR (35) 6th meeting, 5 Sept. 1935, CAB 16/136. Hoare later assured the Committee that he had this principle 'continuously in mind'. DPR (35) 9th meeting, 23 Sept. 1935, CAB 16/136.

waters of the Mediterranean. The only docks available would be those at Gibraltar, which could not take capital ships, and one at Alexandria, which could take nothing larger than a small cruiser. Repair facilities would be similarly limited. Damaged ships most probably would have to return to England for repairs, if they were able to do so, or remain out of action for an indefinite period. The availability of the French naval bases of Toulon and Bizerta would have solved this problem. (2) Offensive French air operations (with the participation of an RAF contingent) against suitable targets in northern Italy would divert to an important degree the Italian air threat to Malta and to the Mediterranean Fleet when operating in the central area. (3) Allied French naval forces in the western Mediterranean, along with the Gibraltar force, would constitute a threat to Italy's west coast that would prevent her withdrawing all her warships from that coast and concentrating them against the British Mediterranean Fleet.

Discussions with the French Naval Staff with a view to concerted action were started in Paris on 18 September. The question became pressing after Italy went to war. Eden had obtained a resolution 'from both the Committees concerned' that all nations that had adopted sanctions would carry out Article 16, paragraph 3: 'The Members of the League will mutually support one another in resisting any special measures aimed at one of their Members by the Covenant-breaking State.' Pressed by the British, Laval had pledged on 15 October that France fully subscribed to the paragraph, but his reservation baffled them and 'made a deplorable impression'. He would not consider Article 16 applicable if the Italians alleged that the British naval build-up in the Mediterranean went beyond the steps agreed upon at Geneva for the execution of Article 16. In addition, the French Admiralty refused to discuss the question of co-operation with the British Naval Attaché. Hoare was particularly annoyed at Laval's reservation because the French Premier had in early September not only concurred in the British naval reinforcements but had expressed surprise that they had not been sent out earlier. 'Moreover, he seemed to be constantly intriguing behind the back of the League of Nations and ourselves with a view to some accommodation with Signor Mussolini.' Anger against Laval mounted in the course of the Cabinet discussion. It was brought out that his attitude, of which the Italians would be almost certain to learn, would lead to a breakdown of the whole scheme of sanctions.

It was suggested that it was necessary in these circumstances to let the French know that if the Covenant were to break down for this reason the

Locarno Treaty would also break down and there would be left no effective obligations. If it was arguable that our reinforcement of the Mediterranean Fleet was so provocative as to enable Italy to attack us without bringing paragraph 3 of Article XVI into operation, it might be argued that in the event of a German attack on France the French fortifications and other defensive preparations were equally provocative to a German attack.

With the First Lord taking the lead in urging that Laval be made to clarify his position, the Cabinet agreed (1) that the British Ambassador should 'insist on a categorical and explicit withdrawal' of his reservation to paragraph 3 of Article 16, and explain to Laval 'what were likely to be the consequences and reactions of adherence to his present attitude on the sanctity of international engagements', and (2) that until the French position was cleared up, 'it would be desirable not to press sanctions too actively at Geneva'.[56]

Pressured by the British, Laval gave them an assurance of military support on 18 October and agreed a few days later to conversations between the two naval staffs. At a meeting in London on 30 October between Chatfield and Rear-Admiral Decoux, representing the French Naval Staff, it quickly developed that, although the collaboration of the two navies was assured, and France would mobilize her forces simultaneously with Britain's, the French armed forces were so unready that they would be in no position to go to war for several weeks after the outbreak of an Anglo-Italian war. This did not much disturb the Admiralty. French mobilization in itself would contain Italian surface and air forces and thereby have 'the same effect as the proposed operations off the Western coast of Italy'. Moreover, Decoux had been able to assure Chatfield that French bases, 'either in France or North Africa', would be at the disposal of the Royal Navy in time of war for docking, repair, and, if need be, operational purposes. The Sub-Committee on Defence Policy and Requirements agreed with Chatfield's evaluation that this being the best that could be hoped for—simultaneous mobilization, French entry into the war when ready, and the use of French bases by the Royal Navy—they should not try, in his words, to get France 'to commit herself irrevocably as soon as we were attacked'.[57] Soon afterwards an agreement was reached in principle that the British Mediterranean Fleet would be responsible mainly for the eastern Mediterranean, the French Fleet mainly for the western Mediterranean, from Cape de Gata in the west to the Cape Bon—

[56] Cab. 46 (35), 15 Oct. 1935, CAB 23/82.
[57] DPR 45, 'French Naval Co-operation in the Mediterranean', 2 Nov. 1935, CAB 16/139.

Sicily line in the east, with the Gibraltar force free to co-operate with either fleet as required.[58] On 22 November the French Naval Staff indicated willingness to exchange information on naval bases in the Mediterranean. The Admiralty suggested a questionnaire that included information on the defences, fuel supplies, and fuelling arrangements at the French bases—Toulon, Bizerta, Philippeville, Bona, and Algiers. The information was forthcoming.

Yet the situation at the end of November was, from the British point of view, far from satisfactory. The French Ministry of Marine had agreed that military and air conversations would be required, yet conversations between the military and air staffs had not begun. Chatfield found it disturbing that in the naval conversations the French representatives had stressed the need to ensure complete secrecy as regards the talks, claiming that the repercussions in France, if they became known, would, in Chatfield's words, 'queer the pitch'. They were even concealing the existence of the talks from their own Foreign Office. Moreover, they did not wish to pursue the talks further for the time being, but were willing to resume them at the London Naval Conference that was to begin on 9 December, when secret talks could be carried on without the possibility of a leak. After accepting this plan, the First Sea Lord had discovered on 25 November that the French representative would not be their Deputy Chief of Naval Staff, as had been first proposed, but an officer who was not a member of the French Naval Staff. This looked to Chatfield 'as if after all the French again wished to burke the issue. . . . Generally, the conversations had brought quite clearly to light the acute anxiety of the French not to become involved in hostilities with Italy.' It was his belief that if the French entered an Italian war as Britain's ally, the only advantage the British would gain would be the use of French bases. He appreciated that 'the exchange of naval information did not, of course, carry with it any executive [that is, official approval to implement in the event of war agreements reached now], and while we knew what the French Naval Authorities could do in the event of hostilities it did not ensure that they would be permitted to carry out the co-operation they envisaged'. There appeared to be a consensus at this meeting that Britain could not rely on French co-operation in the event of Italian aggression against her. What emerged was agreement that the time had come to know precisely where they stood with the French and that if they received no satisfaction, they should adopt a go-slow policy on sanctions and,

[58] Telegram no. 1544/2, Director of Plans, Admiralty (Captain T. S. V. Phillips), to C-in-C, Mediterranean, 2 Nov. 1935, ADM 116/3038.

as Monsell put it, 'try and approach the whole problem from another angle—that of finding ways and means of improving the general international situation'.[59]

In the course of the next few days the British Ambassador saw Laval and received from him a 'categorical affirmative' in reply to the specific question whether they could count on French assistance if Italy attacked, and whether the French would in that eventuality regard themselves as in a state of war with Italy. Laval had gone a step further and repeated his assurances to the Italian Ambassador. This was reported at the Cabinet of 2 December. The 'efficacy of the French undertaking' would be checked by their readiness to continue the naval conversations and to extend them to military and air talks, though from the General Staff's point of view the military talks were not essential. At the same Cabinet, which accepted an oil sanction in principle, it was 'strongly urged, from the point of view of the Defence Services, that no decision to apply [oil] sanctions should be taken until effective co-operation by France had been secured, in accordance with previous Cabinet decisions'.[60]

At his notorious meeting with Laval on 7 December, and before they got down to working out the details of their Ethiopian scheme, Hoare asked the wily Frenchman 'categorically whether in the event of an attack we could depend upon French help. His answer, though it was in general terms satisfactory, avoided any undertaking to make military preparations, and obviously assumed that French co-operation would depend upon Anglo-French agreement as to our immediate policy.'[61] Laval did agree to open military and air staff conversations, but these, held on 9 and 10 December, were unproductive.[62] The military conversations made it clear that 'the French can, if they wish, carry out certain measures which will not only shew that they are prepared to come to our assistance if we are attacked by Italy, but that they themselves are committed to stand side by side with us on an equal footing'. The air conversations were equally barren, it being obvious that 'the French wished to limit the war to the Mediterranean and to avoid any action

---

[59] DPR (35) 14th meeting, 26 Nov. 1935, CAB 16/136.

[60] Cab. 50 (35), CAB 23/82.

[61] Templewood, *Nine Troubled Years*, p. 179.

[62] British reports on the conversations are in DPR 75, 'Report on Conversations between Representatives of the British and French General Staffs in Paris on 9th and 10th December, 1935', 18 Dec. 1935, and DPR 77, 'Report on Air Aspects of the Conversations in Paris, 9th and 10th December 1935', 10 Jan. 1936, CAB 16/140. These reports were later circulated to the Chiefs of Staff for their consideration as COS 423, CAB 53/26.

which would entail retaliatory measures against France itself. This was made more evident by the way in which they suggested that they might take action from Tunisia against Sicily, but were reluctant to take any action against Northern Italy unless France was first attacked.' Neither French Service was prepared to concert any concrete measures beforehand. This *non possumus* cast suspicion on the sincerity of Laval's assurances of French military support in the event of an Anglo-Italian war, besides compounding the difficulties of Allied co-operation in this contingency. Nor, with the exception of Turkey, were assurances forthcoming from the other Mediterranean powers of active military co-operation.

The situation as of mid-December was summarized in a telegram from the Chiefs of Staff to the three Commanders-in-Chief in the Mediterranean:

It appears that our own forces will have to sustain the war for a not-inconsiderable period. France and Greece, however, have promised full use of their ports, and Turkey is willing to co-operate with her limited air forces. The situation as regards the military co-operation of France is at the present time profoundly unsatisfactory. She has made no preparations for a war with Italy, and it is very unlikely that any precautionary measures will be taken before an emergency rises, as this involves mobilisation, which, under the existing political situation in France, is not feasible.[63]

The naval, military, and air conversations, which continued into January, only confirmed the hopelessness of expecting active military support from the French. The French Air Staff confessed that they wanted to assist but could not get their Government's permission to take the steps they wished to take. The French Naval Staff, Chatfield was informed by his opposite number, were anxious to co-operate fully, but the preparatory steps their Navy was taking were being kept from their own Minister of Marine! Chatfield, who with the other Chiefs had by now practically given up hope of active French support in a showdown with Italy, had second thoughts about the value of getting a firm commitment. 'If ultimately the threat of hostilities with Italy was likely to disappear, then it would clearly be best that we should have committed France to as little as possible. The more she was committed, the more likely would she be to use her co-operation as an argument for similar aid on our part in the event of French difficulties with Germany at some future date. The alternative was merely to express dissatisfaction with the steps France had taken to-date.'[64]

[63] COS (35) 159th meeting, 13 Dec. 1935, CAB 53/5.
[64] COS (36) 161st meeting, 13 Jan. 1936, CAB 53/5.

The last important contact with the French naval authorities occurred in mid-January, when two French senior officers met at the Admiralty with Chatfield, the Deputy Chief of the Naval Staff, and the Director of Plans.[65] These agreements were reached: (1) British naval assistance would cover the transport of two divisions from North Africa to France (Bordeaux), beginning some ten days after the outbreak of war; (2) liaison officers would be appointed to the staffs of the Commanders-in-Chief of the two countries, effective 'in emergency or on the outbreak of war'; (3) as regards operations in the western Mediterranean, the French might send a destroyer force to assist in anti-submarine work in the Straits of Gibraltar, and, once their transport operations were over, they would be ready to carry out offensive operations against the Italian coast or ports; (4) they might co-operate in the eastern Mediterranean by sending one or two submarine flotillas to attack Italian communications with Libya; (5) the Mediterranean would be divided into an area east of the line from Cape Bon in Tunisia to Maritime Island, some twenty miles west of Sicily, where the British would be responsible, and the western basin of the Mediterranean, which would come under the French Commander-in-Chief, except for the area westward of a line drawn 180 degrees from Cape de Gata, Spain, where the British Home Fleet would be responsible. This line hits the African coast almost exactly on the frontier between Morocco and Algeria.

This, for the duration of the crisis, was as far as conversations with the French got. Arrangements for co-operation in war were left in general terms, and even these were not worth much, since they were never officially approved by the French Government, and there was no certainty when, if at all, France would enter an Anglo-Italian war provoked by Italy. The negotiations with the other Mediterranean powers early in 1936 showed some progress. Greece, Turkey, and Yugoslavia accepted the British interpretation of Article 16—that in case of an unprovoked attack by Italy, they had an obligation to support Britain. 'Unqualified assurance that we should have the use of Greek harbours and repair facilities and the support of the Greek forces. The extent of military co-operation from Turkey and Yugo-Slavia must depend on conversations between General Staffs.' From Spain only vague assurances were received.[66]

On 7 March 1936 the Germans took advantage of the Ethiopian

---

[65] 'Record of Meeting held in C.N.S.'s Room on Wednesday, 15th January, to discuss questions of co-operation with the French in the event of hostilities', ADM 116/3398.   [66] 'History of the Emergency', pp. 22–3.

Crisis to denounce the Locarno Pacts and reoccupy the Rhineland. On 12 March Britain, France, Italy, and Belgium in turn denounced Germany's violation, which meant nothing to the Germans. For the Royal Navy the Rhineland Crisis was very nearly the last straw, since it highlighted the precarious position of the Navy in the event of a war with Germany while so much of its strength was disposed in the Mediterranean. There was insufficient naval force in Home waters effectively to protect British trade routes or to prevent German naval bombardment of British coasts. And there was the patent impossibility of simultaneously fighting in East Asia against Japan and in Home waters against Germany, unless Britain could count on a friendly, or at least a neutral, Italy.

The Chiefs of Staff reported on 12 March that

> any question of war with Germany while we are as at present heavily committed to the possibility of hostilities in the Mediterranean would be thoroughly dangerous. As regards naval operations against Germany, our minimum requirements could only be carried out by weakening naval forces in the Mediterranean to an extent which would jeopardise our position there *vis-à-vis* Italy. Even so, there would not be sufficient naval forces available to ensure that we could safeguard our coasts or trade against serious depredations of the German Fleet, small as it is.

The resources of the Army and Air Force had been stretched so thin by the Mediterranean crisis that they would not be able to dispatch a field force or provide 'any proper defence in the air'; anti-submarine defences were lacking at various important ports; anti-aircraft guns and searchlights were inadequate to deal with the German air threat. The conclusion was that 'if there is the smallest danger of being drawn into commitments which might lead to war with Germany, we ought at once to disengage ourselves from our present responsibilities in the Mediterranean, which have exhausted practically the whole of our meagre forces'.[67] The

[67] COS 442, 'The Condition of Our Forces to Meet the Possibility of War with Germany', 18 Mar. 1936, CAB 53/27. The conclusion of the Joint Planning Sub-Committee of the Chiefs of Staff was: 'If war with Germany were to break out while our forces are disposed as at present, we should be perilously exposed in the air and completely open to attack at sea. The French would be equally susceptible to naval attack. It would be impossible to send overseas any army formations. If mobilisation is ordered without withdrawal from the Mediterranean the situation on the naval side would be considerably improved, but the forces available would still not be sufficient to secure the British Isles and our trade routes (or those of the French). The increase in our air strength and improvement to our air striking power at Home which would result from mobilisation would do little to reduce the seriousness of the air defence situation. A small Field Force, but lacking in modern equipment, could be despatched overseas.' 'The Condition of our Forces to Meet the Possibility of War with Germany', amended and approved by the Chiefs of Staff at

nub of the matter for the Navy was the fact that the battle cruisers at Gibraltar, the *Hood* and *Renown*, were the only capital ships in European waters that could deal with 'Deutschland'-class 'pocket battleships', three 10,000-ton battleships with long endurance and heavy guns. But to withdraw them from the Mediterranean would jeopardize Britain's security there. The Service Chiefs deemed the country to be so 'defenceless' while a large proportion of their forces was locked up in the Mediterranean that they saw little point in staff conversations with the Locarno powers. 'Conversations were of little practical value as a means of assessing our effective contribution to the allied cause.' The upshot was the affirmation: 'If we are seriously to consider the possibility of war with Germany, it is essential that the Services be relieved of their Mediterranean responsibilities, otherwise our position is utterly unsafe.'[68] When Eden expressed his anxiety over the naval position in Home waters and asked if it would be possible to withdraw some ships from the Mediterranean, the Committee of Imperial Defence decided it would be undesirable 'at the present time, and in the existing political situation' to bring naval units home from the Mediterranean.[69]

The Rhineland Crisis focused attention on the German naval threat in Home waters and confirmed the Admiralty in their view that 'we must recover our relations with Italy, if such a thing is possible; that Italy must, for the stability of Europe, be persuaded to come back into military alliance with France. Should we not be taking steps now to implement this *recovery* policy?'[70] In passing, we should note that the Mediterranean situation helps to explain the British unwillingness to resort to military action in defence of the Locarno treaties.

During April and May the sanctionist front began to crack. Ecuador lifted sanctions, and others appeared eager to do likewise. The Italian entry into Addis Ababa on 5 May for all practical purposes ended the war. Yet the state of tension for the Services was not relaxed. In particular, the efficiency and well-being of the Mediterranean Fleet, on a war footing since August, was bound to suffer as the weather turned hot and the terrible strain on personnel

their 168th meeting, 17 Mar. 1936, enclosure to COS 442. The existing position was that the only forces readily available in Home waters were one 6-inch cruiser, 17 destroyers, and 9 submarines.

[68] COS memorandum, 'Staff Conversations with the Locarno Powers', 1 Apr. 1936, CID 1224-B, CAB 4/24.

[69] CID minutes, 3 Apr. 1936, CAB 2/6(1).

[70] DCNS memorandum for the Board, 'Easement of Mediterranean Situation', 22 Apr. 1936, ADM 116/3042.

continued indefinitely. Chatfield viewed the prospect of 'a further period at concert pitch' with deep concern. If the existing situation continued, it would be necessary gradually to call up 6,000 reservists.[71] It made little strategic sense to continue the Fleet in a highly keyed-up state throughout the summer at a time when the political necessity no longer existed and when the Fleet must be ready for use elsewhere. Actually, the Admiralty, without Cabinet approval, had started to bring ships home for repair and to give leave and relaxation, but not all the ships were so fortunate. Many men had had neither Christmas nor Easter leave.

The Admiralty put pressure on the Foreign Office late in April to agree to an easing of the naval situation through such measures as returning the bulk of the Mediterranean Fleet to Malta and the Home Fleet detachment at Gibraltar to England. The Cabinet, however, decided against any major redistribution of the Fleet, though they had no objection to some relaxation of the state of 'instant readiness' in the Mediterranean, nor to the 'unostentatious movements of ships' of the sort the Admiralty had been carrying out, 'providing that these were not on such a scale as to reflect on our foreign policy'.[72] The Admiralty almost immediately (1 May) took advantage of this policy to put into effect a relaxation of fleet routine on the Mediterranean, East Indies, and Home stations: the notice for 'steam of ships' (readiness to sail) was extended and ship leave was liberalized. Further pressure was applied through an Admiralty memorandum for the Cabinet over the First Lord's signature. It urged that the grave personnel situation be solved either by liquidating British commitments in the Mediterranean, thereby enabling the Fleet 'to return to its normal peace-time routine of recommissionings and training', or by recognizing that, though the country was not at war, the Fleet was being maintained on a war footing, and accordingly authorizing the Admiralty to call up sufficient reserve men to ease the manning situation. '. . . we cannot make bricks without straw, and nine months on a war footing without mobilisation is more than even the most willing administration can cope with without help.'[73] No further relaxation was possible, however (the Admiralty would have liked, for instance, to return the cruisers *Sydney* and *Achilles* to Australia and New Zealand, respectively), in the face of Eden's strong statement that

[71] COS (36) 174th meeting, 13 May 1936, CAB 53/6.
[72] Cab. 31 (36), 29 Apr. 1936, CAB 23/84.
[73] CP 134 (36), 'Position of the Fleet in the Eastern Mediterranean', 14 May 1936, CAB 24/262. The CP series (PRO) contains memoranda and other papers circulated to the Cabinet.

'the present time was still very inopportune for giving any impression to the world that we were weakening our position in the Mediterranean'.[74]

In the early days of June, when it became apparent that an Ethiopian government no longer existed, that sanctions were not serving any useful purpose, and that the sanctionist front was disintegrating anyway, a speech on the 10th by Neville Chamberlain, the Chancellor of the Exchequer, with its reference to the continuation or intensification of sanctions as 'the very midsummer of madness', was a turning point, the beginning of the end. In addition to political and strategic arguments, there were economic pressures on Britain to abandon the sanctions: unemployment was high, especially in South Wales, which was suffering from the embargo on coal exports to Italy. The Chiefs of Staff contributed to this dénouement with these conclusions:

(1) Our interests lie in a peaceful Mediterranean, and this can only be achieved by returning to a state of friendly relations with Italy. This should be our aim even in the earliest steps we take to liquidate the Mediterranean situation.

(2) One of the objects of raising sanctions is to enable us to withdraw our extra forces at present in the Mediterranean, and to return to a state of normal distribution which will permit us to be more ready to defend our interests at Home or in the Far East.[75]

On 19 June the Admiralty stated their general intentions to all Commanders-in-Chief as regards the movements and disposition of the Fleet, should a change in the international situation make it no longer necessary to maintain the existing state of readiness in the Mediterranean and Red Seas. On 4 July, with 44 votes for, 1 against (Ethiopia), and 4 abstentions, the League Assembly lifted the sanctions against Italy. On 8 and 10 July, after reaching agreement with the Foreign Office, Admiralty signals went out to implement the 19 June directive. The main body of the Mediterranean Fleet left Alexandria on 18 July (just as soon as their annual regatta was finished, not a day earlier!), the reinforcements from the China

---

[74] Cab. 37 (36), 18 May 1936, CAB 23/84. In his memoirs Eden wrote that it was not 'acceptable for Great Britain to reduce her strength in the eastern Mediterranean. Our position in Egypt, the Persian Gulf, the Mediterranean and Red Sea basins, and the Middle East, had been assured by British sea power. Events had now placed in doubt our ability and determination to maintain that predominance and I refused to agree to any weakening of our position.' The Earl of Avon, *The Eden Memoirs* (3 vols., London, 1960–5), ii, *Facing the Dictators*, p. 383.

[75] COS (36) 178th meeting, 16 June 1936, CAB 53/6. These conclusions were contained in a report of 18 June that was put before the Cabinet on 23 June. COS 477, 'Problems Facing His Majesty's Government in the Mediterranean as a Result of the Italo-League Dispute', CAB 53/28.

Station were sent back, and other measures were taken to end the state of war readiness.

* * *

And so the crisis had run its course, and the might-have-beens have been warmly debated ever since. Generally, it has been claimed that it would have been wiser had the British adopted a strong sanctionist position, lead where it would, since Italy was highly vulnerable to a blockade with teeth in it, and that, had the British made the right turn in 1935–6, the League and the system of collective security would have been strengthened. This would have discouraged Hitler from marching into the Rhineland. Writing in his diary in 1943 on receiving the news of Mussolini's resignation, Eden reflected: 'Looking back the thought comes again. Should we not have shown more determination in pressing through with sanctions in 1935 and if we had could we not have called Musso's bluff and at least postponed this war? The answer, I am sure, is yes.'[76] To the question 'Why was not more determination shown?' the reply usually given is that 'faint-heartedness' on the part of the Government and the Services was responsible.

Faintheartedness there was—there is no denying that the Service Chiefs badly wanted to postpone a war—but it was not of the pusillanimous sort. It was founded on compelling considerations of strategy and fleet efficiency. The Far Eastern strategic factor, the German problem, the personnel situation, and the failure to secure a definite guarantee of French naval co-operation—these factors complicated tremendously the British naval problem and argued strongly for a restoration of a friendly Italy and a secure Mediterranean. The attitude of the Services and more particularly of the Admiralty contributed powerfully to the Government's weak sanctionist policy and the decision to liquidate the whole venture. One cannot read the minutes of the Cabinet or of the Defence Policy and Requirements Sub-Committee without appreciating that military considerations, mainly naval factors, were very much in the minds of the decision-makers. They were just as anxious as the Service heads not to challenge Mussolini or incite him to anger.[77]

[76] *Facing the Dictators*, p. 311. Similarly, Liddell Hart: 'That wobbling course was bound to bring the maximum risk with the minimum insurance. Never again would there be so good a chance to check an aggressor so early, and the failure to do so in this case was the most fateful turning point in the period between the two world wars.' *Memoirs*, i. 290.

[77] As Baldwin's biographers point out: 'Up to 22 August, he was inclined to play a strong hand but was then much deterred by the military advisers, whose recommendations about the threat to Imperial Defence, both then and in the autumn [and

So far as the Navy was concerned, the principal lessons of the crisis were, in Chatfield's opinion: (1) Their 'foreign policy had not been in line with our defence policy of the last few years', and (2) 'Collective Security thus showed itself but a heavenly dream, as it was the British sailor's nightmare'.[78] The former point was made by Hoare, who 'continually complains on the limitations imposed by our known weaknesses'.[79] It was made by the Military Assistant Secretary of the CID in terms the Services would have wholeheartedly endorsed:

Ministers are grumbling, especially Hoare and Eden, that the Services have done so little since September to put themselves right. . . . deficiencies and financial starvation over 15 years *cannot* be put right in three months —they will not believe it though they have been told so over and over again. Goodness knows enough warnings have been given by the Chiefs of Staff—and now the 'Frocks' turn round and ask, 'Why aren't you ready —we told you in September.' To which the reply is, '*We* told *you* in 1925 and every year afterwards and you paid no attention.' A Royal Commission on why the Services are what they are, *why* they are unable to

beyond, I would add], he took as more important than any other consideration.' Middlemas and Barnes, *Baldwin*, pp. 898–9. An incident that occurred early in 1936 is revealing of the Foreign Office position. The DCNS afterwards recalled: 'The Foreign Office were very anxious not to provoke Mussolini. I had an odd experience in connection with this. Fisher had asked that the *Hood* should be sent to him as a reinforcement. Chatfield was not well and told me to go over and obtain the consent of the Foreign Office. During periods of diplomatic crises the Admiralty are not free to move ships from one area to another without F.O. consent. I found Eden in his room and told him that I wanted his concurrence to ordering *Hood* to join Fisher. He at once demurred and said that the situation was very inflammable and that Mussolini's reactions when he heard that *Hood* might join Fisher might cause a flare up. He then rang for Sir Lancelot Oliphant [Assistant Under-Secretary of State], who was, I suppose, dealing with the crisis, and asked his view. He seemed to me rather an *ass* when he said, "I believe that Mussolini is far more afraid of a battle cruiser than a battleship." Then he rang for Vansittart, the Permanent Secretary, and he supported me. So I came away with my mission fulfilled. The situation changed and so far as I can remember the *Hood* did not join Fisher. But I had an insight into the anxiety of the F.O. to avoid a showdown with Mussolini at all costs.' Admiral Sir William James's letter to the author, 7 Nov. 1963. See his earlier, briefer version: *The Sky Was Blue* (London, 1951), p. 184.

[78] Respectively, COS (36) 174th meeting, 13 May 1936, CAB 53/6, and Chatfield, *It Might Happen Again*, p. 90.

[79] Pownall's diary, 7 Oct. 1935, Bond, *Chief of Staff*, p. 84. A week after the Hoare–Laval Plan was hatched, the British Ambassador in Paris wrote to Hoare: 'It will probably be neither possible nor expedient to expose, in public debate in the House of Commons, all the factors which surrounded your recent conversations in Paris with the President of the Council, but I think that the archives of the Foreign Office should contain a record of the manner in which your discussions with M. Laval were conditioned throughout by our own naval, military and air position and by the situation in France.' Sir George Clerk to Hoare, 15 Dec. 1935, FO 371/19170. Miss Rosaria Quartararo kindly brought this document to my attention.

back a vigorous foreign policy, would have some terrible things to say. The warnings are there year after year and no effect till 1934. Even then they scaled down the D.R.C. Report on our 'worst deficiencies'.[80]

The second of Chatfield's two lessons was spelt out by the Joint Planning Sub-Committee of the Chiefs of Staff: 'The whole theory of collective security rests upon the assumption that each Member of the League . . . will be prepared in the last resort to take up arms to repel aggression against any other Member, irrespective of whether the particular aggression seems to be a matter of vital concern to himself. The fallacy of this assumption has been proved by the events of the past four years.' Moreover, 'the indefinite liabilities entailed in the League Covenant hold great dangers for us', and therefore their military liabilities ought to be limited to a clear recognition of the vital interests for whose protection they should be prepared to go to war, 'freed from the vague, wholesale and largely unpredictable military commitments which we at present incur under the League Covenant'.[81]

The practical consequences of these lessons for the Navy were the conviction that Britain must look after her own interests, be prepared to go it alone if need be, and, above all, speed up her naval rearmament.[82]

A Note on the Naval War Plan

A fact not generally known is that the first offensive action planned by the Rear-Admiral, Aircraft Carriers, the Hon. Sir Alexander Ramsay, if Britain found herself at war with Italy, was a Fleet Air Arm attack with bombs and torpedoes on the Italian naval base at Taranto. It did not seem to be heavily defended, and they knew that the bulk of the battle fleet was based there. The aircraft available were Fairey III Fs with bombs and Blackburn Ripons with torpedoes. The fighters available were too short-legged for the

[80] 4 Dec. 1935, ibid., pp. 91–2. The DRC was the Defence Requirements Committee of the Cabinet, which was superseded by the DPR.

[81] COS 491 (JP), 'Strategical Review by the Joint Planning Sub-Committee', 3 July 1936, CAB 53/28.

[82] Naval rearmament now went into high gear. A White Paper of 3 March 1936 announced that it would be 'necessary not only to proceed with new construction at a more rapid rate than in recent years, but also to make good existing deficiencies in ammunition and stores of all kinds'. When the London Naval Treaty of 1930 expired on 31 December 1936, capital-ship building would become possible: two new capital ships (battleships) would be laid down early in 1937. Cruiser strength would be increased from 54 to 70, beginning with 5 in the 1936–7 programme (increased to 7 in July). The Navy Estimates, introduced on 4 March 1936, were, at £69,930,000, nearly £10 million above those of 1935–6; they were raised to £80,230,000 by Supplementary Navy Estimates on 30 April. The Estimates made heavy provision for expediting ships under construction and for the Fleet Air Arm. Obviously, all that was set in motion in 1936–7 would need time—much time.

distances involved. The main problem was how to launch the attack at night and recover the aircraft in daylight, while keeping the ships at a respectable distance from the Italian air force during the latter operation. The solution was for the squadrons to fly to Janina airfield in north-west Greece to refuel after the attack, and then rejoin their ships, which in the meantime were to retire to a position off Zante, the southernmost of the Ionian Islands, the next morning. The use of Janina and the stocking of fuel and oil for this specific purpose were to be negotiated by the British Embassy in Athens with a sympathetic Greek Government. There was, of course, no war with Italy in 1935–6; but the germ of the idea remained in being and, modified to suit the conditions, evolved into the actual attack on Taranto harbour in World War II (November 1941).[83]

The establishment of Port X was to be the Mediterranean Fleet's chief preoccupation at the commencement of hostilities. (See above, p. 70n.) After it had got the MNBDO (above, p. 72) to Port X, about eight or nine days after the fleet left Egypt, it would proceed to carry out operations in southern Italian and Sicilian waters. Light forces under Cunningham's command would carry out inshore sweeps by night in Sicilian waters between Syracuse and Cape Spartivento, covering the bombardment by an 8-inch cruiser of the railway near Taormina, and possibly attacking ships in Port Augusta if there were enough of them. With battleships and destroyers furnishing protection for the carriers, the Fleet Air Arm would make dawn bombing attacks on Port Augusta and Catania air bases, if such retaliatory action were authorized as a reply to air or naval bombardment of Malta.[84] On conclusion of this 48-hour operation, which was designed 'generally to make ourselves obnoxious', Cunningham wrote, light forces would fuel from two oilers at Scutari on the Albanian coast and the fleet would make for Port X.

Concurrently with Fisher's operation, the Admiralty envisaged a sweep by the Gibraltar Force off Italy's west coast, making minor attacks on military objectives by air or sea bombardment, intercepting Italian warships, and 'to spread alarm in Italy and cause dispersion of effort'. The Gibraltar and Alexandria fleets might carry out a joint operation (mainly by cruisers and destroyers, with larger units and carriers at a distance) in the Malta Channel. A concerted sweep from east to west would catch the

[83] A highly reliable informant, an officer on Ramsay's staff, is my source for this 'first offensive action'. The Admiralty records make no mention of it, leading one to suspect that the plan did not get very far up the line and was scrapped.

[84] 'Even if we went to war it is considered much preferable to leave the initiative in starting such attacks to Italy.' Director of Plans (Captain Tom Phillips), minute of 2 Sept. 1935, ADM 116/3038. As a general principle, Italian shore objectives were not to be bombarded if the Italians did not bombard Malta, but rather would they attack enemy shipping and naval forces. The Chiefs of Staff defined the principle in these terms: '. . . we must avoid taking the initiative in any action calculated to expose the civilian population to losses from naval or air bombardment in order that Italy should not be provided with a case for stating that we had broken humanitarian practice and that consequently she was entitled to take similar action.' An exception was made for British air attack upon military objectives in Libya and Eritrea immediately on the outbreak of war. COS (35) 156th meeting, 3 Dec. 1935, CAB 53/5.

expected Italian naval concentration in the Channel and bring this force to battle or chase it into port. However, the most important duties of the Gibraltar Force were to prevent Italian warships or armed raiders passing out into the Atlantic, and to prevent submarine operations in the Straits of Gibraltar and its approaches. There would also be a vigorous anti-submarine offensive to drive the large Italian submarine forces out of the eastern Mediterranean and back to their bases, submarine raids on the coast of Sicily, an attempt to cut Italian communications to Libya, and an offensive by air, submarine, and light forces on the Libyan coast. 'The object would be to clear one flank, provide increased security for our shipping and our own forces and induce the Italian Fleet to come out to relieve the situation.'[85] The Admiralty and Fisher were in agreement on the 'main principle', which was 'to make the fleet felt at widely separated places at the very beginning while keeping important heavy ships outside areas of air concentration until danger from these can be estimated'.[86]

A Fisher paper of 30 November convinced the Admiralty that the advantages of establishing a base at Port X in the earlier stages of a war did not justify the risk of trying to establish it in the face of the Italian air threat, whose strength could not be estimated. He proposed that Alexandria be considered the main fleet base in the event of war. The Chiefs of Staff accepted this recommendation (13 December) and earmarked the AA guns and searchlights of the MNBDO for defence of the base at Alexandria. Chatfield was unhappy over one important facet of the new situation—that Fisher might try to retain continuous control over the central Mediterranean from Alexandria, and this, he felt, would be impossible for any length of time. A blockade could not be achieved by patrol, and detached forces were liable to be attacked by the full force of the enemy at their discretion, if the Italian Navy 'has any enterprise, which I dare say it has not'. He believed that Fisher's best strategy would be to employ his full strength at one time in Italian waters, withdraw it for reconditioning, then return to the central Mediterranean. 'This would not achieve a perfect blockade, but would be effective and complete during the periods when the Fleet was at sea.' He anticipated that it would become necessary—the timing to be decided by the C-in-C—to establish the fleet at Port X in order 'to advance closer to Italy in order to force things to a conclusion'. This time might arrive when the French were prepared for full military co-operation and were to put pressure on Italy by air attacks on northern Italy.[87]

With the temporary abandonment of the establishment of a base at Port X, the war plan underwent various alterations in December which did not change it fundamentally.[88] The revised plan called for the whole fleet to leave Alexandria on, or as soon as possible after, the outbreak of war, and to take control of the area to the westward of Crete, as far as the Malta Channel. The objective was to cut off supplies to Italy and, in order

[85] 'History of the Emergency', p. 11.

[86] C-in-C, Mediterranean, to Admiralty, 19 Oct. 1935, ADM 116/3038.

[87] COS (35) 159th meeting, 13 Dec. 1935, CAB 53/5, Chatfield to Fisher, 19 Dec. 1935, Chatfield MSS.

[88] 'History of the Emergency', pp. 18–21.

to reduce the menace to Egypt, to her army in Libya. *En route* to the central Mediterranean the 3rd Cruiser Squadron and 1st Battle Squadron would, in synchronization with an air attack, bombard Tobruk, while the 1st Cruiser Squadron and aircraft carrier proceeded to the central area, to be joined there by the 3rd Cruiser Squadron. The 1st Battle Squadron would return to Alexandria under escort of the Local Defence Flotilla. The main body of the fleet, joined by the two destroyer flotillas at Malta, would carry out offensive operations against the Italian and Sicilian coasts for 8 hours, occupy the area for 6 days more, then withdraw to Alexandria for rest and refuelling. One battleship and several destroyers, stationed in the Suez Canal, would deny its use to Italian ships and thereby cut the Italian communications to Ethiopia.

As regards protection of trade, the difficulties of instituting a convoy system in the Mediterranean were such that the diversion of through shipping round the Cape appeared to be the only practical solution. As for the protection of British shipping outside the Mediterranean and Red Sea, the Admiralty did not think the Italians could pass a raider through the Straits of Gibraltar or the Red Sea. Even if they sent raiders (probably disguised) into the Atlantic or Red Sea in advance of a war declaration, or supplied guns to some of their merchant ships, to be mounted when they were beyond the Mediterranean and after war had been declared—even then, the difficulties of refuelling the raiders were such as to bring their careers to an end before long, provided they did not make captures of fuel. It was not expected that the Italians would send submarines into the Atlantic. 'To achieve important results submarines will have to adopt unrestricted warfare and it is not sure that Italy would do this.' If they did, to achieve success they would have to operate about 2,000 miles from Italy to be in an area where they might meet a large number of ships. But they only had eight large ocean-going boats (9,500-mile radius)—too few to maintain a large-scale attack at such a distance. Also Italian submarines could be employed more effectively in attacking the lines of communication of the Mediterranean Fleet. There is no mention in the war plan of convoy for merchant shipping. An effective anti-submarine organization in the Gibraltar Straits, together with routing of ships away from the Portuguese coast (submarines might be sent out to intercept ships off this and the Spanish south-west coast), would be adequate anti-submarine protection for shipping in the Atlantic and Indian Oceans.[89]

The main lines of supply for the fleet in the Eastern Mediterranean and for the Army and Air Force in Egypt would be from the Black Sea or through the Red Sea, with the C-in-Cs Mediterranean and East Indies, respectively, responsible for their protection. As regards the possibility of passing military convoys through the Mediterranean, Chatfield saw no difficulties with the smaller and faster convoys, but he was sceptical about the practicability of escorting large convoys, whose speed was slow, and it would be impossible to pass them through the whole length of the Pantelleria Straits bottleneck in dark hours. With sufficient notice, however, he thought the Navy could clear areas of enemy ships and open the way for convoys.[90]

[89] Admiralty memorandum, 'Protection of Trade', 28 Sept. 1935, ADM 116/3049.
[90] COS (35) 150th meeting, 13 Sept. 1935, CAB 53/5.

Chapter Four

'Winston is Back'

Churchill at the Admiralty, 1939–40[1]

(Chart 3)

T HE famous 'Winston is back' signal from the Board of Admiralty
to the Fleet on 3 September, the day Britain entered the Second
World War, heralded Churchill's return to the Admiralty as
First Lord. On that Sunday evening he 'came again to the room
I had quitted in pain and sorrow almost exactly a quarter of a
century before, when Lord Fisher's resignation had led to my removal from my post as First Lord and ruined irretrievably, as it
proved, the important conception of forcing the Dardanelles'.[2] The
first Board meeting (an informal one) was held that evening—an

[1] I cannot overstress that this chapter is, except for the few instances where
I expressly state otherwise, concerned only with Churchill as First Lord of the
Admiralty, that is, between 3 September 1939 and 10 May 1940. After going to
No. 10 as Prime Minister and Minister of Defence, he was able to do, and did, things
quite differently. Thus, in the later period he interfered, or tried to interfere, with
naval operations much more than when he was at the Admiralty. This chapter is
based on the Admiralty records at the Public Record Office—the ADM 1, 116,
199, and 205 classifications, but especially ADM 199/1928–9 and ADM 205/1–6
(respectively, the 'Personal War Records, 1939–1945', of the First Lord and the
First Sea Lord)—and the Cabinet Office records at the P.R.O.: War Cabinet minutes
(WM series, CAB 65/1–7: 'Conclusions', and CAB 65/11–13 'Confidential Annexes'
to the Conclusions) and papers (WP series, CAB 66/1–7), Ministerial Committee on
Military Co-ordination minutes and papers (MC series, CAB 83/1–5), and Chiefs of
Staff (COS) Committee minutes (CAB 79/1–4, 85) and papers (CAB 80/1–10, 104–5).
I am deeply indebted to the following gentlemen, who provided information or side-
lights of value: Admirals of the Fleet Lord Mountbatten of Burma and the late Sir
George Creasy, Admirals Sir Harold Burrough, Sir Charles Daniel, the late J. H.
Godfrey, Sir Guy Grantham, the late Sir William James, and Sir Henry Moore, Vice-
Admirals Sir Geoffrey Barnard, Sir Ronald Brockman, Sir Peter Cazalet, the late Sir
Gordon Hubback, R. D. Oliver, R. M. Servaes, and J. Ashley Waller, Rear-Admirals
R. M. Dick and A. D. Nicholl, Captains G. R. G. Allen, G. O. C. Davies, J. S. S. Litch-
field, the late G. H. Oswald, and Sir Richard Pim, Marshal of the Royal Air Force Sir
John Slessor, Lieutenant-General Sir Ian Jacob, Major-General J. L. Moulton, Sir
Clifford Jarrett, and the late Sir Eric Seal.
[2] Churchill, *The Second World War* (6 vols., London, 1948–54), i, *The Gathering
Storm*, pp. 320–1. Note that the paginations in the English and American editions
are completely different.

unforgettable experience, the Third Sea Lord and Controller after-wards wrote. 'As he once again took the First Lord's chair in the famous Board Room, Churchill was filled with emotion. To a few words of welcome from the First Sea Lord he replied by saying what a privilege and honour it was to be again in that chair, that there were many difficulties ahead but together we would over-come them. He surveyed critically each one of us in turn and then, adding that he would see us all personally later on, he adjourned the meeting, "Gentlemen," he said, "to your tasks and duties".'[3] He himself lost little time in getting to work. '. . . from the morning of the fourth I laid my hands upon the naval affairs.'

His energy and stamina were prodigious.[4] A stream of memo-randa, virtually ultimata, issued from the private office covering every aspect of the war at sea and leaving the recipient in no doubt as to what the First Lord wanted. Known irreverently as 'the First Lord's prayers', they frequently opened with 'Pray inform me . . .' or 'Pray why has . . . not been done?', with an answer usually de-manded by a certain time. Churchill stimulated, inspired, indeed electrified the whole machinery of the Admiralty, partly because no one was safe from his probing inquiries and might at any moment be called to account. The then Deputy Director of the Trade Division writes:

One thing that remains firmly in my mind about Winston's arrival in the Admiralty was the immediate impact which his personality made on the staff at all levels, both service and civilian. From the very first day even I in my subordinate situation became aware of this presence and I amongst others began to receive little notes signed W.S.C. from the private office demanding weekly reports of progress direct to him. If the required report

[3] Admiral of the Fleet Lord Fraser of North Cape, 'Churchill and the Navy', in Sir James Marchant (ed.), *Winston Spencer Churchill: Servant of Crown and Common-wealth* (London, 1954), pp. 78–9.

[4] It is well known that the secret lay in his habit of undressing and taking an afternoon nap in bed of at least an hour, exploiting 'to the full my happy gift of falling almost immediately into deep sleep. By this means I was able to press a day and a half's work into one.' He regularly worked through the night until two or three in the morning and was ready for more between eight and nine. 'If he finished by two a.m. he was more wide awake than ever. We vainly suggested it was time for bed. He usually had other ideas. "What about a visit to the war room?" He loved looking at the flags denoting the position of our warships on the oceans of the world. "Where is the oil?" he asked his yawning secretary one night. "What oil, sir?" "Wake up," said Churchill, "I want the oil (Earl) of Cork and Orrery." It was nearly three a.m. by the clock.' Sir Geoffrey Shakespeare (Parliamentary and Financial Secretary to the Admiralty in Churchill's time there), *Let Candles Be Brought In* (London, 1949), pp. 228–9. 'Where is the oil?' reminds me of an occasion when Churchill was Prime Minister. It was the middle of the night and he wanted Seal, his Principal Private Secretary, who had gone to sleep in the shelter at Downing Street. 'Fetch the seal from his ice floe!' was his command.

was a good one (and it would not necessarily be one's fault if it were not) one might get a reply in red ink—'v.g. press on.' It was like the stone thrown into the pond, the ripples got out in all directions, galvanising people at all levels to 'press on'—and they did.[5]

The same stimulation was at once felt in the Fleet. Conveniently forgotten were recollections of Churchill's frequent interference in professional concerns and disregard of naval opinion when First Lord in 1911–15, and his role in scaling down the Navy's cruiser-building programme when Chancellor of the Exchequer in 1924–9. Remembered were his experience of the Admiralty, his love of the sea and the Navy, his deep knowledge of the role of sea power in British history, and his reputation for getting things done. Also in his favour was the complete contrast with his immediate predecessor, Lord Stanhope, a splendid gentleman, but slow-moving and lacking any real knowledge of the sea and ships, or of strategic matters. From the beginning the new First Lord went everywhere, visiting training establishments, naval bases, dockyards, experimental stations, and the Fleet itself. His impact on the officers and men of the battle cruiser *Hood* is typical. 'We received a visit from Winston, who made the sailors an excellent speech. We were much impressed, and feel we have got the right man in the right place.'[6]

And how Churchill loved his job! There is, for example, an incident of February 1940, reported by an officer on the Joint Planning Staff. He is writing of the return to London from a meeting of the Supreme War Council in Paris.

Chamberlain led our party, with Churchill in company. On the way home we crossed the Channel in a destroyer. When we embarked at Boulogne, Churchill ordered the Admiralty Flag to be hoisted and clearly regarded himself as Chamberlain's host afloat. Mr. Chamberlain looked decidedly put out, no doubt regarding himself as No. 1 ashore *or* afloat. They both put on tin hats: somehow Mr. Chamberlain looked most incongruous in a steel helmet and a naval duffle coat, whereas Churchill, of course smoking a cigar and grinning, looked everything that any cartoonist had ever made him out to appear. During the crossing a floating mine was sighted.

---

[5] Captain G. R. G. Allen's memorandum for the author, n.d. (1966).

[6] Vice-Admiral W. J. Whitworth (commanding the Battle Cruiser Squadron, Home Fleet) to Admiral Sir Andrew Cunningham (C-in-C, Mediterranean Fleet), 5 Oct. 1939, Cunningham MSS., British Museum Add. MSS. 52568. Admiral Sir William James, then C-in-C, Portsmouth, wrote after Churchill's visit there on 13 January 1940: 'The Dockyard men love him, and turned out in thousands to cheer.' 'Wherever he was, frowns gave way to smiles.' When they returned to Admiralty House, Lady James asked Churchill if he would have tea, and he replied, 'My doctor has ordered me to take nothing non-alcoholic between breakfast and dinner'! James, *The Portsmouth Letters* (London, 1946), p. 30, *The Sky Was Always Blue* (London, 1951), p. 207.

Instantly Winston personally ordered it to be destroyed, and it was duly potted by a rifle and exploded with a huge bang. Winston was overjoyed, and no doubt felt he was really in the war.[7]

It would be foolish to deny that he enjoyed the war—in the sense that he liked doing what he knew he was superbly equipped by temperament ('he was a warrior at the bottom of his being'), knowledge, and experience to do. 'He loved, too,' Shakespeare points out, 'the excitements and the tense situations which war always brings in its train. "What a dull war this will be," he said to me once with a spark of prophetic intuition. "We have only Germany to fight. Now if we fought Germany, Italy and Japan together, that would be much more interesting." It certainly was.'[8]

Before proceeding, a few words on Churchill's rights and responsibilities as First Lord are essential. The members of the Board of Admiralty, professional and civilian, had collective responsibility for all matters concerning the Navy. In the spring of 1940, they were the First Lord, the five Sea Lords, the VCNS, the Controller of Merchant Shipbuilding and Repairs, the three ACNS, the Civil Lord, the Parliamentary and Financial Secretary, and the Permanent Secretary. They were appointed by Letters Patent as 'Commissioners for executing the office of Lord High Admiral'. But Churchill as First Lord was the Supremo of the Board. He did not have to accept Board decisions or recommendations: under the doctrine of the First Lord's final and individual responsibility (laid down by Goschen when he was First Lord in 1871) the final say was his, and his alone. He was the one man responsible to Parliament for all the actions of the Board. The Board met to discuss and perhaps approve major matters of policy, for example, the warship-building programme, characteristics of new ships, and the entry and training of naval personnel. Operational matters, however, were not referred to the Board. They were the province of the Naval Staff, consisting of the First Sea Lord, who was Chief of the Naval Staff, the VCNS, and the three ACNS, aided by the Directors of the Plans, Operations, Intelligence, Trade, and other divisions and their staffs. A wise First Lord chose and relied upon his professional advisers in the shape of the Naval Staff, but this did not absolve him from the ultimate responsibility for all the actions of the Naval Staff. I am sure that Churchill knew all this probably better than any other First Lord of this century; after all, he had 1915 as a permanent reminder.

It is the opinion of some officers who were fairly close to the naval high command that Churchill, even before he became Prime Minis-

[7] Captain J. S. S. Litchfield's memorandum for the author, 26 Feb. 1970.
[8] Shakespeare, *Let Candles Be Brought In*, pp. 230–1.

ter and Minister of Defence, dominated the professional heads of the Navy. One would have expected this sort of relationship, remembering Churchill's extreme view of his prerogatives as the minister responsible. The fact is that, notwithstanding his great influence as First Lord (for better or worse), he did *not* dominate his professional advisers. To be sure, on relatively unimportant matters he often overrode the experts. First Lords, almost invariably civilians, were not supposed to concern themselves in purely professional concerns. But Churchill, feeling himself expert in naval matters because of his long service as First Lord before and in the First War, and his sustained effort between wars to remain *au fait*, regularly put his oar into seas which were *maria incognita* to all his civilian predecessors. Note, for instance, the minute below on naval cadets and the story of the introduction of the U.P.s. But in matters pertaining to strategy and operations, he rarely failed to abide by expert advice, however much he may on occasion have been critical of it. On all matters he would listen to the opinions of others, even those of junior officers, and if approached sensibly and with sound arguments, was always open to conviction. There was nothing rigid about his mind. It could, however, be an exhausting process for the opposers, who often got intensely irritated by Churchill's extraordinary powers of argument. 'To get his own way [writes the first wartime DNI] he used every device and brought the *whole* battery of his ingenious, tireless and highly political mind to bear on the point at issue. His battery of weapons included persuasion, real or simulated anger, mockery, vituperation, tantrums, ridicule, derision, abuse and tears, which he would aim at anyone who opposed him or expressed a view contrary to the one he had already formed, sometimes on quite trivial questions.'[9]

Churchill's relations with Sir Dudley Pound, the First Sea Lord throughout the war until his death in October 1943, were crucial to a successful administration of the Navy. The omens at first were not favourable. On Good Friday, 1939, when Mussolini grabbed Albania, the Mediterranean Fleet, Pound, C-in-C, was dispersed in the various ports around the Mediterranean. Churchill in the House of Commons was very critical of this failure in concentration. He was not satisfied with the explanation that a failure in Whitehall intelligence, and not lack of forethought by the C-in-C, was to blame. With this background, relations between the two men were cool at the beginning. 'We eyed each other amicably if doubtfully', Churchill wrote of their first meeting (3 September). The

[9] Admiral J. H. Godfrey, 'Mr. Churchill', a paper of 1964; copy in the author's possession.

considerable temperamental differences promised slight improvement in their relations. Pound was reserved, seldom showed any
emotion as regards anyone or anything, and was without much
sense of humour. Yet in a short time Churchill formed a close attachment to, and trust in, Pound. He was impressed with the Admiral's
energy, keen intellect and analytical mind, and mastery of his profession. He respected this non-political sailor of unimpeachable
character who was able to state his case to ministers in a dry and
factual manner and without ever losing his temper, and to stand
up firmly when necessary to the prodding of the arch-prodder.
Pound feared neither God, man, nor Winston Churchill. Churchill
had no great opinion of the planners ('the machinery of negation',
he once called them), but he was ready and willing to accept Pound's
judgement, which he trusted. On his part, Pound recognized that
Churchill's qualities of leadership were so exceptional as to justify
extraordinary effort to co-operate with him and to support him. He
accordingly quickly developed an intense loyalty towards Churchill.
He was never heard to criticize him or to complain about him. 'I have
the greatest admiration for W.C., and his good qualities are such
and his desire to hit the enemy so overwhelming, that I feel one
must hesitate in turning down any of his proposals.'[10]

Pound was masterly at handling Churchill. He had the common
sense to know that a head-on collision merely increased Churchill's
obstinacy. He would never defy him or flatly contradict him in
front of others. 'There could have been friction between 1st Lord
(and later as P.M.) and a different 1st S.L., but Pound's temperament, calm and deaf as required—never getting into heated argument—made for peace',[11] as did his willingness to permit Churchill
to nag and bully him over small things. Pound decided early that
he would fight Churchill only on the really vital matters. The First
Sea Lord was a master-hand at patiently weaning or diverting
Churchill from his wilder, or shall we say more imaginative, projects, usually perfectly desirable tactically or strategically, but completely impracticable from entire lack of resources. This was, in the
judgement of a postwar First Sea Lord, Sir Charles Lambe, Pound's
'greatest accomplishment'. The *modus operandi* was never to show
any obstructive response, but to indicate that the proposition would
be fully investigated. This was done, by a groaning staff, who

[10] Pound to Admiral Sir Charles Forbes (C-in-C, Home Fleet), 20 Jan. 1940,
Cunningham MSS., Add. MSS. 52565. To his last days Pound carried his great
respect for Churchill to the point of addressing him as 'Sir', instead of the traditional
'First Lord' (or 'Prime Minister').

[11] Captain Sir Richard Pim's letter to the author, 21 Mar. 1970. Pim was in charge
of Churchill's map room in Admiralty House.

already had more on their plate than could be done efficiently. They produced an 'appreciation' and a statement of 'forces required' which argued against the project. This method, instead of provoking obstinacy, usually allowed the project to die quietly. There are far more instances of this after Churchill went to No. 10. 'Operation Catherine' (below) is the best example for the earlier period. In passing, one may speculate that Pound, when Additional Naval Assistant to Fisher for nearly two months (late March to mid-May) in 1915, would have seen how to handle, and how *not* to handle, Churchill.

We have here a most interesting, even an odd, situation—of two men with a very high regard and affection for each other and who established a good working relationship, though they were so different: a busy, plodding First Sea Lord, with all the worries and problems associated with a Fleet stretched to the full, and a First Lord, imaginative, enthusiastic for his ideas, and 'always with a wide canvas before his eyes, even if the scale of sea-miles was not evident'. Churchill was visibly very sad after Pound's death. There were only four men, he said (winter of 1942–3), whose minds were attuned to his: Smuts, Beaverbrook, Bracken—and Pound.[12] When Pound was gone and Churchill was dealing with Cunningham, he would sometimes say, 'I wish Pound were here.'[13]

Churchill's relations with the sailors afloat were, generally speaking, excellent, even if he sometimes thought the admirals were too stereotyped, too plodding, and at times lacking in fire. This feeling, and the attendant friction, became more pronounced after he became Prime Minister and stepped up his production of interesting ideas. We know that Sir Andrew Cunningham, C-in-C, Mediterranean, had a poor view of Churchill's constant interference with detailed operational matters, telling him (and other Cs-in-C abroad) not only what to do, *but how to do it*, without any regard to the local resources available and what other commitments the Fleet had. But this refers to the war in the inland sea *after Churchill became Prime Minister*, especially in 1940–1. (Even then Churchill never gave an order direct to any C-in-C: all signals came through the First Sea Lord, but many a signal bore an unmistakable Churchillian imprint in its phraseology.) I can find no earlier instances of Churchill's interference in the Mediterranean, if only because the Mediterranean Fleet had little to do prior to Italy's entry into the war (10 June 1940) 'but', in Cunningham's words, 'to watch the Italians to see

[12] Interview with Captain Sir Richard Pim, 10 Jan. 1968, McLachlan MSS.
[13] Interview with J. R. Colville (Private Secretary to Churchill when Prime Minister, 1940–1, 1943–5), 20 May 1968, McLachlan MSS.

that they really mean to remain neutral'. Indeed, the fleet had 'melted away' in the autumn of 1939, as many of its ships were needed for duty elsewhere. The build-up of the fleet did not commence seriously until April and May 1940, when there was fear that Mussolini might be tempted by Britain's Norwegian difficulties into entering the war. Churchill's relations with the C-in-C, Home Fleet, are a moot point, we shall see.

*   *   *

There were few matters pertaining to the naval war that did not enlist Churchill's keen interest and intimate involvement. They included all manner of personnel questions. Take the problem of the employment of Indians or colonial natives in the Navy, whether those resident in the United Kingdom or those who might volunteer abroad. Churchill's position tells us something about his comparatively broadminded views on race. At the start of the war it was, the Second Sea Lord, Admiral Sir Charles Little, explained, the Admiralty's 'intention under the Military Training Bill to reject any coloured man who gave a preference for the Navy on account of the well known difficulties we have in associating coloured men with British ratings on the Lower Decks of His Majesty's ships. In the case of the National Service Act, we had proposed to follow the same course, but in view of the attitude now being adopted by the War Office and Air Ministry, you may consider it politically expedient that we should follow the same line as them and accept a certain number of these non-Europeans (coloured men) in the Navy.' However, the Admiral continued, it was not intended to grant the coloured men commissions as temporary officers until the lists of RNVSR (Royal Naval Volunteer Supplementary Reserve) and university candidates, etc., had been exhausted. 'Should the war continue long enough, however, it was the intention to commission recommended "Hostilities Only" ratings, but it is clear that it is most unlikely that Commanding Officers will recommend for commissions any of the coloured ratings. It would be, therefore, hardly fair to hold out any prospect to non-Europeans (coloured men) of obtaining commissions in the Royal Navy except in most exceptional cases and only then if the war goes on long enough.' The First Lord found this policy objectionable—up to a point. 'There must be no discrimination on grounds of race or colour. In practice much inconvenience would arise if this theoretical equality had many examples. Each case must be judged on its merits, from the point of view of smooth administration. I cannot see any objection to Indians serving in H.M. Ships where they are qualified and needed, or if their virtues so deserve rising to be Admirals of the Fleet. But not too many of them, please.'[14]

Churchill's democratic instincts and deep concern for the welfare of the personnel, which had been well ahead of Service opinion when he was first at the Admiralty, are revealed in a number of minutes which he reproduces in *The Gathering Storm*.[15] In one case he ordered that cadetships be granted to three candidates who had been rejected, though rated fifth, eighth, and seventeenth of the ninety who had been successful in the educational examination. To the Second Sea Lord he declared (7 April 1940), in words that would have warmed the cockles of 'Jacky' Fisher's heart, 'It is quite true that A has a slightly cockney accent, and that the other two are the sons of a chief petty officer and an engineer in the merchant service. But the whole intention of competitive examination is to open the career to ability, irrespective of class or fortune.'[16] On another occasion (7 October 1939) he asked for 'the reasons which debar individuals in certain branches from rising by merit to commissioned ranks. . . . If a telegraphist may rise, why not a painter? Apparently there is no difficulty about painters rising in Germany!' He wished small-ship crews to be 'comforted' 'to the utmost extent that operations will permit'. And so he urged (12 December 1939) that 'every effort should be made to ease the strain upon the destroyer crews' who took their 'brief spell of rest' at Scapa Flow and Rosyth, whose amenities were well below those of the naval ports. Already, on his initiative (21 September), a ship had been fitted with theatre and cinema facilities as 'a most important adjunct of naval life at Scapa'.

Another illustration of Churchill's wide-ranging interests relates to food production. The Parliamentary Secretary found an 'Action This Day' memorandum on his desk one morning in October 1939: 'I am concerned about the shortage of fish. Parliamentary

[14] The Second Sea Lord's minute of 11 Oct. 1939 and Churchill's of 14 Oct. 1939, ADM 1/10818. Churchill, *The Gathering Storm*, p. 607, prints only the latter. Churchill won the consent and co-operation of the War Office, Air Ministry, India Office, and Colonial Office. On 15 March 1940 the Director of Naval Recruiting notified all recruiting staff officers that coloured men, resident in Britain or in the colonies, were now eligible for entry into the Royal Navy 'for hostilities only'. This applied both to volunteers and those called up under the National Service Act.

[15] See pp. 582, 592, 605–10.

[16] Admiral Gretton has traced the subsequent careers of the three officers. As of 1967, 'two are still serving, and after useful, honourable careers have reached the rank of Commander. The third resigned his commission in 1948, after service in which he always received reports of above average merit . . .' Gretton, *Former Naval Person: Winston Churchill and the Royal Navy* (London, 1968), p. 260. In an earlier instance the First Lord had warned (8 February 1940): 'One has to be particularly careful that class prejudice does not enter into these decisions . . .'

Secretary will immediately take up the matter with the A.C.N.S. and the head of the Mine Sweeping Division to see if any trawlers can be released for fishing. We must have a policy of "utmost fish". Parliamentary Secretary will report to me by midnight with his proposals.' Shakespeare went into action at once and before the day was out had initiated a programme of 'utmost fish' which was acceptable to the First Lord.[17]

Admiral Godfrey has observed: 'Anything unusual or odd or dramatic intrigued him: Q ships, dummy ships, the stillborn operation "Catherine", deception, sabotage, and, no doubt influenced by Professor Lindemann [see below], the application of novel scientific methods.'[18] We shall be concerned with the more offensive of these outlets for Churchill's demonic energy and extraordinary imagination. Here I would mention certain of his devices that were essentially defensive in character. His recollection of the use of dummy ships early in the 1914 war (about a dozen to mislead enemy reconnaissance as to the whereabouts and strength of the Fleet) led to his resurrection of the idea. On his third day in office he put his proposal before the First Sea Lord. 'The experiment cost a good deal of money, and was not really tried out. Now the argument for it is vastly increased. Air reconnaissance can sweep over every harbour, and obtain a photograph of the deck plan, though not of the silhouette, of almost every vessel. In a few hours they can know what we have at Scapa, or the Thames, or Portsmouth. It therefore becomes all the more important to introduce this element of mystery which, if rightly used, might draw long, exhausting and futile attacks upon futile targets, while the real ships are doing their work elsewhere.' His concrete proposal was that they reproduce the deck plans, sufficiently to deceive air reconnaissance, of the battle cruisers *Hood* and *Renown*, the battleship *Nelson*, two 'Queen Elizabeth' battleships, and a 'Royal Sovereign' battleship, as well as two 8-inch cruisers. These vessels would not go to sea, so that all that was needed were 'some large barges fastened together in a light steel framework which will support a mock-up to aerial observation of the aforementioned vessels'. Pound accepted the proposal with one change, in which Churchill concurred—that, since air photographs would show the dummies to be dummies, 'the man o'war superstructure should be built on merchant ships. This would have the great advantage that the dummies could move from place to place under their own steam.'[19] Three were agreed to.

[17] Shakespeare, *Let Candles Be Brought In*, pp. 231–2.
[18] Godfrey, *Naval Memoirs*, vi, Pt. I, p. 35.
[19] Churchill and Pound minutes of 5 Sept. 1939, ADM 205/2.

For Churchill this was but a start. 'I also feel tonight [21 October] very much the need for more images—the three are not enough and another five or six should be started at once.' But two 'battleships' and one 'aircraft carrier' was the sum total; they were employed at Scapa and in the Firth of Forth. They served no useful purpose except on one occasion shortly before they were dissolved. In May 1941 the *Bismarck* was encouraged to push on into the north Atlantic among other factors by reconnaissance reports that three heavy units were still in Scapa Flow, when two were actually dummies.

Less fortunate was the dénouement of another Churchillian foray into professional realms. It also illustrates how he could override a technical department. This is the story of the anti-aircraft device that came to be called the 'Naval Wire Barrage' (NWB). It was a multiple launcher—in appearance, like a large umbrella-stand—into which were crammed fourteen 3-inch rockets (known as U.P.s, standing for unrotating projectiles). Each rocket projected a 7-inch container carrying 2,000 feet of wire with a small parachute at one end and a 2-lb. bomb at the other. The rockets ejected their loads at a predetermined height (about 4,000 feet), allowing the bombs to fall to their full scope and then drift downwards fairly rapidly, the small parachute acting as a drogue, so that if an aircraft struck the wire, the bomb might be drawn upwards into its wing and explode on contact. It was Professor Frederick Lindemann's statistical branch at the Admiralty (part of the First Lord's personal staff) that took up the device early in the war. The 'Prof', a brilliant Oxford physicist and mathematician, and close friend and scientific adviser to Churchill since the thirties, had the bee in his bonnet that AA guns were not a sufficient deterrent to low-flying enemy aircraft passing overhead and that the answer lay in rocket devices. 'In theory', says Rear-Admiral A. D. Nicholl, 'he may have been right, but his practical solution in the form of the NWB was considered by everyone, except Winston, as plumb crazy.'[20] The DNO's department opposed the scheme on the grounds of its impracticability, due to the impossibility of firing the barrage in sufficient time to establish the protective screen in the right place against a dive bomber, for which it was intended. The competent staff department (Training and Staff Duties) fully supported them in this view. Nevertheless, due to Churchill's backing (note

[20] Admiral Nicholl's letter to the author, 30 Dec. 1967. He was then a captain serving as Naval Assistant Secretary to the War Cabinet (1939–41). He, as well as Captain G. H. Oswald, who was in the department of the Director of Naval Ordnance at the time, and Lieutenant-General Sir Ian Jacob, Military Assistant Secretary to the War Cabinet, 1939–46, are quite certain that Churchill overrode the DNO's department.

that he was by this time Prime Minister and Defence Minister), and the apparent disinclination of the Chiefs of Staff to dig in their toes over something of relatively small cost in equipment and manpower, mad though it might be, the device was proceeded with. Churchill instructed that it should be produced at high priority and fitted in ships large enough to take the cumbersome contraption. It was also mounted on shore. By the autumn of 1940, 40 Naval Wire Barrages had been mounted: 29 in capital ships and cruisers of the Home Fleet, and 6 at Dover, 4 at Gibraltar, and 1 at Aberporth. They accomplished next to nothing.[21] In Admiral Nicholl's opinion, 'It was just part of the price–and not a very high one–that had to be paid to keep Winston going. Without him Britain and the Free World were sunk.'

---

[21] On 17 August 1940 Churchill, now Prime Minister, asked for a report on the experience gained with them in action with enemy aircraft. 'The results have been somewhat meagre. There have been no occasions on which U.P. equipments mounted in H.M. Ships have been in action with the enemy and on only four occasions have U.P. equipment mounted ashore at Dover been fired at enemy aircraft. . . . The only casualty obtained by the U.P.'s has been one "Probable" at Dover on 14th November when a Ju. [Junker] 87 was seen to become entangled in a U.P. wire and is thought to have crashed later. In the same raid 15 confirmed casualties (plus 8 probables) were obtained by two "Spitfire" Squadrons and 2 confirmed casualties were obtained by the Bofors gun.' A. V. Alexander (First Lord) to Churchill, 5 Dec. 1940, ADM 199/1931. Five of the U.P.s were mounted in the battle cruiser *Hood*, whose loss (24 May 1941) in the action against the *Bismarck* may have been due to them, in part anyway. Captain J. C. Leach and Commander H. F. Lawson of the battleship *Prince of Wales* (the former had been DNO, 1939–41, just prior to his *Prince of Wales* appointment), which had participated in the action, believed that the *Hood*'s rocket weapons were the cause of her loss. The size and number of the cordite-filled rockets made the stowage of the ammunition extremely difficult and dangerous: the refill ammunition was stowed immediately below the launchers in splinter-proof lockers *above* all armour. Leach and Lawson were convinced that the rocket weapons and their unsafely stowed ammunition were the cause, probably through the explosion of the ready-use cordite penetrating the flash proofing of 'X' turret. I have this on the authority of Captain G. H. Oswald (memorandum for the author of 15 Dec. 1966), who went on board the *Prince of Wales* at Scapa Flow not long after the loss of the *Hood* and received a most graphic account of the loss from the two officers. No further NWB contraptions were fitted in ships, and the few already fitted were taken out. Cf. Roskill, *The War at Sea*, i. 406, and his 'Marder, Churchill and the Admiralty, 1939–42', *RUSI Journal* (formerly *Royal United Service Institution Journal*), cxvii (Dec. 1972), 51. In the latter Roskill asserts: 'The two very long inquiries [1941] conducted by Admiral Sir Geoffrey Blake concluded that this was not so.' These inquiries, soon after the disaster, decided that the cause of *Hood*'s loss was a 15-inch shell penetrating her armour and exploding in or near her after magazines. There could have been a hundred long inquiries without getting nearer the truth, for there was no substantiative evidence. Of course, what Leach and Lawson saw and thought could not have been conclusive, either. There is a complication in that Leach did not suggest in his testimony at both inquiries that cordite fire was the cause of the loss of the *Hood*, and that we have no way of ascertaining whether the conversation with Oswald preceded or followed his appearance at the inquiries.

Churchill's profound interest in the technological side of the war had at least one major positive result. Losses from magnetic mines, which the Germans were dropping by parachute in shallow waters of harbours and channels, and which were activated when a ship passed over them, were suspected as early as the first weeks of the war. They became one of the worst menaces to shipping. The First Lord threw himself into the search for effective antidotes. The turning point came with the recovery, intact, of one of these mines in the mud of the Thames estuary off Shoeburyness on 23 November. One counter to the magnetic mine was the 'degaussing' or de-magnetizing protection fitted to all ships—a method that was not fully developed until soon after Churchill became Prime Minister.

Churchill's considerable influence on his professional advisers is clearly seen in construction policy. In common with the Service he attributed to the battleship a power which war experience was to prove exaggerated. Twelve battleships were in commission at the outbreak of the war: *Nelson, Rodney,* five 'Royal Sovereigns', and five 'Queen Elizabeths'. There were, in addition, the old battle cruisers *Hood, Renown,* and *Repulse.* In 1937 five new 14-inch-gun battleships, of the 'King George V' class, had been laid down: they were due to come into service in 1940–1. (1936–7 programme: *King George V, Prince of Wales;* 1937–8 programme: *Duke of York, Jellicoe* (later *Anson*), *Beatty* (later *Howe*).) Four more, the 'Lion' class, were authorized in 1938 and 1939: the 16-inch-gun *Lion* and *Temeraire* (1938–9 programme) and *Conqueror* and *Thunderer* (1939–40 programme), the first battleships comparable in gun-power to the contemporary battleships of the other naval powers. The first two were laid down in June and July 1939 and the latter two ordered in August 1939.

The war was scarcely a week old when Churchill proposed a year's suspension of all battleships that could not be in service by the end of 1941 (meaning the four 'Lions') and concentration on the first three of the 'King George Vs', *King George V, Prince of Wales,* and *Duke of York,* plus the *Jellicoe* if she could be completed by 1941. But a staff conference on 12 September decided that all five 'King George Vs' should be advanced as swiftly as possible, and similarly the four 'Lions', work on which was suspended for about three months while the armed merchant cruisers were being brought out. The First Sea Lord 'felt he could not accept postponing the construction' of any of these ships, 'as, if once abandoned, we should not easily get the work restarted. It would be fatal to the Empire to emerge from this war only with old battleships, when we might be faced with sending a fleet to the Far East.' Churchill was not to be put down so easily. There was no question of 'abandoning' the four 16-inch ships, but they 'must have all armour capacity which can be spared for strengthening H.M. Ships against air attack', and he repeated the proposal for a year's suspension of battleships that could not be completed by the end of 1941, with an exception for the *Beatty,* if she could be finished in the first quarter of 1942.[22] 'It is far more important to have some ships to fight with, and to have ships that Parliament has paid for delivered to date, than to squander effort upon remote construction which has no relation to our dangers!'[23]

The debate came to centre upon the *Conqueror* and *Thunderer,* on which no work was yet being done. Churchill continued to argue the importance of concentrating personnel and *matériel* resources on the production of ships that could be used in this war: *Conqueror* and *Thunderer* could not qualify. He would instead have a battleship laid down in 1940, using the four spare 15-inch-gun turrets of the 'Royal Sovereign' class which were lying idle since the conversion of the *Courageous* and *Glorious* to carriers. (These turrets were kept as replacements in case ships of this class suffered damage in action.) He was resisted on both issues by the Naval Staff, including the First Sea Lord, and by the Controller. The Staff repeated earlier arguments about the need for a strong battle fleet after the war, especially in view of Far Eastern contingencies and the necessity, as the DCNS, Phillips, declared, of achieving the prewar goal of maintaining 'an adequate fleet to go to the Far East plus the necessary minimum to retain in Home Waters to balance any one European Power. . . . War is a wasteful thing. At the end of the war there are sure to be millions upon millions of pounds' worth of Army and Air Force material which will be utterly and absolutely wasted. Not one penny put into our capital ship strength will ever be wasted.' No, they must not give up the *Conqueror* and *Thunderer.* Pound strongly endorsed this statement. 'I entirely agree with the above and it must be taken into account that before the war is over the scales may be more heavily weighed against us if we lose any capital ships.' Churchill held his ground.[24]

In the end the First Lord pretty much had his way. No work would be done on the *Conqueror* and *Thunderer,* whose future would, however, be reconsidered in the autumn. 'The Sea Lords, however,

---

[22] Captain W. G. Tennant's notes and 'First Lord's Comments on Captain Tennant's notes of Staff Conference of September 12', ADM 205/2.

[23] Churchill to the First Sea Lord and others, 8 Oct. 1939, ADM 205/2.

[24] Churchill's minute and memorandum for the War Cabinet, 1 Feb. 1940, Phillips's and Pound's minutes, 2 Feb., and Churchill to the Controller, 7 Feb., ADM 1/10850.

had agreed to this postponement with great reluctance . . .' The *Lion* and *Temeraire* would be proceeded with, also the *Vanguard* (using the spare 15-inch turrets): she could be completed six months earlier than ships of the design of the *Conqueror* and *Thunderer*, and at a saving of £2,000,000.[25] In the event, construction of all four 'Lions' was abandoned in 1940. The five 'King George Vs', launched in 1939–40, were completed between December 1940 and August 1942. The *Vanguard*, which it was hoped to build in no more than $3\frac{1}{2}$ years, was not laid down until October 1941 and was not ready until after the war (August 1946). Churchill's advocacy of the suspension of work on warships that could not be ready by the end of 1941, and concentration instead on ships that could be completed fairly rapidly, was an insight not without shrewdness.[26]

It is to Churchill's credit that from the beginning he appreciated the vital importance of trade defence and that defeating the U-boat was the key to winning the war. Among his happy initiatives were the high priority given to an emergency programme of trawler conversions to anti-submarine work, the emphasis on destroyer and other small-craft construction, and the development of the Fleet Air Arm 'as an adjunct of the Fleet both for cruiser reconnaissance and in the anti-U-boat warfare . . .'[27] His anti-U-boat policies and interventions were not always sound, particularly as regards his ambivalent attitude towards the convoy system. Speaking in the Commons on 24 September 1939, he mentioned the convoy system, the arming of merchant ships, and the counter-attack on the U-boats as the principal means of coping with the menace. But it was on

[25] WP 53 (40), Churchill, 'Naval Programme 1940–41', 2 Mar. 1940, CAB 66/5, WM 67 (40), 13 Mar. 1940, CAB 65/6.

[26] One very important reason for 'straining every nerve' to finish the *King George V* and *Prince of Wales* in 1940, by the autumn if possible, was the expected arrival of the formidable battleship *Bismarck* (eight 15-inch guns). If ready before the first two 'King George V's', she would, it was feared, range freely throughout the oceans, rupturing the trade routes. She could not be caught by any British ship that could destroy her. This was the particular reason why Churchill was so exercised over the progress of the two battleships in the winter of 1939–40, as well as over their ten 14-inch main armament. The situation took a grave turn in the latter part of January 1940, when photographs obtained of the *Bismarck*, building at Hamburg, showed her to be more advanced than had been thought and likely to be in service in June. Churchill's apprehensions led him to suggest (28 January) an air strike against the *Bismarck* in harbour (as well as the aircraft carrier *Graf Zeppelin*, building at Kiel and expected to be ready in May). The status of the *Bismarck* revealed late in March removed some of the urgency, and together with the unfolding Norwegian campaign in the spring took Churchill's mind off the subject of German surface raiders. Work on the *Graf Zeppelin* was suspended in April, and the *Bismarck* was not in service until August.

[27] WP 36 (39), 'Report of the First Lord of the Admiralty to the War Cabinet. No. 1', 17 Sept. 1939, CAB 66/1.

the effectiveness of the third that he dwelt then and later. In his view the development of asdic (the device introduced since the First War as the answer to the problem of locating submarines) strengthened the case for an offensive U-boat strategy. Asdic 'certainly are very remarkable in results', he wired President Roosevelt, 'and enable two destroyers to do the work that could not have been done by ten last time.'[28] Churchill's exaggerated confidence in asdic reflected the general view of the Navy, but it accorded with his private inclination.

Early in the war he began to urge the formation of 'attacking groups', or 'hunting groups', of destroyers, at the expense of convoy escorts, to seek out and destroy U-boats. It was argued by the Naval Staff, Pound included, and strongly supported by Churchill, that such action was 'aggressive', whereas waiting to counter-attack from convoys was 'passive'. On 9 November, in an 'Action This Day' minute to the First Sea Lord and others, the First Lord expressed his deep concern at the serious decline in imports and exports, which threatened 'grave shortages'.

We shall have failed in our task if we merely substitute delays [arising from the convoy system] for sinkings. . . . We must secretly loosen-up the convoy system (while boasting about it publicly), especially on the outer routes. . . . a higher degree of risk must be accepted. This is possible now that so many of our ships are armed. They can go in smaller parties. Even across the Atlantic we may have to apply the principle to a certain degree. If we could only combine with it a large effective destroyer force, sweeping the Western Approaches as a matter of course instead of providing focal points on which convoys could be directed, we should have more freedom.

And on 20 November to the First Sea Lord: 'Nothing can be more important in the anti-submarine war than to try to obtain an independent flotilla which could work like a cavalry division on the approaches, without worrying about the traffic or U-boat sinkings, but could systematically search large areas over a wide front. In this way these areas would become untenable to U-boats . . .'[29]

This strategy was, in fact, almost a complete failure and led to heavier convoy losses than might have been the case, since convoys were weakened to permit offensive sweeps that might as well have been searching for the proverbial needle in the haystack.

[28] 16 Oct. 1939, ADM 199/1928.
[29] Churchill, *The Gathering Storm*, pp. 589–90. A footnote to the 20 November minute stating that 'this policy did not become possible until a later phase in the war' presumably refers to the later, and successful, strategy of the 'support groups' (from late 1942). But these were a different matter. They were placed to go to the aid of a convoy under attack or threat of attack and bore no relationship to independent flotillas sweeping the Western Approaches.

Churchill never completely grasped the nature of maritime war. He says he always sought to rupture the Navy's defensive obsessions, was never content with the policy of 'Convoy and Blockade', and always looked for counter-offensives.[30] But convoy was a vital *offensive* measure, as proved by the First War, if that war proved anything,[31] and the practicable large-scale method of destroying submarines. Actually, it did not matter how many U-boats the Germans had, if they were forced to keep them out of the way and British merchantmen remained afloat. This was the position of the DCNS. But the First Sea Lord was on a 'hunt 'em down' racket and pressed this on the DCNS and the DA/SW. It was not until 1942, when the proof of the efficacy of the convoy system had been demonstrated to Churchill's satisfaction, that he accepted it without reservations.

The results of Churchill's anti-submarine policies were equally unfortunate in another direction. At an early date we find him pressing a Northern Mine Barrage on the War Cabinet. The proposal, it is clear, originated with Pound in mid-October. Churchill writes: 'I did not like this kind of warfare, which is essentially defensive, and seeks to substitute material on a vast scale for dominating action. However, I was gradually worn down and reconciled.'[32] He submitted the barrage proposal to the War Cabinet on 19 November. The barrage was to be similar to the one laid down in 1918 between the Orkneys and Norway, which was supposed to have accounted for six U-boats in just under six weeks towards the end of the war, with three others damaged. (In fact, a mere three U-boats had been sunk for certain.) His proposal called for four lines of mines at each of seven depths (down to 50 fathoms); 181,000 contact mines would be required.

The Northern Barrage is a huge project [six months were needed for preparation, then a year for completion], but like any minefield which cannot be swept up, it is an offensive operation of which there are so few which are practicable. Unless we lay the Northern Mine Barrage we shall not have done everything possible to protect the trade which is vital to this country. . . . the minefield will be partially and progressively effective

[30] ibid., pp. 362–3.
[31] See Marder, *From the Dreadnought to Scapa Flow*, iv and v, especially v. 85–91.
[32] Churchill, *The Gathering Storm*, p. 306. He told Pound in a minute of 18 Oct.: 'You will find me very reluctant to embark on the big barrage, having regard to the immense drain upon explosives which the Army will need. When we think how little the Germans spend on their handful of ships and few score of U-boats, and vast establishment and forces under the control of the Admiralty, we must be careful not to take more than is absolutely necessary from the common pot.' ADM 205/2. And see further his minute of 23 Oct. to the First Sea Lord and Controller, *The Gathering Storm*, p. 587.

from the time that the first mines are laid (as was the case in 1918). Its moral effect will start from the declaration of the mined area and the laying of navigational marks.[33]

The War Cabinet on 30 November authorized preparations for the barrage. The end result was the fantastic reintroduction, beginning in July 1940, of a scheme similar to the one of 1918, with the same shockingly inefficient and unreliable antenna mines.[34] It was made even more fantastic when the Orkneys–Norway line in about 40 fathoms was no longer feasible (after the German occupation of Norway) and it was shifted to the much deeper waters of the Faroes–Iceland line. Only by a good deal of ill-judged enthusiasm could it be imagined that a minefield could be efficient in 200 fathoms, for the dip caused by the tidal streams would have been so much greater. The so-called Northern Barrage cramped the freedom of action of the C-in-C, Home Fleet, absorbed about 90,000 mines and many destroyers (escorts for the minelayers as well as for the Home Fleet, which provided cover for the minelaying operations) that could have been put to better use. The results were dismal: one U-boat was sunk, *U-702*, in September 1944. There is no evidence to show that the barrage influenced U-boat operations or movements to any noticeable degree.[35]

We cannot leave the subject of anti-submarine strategy without mentioning the peculiar business of Churchill and the statistics of U-boat kills.[36] The First Lord made exaggerated claims: on 12 November 1939, in a broadcast, that 'the attack of the U-boats has been controlled and they have paid a heavy toll', and on 20 January 1940, in another cheerful broadcast, that it 'seems pretty

[33] WP 126 (39), 'The Northern Barrage', CAB 66/3. For the 1918 barrage, see Marder, *From the Dreadnought to Scapa Flow*, v. 65–75.

[34] Captain J. S. Cowie, a mine specialist who was then a commander in the Operations Division, claims that Churchill was converted to it 'by a man who could draw pretty pictures showing that if "antenna" mines were used the number required would be greatly reduced. True enough, if antenna mines worked, but they didn't!' Captain Cowie's letter to the author, 6 Aug. 1971.

[35] It may well be asked why Pound had proposed this nonsense. The natural inclination of Pound, a torpedoman (that is, a specialist in under-water weapons), towards mining, as well as the incomplete knowledge of the 1918 results, may have contributed to his decision. His weak excuse, when tackled on the subject by Cowie, was that 'the Admiralty would never have been forgiven had they failed to make the attempt to mine these waters. He also emphasized that the minefields, in addition to being no more than a hazard to U-boats, were intended to have a restrictive influence on the operation of enemy surface vessels against shipping in the Atlantic. This they undoubtedly did, as well as acting as a flanking protection to the Iceland convoys.' Cowie, *Mines, Minelayers, and Minelaying*, p. 135.

[36] This paragraph is based on Admiral Godfrey's *Naval Memoirs*, v, Pt. 2, pp. 259, 262–70, vii, Pt. 2, pp. 225–6.

certain' they had sunk half the U-boat force with which Germany had begun the war. The correct figure on 12 November, we now know, was 6 boats lost out of 57 in commission when the war began. The NID estimate was 6 out of 66. On the second occasion, the figure of the DNI and DA/SW was 9—just balancing the number of boats added between 1 September and the end of the year. Churchill got his 'half' by combining the 16 'probably sunk' with the 9 'known sunk', and then very likely with the help of Professor Lindemann's statistical section, by throwing in another 10, for a grand total of 35. This manipulation did raise the total kills to over half the number, 66, which NID estimated the Germans possessed at the outbreak of war. The 9 U-boats 'known sunk' on 20 January was the correct total figure; the First Lord's 16 'probables' had returned safely to harbour. This was not the last of the First Lord's exercises in inflation. When the First Sea Lord, on grounds that are not clear, estimated in February that 35 U-boats had been disposed of, the First Lord challenged it: 'A working hypothesis: but I think 45 will be nearer the truth' (17 February). The DNI's estimate was 10; the true figure, 11. 'Both Churchill and Pound were being wishful and disinclined to believe D.N.I.'s monthly estimates.' Churchill's figures had the U-boat fleet down to a piddling 12; Pound's, to 22. NID knew the enemy had at least 40 afloat.

How are we to explain Churchill's flights of fancy, especially in view of what he had told the DNI on 6 September 1939: 'It is of the highest importance that the Admiralty bulletin should maintain its reputation for truthfulness . . .'?[37] 'You can see what was going on', Donald McLachlan has commented. 'The First Lord had a morale role to play. The Navy was the only Service which was fully engaged at the time; it must not be discouraged by too rigorous a method of assessing "kills"; it was essential that the nation should have some sense of action and success and achievement; and the only material that was really available at that time came from the U-boat war. It was essential to make the most of what was happening, but in the process truth suffered.'[38]

One can understand Churchill in his role of morale-builder and make some allowance for his exaggerations. But what are we to make of the Talbot affair, where national morale was not involved, only the truth? Captain A. G. Talbot, the DA/SW since 15 November 1939, had a first-class row with Churchill, who kept claiming large

[37] Churchill, *The Gathering Storm*, p. 577.
[38] McLachlan, 'Naval Intelligence in the Second World War', *Royal United Service Institution Journal*, cxii (Aug. 1967), 224.

numbers of U-boats sunk. Talbot, whose responsibility it was as head of the Assessment Committee, abstained from wishful thinking. He claimed a considerably more modest and realistic figure, and postwar knowledge has proved that he was right—almost exactly right.[39] But he 'argued the toss' with the First Lord just one stage too far and so he had to go. Talbot's report of 24 April 1940 brought matters to a head. It concluded with these statistics on the state of the U-boat fleet on 10 March 1940: destroyed, 19; under repair, 2; available, 43. Churchill's minute (25 April) was crisp and decisive:

> As we know from wrecks, corpses or survivors, that we have 15 U-boats sunk for certain, Captain Talbot's estimate of 19 in all indicates that only 4 others have been sunk by the British and French activities. The ordinary accidents of the sea and the Service would, according to the figures of the last War, have accounted for this number. Therefore the conclusion to which this officer comes is that all the attacks, except the actual 15 of which we have remnants, have failed. This conclusion leads me to think that it might be a good thing if Captain Talbot went to sea as soon as possible.[40]

This turned out to be September 1940. Captain Creasy succeeded Talbot at ten minutes' notice.[41]

The U-boat menace turned Churchill's thoughts from his first days in office to the possibility of getting the use of bases in southern Ireland to which Britain had renounced all rights in 1938: Berehaven, in particular. He realized with the Naval Staff how invaluable this would be in facilitating the work of the destroyers operating in the Western Approaches from Milford Haven by increasing their radius of action. The shortage of these craft underscored the importance of this consideration. Churchill informed the War Cabinet on 18 September that 'the position was profoundly unsatisfactory' from the Admiralty's point of view. The War Cabinet felt 'it would

[39] An officer remembers following Churchill down the passage from Admiralty House to his room one day. The First Lord came across Talbot, coming in the opposite direction. He gave his version of the U-boat score, and Talbot cheerfully said, 'No, Sir, it's ——.' Churchill, furious, shouted at him, 'Stop grinning at me, you bloody ape!'

[40] ADM 205/6. Marked 'Action This Day'. Admiral Sir Frederic Dreyer's U-Boat Investigation Committee, which was appointed in September 1940 to inquire into the methods of assessing U-boat losses, to review the estimates of those losses, and to consider proposals for improving those methods, gave high marks to Talbot and his Assessment Committee in their report (10 Oct. 1940). ADM 199/138.

[41] Admiral of the Fleet Sir George Creasy's letter to the author, 28 May 1970. The Admiral added: 'I think, personally, that it was Winston in one of his naughtiest moods and the less said about it the better', which advice I am happy to follow. Other factors may have been involved than arguments about estimates of U-boat sinkings.

be very undesirable that there should be an open difference between this country and Eire at the present moment', and expressed the hope that the Irish would come to see that co-operation was in their own interest.[42] The situation worsened by mid-October with the U-boats now operating off the Irish coast. On the initiative of the War Cabinet an approach was made to Dublin. De Valera, the President of Eire, was not to be budged, claiming that Irish public opinion would not stand for any concession to the British. At a War Cabinet meeting on 24 October, Churchill proposed that they 'should challenge the constitutional position of Eire's neutrality. We should not admit that her neutrality was compatible with her position under the crown . . . [and] insist on the use of the harbours.' Though impressed with the First Lord's case, Chamberlain was not prepared to sanction force yet. It was not certain that the use of southern Irish ports was 'a matter of life and death'; seizure would have 'most unfortunate repercussions in the United States and in India, where it would be hailed as a high-handed and unwarranted action'; consequently, there would be no justification for seizure 'until the situation became much worse'. The War Cabinet could agree on little more than to have Eden, the Dominions Secretary, 'take every opportunity of bringing home to the Dominions that the use of ports in Eire by the Royal Navy was essential for the security of the Empire, and that the present attitude adopted by Eire in the matter was intolerable'.[43] On 23 November the War Cabinet stated that, with the U-boat menace in the Western Approaches now under control, the use of Berehaven no longer 'constituted a vital interest'.[44]

As matters developed, the British really lost little from having given up the southern Irish bases. The German U-boat wolf packs did not start until after the fall of France, and by that date it would have been foolish to have tried using the Southwest Approaches. As Captain Roskill has brought out:

With the German U-boats and bombers based on the French Biscay coast we were forced to bring *all* our seaborne traffic in through the northwestern approaches to this island, instead of some ships using the southwestern approaches. This greatly reduced the value of the bases in southern Eire, but vastly enhanced the importance of those in Ulster, without which we could hardly have survived. . . . Though the decision not to use force was unquestionably correct it none the less remains true that, had we enjoyed the use of the Eire bases, many Allied ships and seamen's lives would have been saved, and perhaps the Atlantic Battle won earlier.[45]

---

[42] WM 19 (39), CAB 65/1.   [43] WM 58 (39), CAB 65/1.
[44] WM 92 (39), CAB 65/2.   [45] Roskill's letter in *The Times*, 7 Jan. 1970.

The U-boat factor partly conditioned Churchill's Mediterranean policy early in the war. He believed in the overriding importance of drawing Italy to the Allied side. 'Everyone can see how necessary it is to have Italy friendly and how desirable to have her an Ally. The best way to work up good relations with a country or with a person is to develop common interests and, as far as possible, partnership in a common policy. Once engaged on this path, one thing leads to another, and confidence ripens into comradeship.' To this end, and, secondarily, to keep the U-boats out of the Mediterranean, he proposed to the War Cabinet an Anglo-French naval arrangement with Italy that would 'neutralize' the Mediterranean. The 'essence of such a plan is that no submarine craft except those belonging to the Mediterranean Powers should be allowed in these waters. This would free the inland sea from the disturbance of U-boat warfare. . . . The mere process of Italian ships acting with ours would be of extreme value.'[46] Churchill had proceeded with this quixotic proposal over criticisms of the Naval Staff, which he never hesitated to ignore when political considerations were important. The Staff advanced the traditional naval argument against anything that restricted belligerent rights in time of war. '. . . it would be a very bad precedent to set,' declared the DCNS (6 October), 'as it might be used against us in the future in an effort to *restrict the rights* of those *who live by sea power* . . .'[47] And the Chiefs of Staff declared that 'it would be impossible to neutralise the Mediterranean since the Germans are fully entitled to extend their submarine activities into that sea. In any event the neutralisation of the Mediterranean and the abandonment of Contraband Control within that sea would result in a breakdown of the economic pressure upon which we mainly rely for the ultimate defeat of Germany.'[48] Nothing came of the First Lord's initiative.

Almost from the day he took over, Churchill was anxious about the safety of the Home Fleet in the main fleet anchorage at Scapa Flow. The defences of Scapa were discussed at an Admiralty conference on 5 September, as a result of which orders went out for additional blockships and nets. The First Lord was not entirely happy with what he learned during a visit to Scapa on 15–16 September, when he conferred with the quite confident C-in-C, Admiral Forbes, in the flagship *Nelson*. The entrance channels were not effectively netted, etc. His thoughts went back to that day almost

---

[46] WP 92 (39), Churchill, 'Possible *Détente* with Italy in the Mediterranean', 18 Oct. 1939, CAB 66/2.   [47] ADM 116/4177.
[48] COS (39) 84, 'Possible Detente with Italy in the Mediterranean', 17 Oct. 1939, CAB 80/4.

twenty-five years earlier when he had visited the Grand Fleet at Scapa. There was in 1939 the same threat from the U-boat, to which had been added the new threat from the air. His worst fears were realized when, in the night of 13–14 October, U-47 successfully torpedoed the battleship *Royal Oak*, at anchor in Scapa. As luck would have it, U-47 had entered the Flow through the Kirk Sound, which channel was to have been blocked the next day with the arrival of a blockship for that purpose. Vice-Admiral R. M. Servaes remembers 'only too well the morning after the *Royal Oak* was torpedoed. I was with Sir Dudley Pound when Churchill came into the room to be given details of this disaster. Instead of recriminations as to why the base was not better defended, all he said was, "What a wonderful feat of arms." A good example of a fighting man's admiration for another fighting man, and also of his magnanimity in the hour of defeat.'[49]

It was at this moment, the latter half of October, when the East Coast was bare of major units of the Fleet (they were using the temporary base of Loch Ewe in the north-west of Scotland), and most of the destroyers were busy in convoy work, that the danger of a German 'gamble'—an invasion or raid, with perhaps as many as 80,000 men, or of a surface-ship raid against the East Coast—gave the First Lord many uncomfortable moments. He kept reminding the Admiralty and the Navy of the need for special alertness and endorsed various precautions such as strengthening the destroyer force on the East Coast and stationing a submarine screen across the probable route of an invading force.

The overriding problem after the *Royal Oak* disaster was where the Home Fleet's base should be. The Chief of the Air Staff argued for the Scottish west coast 'from the point of view of air attack'.[50] The Admiralty agreed: the Clyde was their preference, and there the fleet, with War Cabinet approval, was dispatched on 31 October. Churchill was in accord with his professional advisers as regards the Clyde, but only as a 'temporary disposition'. He believed an East Coast base, meaning Rosyth, to be *'essential'*. Rosyth had important advantages, being better placed geographically for a fleet whose primary duty was to secure the Island against invasion or a naval sortie in force. Rosyth was, moreover, their best-defended war harbour against both air and submarine attack. At the least, Churchill wanted to base one heavy ship there to deter

[49] Admiral Servaes's letter to the author, 20 May 1965. The pre-Churchill Admiralty and Treasury must share the principal blame for the deficiencies in the defences of Scapa. See Roskill, *The War at Sea*, i. 78–80, and above, pp. 51–2.

[50] WM 51 (39), 18 Oct. 1939, CAB 65/3.

the enemy from attempting to dominate the North Sea with surface craft.[51]

The C-in-C was also giving trouble. In reply to a message informing him that the Admiralty considered the Clyde should be his base, Admiral Forbes had stated in his first sentence: 'I totally disagree' (the fleet would need an additional day to reach the North Sea), and went on to say why he wanted Scapa as his main base. The First Lord deemed it 'indispensable' that they confer with him. On 31 October Churchill, the First Sea Lord, and the Deputy Chief of the Air Staff (Air Vice-Marshal R. E. C. Peirse) came aboard the *Nelson* in the Clyde for a conference with the C-in-C. 'After we had sat down round my dining table,' Forbes wrote afterwards, 'Churchill turned to me and said, "We made a perfectly polite signal to you for good reasons, and you replied, 'I totally disagree'."' We went at it hammer and tongs until 12.30 when Churchill turned to me and said he wanted to speak to me in my after cabin. When we got there he said "You have converted me [to Scapa as the only proper base for the fleet]; now you have got to convert the other two." The day ended happily with the First Lord promising that everything should be done to make Scapa properly secure.'[52] The C-in-C had, however, been shown why it was not practicable for him to use Scapa for some time to come. Apart from the agreement 'to proceed with all possible speed' upon the defences of Scapa, with the measures to be taken specified, it was decided that Scapa could in the meanwhile be used as a refuelling base, and that Rosyth would be the principal fleet base, pending completion of Scapa's defences, with everything done to bring Rosyth 'to the highest possible efficiency'. The specifics were set down.[53] As between Rosyth and the Clyde, the C-in-C had expressed a strong preference for the former, largely because he believed that the fleet had better anti-submarine protection there than in the Clyde. The War Cabinet approved Rosyth and the other arrangements of 31 October after hearing the First Lord's report on the conference.[54]

The troubles over the fleet base had only begun. The fleet continued to use the Clyde as its base. Churchill's impatience spilled over:

This quitting of the North Sea has not saved our great ships; for two accidents which might well have been fatal have occurred to principal

[51] See, for example, Churchill to Pound, 28 Oct. 1939, ADM 205/2.

[52] Quoted in Roskill, 'Churchill and His Admirals', London *Sunday Telegraph*, 11 Feb. 1962.

[53] Churchill's memorandum of 1 Nov. 1939 for the DCNS and others, Churchill, *The Gathering Storm*, pp. 556–7.   [54] WM 67 (39), 1 Nov. 1939, CAB 65/4.

units.[55] All the dangers of entering the Clyde and leaving it, all the defects of its bad strategic situation, all its feeble gun and harbour defences, all the demoralisation that is caused by its proximity to Greenock, are now apparently to be endured for another two or three months [until Scapa was ready]. I really cannot think that this is the best way of treating the problem, and I would ask that a definite date should also be fixed for the Fleet to work from Rosyth, and have the mine-sweeping arrangements ready by then. Could they not be ready by February 1?[56]

Meanwhile, the programme for the defence of Scapa ('Plan R') was proceeding with dispatch. It was an elaborate one, involving minefields, booms, nets, blockships, patrol craft, guns, anti-aircraft guns, searchlights, barrage balloons, and fighter aircraft. The goal was to have the work so far advanced as to permit the fleet to return to a safe home by the end of March 1940. Churchill kept after the First Sea Lord, Civil Lord, and others concerned to ensure that all was going forward with the utmost speed. This exhortation is typical:

> . . . experience shows that contractors are much more ready to book work for Government than to carry it out punctually. I therefore wish to know how many men are at work at Scapa, and how many will be working every Monday in January. Also reports whether in fact that number are at their posts. . . . My general impression is that we are making very little progress at Scapa. Two and a half months have passed since the *Royal Oak* was torpedoed. What, in fact, has been done since? How many blockships sunk? How many nets made? How many men have been in work for how many days? What buildings have been erected? What gun sites have been concreted and prepared? What progress has been made with the run-ways of the aerodrome? I thought we settled two months ago to have a weekly report. The Civil Lord should draw up a form of weekly report, which would enable every aspect of progress to be seen at a glance each week. Up to the present I share the Commander-in-Chief's anxieties about the slow progress of this indispensable work.[57]

'With his backing', writes Admiral Oliver, then a captain and the officer initially in charge of 'Plan R', 'it was amazing how bureaucratic obstruction melted.' The target date was realized: the fleet was able to return at the beginning of March from its long period of exile. The First Lord came north on the 9th to see the new Scapa.

---

[55] The new cruiser *Belfast*, mined in the Firth of Forth, 21 November, and the *Nelson*, mined in Loch Ewe, 4 December.

[56] Churchill to Pound, 6 Jan. 1940, ADM 1/10317. It transpired that the fleet had made little use of Rosyth, especially after the discovery of magnetic mines when the *Belfast* was mined. Pound did not consider it safe to have the fleet use Rosyth as a base until this difficulty had been overcome, whether through a successful demagnetizing of all important vessels or the sweeping of a 50-mile-long channel. Pound to Churchill, 11 Jan. 1940, ADM 1/10317. The fleet remained in the Clyde.

[57] Churchill to Pound and others, 1 Jan. 1940, ADM 205/6.

Oliver and his successor, Rear-Admiral A. L. St. G. Lyster, accompanied him on his tour of the defences in a motor launch, finally lying off Hoxa Sound to watch Forbes in the *Rodney* and the *Repulse* and *Renown* enter harbour. 'It was very cold', Oliver remembers, 'and he went below to get warm. I remember so well the gestures of his white podgy hands as he warmed them before the fire and declared, "They will hang us all if it happens again." I was accustomed to think that Winston took everything in his stride without regard to the consequences to himself. I was surprised to hear him express such acute regard for his responsibility should our estimation of the efficacy of the defences have proved false.'[58]

*   *   *

Linked with Churchill's restless energy was his itch for the offensive. The so-called 'Phoney War' galled him. The classical theory of a 'Fleet in Being' had little attraction for him, though in many respects he had a remarkable grasp of sea warfare and often appeared to see a little further ahead than his professional advisers. The truth was that the 'Phoney' or 'Twilight' war was a very real war at sea from the first day, as he more than others was in a position to realize. His inability to endure inaction made him something of a trial to the Naval Staff. His fertile imagination never ceased to conjure up, and to press on his advisers, ideas for carrying the war more effectively to the enemy. He could be impatient with sailors who pointed out the dangers in a proposed offensive operation. He tended to disregard, or to underestimate, the risks. Although this offensive cast of mind sometimes created, as we shall see, work which proved useless and even potentially dangerous, it imparted a tremendous impetus to the search for, and the discovery of, ways to eventual victory. And it had a positive effect on morale, as Churchill's then Principal Private Secretary brings out:

. . . his personal minutes and 'prayers' made everyone feel that he was watching them, but these would have been of little use if we had not felt that he was imbued with the spirit of pugnacity, and with the offensive spirit and the desire to be 'up and at 'em'. In some mysterious way this spirit was conveyed to everyone with whom he came into contact, directly or indirectly. I sometimes think that some of his wilder projects, which might have been very costly if put into effect, nevertheless served an even more useful purpose in the hearts and minds of those who found in them indications of his burning desire to come to grips with the enemy.[59]

Churchill married his love of gadgetry to his love for the offensive.

[58] Vice-Admiral R. D. Oliver's letter to the author, 20 May 1965.
[59] Sir Eric Seal's unpublished memoirs.

An inordinate amount of time and energy went into examining and encouraging these often impracticable devices, especially when working models were produced. One of his brain waves when at the Admiralty was a 'trench-cutting tank' for military use, in the event of a First War-type of deadlock in the land fighting—a project dubbed by him 'White Rabbit Number 6' (afterwards rechristened 'Cultivator Number 6'). His experience with the caterpillar tractor in the First War, an imaginative idea of his which eventually led to the tank, may have been responsible. The machine was to be capable of excavating a trench 6 feet deep by 3 feet wide at the rate of one mile an hour. The idea was to use the hours of darkness to effect by way of this groove a surprise penetration of enemy-held territory. By dawn they should be 10 miles inside the enemy defences on a 20- to 25-mile front. Churchill had Sir Stanley Goodall, the Director of Naval Construction, design the machine. After six weeks a 3-foot-long working model was made and successfully demonstrated in a basement of the Admiralty (this was one of his celebrated 'Midnight Follies' meetings to inspect new weapons), with the Prime Minister, Chancellor of the Exchequer, and the Chief of the Imperial General Staff, among others, in attendance. Churchill was ecstatic. He quickly secured Cabinet approval (7 February 1940) for 240 of these monsters—in their final form, 130 tons, 8 feet high, and nearly 80 feet long. The amount of noise they would make did not seem to occur to him. As things turned out, the end of the 'Phoney War' period and the onrush of the German panzers put paid to the idea after the Ministry of Supply had completed a few units. Admiral Gretton holds that this was the only example of Churchill's 'interference' in another Service, i.e. during his time as First Lord. His own last word on the subject: 'I am responsible but impenitent.'

Operation 'Royal Marine' is the major illustration of his combination of interesting devices with an offensive strategy. Enraged by the magnetic-mine sinkings in the mouth of the Thames in a three-day period in mid-November, Churchill's thoughts turned to retaliatory measures against 'this odious practice. The most cowardly that can be adopted whereby merchant ships of neutral nations are sunk without mercy or discrimination in the fairways.' He advanced a scheme that had first occurred to him during a visit to the Rhine sector of the French defences on the eve of the war. It called for paralysing the barge traffic on the Rhine, Germany's main artery of internal communications, which directly sustained her huge armies lying along the French frontier. This would be achieved by aircraft dropping large numbers of fluvial mines into the river. Devised to explode on contact, they would float down, a few feet from the surface, from just inside French territory below Strasbourg, destroying barges and floating bridges. Churchill had not proposed the scheme earlier because of the considerable neutral shipping that used the Rhine. But the situation had changed with the 'indiscriminate warfare' the Germans had launched by depositing magnetic mines at the entrance to British harbours. The First Lord now proposed that 'a steady process of harassing this main waterway of the enemy should be set on foot. . . . Not a day should be lost.'[60] On 24 November the War Cabinet approved the project in principle on the understanding that they would reserve a final decision until it was ready for execution. An Admiralty committee which included the First Lord, First Sea Lord, and Controller, together with RAF and War Office representatives, went into action without delay. Churchill was fascinated by the possibilities of 'Royal Marine'. 'He would call for a bucket full of water and insist that everyone should watch the model [of one of the fluvial mines] work.' The committee agreed on 27 November to launch the operation on the January full moon, the 21st, by which time they expected to have 10,000 mines. By 4 December the scheme had been expanded into a large-scale campaign on the inland waterways of Germany, canals and rivers both, and involving the Navy and the RAF.

The First Lord fought off the objections raised by Sir William Malkin, Legal Adviser to the Foreign Office, in a paper of 7 December attached to the Air Staff's study of 'Royal Marine' and which might have destroyed the scheme if left unanswered. To Malkin's argument that 'Retaliation does not arise, since the enemy have not yet attacked an inland waterway or any other form of inland transport', Churchill riposted: 'But they seek to choke our estuaries, and if they succeed we shall starve.' To Malkin's assertion that the plan amounted 'in effect, to indiscriminate air action, and could only legitimately be undertaken, if at all, in the event of the enemy first committing some new outrage which would justify it on the score of reprisal' (an Anglo-French declaration on 3 September had stated that Allied naval and air action would be confined to military targets), Churchill countered: 'What does Malkin suggest would qualify us?' To the argument that 'the action proposed is certain to give rise to retaliation or reprisals by Germany', the First Lord's

---

[60] Churchill to the First Sea Lord and others, 19 Nov. 1939, ADM 205/2. The formal proposal was first made on 17 November. Much of the source material on 'Operation Royal Marine', as it came to be called ('R.M.' for short), is in ADM 116/4239, 4240. Material quoted below is from these files, if not otherwise indicated.

scornful reaction was: 'Don't irritate them dear!' Malkin pointed out: 'Owing to the need for notification to neutrals surprise is, in any circumstances, likely to be prejudiced. It is, therefore, doubtful whether the project is sound.' Churchill's marginal comment was simply: 'rubbish'. He was 'much distressed' by Malkin's paper, but relieved to discover at the 10 December War Cabinet that the Air Ministry were not committed to its views.

It would [he wrote to the Air Secretary] be better to have the operation argued out solely as to whether it could be carried out with success, and what the military retaliation would be. If this study of the technical aspects in their integrity and in isolation reveals a good case, it would then be for the Cabinet to consider the wider aspects of law and policy involved. . . . Let us see if we can make the ship float, and then let the War Cabinet decide whether she is to be sent to sea, and in what circumstances, and when. . . . The offensive is three or four times as hard as passively enduring from day to day. It therefore requires all possible help in early stages. Nothing is easier than to smother it in the cradle. Yet here perhaps lies safety.[61]

For Churchill, as he informed General Gamelin, the French Commander-in-Chief (21 February 1940), 'the moral and juridical justification appears to me complete. The Germans having assailed the ports of Great Britain and their approaches with every form of illegal mining, having constantly bombed and machine-gunned from the air unarmed merchant ships and even fishing boats and lightships, and waging all the time a ruthless U-boat warfare, not only upon belligerents but still more upon neutrals, are an enemy against whom stern reprisals are required.' Note how he had expanded the original *raison d'être* of 'Royal Marine'.

By mid-January 1940 the committee had agreed on four kinds of mines—the first two, the non-aerial mines, the responsibility of the Admiralty, the latter two, of the Air Ministry: drifting mines to be put into rivers from the banks, mines for estuaries, drifting mines to be laid in rivers from aircraft, and mines to be laid in still waters (canals, etc.) from aircraft. Design problems forced a postponement of the plan (12 January) until the March full moon (15 March). The French attitude was an additional reason for postponement. Their military and naval authorities accepted 'Royal Marine' (it would be

[61] Churchill to Sir Kingsley Wood, 11 Dec. 1939. He dealt with the purely juridical aspects of Malkin's paper in a memorandum of 17 Dec. for Wood. The heart of his argument lay in these statements: 'Breaches by the enemy of any particular rule of International Law may be taken as abrogating that rule for the duration of the war, so far as needless suffering is not inflicted.' He cited Germany's use of poison gas in the First War as a precedent. 'It was accepted that the rule [against the use of poison gas] had been abandoned by the enemy, and that in this field no rule or convention any longer fettered the Allies. No-one has ever impugned their action.'

'a most valuable diversion in the rear of the enemy during an offensive', Gamelin told Churchill), but were convinced that action should be delayed until a large supply of mines was available. Planning did not let up. Production schedules were revised, mines were tested, and so on, and always there was the First Lord's invigorating presence—encouraging, prodding, goading the Admiralty, Air Ministry, and French military authorities. He was absolutely convinced of the immense success and strategic consequences of 'Royal Marine', and, therefore, that no time should be lost.

The War Cabinet approved 'Royal Marine' on 6 March 1940. The Government planned to issue with the French on 11 March a declaration setting forth 'the many breaches of the customs of civilised war of which the Germans have been guilty', and particularly those committed in British coastal waters, and warning that they intended to retaliate upon the Rhine and inland waterways of Germany. The Royal Navy would then loose the first 2,000 fluvial mines on the Rhine from the various places chosen, at the rate of 300–400 a night, and maintain a rate of discharge of 1,000 a week, rising shortly to 2,000 for an indefinite period. The RAF (delayed by production difficulties in the mines designed for aircraft) would from mid-April begin to discharge their mines into the lower reaches of the Rhine where there were no anti-aircraft defences, and, later, a different type of mine into the still-water canals. Finally, the other type of naval mine would be laid in the river mouths. The operation, Churchill stressed in a letter to Gamelin (6 March), was to be 'not a temporary or occasional blow, but is designed to be a permanent feature of the war . . .'.

Everything appeared to be set. Rear-Admiral J. U. P. FitzGerald, in charge of the execution of 'Royal Marine' under the Fifth Sea Lord (Vice-Admiral G. C. C. Royle), and a force of British marines and naval officers, 'each man aflame with the idea of a naval stroke in the war' (Churchill), were on the upper reaches of the Rhine awaiting the word to strike. The Naval Attaché in Paris reported that Admiral Darlan, the Commander-in-Chief of the French naval forces, was 'enthusiastically in favour of the operation, which he thought might have a decisive effect upon the war in, say, a year's time'.[62] Only the (*pro forma*, it was expected) concurrence of the French Government in the operation was lacking. Then, at the last moment almost, the troubles began.

Reports from the Fifth Sea Lord on 8 March (he had gone to Paris to make the final arrangements) and the Naval Attaché on 9 March revealed that Gamelin had developed cold feet. It tran-

[62] Pound at the 6 Mar. War Cabinet, WM 61 (40), CAB 65/12.

spired that what the French now feared was retaliatory German air attacks on the French aircraft factories, particularly at that time, when there was congestion in them. They envisaged a delay of as much as two months. An upset First Lord worked feverishly to re-convert the French. He hustled over to Paris on the 11th. On his return he wrote to Gamelin (16 March):

My colleagues in the War Cabinet are greatly concerned at the enforced delay in this operation. It appears timely, first, because the condition of the River and its tributaries is more favourable than it will be when the snow melts in the Alps later in the year. In fact it will never be so good again until the late summer. Secondly, by all accounts the traffic on the Rhine is now exceptionally heavy, and the strain produced on the German railways would be proportionately increased. Thirdly, after the fiasco in Scandinavia and of the sinister lull now prevailing, the effect of our appear-ing bankrupt in all forms of positive or offensive action may be bad upon the neutrals, and give encouragement to the movements for a patched up peace, which gather around the mission of Mr. Sumner Welles [the Ameri-can Undersecretary of State]. For all these reasons, and others with which I do not burden you, we deplore the delay. . . .

The enemy might naturally reply by an attack on British or French inland waterways. We recognise that this affects France far more than Great Britain on account of geography. However if the Germans have not already prepared contact mines of the kind we propose to use, four or five months would have to elapse before they could retaliate in that way. They might of course drop magnetic mines in British and French waterways; but we should have no difficulty in exploding these by the various anti-magnetic devices now coming forward in a broadening stream. . . .

If the Germans should retaliate as is feared by attacking French Air factories, they would thereby open a new chapter, and expose themselves to our attacks on the many military targets in Germany which have been carefully studied. This they have not shown any desire to do, and we do not see how the reasons which have hitherto restrained them would be .altered by the adoption of R.M.

But Churchill was willing to postpone the operation until 15 April to meet Gamelin's argument that it would be advantageous to have the RAF part of the operation combined with the naval. (The RAF would have 10,000 mines of their patterns by that date.) He was also ready to accede to the French desire that there be no public declaration; instead, at the moment of launching the mines, they would secretly warn the Dutch and Belgian governments to recall their barges. On 22 March he wrote to the new French Premier, Reynaud, enclosing a copy of the letter to Gamelin and begging him to give 'Royal Marine' his 'immediate sympathetic considera-tion'.

Chamberlain's personal and powerful promotion of the scheme

at a Supreme War Council meeting in London on 28 March—he assured the French that retaliatory attacks were not likely—led to an agreement to begin 'Royal Marine' on 4 April, with fluvial mines launched in the Rhine from land, and on 15 April, with aerial mines to be dropped on the German canals. This decision was subject to concurrence by the French War Committee (similar to the British War Cabinet). The rejoicing at the Admiralty was short-lived. On 1 April the news reached London that the War Committee wished a three-month postponement, in order, through a policy of dispersion, to render French munitions and aircraft factories less vulnerable to air reprisals. Chamberlain sent Churchill to Paris to try to win over the former Prime Minister and now Minister of War and Defence, Daladier, 'who was evidently the stumbling-block'. Churchill met him and Reynaud on 4–5 April. He was unable to budge Daladier, who insisted that they needed three months in order to take the necessary security measures. Churchill telephoned this information to the War Cabinet meeting on the 5th, adding that it would be 'a very great mistake' to put further pressure on their Allies.[63] Four days later the German invasion of Norway prompted him to make a fresh attempt to secure a French reconsideration of their veto 'in the light of events' through an urgent Foreign Office telegram to Reynaud over his signature. Again there was no moving the French.

The French did at last bestir themselves with the German invasion of the Low Countries on 10 May. Between 10 and 31 May, 2,466 mines were laid in the Rhine, 400-odd in the Moselle (10–17 May), and some 368 in the Meuse (19–28 May). 'Evidence that the Operation has been successful is chiefly circumstantial', an Admiralty official reported on 10 June. 'As regards the Rhine, on 15th May the French reported that from photographs it was apparent that extensive damage had been done to the Karlsruhe Barrage [74 vessels of all sorts spanning the river, to protect against mines sent down from the upper Rhine]. . . . There were [according to an RAF reconnaissance on 4 June] only some 8 barges moving on the whole of the 100 miles between Karlsruhe and Mainz: below Mainz there was normal barge traffic. . . . There is still a considerable number of the mines which have not yet been used . . .' This fairly auspicious start came late in the day and was not followed up, due to the French collapse in June. It is impossible to say how much havoc this ingenious scheme would have raised with the German transport system; but one can sympathize with Churchill's postwar lament, 'Good, decent,

[63] WM 82 (40), CAB 65/6.

civilized people, it appeared, must never themselves strike till after they have been struck dead'.[64]

*   *   *

Pound, the supreme centralizer, kept a tight grip on operations which Churchill was not disposed to challenge. Sensitive to the criticism at the time of the Dardanelles in 1915, and for years afterwards, that he had interfered unduly in the naval strategy and operations, Churchill leaned over backwards now, as First Lord a second time, not to lay down the law upon strategy or operational matters to the sailors. The only exceptions were his personal intervention in the *Altmark* episode and *possibly* in one or two instances during the Norwegian campaign. In the former case political considerations were involved. Churchill's intense interest in, and the usual extent of his influence on, purely naval strategy and operations is best illustrated by the action off the River Plate.

Any German raider or blockade-runner reported to Churchill brought him to his map room, which had been the library in Admiralty House, overlooking the Horse Guards Parade. There he would work out what force and dispositions were needed to bring about the destruction or capture of the enemy ship.

He would [writes the then Naval Assistant to the First Sea Lord] often suggest the type and names of ships which should be employed, regardless of their immediate availability, and it was interesting to watch Dudley Pound on these occasions. The First Sea Lord normally would appear to agree with what Winston proposed: he would never argue that such proposals were impracticable or that less force would be adequate. After leaving the map room, Pound would work out with the Naval Staff what could be done and then signal the necessary operation orders. He was always ready to face afterwards any complaint of Winston's that changes had been made. Pound was always loyal to Winston but could be firm when he did not agree with any particular suggestion.[65]

[64] Churchill, *The Gathering Storm*, p. 454.
[65] Admiral Sir Guy Grantham's memorandum of 19 Aug. 1966 for the author. More specifically, Churchill had the right to be kept informed on operations. It is true that he was frequently in the Duty Captain's office throughout his time as First Lord, rarely hesitating to express his opinions. This he had a right and a duty to, as well as the right to suggest possible operations in pursuance of government policies, and, if it came to it, of imposing a veto. All this was implicit in his appointment as First Lord; but, as I have said earlier, a wise First Lord, which Churchill was, usually accepted, after proper examination, the advice of his Naval Staff. *There is no hard evidence that as First Lord he overrode or attempted to override Pound on operational decisions.*
Apropos (remotely) of Churchill and his keeping *au fait* with strategy, this charming story begs to be mentioned. Rear-Admiral Davies, Assistant Chief of the Naval

Churchill took a keen interest in the entire operation against the 'pocket battleship' *Graf Spee*. Eight hunting groups, British and French, composed of battle cruisers, aircraft carriers, and cruisers, scoured the Atlantic for the surface raider from mid-October 1939. Damaged by three British cruisers in an action off the River Plate on 13 December, the *Graf Spee* sought refuge in Montevideo harbour and eventually scuttled herself outside the harbour. Throughout the 13th Churchill hardly left the First Lord's map room. It was a centre of action, with the First Lord, First Sea Lord, and Operations Division chiefs all sitting round the table watching the charts being plotted. Churchill was in terrific form. Here was the first prospect of a victory at sea after many disasters. We have a picture of him bursting with strategic ideas which had to be deflected by Pound.

The earliest information which reached the Admiralty, and particularly when the *Graf Spee* was approaching Montevideo [during the 13th], was in harbour for repairs and sailed to her final end [she blew herself up outside the harbour on the 17th], came from American broadcasting sources. It must be remembered that Commodore Henry Harwood's reports were enciphered and were relayed through W/T stations in the Falkland Islands, Sierre Leone, Gibraltar and Whitehall W/T. They then had to be deciphered and all this took six hours and more. On the strength of the U.S. reports, Winston was most anxious to send telegrams to Harwood about the dispositions of the three cruisers off the River Plate, and various other instructions. Pound insisted that Harwood should be allowed to deploy his ships as the situation demanded, and that information from the Admiralty should be confined to the reinforcements being sent, oil tankers, repair facilities, etc. He pointed out that it would be particularly dangerous to initiate any action on the strength of American radio broadcasts, which were concerned with what could be seen from landward only.[66]

Air Service (1942–3), was horrified one morning by the tremendous pile of signals dumped on his desk. 'Good heavens! Have I got to read all those?' The reply of the senior messenger attached to the office, a naval pensioner named York, was: 'I got to bring 'em to you. Whether you reads 'em or not is up to you. That reminds me of Mr. Churchill early in the war when 'e was First Lord. I was First Lord's messenger and one day I brings 'im a lot of signals, same as I 'ave you. 'E looks up and 'e sez, "Take 'em away, York," 'e sez. "I don't want no more signals today," 'e sez. Well o'course I didn't bring 'im no more signals; and d'ye know, sir, the war went on just the same.' Vice-Admiral Richard Bell Davies, *Sailor in the Air* (London, 1967), p. 238.

[66] Admiral Grantham's memorandum of 19 Aug. 1966. Grantham spent many hours in the First Lord's map room during the entire operation. Admiral Godfrey writes of a scene in the OIC (Operational Intelligence Centre) on the night following the Battle of the Plate: 'The First Lord clad in his strange night garment and wondering what would happen next, was itching to emit a series of instructions to Bobby Harwood, and would have done so but for the presence of Admiral Pound who, in his quiet way, was able to convince him that Harwood knew what he was about.' Godfrey, *Naval Memoirs*, v, Pt. 1, p. 27. See also Godfrey to Donald McLachlan, 2 Dec. 1966, Godfrey MSS.

Nobody could have been more excited than Churchill when the news of the scuttling came through. He at once sent personal messages to the ships involved in the action, and to Pound: 'Let me congratulate you, and the Naval Staff on this fine and timely success, which may go far.' He then proceeded to suggest to the First Sea Lord how the ships might be redisposed.[67]

The German tanker *Altmark*, supply ship to the *Graf Spee*, had got away. On board were 299 men from captured British crews who had been in the *Graf Spee*. The *Altmark* hid in the south Atlantic, then, on 14 February 1940, took refuge in Jössing Fiord on the south-west coast of Norway, where two British destroyers under an unknown Captain, Philip Vian (HMS *Cossack*), kept watch on her. Churchill intervened decisively (16 February). The story is graphically told by the Duty Captain in the War Room:

At 5 o'clock Winston, still First Lord, came down to the War Room—then a dingy hole in the old Admiralty basement—accompanied by his P.P.S. [Seal] and by Tom Phillips, then V.C.N.S.

He called for the Duty Signal Officer and dictated a signal of precise instructions to Vian. 'Get that cyphered up,' he said, 'and be quick about it. I've told the Secretary of State that those orders are going at a quarter to six unless we hear to the contrary.'

Then he walked up and down, flapping his coat tails and chewing his cigar. At 5.20 he said to me (I was Duty Captain), 'I can't wait. Get me Lord Halifax.'

I got him the Foreign Secretary in a few seconds and he sat down with the telephone in the little green armchair which used to stand alongside our desk. He talked to Halifax for about a minute. We didn't hear what Halifax said to *him*, of course, but we heard what he said to Halifax and that was an education. Then he called for the Duty Signal Officer again and dictated one more sentence to add to the signal. I forget the exact wording, and I haven't had time to unearth the signal today, but roughly it was this: 'and tell the Norwegians that submission to force majeure is no derogation of their sovereignty.'

'Now get that off at once,' he said, and lounged off upstairs. At the door he turned, and said to all of us, 'That was *big* of Halifax.' The Signal was made a few minutes later, and within an hour Vian went in and did his stuff.

It was a perfect example of the much maligned British Government system working at its best in an urgent war crisis. The *Altmark* story was the foundation of Vian's fortunes, and rightly so, but I have always thought of it as one of the unknown personal triumphs of the man who became Prime Minister three months later.[68]

[67] Churchill to Pound, 17 Dec. 1939, ADM 205/2. The second minute to Pound, also of 17 December, is in Churchill, *The Gathering Storm*, p. 416.

[68] 'Winston and the Altmark', A. V. Alexander (Lord Alexander of Hillsborough) MSS., 5/4/1 (Churchill College).

What had happened was that, with Halifax's concurrence, but without troubling even to inform Admiral Forbes, under whom Vian was operating, Churchill had the Admiralty signal Vian to board the *Altmark* and free the prisoners, if the Norwegians refused to convoy her to Bergen with a joint escort. 'I did not often act so directly', he afterwards confessed. Vian took the *Cossack* into the fiord that evening and carried out his orders after a short sharp fight and without interference from the Norwegian gunboats in the area. It was a minor operation of no importance except for its considerable moral effects.

With all his display of energy and all his imagination, Churchill at times carried his offensive ideas too far. Impatient of what one might call the progressive approach to an operation, he had a desire for short cuts. This habit of mind was of inestimable value in many circumstances, but not always; it could be dangerous. The best example of this trait while he was at the Admiralty was the notorious 'Operation Catherine', which Churchill calls 'the sovereign plan if it were possible' in the period of the 'Twilight War'. This operation also illustrates what Generab Jacob has called 'the fury of his concentration. When his mind was occupied with a particular problem, however detailed, it focused upon it relentlessly. Nobody could turn him aside.'[69] There can be no doubt that a disproportionate amount of time was taken in the early months of the war countering the First Lord's cherished plans for a Baltic operation that, most senior naval officers of the time were agreed, could only have ended in catastrophe. As indicated, Churchill could be exasperatingly obstinate and perverse over his ideas. The Baltic, and increasingly the Norwegian facet, became almost an obsession with him.

Churchill named the plan 'after Catherine the Great, because Russia lay in the background of my thought'.[70] It surfaced on 6 September, when the new First Lord asked for a Staff appreciation on forcing a passage into the Baltic with naval forces. In its elaborated form on 12 September the plan called for sending into the Baltic a self-supporting force of two or three 'Royal Sovereign' battleships, an aircraft carrier, five cruisers, two destroyer flotillas, a detachment of submarines, and fleet auxiliaries, including supply ships: 'turtlebacked blistered tankers' carrying a three-months' oil supply for the squadron. The battleships would be strengthened to

[69] Lieutenant-General Sir Ian Jacob, 'Churchill as a War Leader', in *Churchill by His Contemporaries. An Observer Appreciation* (London, 1965), pp. 75–6.

[70] Except where otherwise noted, my account of 'Catherine' is based on the documents in ADM 205/4 and ADM 199/1928.

withstand torpedoes by anti-torpedo bulges, and air attack, by stronger armoured decks and a heavier AA armament. (Two of the four 15-inch turrets would be removed to provide 2,000 tons of deadweight needed for the extra armour and armament.) A dozen specially prepared vessels fitted as mine-bumpers were to precede the battleships during their passage into the Baltic.

For Churchill this was 'the supreme naval offensive open to the Royal Navy'. It would, he expected, isolate Germany from Scandinavia, thereby cutting off her supplies of iron ore (vital to her), food, and other trade; the establishment of command in the Baltic might bring the Scandinavian states in on the Allied side, so providing the British with a convenient base; and it just might induce Russia to forsake her neutrality. Other strategic objectives were added as time went on. To the ore-trade and Scandinavian neutrals arguments Lord Cork (see below) added (28 October) the strong possibility that the operation would bring on a clash with the German Fleet. 'This might of course mean the defeat of the British force, but the successful fleet would be in no condition for further service after such a result had been achieved. [In narrow waters submarines and mines would inflict heavy damage.] It would be the disablement of the whole German fleet: to us, the destruction of merely a detachment.' And the operation 'would enormously hearten the Navy and the Nation ... Even if the operation was not completely successful, the very fact that such a feat of arms had been attempted would surely have the same results.' Churchill was delighted: 'It is not possible to express the objects more forcefully.'

'Catherine' was not at first regarded as a wildcat project by the Naval Staff. The Plans Division declared (12 September) that the operation was feasible only if Japan and Italy remained neutral, and that the threat of air attack appeared to render it impracticable; but 'apart from air attack, the possibilities of the operation justified detailed planning'. The First Sea Lord, too, did not oppose 'Catherine' outright, apparently viewing the passage into the Baltic as a practicable military operation. But the conditions that he laid down as required for success (20 September) were formidable: that Russia should not join Germany and that Swedish '*active* co-operation' should be forthcoming 'within a measurable time of our arrival in the Baltic', since the expeditionary fleet would need oil and the use of a base and repair facilities. Pound added the condition that they had to be able to win the war against any probable combination of powers without the assistance of the 'Catherine Fleet', also that the plan must deal with the air menace. Churchill agreed (20 September). At present the plan was for exploration only. 'But the search for a naval offensive must be incessant.'

The next day Admiral of the Fleet the Earl of Cork and Orrery was appointed C-in-C designate to plan the operation. He was given a small staff soon afterwards. The offensive-mindedness of Cork, who was grand as both man and seaman, appealed to Churchill, whose nominee he was. Cork's preliminary appreciation (26 September) rated the operation as perfectly feasible but hazardous because of the losses to be expected in the passage. His plans called for a larger force than in Churchill's project: *three* destroyer flotillas, *two* carriers, *nine* cruisers, etc. It was taken for granted that a Swedish base in the Gulf of Bothnia would be available: Gävle, until ice conditions permitted the use of Harnösand, farther to the north, with Lulea as a northern anchorage. A date was soon fixed: the naval force would assemble in the second week of January, the 'working up' of individual ships would then commence: intensive gunnery practice, rehearsal of the passage of the Sound, etc., and the force would set off on 15 February. The date proved unrealistic. The bows of the destroyers and other ships of the special squadron needed strengthening against the Baltic ice, the battleships had to be prepared, and so forth, all very time-consuming and having to compete for the resources required for the large construction programme. Besides, many of the ships earmarked for 'Catherine' could not be spared from their current employment. The battleships, for instance, were required as escorts to ocean convoys, should any powerful enemy surface raiders break loose. On 22 November Churchill postponed 'Catherine' until 30 April, with the squadron to assemble on 31 March for the necessary working up together.

The air factor weighed heavily. There was little doubt at the Admiralty that the battleships could be taken into the Baltic; but Churchill generally appeared quite oblivious to the heavy air threat that could be expected from nearby land bases. In Sir Eric Seal's view, 'Operation "Catherine" appealed to the cavalryman in him; he wanted to disregard the danger of air attack as the famous "Light Brigade" had disregarded the Russian artillery at Balaclava.' The RAF could not provide fighter cover against Luftwaffe bombers, yet Churchill assumed that the AA guns of the Fleet alone could cope with bombing (dive-bombing) attack. The poor results achieved by both the RAF and the Luftwaffe in their attacks on warships helped to conceal from him the real possibilities of air attack. 'We have not been at all impressed with the accuracy of the German air bombing of our warships', he confided to President Roosevelt on 16 October. 'They seem to have no effective bomb sights.' He later confessed: 'In common with prevailing Admiralty belief before the war, I did not sufficiently measure the danger to, or the consequent deterrent upon, British warships from air attack.'[71] He admits that 'Catherine' was 'vetoed by the growing realisation of the air power'.[72] Moreover, he does not seem to have realized that the German Army held the gate of the Baltic in its hand. It could have quickly invaded southern Denmark and supported the minefields in the Kogrund Channel and the Belts by artillery fire, just as the Turks had done in the Dardanelles in 1915.

The modest measure of support for 'Catherine' in the Naval Staff initially had pretty well evaporated by December. 'The main objection of the Naval Staff to the operation', according to an officer in the Plans Division who joined Cork's staff, 'was the large slice of the British fleet which would be locked up in the Baltic. It would have stretched us too far elsewhere. An unanswerable argument unless the entry of Norway, Sweden and possibly Russia in the war would have brought it to an end.'[73] Churchill writes: 'I had strong support in all this from the Deputy Chief of Staff, Admiral Tom Phillips . . . and from Admiral Fraser, the Controller and Third Sea Lord.'[74] This claims too much. Fraser joined the opposition when he was told to convert several valuable 17,000-ton 'Glen'-class ships to carry fuel and ammunition. He was certain that if he did this, he would have to reconvert them again later.[75] As regards Phillips's alleged support, Admiral Godfrey comments tersely: 'Nonsense', and goes on to assert: 'It is questionable if Pound was right to give lip service to a project in which he cannot have believed. He said . . . "Don't worry. It will never take place," but his acquiescence in its planning cannot but have given Churchill a feeling of ascendancy and was akin to appeasement.'[76]

This 'appeasement', if such it was, did not survive the year. On 3 December Pound, in a 'most secret' memorandum for the First

[71] Churchill, *The Gathering Storm*, p. 325. On the other hand, in his Christmas Day minute (see below) he wrote: '. . . the German Air Force would certainly establish advance operational air bases, on Finnish territory, and strike at us from there. This seems to be a very serious adverse factor to Catherine, which I in no wise underrate. I hope however that the U.P. weapon with the multiple-projector, may be a great help.'

[72] Churchill, *The Gathering Storm*, p. 458. On air power see further, below, pp. 166–7.

[73] Vice-Admiral Sir Gordon Hubback's letter to Major-General J. L. Moulton, 16 Nov. 1964; copy in the author's possession. The strong opposition to 'Catherine' of the able and self-confident Director of Plans, Captain V. H. Danckwerts, was, his successor believes, 'largely the reason for his going' at the beginning of March 1940. Admiral Sir Charles Daniel's letter to the author, 2 Oct. 1971.

[74] Churchill, *The Gathering Storm*, p. 365.

[75] Interview with Admiral of the Fleet Lord Fraser, 13 Oct. 1967, McLachlan MSS.

[76] Godfrey, *Naval Memoirs*, vii, Pt. 2, pp. 223–5.

Lord, reiterated his serious reservations about 'Catherine'. It will be instructive if we contrast his principal points and Churchill's rejoinder of 11 December. They bring out fundamental differences in attitudes towards strategy that transcended 'Catherine'.

[Pound] 1. It has been suggested that the attitude of Sweden would be the determining factor as regards the possibility of carrying out Operation 'C'. It appears to me, however, that it is the attitude of Russia and not of Sweden which is the determining factor. Whilst Russia is nominally working in with Germany there appears to be no possibility whatever that Russia would welcome an intrusion in the Baltic of the British Fleet.

[Churchill] No opinion can be formed on this at present. It may be that we may find ourselves at war with Russia, and Allies of Sweden, Norway, Finland, and Italy. In this case the Baltic would assume capital importance. Bases would be forthcoming, and Air protection from England might be available. Action might become urgent, and it would be grievous if the need and opportunity came and found us without the necessary preparation. It is more likely however that the situation will remain obscure.

[Pound] 4. According to present arrangements, the working-up period commences on the 31st March and hence all arrangements should be completed by then, and on this basis you requested that a programme should be drawn up. No programme has been drawn up as it is quite impossible to do so under existing conditions when every available ship of whatever class is required with the Fleet.

[Churchill] Owing to our having been thrown so completely on the defensive, and the initiative having passed to the enemy, we have suffered heavy disablements in ships, and are forced to disperse our strength. The possible presence of even only one 10,000-ton armoured ship in the Atlantic is sufficient to draw five or six of our largest capital units to Halifax for convoy duty. The strain on the Fleet is very severe, and we have both agreed how necessary it is to give them a rest. We have, for the time being, evacuated the North Sea. Our harbours are insulted and mined with impunity, requiring terrific efforts merely to keep the traffic moving. While these conditions oppress us, I recognise the difficulty of finding opportunity to fit vessels for Catherine, but this should be reviewed at leisure, and certainly before the end of the year.

[Pound] 5. There are signs that the continual cruising in heavy weather is causing defects to develop in all classes of ships, and as we have many months of winter weather yet to get through it is only reasonable to suppose that these defects will increase, thus throwing a lot of additional work on the dockyards and private firms.

[Churchill] I agree, and have indeed been surprised to see how well our ships have so far stood up to the tremendous cruising demands made upon them. This is very much better than last time.

[Pound] 6. I would suggest, therefore, that we face up to realities and make no attempt at the present time to achieve the impossible by endeavouring to work to any date.

[Pound] 10. It is also questionable whether Lord Cork's Committee should not be disbanded for the time being as a considerable number of the officers now employed on the Committee are urgently required for other duties.

[Churchill] I could not agree to the disbandment of Lord Cork's Committee. On the contrary, I would suggest to you that its functions might be extended. I went through the offensive plans of the Plans Division with Captain Edelsten [the Deputy Director], and I must say I was not greatly impressed with the force, ingenuity and will-power behind them. I am by no means satisfied that the offensive side receives the full effort which it requires. . . . It is very difficult for you and me and also for the D.C.N.S. charged with the hour-to-hour weight of business, to give the life and thought to overcoming the difficulties of offensive plans, until the whole ground has been thoroughly explored beforehand by others. I therefore propose to you that Lord Cork, assisted by his group of officers, should go through all the offensive ideas of our Plans Division. . . .

[Pound] 12. The time when [the committee could be reassembled] . . . will not only depend on the attitude of Russia but also on the general situation at sea. Until the trade route has been cleared of raiders, and the U-boat menace, whether from torpedoes or mines, has been destroyed, it will be quite impossible to spare the force which will be required for 'C.' This question alone, apart from the attitude of Russia, will determine the date on which it is possible to carry out the operation, and is one which will give us adequate warning.

[Churchill] Our dominant strategy must be shaped by events. The entry of the Baltic for instance, would soon bring measureless relief. If we allow ourselves indefinitely to be confined to an absolute defensive by far weaker forces, we shall simply be worried and worn down while making huge demands upon the national resources. I could never become responsible for a naval strategy which excluded the offensive principle, and relegated us to the keeping open the lines of communication and maintaining the blockade. Presently, we may find the U-boats in the outer sea, and what is to happen then?

The position of the Board of Admiralty at the end of December was, as Churchill notified Cork on the 29th, that 'the study of the project is to continue, and that all preparations are to be pressed forward, subject to the inevitable demands of the naval war from day to day; but that neither this study nor these preparations in any way commit the Admiralty or H.M.G. to authorise action. The position remains, as I said, "the gun is to be loaded for firing." This, and no more.' Pound weighed in with a blunt minute to Churchill on the 31st. ' "Catherine" is a great gamble, even if there were adequate fighter protection for the Fleet, and if Russia were on our side and we had the use of Russian bases. As neither of these conditions will be present, I consider that the sending of a Fleet of surface ships into the Baltic is courting disaster.' All he was prepared to sanction . was, with special reference to the Swedish ore problem (on which more below), the dispatch of a strong submarine force into the

Baltic immediately the Germans had landed in, or were at war with, Sweden.

The advantage of sending submarines as opposed to surface ships is that we are not dependent on either Russian assistance or Air co-operation. If we do establish a force at Lulea our submarines should not only be able to interrupt the lines of communication between Germany and the South of Sweden, but we should also be able to prevent German forces being landed anywhere on the East Coast of Sweden. On the other hand if we had not landed forces at Narvik, our submarines should be able to ensure that we had time to do so before the Germans had time to reach Lulea by land from the South of Sweden. It is possible that we might lose all our submarines, but this would not prevent us from waging the war with full intensity inside the Baltic, nor would it jeopardise our general Naval position in the world.

Churchill replied (1 January): 'I remain very deeply impressed with the risks and dangers of "Catherine". It must be remembered however that if a British Fleet were placed in the Baltic, it would act as a magnet to draw in German vessels from the outer seas and that very great relief would come thereby.' He agreed that sending in a strong submarine force was 'a much less serious, but at the same time quite hopeful, operation', and suggested that it be studied.

On 10 January Pound sent a paper to the First Lord calculated to make his flesh creep. It described the probable 'menaces' the fleet would encounter in forcing an entry into the Baltic: severe air attack before reaching the Great Belt, then the hazards of minefields and possibly U-boats, followed by the fire of powerful shore batteries. The result would be 'a severe buffeting' of the fleet and losses. 'This battered and mauled force' operating without a secure base would have to proceed to a Swedish anchorage lacking in net defences and fighter protection, where it would face continual air and submarine attack, and be exposed to mines when at sea. Most importantly: 'The loss of such a large proportion of our Fleet would be the surest inducement to either Italy or Japan to come in against us.' Pound's conclusion, which he presented 'most strongly', was that all special preparations for 'Catherine' should be discontinued, apart from planning. Again he stated the two essential conditions that must be fulfilled to make the operation a reasonable gamble at a future date: that they enter the Baltic at Russia's invitation and have the use of her bases; and that they have sufficient naval force outside the Baltic to win the war even if the force inside the Baltic were annihilated. For the present the desired object could largely be achieved by a strong force of submarines, which could operate in the Gulf of Bothnia and the southern part of the Baltic. He concluded: 'Our first object must be to win *this* war, but it is important that we should if possible end the war with our sea supremacy un-challenged. Even if we lost the whole of the submarines we sent into the Baltic it would not really matter, whilst if we lost a consider-able part of our surface fleet the story would be a very different one.'

Churchill fought back. They would, he believed, soon master the U-boats and the surface raiders and consequently have a super-fluity of force for the Baltic. As for Russia, she might veer towards the Allied side at any moment. These arguments could not sway a hard-headed First Sea Lord. Finally, when it was clear from a Cork statement on 10 January that little progress had been made in preparations during the preceding three and a half months, Churchill gracefully accepted the inevitable. He 'reluctantly' agreed with Pound on the 15th that 'Catherine' would not be practicable that year but that preparations for the operation were to be kept under continuous review by a reduced committee. The German invasion of Denmark and Norway on 9 April wrote *Finis* to Churchill's hopes, at least for some time to come. The conception may have been brilliant, as Admiral Hubback believed, and had it been practicable and successful, the whole future of the war might well have changed. The risks, however, were enormous, since the conditions for success were utterly lacking.

The cost of 'Catherine' in wasted hours had been prodigious. But, as it happens, the £12,000,000 invested in equipping special craft for the operation was not wasted. Just as Fisher's abortive Baltic scheme in the First War had produced the self-propelled lighters that had such a useful role at the Dardanelles, so the four fast Glen Line cargo ships converted to carry 5,000 tons of fuel and 2,000 tons of ammunition eventually found a home in the Mediter-ranean. The C-in-C, Mediterranean, put them to excellent use when the supplying of Malta was proving so difficult (1941–2). One officer remembers Churchill, by then Prime Minister, 'muttering discontentedly, "If only you'd had the 'R' class battleships re-armoured when I suggested it, how useful they would be now".' He had in mind the 'need' at this time of bombarding Italian ports, in particular Tripoli. But he got a great deal of satisfaction from the fact that the converted merchantmen were proving their worth in running supplies to Malta.[77]

* * *

Churchill had an alternative to 'Catherine' for a Baltic strategy

[77] Rear-Admiral A. D. Nicholl's letter to the author, 31 May 1967. And see Churchill, *The Gathering Storm*, p. 367. The tremendous congestion in the yards had posed too great difficulties in carrying out Churchill's plan of giving the 'Royal Sovereigns' super-blisters and special deck protection, and the work was never done.

that would win the war. Normally, Germany imported about 20 million tons of iron ore annually, about half of which came from Sweden and half from the French Lorraine fields. With the latter source shut off, German war industry was vitally dependent on supplies of Swedish ore. The great bulk of it came from the mine-fields at Gällivare in the north, shipped in the summer from the Swedish port of Lulea at the head of the Gulf of Bothnia, and in the winter (mid-December to mid-April), with Lulea ice-bound, shipped by rail to Narvik, in the north of Norway, which was open. (Ore of lower quality from the southern fields was shipped out of Oxelö-sund, the main Swedish ice-free port in the Baltic, during the winter.) The Narvik ore ships proceeded to German North Sea ports down the west coast of Norway, using territorial waters, within the chain of outlying islands (the 'Leads'), until inside the Skagerrak. It was reminiscent of the situation in the First War, when the U-boats circumvented the North Sea Barrage by using these sheltered waters. It was not until towards the end of the war that the Allies had been able to persuade the Norwegian Government to mine their territorial waters.

From the beginning Churchill and the Naval Staff were much exercised over the German use, or misuse, of this neutral corridor. If action to cut this traffic were not taken by April, when the ice in the Gulf of Bothnia would melt, Germany would have ample sup-plies for some time to come. At least this was the general belief at the Admiralty. It must be stressed that the many Scandinavian schemes Churchill proposed or supported while First Lord had a common great objective—depriving Germany of the bulk of her Swedish ore imports, and thereby providing 'a great chance of shortening the war and possibly saving immeasurable bloodshed on the Western Front'. As early as 19 September he raised the matter in the War Cabinet, urging the laying of minefields at strategic points in Norwegian territorial waters to force the German ore ships out to open waters, where their cargoes could legitimately be con-fiscated as contraband or the ships captured as enemy prizes. Although Churchill pressed his point 'by every means and on all occasions', he was unable to overcome the reluctance of his col-leagues to infringe Scandinavian neutrality in the face of Foreign Office arguments against this course and continuing opposition to the mining proposal. The Russian invasion of Finland on 30 Nov-ember opened up fresh possibilities. Churchill was in sympathy with a current of opinion in the Government that favoured a demand upon Norway and Sweden for the free passage of men and supplies to aid the Finns in their heroic struggle. He saw a chance to work it in with the larger goal of depriving the Germans of Swedish ore. 'If Narvik was to become a kind of Allied base to supply the Finns, it would certainly be easy to prevent the German ships loading ore at the port and sailing safely down the Leads to Germany.'[78]

He stated 'the case in its final form as I made it after prolonged reflection and debate' in a paper of 16 December which called for mining the Leads, bottling up Lulea, as through the laying of mines off the port by submarines, and if Germany 'fired back', occupying Narvik and Bergen and closing them completely to Germany. He concluded with an appeal to a higher law to justify any breach of international law. 'Small nations must not tie our hands when we are fighting for their rights and freedom.'[79] The idea of minelayers closing Lulea was absurd. Not only was the entrance to the Baltic heavily mined and patrolled, but a base and supplies of mines would have been necessary in the Baltic. The Germans could have easily maintained swept channels through these small minefields if they were laid. On 20 December Churchill advocated that they 'should not nibble at the problem, but go wholeheartedly for stopping Germany's supplies' by dispatching an expedition to Sweden to hold the Gällivare mines.[80] What he appears to have had in mind was the occupation of Narvik, which would not only cut the Narvik ore traffic, but would permit the dispatch of troops over the iron-ore railway across northern Norway into Sweden—both to succour the Finns and to dominate the Gällivare ore fields and prevent their acquisition by Germany. At the War Cabinet of 22 December Churchill shifted his position somewhat. He now favoured sending destroyers in to stop the Narvik ore traffic, and that they be prepared to occupy the Gällivare ore fields—presumably from Narvik, if the Germans attempted to land a force at Lulea to acquire them. The War Cabinet would only invite the Chiefs of Staff to give further consideration to all the military implications of a policy which aimed at bringing a halt to the ore traffic.[81]

In a Christmas Day minute to the First Sea Lord Churchill raised the question of what the Navy could do in this contingency: if they occupied the Gällivare iron fields with a military force and it was

[78] Churchill, *The Gathering Storm*, p. 430.

[79] 'Norway–Iron-Ore Traffic. Note by the First Lord of the Admiralty', ibid., pp. 430–3.

[80] At the Military Co-ordination Committee, 20 Dec., MC (39) 10th meeting, CAB 83/1. This Committee consisted of Admiral of the Fleet Lord Chatfield (Minister for the Co-ordination of Defence) as Chairman, the three Service ministers, and the Minister of Supply, with the three Chiefs of Staff in attendance. Lieutenant-General Sir Henry Pownall, Chief of the General Staff of the Expeditionary Force, sarcastically termed the Military Co-ordination Committee 'the Crazy Gang'.

[81] WM 122 (39), CAB 65/4.

attacked by a large German army, as it certainly would be as soon
as the ice melted and Lulea was open for its disembarkation. Pound's
reply, the same day, a restatement of the anti-'Catherine' case, gave
Churchill little comfort.

> . . . the only manner in which Naval action could ensure against any
> reinforcements reaching the Head of the Gulf of Bothnia by sea would be
> to send into the Baltic a sufficient force to beat or contain the German Fleet.
> Owing to the great hazards to which it would be subjected during its pas-
> sage into the Baltic, and by submarines, mines and aircraft after its arrival,
> we must be prepared to write off this force and be quite certain that we
> cannot lose the war at sea with the reduced forces we should have outside
> the Baltic.

The difficulty, he pointed out, was that they could not spare the
necessary force. The U-boat menace, the need for destroyers to
escort the troop and supply ships after an expeditionary force had
been landed at Narvik, and the possibility of that landing bringing
Russia into the war and thereby intensifying the war against British
trade, would prevent the detachment of any flotillas to the Baltic;
cruisers could not be spared from the Northern Patrol; and the dispatch of capital ships would largely depend on Russia's attitude and
whether a force would be needed in the eastern Mediterranean.
'I am unable to visualise therefore, a situation in 1940 in which we
could spare the necessary forces to enter the Baltic, unless we were
assured of Russian co-operation and could enter the Baltic at the
invitation of that country.'[82]

Possibly influenced by Pound's unwillingness to commit the Navy
to the support of a Gällivare operation, at the War Cabinet on
27 December Churchill denied that he favoured landing troops in
Narvik or sending an expedition to the ore fields 'at the present
stage'. He was merely proposing that, after notification to the
Scandinavian governments, they send in a destroyer force to intercept the ore traffic in Norwegian territorial waters. The Admiralty
only awaited War Cabinet authorization.[83] This scheme met head
on with one sponsored by the Chiefs of Staff, who on 31 December
responded to the War Cabinet directive of 22 December. The only
way to stop the export from the northern minefields was through
the dispatch of an expedition in the early spring via Narvik to the

[82] Churchill, 'A Note on the War in 1940', and Pound's minute, ADM 199/1929.
An undated draft minute to Pound may refer to the latter's Christmas Day minute:
'. . . although the course of the sea war has been favourable to us we seem less bold
than at the beginning . . . [Pound's minute] showed that you do not foresee any
activities open to the Navy in 1940 beyond keeping open the lines of communication,
enforcing the blockade and laying a great many mines.' ADM 199/1928.
[83] WM 123 (39), CAB 65/4.

ore fields. The gains justified the risks, since the seizure of the Gäl-livare mines could be decisive.[84] At the War Cabinets on 2 and 3 January 1940, which debated both plans, the Service Chiefs opposed the First Lord's 'half-cock scheme', the half-measure of naval action alone. This could, through antagonizing the Norwegians and pos-sibly the Swedes, lessen the chances of their co-operation in the larger project, as would the expected strong German reaction in the form of a demand for Norwegian or/and Swedish bases which might have to be accepted under duress. Churchill fought hard for his 'limited' operation. He did not expect a strong reaction from either the Scandinavians or the Germans, but if the latter invaded southern Norway, it would open the way to the Allied occupation of the northern ore fields by involving Norway in war with Ger-many. The War Cabinet was attracted to the First Lord's scheme and on 3 January authorized the Foreign Secretary, with French concurrence, to inform Norway that, having regard to German naval violation of Norway's territorial waters, British naval forces would 'at times enter and operate in Norwegian territorial waters'. Orders to enter these waters were to wait on the Norwegian reaction.[85]

The War Cabinet heard at its 10 January meeting that the Nor-wegian reaction had been 'bad' (actually, there had been a violent protest); the Swedish reaction, too, was unfavourable. Churchill was all for going ahead anyway.

The need for action was urgent. Every week the prize was melting . . . we had now been considering the proposal to stop the Narvik traffic for some six weeks, and so far we had taken no action. . . . The neutral countries could not be permitted to tie our hands when we were, in fact, fighting to maintain their liberties. . . . This stoppage of German ore supplies might result in shortening the war and saving an enormous number of casualties on the Western Front. . . . It might be true that we required the co-operation of Norway and Sweden if we were to send in our own forces to stop the ore going out from Lulea. But in his view the only way of obtaining this co-operation would be . . . to make them more frightened of us than they were of Germany.[86]

On the succeeding two days he pleaded for his scheme, introducing a larger consideration on the 12th: 'He was not impatient for action merely for action's sake, but ever since the beginning of the war we

---

[84] COS (39) 181, 'Military Implications of a Policy Aimed at Stopping the Export of Swedish Iron Ore to Germany', CAB 80/6.
[85] WM 1, 2 (40), CAB 65/11, Colonel R. Macleod and Denis Kelly (eds.), *The Iron-side Diaries, 1937–1940* (London, 1962), pp. 191–3. Ironside was the CIGS. The Naval Staff also was 'dead against the half measure policy'. Diary, 9 Jan. 1940, Litchfield MSS.   [86] WM 8 (40), CAB 65/11.

had let the initiative rest with Germany. We waited for her to develop each form of attack against us, and contented ourselves merely with devising means of meeting these attacks as they arose. If, however, we opened up a new theatre of operations in Scandinavia, we had a fine chance of forcing Germany into situations which she had not foreseen, and of seizing the initiative for ourselves.' The War Cabinet, to Churchill's disgust, decided to do nothing for the present. The violence of the Scandinavian protests to the naval plan had shaken them. There was also the uncertainty of the dominions' support (especially that of Australia) and the argument of the Chiefs of Staff that stopping the ore traffic in Norwegian territorial waters might endanger the success of the larger project. The War Cabinet would not approve the latter, but merely directed the Chiefs 'to consider the possibility of capturing the Gällivare orefields in the face of Norwegian and Swedish opposition', and what forces would be needed if the operation were practicable.[87]

The *Altmark* incident prompted Churchill to revert to his original mining proposal, but now linked to the larger project. He would take advantage of this fresh illustration of Norway's inability to guard its neutrality to lay a minefield in her territorial waters. His hope was that the minelaying would provoke Germany to reprisals against Norway which 'might provide the Allies with a favourable opening', viz. a pretext to seize Narvik. He would have them 'strike while the iron is hot!', that is, while indignation was high over the abuse of Norwegian neutrality. The War Cabinet would only authorize the First Lord 'to make all preparations, so that, if it were subsequently decided to lay a minefield in Norwegian territorial waters, there would be no delay in carrying out the operation'.[88]

At about this time the Finnish aspect of the Scandinavian problem came to the fore, with the provision of assistance to Finland through Norway and Sweden being added to the original Narvik/Gällivare conception. The Service Chiefs' plan was to land an Anglo-French force in Narvik, which would swiftly secure the railway into Sweden and the Gällivare ore fields (if driven out, this force would first destroy the facilities at Lulea); part of the Narvik/Gällivare force would aid the Finns from northern Sweden; British forces would occupy the southern Norwegian ports of Stavanger, Bergen, and Trondheim, in order to secure Allied bases.[89] Churchill

[87] WM 10 (40), 12 Jan., CAB 65/11.

[88] WP 60 (40), Churchill, 'Stoppage of Traffic in Norwegian Territorial Waters', 18 Feb., CAB 66/5, WM 46 (40), 19 Feb., CAB 65/11.

[89] COS (40) 234 (S), 'The Employment of Allied Land Forces in Scandinavia and Finland', 14 Feb., CAB 80/104.

supported the plan, stressing the importance of putting troops into Finland quickly. The Finnish venture was only the 'pretext for getting a footing in Scandinavia in order to secure these [Gällivare] fields'. Even if they had to retire from Finland, 'they might after all secure possession of the Gällivare ore fields'.[90]

The Narvik expedition was about to sail when, on 12 March, the Finns signed an armistice with Russia. The Allied pretext for intervention was gone. Churchill urged (14 March) that, although shorn of the pretext of helping the Finns, they proceed with the Narvik/Gällivare facets of the operation. They should, no more than the Germans, hamper themselves with the need to find a moral justification for every action they took. But the War Cabinet in effect cancelled the operation.[91]

On the same day, Churchill, as resourceful as ever, proposed that one or two merchantmen of sufficient speed, strengthened in the bows and if possible equipped with a ram, 'carry merchandise and travel up the Leads looking for German ore ships or any other German merchant vessels, and then ram them by accident. This is only another development of the "Q" ship idea.' Vice-Admiral Gordon Campbell, of World War I Q-ship fame, and who was then looking after these decoy ships, submitted (30 March): 'Although it is quite practicable to fit a ship for ramming purposes, so many complications would arise if this proposal was proceeded with, that I cannot recommend it.'[92] The proposal was definitely turned down on 6 April, by which date there had been a startling development: the acceptance, finally, of Churchill's mining scheme!

It was on 28 March that the Supreme War Council decided that minefields should be laid in Norwegian territorial waters. On 1 April the War Cabinet set 5 April as the date for the start of 'Operation Wilfred', so-called, explains Churchill, because 'by itself it was so small and innocent', but tied in with the larger Narvik/Gällivare scheme. Should the expected strong German reaction to the minelaying materialize, namely, an invasion of Norway, 'Wilfred' would be backed by the landing of an Anglo-French force at Narvik. It was to seize the port and advance to the Swedish frontier over the railway, thus preparing the way for the seizure of the northern ore fields. Additionally, small Allied forces were to seize Stavanger (the

---

[90] WM 45 (40), 18 Feb., CAB 65/11.   [91] WM 68 (40), CAB 65/12.

[92] Churchill to the First Sea Lord and others, ADM 1/10795. On 18 March he put before the War Cabinet a Naval Staff scheme for mining the approaches to Lulea with carrier-based aircraft operating from off the Norwegian coast, and torpedoing the ships in port to block it. WM 71 (40), CAB 65/12. The Chiefs of Staff were cool; the scheme, by infringing Swedish neutrality, might antagonize them 'and remove all chances of getting to Gallivare'. COS (40) 64th meeting, 4 Apr., CAB 79/85.

operation to start on the 5th) and, as soon after as possible, Bergen
and Trondheim, to deny the enemy the use of these bases as well
as Narvik. The military operation ('R4') was similar to the one
rescinded on 14 March. It was expected that the landings would
be unopposed by the Norwegians. On 3 April the War Cabinet postponed the date for 'Wilfred' to 8 April, so that a final effort could
be made to persuade the French to agree to the linked 'Royal
Marine' operation. The delay was fatal, since, unknown to the
Allies, Hitler was planning to occupy Denmark and Norway early
on the 9th by a surprise *coup.* On the 5th the War Cabinet decided
to proceed with the mining as an independent operation. The minelaying forces sailed that day; the mines were laid in the morning
of the 8th in the Vest Fiord, the outer approach to Narvik, between
4.30 a.m. and 5.30 a.m. The force which was to have laid the
southern minefield (off Stadtland, below Aalesund) was ordered
back till the situation could be cleared up, for the unexpected was
happening. It was known in the morning of the 9th that the Germans were landing troops under naval escort in various Norwegian
ports: Oslo, Stavanger, Christiansand, Bergen, Trondheim, and
Narvik. Within a day the irresistible invaders were in control of all
the ports. 'Surprise, ruthlessness, and precision were the characteristics of the onslaught upon innocent and naked Norway',
Churchill relates. 'It was obvious that Britain had been forestalled,
surprised, and . . . outwitted.'

There is little that one can say about the Norwegian campaign
that has not already been said. It is perhaps the most completely
researched operation of the war, as well as a classic example of
'divided counsels, contradictory orders, muddle, and improvisa-
tion', or, more succinctly, it was largely 'order, counter-order, dis-
order'. Here, fortunately, I need concern myself only with Churchill's
role during his last weeks as First Lord, specifically, with his influence on the main lines of strategy, on the joint operations,
particularly at Narvik, and, most importantly, with his alleged
interference with naval operations.

For a week Churchill put a cheerful face on the situation. Thus,
on the 9th: '. . . we were in a far better position than we had been
up to date. Our hands were now free, and we could apply our overwhelming sea power on the Norwegian coast. The German forces
which had been landed were commitments for them, but potential
prizes for us.' As late as the 16th he was 'full of confidence in the
strategical error that Hitler had made in going to Scandinavia'.[93]

At the outset Churchill strongly advocated that they proceed with

[93] WM 86 (40), CAB 65/6, *The Ironside Diaries,* p. 263.

'Rupert', the Narvik operation, at the earliest possible moment, with no dissipation of forces by trying to recapture Bergen and Trondheim. He was sanguine about the prospect of having Narvik 'within one or two weeks'. The War Cabinet, appreciating that to the original importance of Narvik as 'the gateway to the Galivare orefields' was now added the consideration that it was a base which must be denied to the Germans, agreed on 10 April with Churchill and the Military Co-ordination Committee that 'the first aim should be the capture of Narvik'.[94] The first convoy of an expedition to seize Narvik sailed on the next day. Exhilarated by the Navy's brilliant effort at Narvik, on 13 April the War Cabinet debated whether to shift the emphasis from Narvik to Trondheim. The Prime Minister and Foreign Secretary urged the seizure of Trondheim from the political point of view. Declared Chamberlain, 'If at the moment we merely concentrate on Narvik, there was a danger lest the Norwegians and Swedes would feel that our only interest was the iron ore. In the event, they might become disheartened and give up the struggle.' The CIGS, Ironside, argued that this would require more troops, which could only come from withdrawing them from France. Churchill backed him up: 'Nothing must be allowed to deflect us from making the capture [of Narvik] as certain as possible.'[95] Actually, the War Cabinet had on the day before declared itself against compromising the integrity of 'Rupert' by other operations.

Churchill and the Admiralty quickly shifted course and came up with a new plan, a direct amphibious assault on Trondheim, or what came to be called 'Operation Hammer'.[96]

At 2 a.m. on the morning of April 14, Mr. Churchill, accompanied only by the Deputy Chief of the Naval Staff, Admiral Tom Phillips, came to Ironside's room at the War Office. 'Tiny, we are going for the wrong place. We should go for Trondheim,' said the First Lord. 'The Navy will make a direct attack on it and I want a small force of good troops, well led, to follow up the naval attack. I also want landings made north and south of Trondheim, one at Namsos and the other at Andalsnes, to co-operate with the assault when it comes off by a pincer movement on Trondheim.' Mr. Churchill was unable to give any date for the naval attack.

Ironside protested that he had no troops available for Trondheim until Narvik had been taken. Mr. Churchill then insisted that the rear half of

[94] WM 87 (40), CAB 65/12. For Churchill's views see also WM 85 (40), 9 Apr., CAB 65/6, and 'Scandinavia. Minutes of Informal Meeting between Representatives of the British Government and French Government . . . 11th April, 1940', ADM 205/4.

[95] WM 91 (40), CAB 65/12.

[96] The quoted matter that follows is by the Editors of *The Ironside Diaries*, pp. 257–8, relying on an account written by Ironside some years later, but confirmed by his Military Assistant with whom he had discussed the incident on 15 April.

the Narvik convoy, which was carrying the 146 Territorial Brigade, should be diverted to Namsos. Ironside again protested, this time with some heat, that Mr. Churchill at least should know how impractical such a diversion would be. If half the Narvik force were removed, the Narvik operation would be ruined. The troops and their equipment had been loaded and the administration organized for a single operation, and everything would be upset if half the convoy was dispatched. There would be no commander for the rear half because the Brigadier, Phillips, had, quite correctly, been taken on ahead by General Mackesy [commander of the Narvik expeditionary force]. It would be better, said Ironside, to abandon Narvik altogether, or at most, to invest it. He was overruled.

Since Churchill made it clear that he was acting as Chairman of the Military Co-ordination Committee, Ironside could only accept the scheme, while protesting he did not like it. After some hemming and hawing, the Service Chiefs accepted the Trondheim plan on the 15th, and the War Cabinet approved it on the same day. The plan, as worked out, called for the commencement of the operation on 22 April. There would be landings of small forces at Namsos and Andalsnes, which 'should be regarded as diversions to confuse the enemy, and as the speediest means of bringing some British troops up to join and encourage the Norwegian forces which stand between us and the enemy'. There would be a combined operation against Trondheim, with the battle fleet, preceding the landing parties, 'smothering' the gunfire from the batteries on both sides of the fiord; and then the troops would be landed in Trondheim— no less than 7,000–8,000, to cope with the perhaps 5,000 Germans in the town.[97]

In *The Gathering Storm* Churchill writes he was 'apprehensive' of 'Hammer'. It was 'a much more speculative affair' than the capture of Narvik and would reduce the chances of success at Narvik. But he appreciated that:

On the broadest grounds of policy and strategy it would be good for the Allies to fight Hitler on the largest possible scale in Central Norway, if that was where he wanted to go. . . . Although Narvik was my pet, I threw myself with increasing confidence into this daring adventure, and was willing that the Fleet should risk the petty ['weak' in U.S. ed.] batteries at the entrance to the fiord, the possible minefields, and most serious, the air. The ships carried what was in those days very powerful anti-aircraft armament. . . . Left to myself, I might have stuck to my first love, Narvik; but serving as I did a loyal ['respected' in U.S. ed.] chief and friendly Cabinet, I now looked forward to this exciting enterprise . . .[98]

[97] MC (40) 77, 'Note by the Chairman [Churchill] on Operation RUPERT', 17 Apr., CAB 83/5, MC (40) 26th, 27th meetings, 16, 17 Apr., CAB 83/3.
[98] Churchill, *The Gathering Storm*, pp. 489, 493.

On the 19th the Chiefs·of Staff underwent a change of heart. The direct attack on Trondheim was unacceptable to the C-in-C, Admiral Forbes, and had already been postponed till the 25th. He realized the dangers to which big ships would be exposed in such narrow, German air-dominated waters—the 39 miles of channel leading to Trondheim. This was the principal consideration behind the C-in-C's serious doubts about the feasibility of 'Hammer' (14 April),[99] which doubts bulked large in the Service Chiefs' reconsideration of 'Hammer'. The other major factor was the highly successful landings on 14 and 17 April at Namsos and Andalsnes, respectively 80 miles north and 150 miles south of Trondheim. At the Chiefs of Staff meeting on the 19th Pound proposed that in view of the conditions which had developed in these areas 'it would be more advantageous and sounder to exploit the pincer movement on Trondheim to the maximum extent, and not to attempt the direct assault in the centre'. And this is what was agreed. The direct assault would be 'very hazardous' and would involve large naval forces; the pincers plan was 'more certain'.[100]

The Military Co-ordination Committee (Churchill in the chair) endorsed the revised operation on the 19th, as did the War Cabinet on the 20th. At the latter Churchill blessed the modified plan. 'Although this change of emphasis is to be deprecated on account of its being a change, it must be recognised that we move from a more hazardous to a less hazardous operation, and greatly reduce the strain upon the Navy involved in "Hammer".' By 'hazardous' he had in mind the danger to the big ships through enemy air action, and of the landing parties suffering heavy casualties. The First Lord on the same occasion turned back to his first love.

Narvik was of vital importance to us, and it was essential that it should be in our hands in good time before the ice melted in the Baltic. Unless we had the area in our control and our forces established on the Swedish frontier, and were in a position immediately to interfere with the orefields if necessary, the Germans would be very likely to demand from Sweden the right to reinforce their troops as soon as their shipping could get up to Lulea. We had therefore only a month in which to liquidate the position at Narvik, and it was of the utmost importance not to have our attention diverted by operations elsewhere from our principal objective, which had always from the very start been the control of the Gällivare orefields.[101]

For some days, however, the spotlight remained on Trondheim.

[99] Captain Roskill stresses other naval considerations in explaining the volte-face. See his *The War at Sea*, i. 186–7.
[100] COS (40) 87th meeting, CAB 79/85. COS (40) 297 (S), 'Operation "Hammer". Aide Memoire', 19 Apr., CAB 80/105, spells out the reasons for the shift to the enveloping movement. [101] WM 98 (40), CAB 65/12.

The Chiefs of Staff emphasized its political and strategic importance. The failure to capture it, with evacuation of the forces from central Norway as the sole alternative, would have grave political repercussions; Trondheim would provide them with the only major line of communication by which to render aid to Norway and eventually to Sweden; it was the only port through which support of forces in southern Norway could be sustained; its aerodrome was badly needed. 'In the hands of the Germans, Trondhjem can easily be made into a strongly defended and important subsidiary naval and air base, from which enemy naval and air forces will be suitably situated to operate against our own bases in the north of England and our sea communications in the North Sea. Moreover enemy air forces operating from Trondhjem will increase the scale of air attack on Narvik and harass our sea communications with that port.' They must have Trondheim; yet the pincers plan was not working. 'In the face of heavy German air attack, to which we have at present insufficient counter, we are unlikely to be able to get adequate and suitably equipped forces into Norway through Aandalsnes and Namsos.'[102] Faced with this grave situation, on Admiralty initiative the Chiefs of Staff urgently considered a reversion to 'Hammer' with adaptations ('Hammer 2') on 25–26 April. Their decision was essentially negative. It would be a 'somewhat hazardous operation', and even if successful, they could not afford the anti-aircraft resources to render it secure against the likely scale of air attack.[103] The Military Co-ordination Committee (the Prime Minister in the chair) agreed on the 26th not to proceed with 'Hammer' and declared that their policy 'should be the ultimate evacuation of Central Norway. . . . it should, if practicable, be postponed until after the capture of Narvik. . . . The capture of Narvik and subsequent advance to the Swedish border should continue to be our primary objective in Norway, and should be pressed forward with all the speed and energy possible.'[104] The next day the Committee, in the light of the latest information, decided that orders should go out immediately for the withdrawal of the troops from the Namsos and Andalsnes areas. The twin attacks had failed, and the two forces were re-embarked between 30 April and 3 May.

The pincers operation could only have ended in defeat or ignominious withdrawal. In view of the free passage allowed to the German Army, hence their presence in superior force, the landing

[102] COS (40) 302 (S), 'Norway: Review of the Situation. Report', 26 Apr., CAB 80/105.
[103] Phillips's minute, 25 Apr., ADM 199/1929, COS (40) 96th, 97th, 98th meetings, CAB 79/85.   [104] MC (40) 34th meeting, CAB 83/3.

of the small, poorly equipped forces at Namsos and Andalsnes was a strategical absurdity, described at the time as putting a kitten at the back door to drive out a tiger at the front door. The Luftwaffe, present in overwhelming strength, ranged without appreciable hindrance over the British positions on land and inflicted serious damage and losses on warships and supply ships.

Churchill was pleased with the final abandonment of 'Hammer' on the 26th. 'Narvik was our principal objective in Norway, and we had only gone into Trondhjem in the hope of being able to bolster up the Norwegians if they seemed to be putting up any sort of resistance. . . . Provided we secured Narvik as a naval base and as a base for operations by land or by air against the ore fields and Lulea, we should be better off on balance than the Germans.'[105]

The CIGS's comment on Churchill's change of emphasis was not entirely fair. They had met at the Paris embassy on the 22nd. 'Winston was very much interested in the Narvik affair. He wanted to divert troops there from all over the place. He is so like a child in many ways. He tires of a thing, and then wants to hear no more of it. He was mad to divert the Brigade from Narvik to Namsos and would hear of no reason. Now he is bored with the Namsos operation and is all for Narvik again. It is most extraordinary how mercurial he is.'[106] The fact is that Churchill had never taken his eyes off the ore factor, meaning the need to control Narvik in the first instance. This helps to explain the bizarre Keyes entr'acte of the latter half of April.

When the war broke out, Sir Roger Keyes was an Admiral of the Fleet without a job. Officers of that exalted rank were at that time retired after holding the rank for five years, though if employed, their retention on the active list might be extended. On 17 November 1939 the Board of Admiralty approved Churchill's proposal that Admirals of the Fleet were to remain on the active list, but this was not made official until 3 March 1940. The new rule suited Keyes perfectly. He was as buoyant and full of fight as ever (his obsession was 'seeking reputation in the cannon's mouth') and grimly determined to reach the battle line somehow. He kept after Churchill, his old friend and admirer, desperate to find a job commensurate to his talents, which he was not one to underrate. He had no success. A week after the German invasion of Norway, Keyes, who had been champing at the bit at his own inactivity and that of the Navy, went to the Admiralty (16 April) and asked for the command of a force which he would lead past the Trondheim

[105] ibid.
[106] 22 Apr. 1940, *The Ironside Diaries*, p. 278.

batteries and then storm the town and capture the aerodrome.[107]
Had Churchill agreed, there would have been a truly Gilbertian
situation. Churchill had already put an Admiral of the Fleet (Cork)
in command of the Narvik operation (see below), and if Keyes had
got his way, there would have been two Admirals of the Fleet
commanding small squadrons in the command of the Commander-
in-Chief, Home Fleet! 'Winston too tired to be interested—expressed
his fears of Italy', Keyes noted in his diary. 'I said the answer to
Italy could be given by a hammer blow on Norwegian Coast.'[108] To
Churchill in the evening, enclosing his outline plan: 'It is sad that
I should be considered unfit for command because I have been
unemployed so long (having commanded the premier fleet [Mediter-
ranean, 1925–8] while still comparatively young). Some of the
great Sea-Captains of old, who were left unemployed for many
years, emerged while older even than I am, and struck a resounding blow at sea, and so would I if I got a chance. Anyhow, I would
have *struck*, and not "looked at it" for a week. . . . I am very devoted
to you, and I only want to help. But you won't let me.'[109] The next
morning: 'I am confident it is a feasible operation—and it is worth
any risk at the moment to hearten the Neutrals. It *can't* and won't
fail if you let me do it and be responsible for it—back my good
fortune. . . . Our stars are linked. Let me do this for you.' Churchill
did not respond and refused to grant him another interview. The
Chiefs of Staff refused to see Keyes. A letter from Churchill on the
25th should have doused his hopes: 'It astonishes me that you
should think that all this has not been examined by people who
know exactly what resources are available, and what the dangers
would be. . . . You will, I hope, appreciate the fact that I have to be
guided by my responsible Naval advisers, and that it is not open
to me to make the kind of appointments you and Eva have in mind
on ground of friendship.' Churchill's intercession secured Keyes an

[107] Keyes and his wife were staying with Admiral Sir William James at Portsmouth
when the Germans invaded Norway. Apparently it was Lady Keyes who originated
this 'bright idea'. She was in bed with measles and asked for the Norwegian charts,
which gave her the idea. James's letter to the author, 25 Mar. 1968. As finally
elaborated by Keyes on 23 April, the force required included two 'Royal Sovereigns',
a carrier, two old cruisers, an AA cruiser, two destroyer flotillas, RAF aircraft
(number not specified), 300 marines, two battalions and two companies of infantry,
and transports. 'Proposal for direct assault on Trondheim', ADM 205/6.

[108] 'Extracts from Sir Roger Keyes Diary. April, 1940', Keyes MSS., 13/12. What
follows is derived mainly from the Keyes MSS., 13/12. Churchill said the 'Royal
Sovereigns' were not available, 'since war with Italy seemed almost inevitable. You
then rang your bell and tried to dismiss me like an importunate beggar.' Keyes to
Churchill, 29 Apr. 1940.

[109] Keyes to Churchill, 16 Apr. 1940, Cecil F. Aspinall-Oglander, *Roger Keyes*
(London, 1951), p. 346. The copies in ADM 205/6 and in the Keyes MSS. vary slightly.

interview with Pound that day, when he learned for the first time that an official plan for a direct naval attack on Trondheim had been turned down by the Chiefs of Staff on the 19th. Pound told him his plan was 'most useful', but that he could say no more about it at present.

Keyes finally managed to see Churchill on the 29th, prior to which he sent him a note which contained this titbit: 'If the scuttle is persisted in the Government will have to go and I shall do my damndest to speed them.' He was as good as his word, as we shall see. The memorandum which accompanied the note was one long bitter wail over 'the shocking inaction of the Navy at Trondhjem, for which you and your pusillanimous, self-satisfied, short sighted Naval advisers must bear the responsibility'. 'This plan can't fail,' he pleaded, 'and if it is done immediately, I am absolutely confident of success. We will strike a blow which will help to decide the issue, cheer our friends, and make the hostile Neutrals pause. For God's sake put your trust in me and don't waste any more time.' The interview itself was friendly, but Churchill made it clear that he did not intend to do anything. Keyes's later version of what had blocked him was that the Naval Staff's 'excuse . . . was that they could not risk ships, owing to the uncertainty about the Italian situation. . . . From information now available, this attack could not have failed, and would have given us a good harbour and the aerodrome, which was the key of the whole situation. . . . it is clear that nothing encouraged Mussolini more than the Naval failure and miscarriages in the Norwegian Campaign.'[110]

Keyes made too much of the Italian factor in explaining the unwillingness of the Admiralty and the Chiefs of Staff to accept his scheme. This was indeed a factor—not exactly an 'excuse'— since the likelihood of Italy entering the war was increasing and a British naval build-up in the Mediterranean was in progress. But the weightiest consideration with the Service Chiefs was, as we have seen, that any direct assault on Trondheim would be too dangerous. There is every likelihood, anyway, that Keyes's 'oddments' would have been sunk by the shore batteries.

At the time, Keyes believed that 'Winston's drive and initiative have been undermined by the legend of his recklessness. Today he cannot dare to do the things he could have dared in 1915.'[111] In the famous Commons debate on 7 May Keyes stated the point bluntly: 'The iron of the Dardanelles had entered into his soul.'

[110] Keyes, 'Notes on the Norwegian Campaign. April 1940', 4 Dec. 1941.
[111] Diary, 30 Apr. 1940, Harold Nicolson, *The War Years, 1939–1945* (vol. ii of *Diaries and Letters*, ed. Nigel Nicolson, London, 1967), p. 74.

Churchill afterwards denied that, on account of having lost office because of his Dardanelles policy, he 'had no longer the capacity to dare'. There are two compelling reasons why Churchill would not back Keyes. One was 'the difficulties of acting from a sub-ordinate position'—he had 'responsibility without power'—meaning that he could not act contrary to the unanimous advice of the Service Chiefs. Again, Pound would have resigned had Churchill preferred Keyes's advice to his, and Forbes might well have joined him.[112] The other consideration is that once the direct assault on Trondheim appeared to be a dead issue, that is, from 20 April, Churchill had 'reverted to Narvik, which seemed at once more important and more feasible'. He approved the objectives of 'Rupert' as set out by the Chiefs of Staff: 'to secure and maintain a base in Northern Norway from which we can: (*a*) deny iron ore supplies to Germany via Narvik; (*b*) interfere so far as possible with ore supplies to Germany from Lulea; (*c*) preserve a part of Norway as a seat of Government for the Norwegian King and people.'[113]

The first convoy of an expedition to seize Narvik had sailed on 11 April. An advanced base was established at Harstad, on an island some 30 miles north-west of Narvik. The commander of the expeditionary force (until superseded on 13 May by General Auchinleck) was Major-General P. J. Mackesy, with Cork as the naval commander. Cork was appointed to the supreme command of the whole operation on the 20th. Mackesy and Cork differed sharply as to strategy: the Admiral wanted to seize Narvik by an immediate frontal assault on the town, putting the troops ashore under cover of a heavy close-range naval bombardment, whereas the General favoured a more gradual advance from the land side, with, finally, a landing on the Narvik peninsula under cover of the guns of the fleet. The rights and wrongs of the rival points of view are not germane to our primary concerns.[114] It is enough to say that the first landing did not take place until the night of 12–13 May (under Mackesy), that is, after Churchill had left the Admiralty for No. 10. The Nazi invasion of the Low Countries and France in effect cut short the Norwegian campaign. Narvik was eventually captured on 28 May, but was held only a few days in order to

[112] Churchill, *The Gathering Storm*, p. 496.

[113] COS (40) 316: annex to WP 144 (40), 'Operation Rupert', 4 May, CAB 66/7.

[114] See Churchill, *The Gathering Storm*, pp. 482–8, 501–3, 514 (where the first landing was credited to the commander of the French contingent, corrected in the U.S. edition), which is very critical of the stalemate at Narvik because of Mackesy's unwillingness to storm Narvik until weeks had passed, and the important rebuttal by Piers Mackesy, 'Churchill on Narvik', *Royal United Service Institution Journal*, cxv (Dec. 1970), 28–33.

destroy the port installations and the railway. The troops were evacuated between 4 and 8 June. It was imperative that all forces be concentrated in Britain and France, where 'tremendous events became dominant'. The attrition that the Fleet was suffering in the northern campaign could no longer be tolerated.

In *The Gathering Storm* (pp. 518–19) Churchill drew comfort from the Norwegian campaign, above all from the fact that the German Fleet had been so badly mauled: no major warship emerged fit for action. 'In their desperate grapple with the British Navy the Germans ruined their own, such as it was, for the impending climax. . . . the German Navy was no factor in the supreme issue of the invasion of Britain.' Also, at Dunkirk in June. And the occupation of Norway tied down 300,000 men for the balance of the war. But the fact remains that British objectives were not achieved, and that the Germans had done pretty much what they wanted, on land, at sea, and in the air. 'Taking the campaign as a whole, the enemy accomplished the safeguarding of his iron ore supplies, tightened his control of the short sea passages across the Baltic and obtained possession of very valuable and well-sited bases from which submarines, surface vessels and aircraft could be sent out on to our trade routes, and from which he could also intensify his operations against our coastal shipping.'[115]

What can we say of Churchill's role in 'this ramshackle campaign', as he later called it? We must first note that his position was strengthened on the eve of the campaign. On 3 April Chatfield had resigned as Minister for the Co-ordination of Defence. (An Admiral remarked somewhat grimly: 'Fancy anybody trying to co-ordinate Winston!') No successor was appointed. Instead, Churchill as senior Service minister took over the chairmanship of the Military Co-ordination Committee, except on the few occasions when the Prime Minister was present. The Committee operated in two ways—making recommendations to the War Cabinet and at other times taking decisions which were presented to the War Cabinet for confirmation. Under a new arrangement, announced by Chamberlain on 1 May, the Chairman's hand was strengthened. He was now responsible on behalf of the Committee 'for giving guidance and direction to the Chiefs of Staff Committee', with the help of a central staff headed by Major-General H. L. Ismay. The first meeting of the new order was on 3 May; a week later Churchill was Prime Minister. Given Churchill's grasp of defence matters and his strong character, it was inevitable that his influence was paramount in the Committee's counsels. There is substance in Sir

[115] Roskill, *The War at Sea*, i. 201.

James Butler's guess 'that the Chiefs of Staff were sometimes induced by the forceful personality of the First Lord of the Admiralty
to lend support to bold enterprises against their better judgement'.[116]
The clearest instance is the adoption of 'Hammer'. Churchill's influence was also important in the launching of 'Rupert', though
here he was not running counter to the strategy favoured by the
Service Chiefs. More important than Churchill's influence on specific
strategic decisions was the fact that he was, in General Jacob's
words, 'the mainspring of a forward policy aimed at trying to throw
[the Germans] out'. He kept fully abreast of all developments by
having all the operational telegrams from Cs-in-C brought direct
to him, even when in Cabinet, as soon as they arrived.

> Although he was in no sense in charge of the conduct of the war, his
> intense eagerness made him so much better informed than his colleagues,
> and so much in hourly contact with events, that he was usually able to
> sway them in the direction he thought the right one at the moment. There
> was no Combined Headquarters directing the campaign with full knowledge
> of the situation throughout the theatre, and reporting to the Chiefs of Staff
> and the Cabinet. The result was a series of *ad hoc* decisions, often arrived at
> on the incomplete information that came to Ministers through telegrams
> from a single commander produced by Mr. Churchill, telegrams that no one
> else had seen.[117]

As regards the actual combined operations, we see Churchill's
direct influence in the diversion of the rear part of the Narvik convoy to Namos (above, pp. 155–6). 'This unexpected disruption sur-
passed in futility the loading, unloading and reloading of the
Dardanelles convoy at Alexandria in 1915.'[118] Churchill's influence
is seen most directly at Narvik. It was his particular show, but his
role was primarily that of gadfly. He took the initiative, stimulating
and prodding mainly, but also suggesting strategy. An example of
Churchill's prodding is his 17 April memorandum for the Military
Co-ordination Committee, which proposed that a strong telegram
be sent to Mackesy and Cork—that 'full consideration' be given to
a naval-supported assault upon Narvik. The Committee approved
the telegram, which was sent but accomplished nothing, the General
refusing to move.[119] Other illustrations are to be found in the
signals exchanged between Churchill and Cork.[120] Thus, on 19 April

---

[116] J. R. M. Butler, *The History of the Second World War. Grand Strategy*, ii (London,
1957), 150.

[117] Sir John Wheeler-Bennett (ed.), *Action This Day: Working with Churchill* (London,
1969), pp. 160–1.   [118] Godfrey, *Naval Memoirs*, viii. 14.

[119] MC (40) 27th meeting, CAB 83/3.

[120] These have been brought together in ADM 199/1929 and cover the period
19 April–22 May.

the First Lord suggested that 'the tongue of land, especially its tip occupied by Narvik port and town, could certainly be dominated by the fire of warships, and that the houses could be occupied with the forces you possess. Once this is achieved we have the trophy at which all Europe is looking, we have a bridge-head for further landings . . .' After more advice, he adds: 'Pray regard this telegram as my own personal opinion to enable you, after consultation with the General, to let me know what you severally and jointly advise, and if you do not agree, what are the main obstacles.' On 21 April Cork reported receipt of a letter from Mackesy that began: 'Before proposed action against Narvik commences . . . I feel it my duty to represent to you that I am convinced that there is not one Officer or man under my command who will not feel shame for himself and his country if thousands of Norwegian men, women and children in Narvik are subject to bombardment proposed.' To this Churchill replied: 'If this Officer appears to be spreading a bad spirit through the higher ranks of the land forces, do not hesitate to relieve him or place him under arrest.' (Cork's response: 'In the event you mentioned I shall not hesitate to assert my authority but do not think need will arise.') Churchill on 4 May: 'Urgency of Narvik is extreme. Trust you will use all available strength and press hard for decision. I shall be glad to share your responsibilities.' And so on. At no time did Churchill order the commanders on the spot to adopt a particular strategy. The CIGS noted in his diary: 'Winston seems to me to be a little weighed down by the cares of being solely responsible for Narvik. He wants it taken and yet doesn't dare to give any direct order to Cork.'[121]

One might add that the appointment, on Churchill's initiative, of Lord Cork to command the naval forces in the Narvik operation was not the height of wisdom. 'He was 67 years old in 1940 and one would have thought a younger man, subordinate to Admiral Forbes, C.-in-C. Home Fleet, would have been chosen for this appointment. Certainly the appointment of an officer so much senior to the C.-in-C. Home Fleet confused the chain of command and blurred the incidence of responsibility.'[122]

---

[121] 5 May 1940, *The Ironside Diaries*, p. 295.

[122] Godfrey, *Naval Memoirs*, vii, Pt. 2, p. 227. 'This is a war of surprises,' wrote Admiral Sir William James at the time (30 April), 'and the latest is the appointment of an Admiral of the Fleet to a command that would normally fall to a Rear-Admiral or a Commodore. He goes with his flag flying in a cruiser, and I do not believe that Solomon in all his glory could devise a chain of command for the occasion.' James, *The Portsmouth Letters*, p. 47. Cork was a product of that perfectly natural but almost disastrous liking Churchill had for being surrounded by elderly officers who had been with him in the First War and who, like himself, had all the warlike gifts: on the naval side, Cork, Keyes (who was in July 1940 to become the first Director of

To sum up, there can be no dispute about Churchill's strong influence on the inept overall strategy of the campaign, including the constant changes of plan, as well as upon the combined operations. At the root of the failure of British strategic thinking was the belief that it was impracticable for the Germans to invade the western seaboard of Scandinavia in the face of superior British sea power. Hitler showed that this conception had become out of date with the advent of air power, and defied convention. As Admiral Forbes put it, 'the scale of air attack that would be developed against our military forces on shore and our naval forces off the Norwegian coast was grievously underestimated when the operations were undertaken'.[123] This blind confidence in sea power was the responsibility of the Chiefs of Staff, specifically, of Ironside and Pound.[124] The Navy itself, from Churchill, Pound, and Phillips down, had excessive faith in the effectiveness of a warship's AA defences. This was a standing source of controversy with the airmen. Vice-Admiral Sir Geoffrey Blake, who was ACNS (Foreign) from 8 April 1940, states that Pound 'was quite as ignorant as we all were before the Second World War as to what aircraft could do to ships. This was quite clear from the Norwegian campaign, where we intended . . . to send a squadron into Trondheim with no reconnaissance, and with the certainty that they would be bombed.'[125] Phillips was perhaps the most dedicated disbeliever in

combined Operations), Dreyer, Evans, and others. Sir John Dill, when CIGS, is supposed to have said to Churchill: 'Prime Minister, we are going to lose *this* war with the heroes of the *last*'! As the war progressed, however, he came to realize this would not do, and he became readier to draw on younger men of vigour.

[123] Roskill, *The War at Sea*, i. 179. The Official Historian of the campaign writes: 'It was the threat from German air power, effective against smaller ships in the narrow waters of the Leads and fiords, which prevented our naval superiority from exercising its accustomed influence on the operations along the Norwegian coastline in the later stages of the campaign. . . . Our home-based bombers were too few to neutralise those enemy-occupied airfields in Norway and Denmark which were accessible to us. . . . The Fleet Air Arm was not designed to fill the gap: trained to operate with and for the fleet, their fighters slower than German bombers, the naval air squadrons were essaying a new (though important) role in their inshore operations along the Norwegian coast. Finally, there was the shortage of anti-aircraft artillery . . .' T. K. Derry, *History of the Second World War. The Campaign in Norway* (London, 1952), pp. 234–5. It should be noted that the German air attacks on the fleet during the Norwegian campaign were generally dive-bombing attacks. There were some high-level attacks, probably because no dive-bombers were immediately available.

[124] Thus, when it was suggested that the small forces that were to occupy Stavanger, Bergen, and Trondheim at the time of the laying of the minefield in Norwegian territorial waters might suffer severely from air attack, the CIGS observed that 'they would be quite capable of looking after themselves after they were landed, and could not be dislodged by German air action'. WM 46 (40), 19 Feb., CAB 65/11.

[125] Blake to McLachlan, 12 Sept. 1967, McLachlan MSS. Another example of

the air threat. This superb and exceptionally hard-working staff officer (DCNS until 22 April 1940, then VCNS), who 'always looks like death and tries to do far too much' (Admiral Somerville, early in 1940), undoubtedly had a great influence on Churchill. The latter would refer to him as 'that little cock-sparrow sitting on the edge of his chair and not caring a damn what I say'. Churchill liked that independent attitude, and his confidence in Phillips was complete.[126] 'Both W.S.C. and Tom Phillips', asserts Admiral Godfrey, 'were obsessed with the idea that a fleet or ship could provide complete aerial protection with its own A.A. guns.'[127]

The sailors were shaken to the teeth by their experience in Norway. Pound had expressed himself early in 1940 as 'rather optimistic about battleships versus aircraft', basing this on 'the improvements in A/A equipment', even though the Fleet had not yet shot down a single enemy aircraft. Four months later, towards the end of the Norwegian campaign, his tune had changed: 'The one lesson we have learnt here is that it is essential to have fighter protection over the Fleet whenever they are within reach of the enemy bombers.'[128]

Finally, what of Churchill's alleged interference with the naval side of the Norwegian campaign? That he was running it was the impression of a number of officers at the Admiralty. Thus, the DDOD(H), Captain Ralph Edwards, confided to his diary during the campaign: 'Winston taking a great personal interest. He wants

Admiralty disdain of the air threat was the dispatch of the cruiser *Suffolk* to bombard Stavanger airfield, which she did on 17 April, suffering heavy damage from a sustained air attack during her withdrawal and just staggering back into port with her decks awash.

[126] That is, until the spring of 1941, when Phillips's refusal to endorse the expedition to Greece cost him Churchill's trust. The Prime Minister now considered him a 'defeatist' and told him so. Rear-Admiral H. G. Thursfield to Rear-Admiral J. H. Godfrey, 24 May 1954, Godfrey to Thursfield, 28 May 1954, Godfrey MSS.

[127] Godfrey to McLachlan, 5 Dec. 1966, McLachlan MSS. Marshal of the Royal Air Force Sir John Slessor, who was Phillips's opposite number in the Air Ministry before the war, when Phillips was Director of Plans, and shared a flat with him, testifies to his scorn of air power. 'They had a pact never to talk about the threat of bombs to battleships because they disagreed so violently. . . . When Tom Phillips was leaving the planning staff to be promoted, Bert Harris [afterwards Marshal of the Royal Air Force Sir Arthur Harris, Bt., C-in-C, Bomber Command, 1942–5] proposed a jocular toast and said, "Tom, when the first bomb hits, you'll say, 'My God, what a hell of a mine!'"' Interview with Slessor, 23 Feb. 1968, McLachlan MSS. Slessor well remembers another occasion when Phillips told him that an aeroplane would be blown out of the sky if it came anywhere near this terrific 'multiple pom-pom'. Slessor's letter to the author, 3 Apr. 1973. And see his *The Central Blue*, p. 277.

[128] Pound to Cunningham, 7 Jan., 20 May 1940, Cunningham MSS., Add. MSS. 52560.

to interfere & I'm sure he's wrong. An astonishing man' (7 April). 'Everyone very indignant with the conduct of affairs. Winston is at the bottom of it all. He will try & be a strategist and run the Naval side of the war' (12 April). 'Winston entered the fray [between Forbes and Cork over the Narvik operation] & decided against the Staff's decision—oh this interference & we aren't strong enough to stand up to him' (29 April). 'They're "crackers" on the project and I'm quite sure we shan't be able to hold it without expending a disproportionate effort on doing so. Winston again—ye gods he's a menace' (1 May).[129] Admirals Godfrey and Grantham felt no differently. Declared the latter: 'We on the Staff felt it was Winston's private operation and that he was running the whole outfit regardless of what the Naval Staff thought.'[130] Admiral Godfrey declares that 'Pound, a Grand Fleet man with no Gallipoli experience, appears to have remained silent and to have accepted Churchill's dictatorial behaviour'. Elsewhere he quotes a senior officer who wrote: 'Pound proved unable to prevent Winston running wild during the Norwegian campaign.'[131] A distinguished Admiral has told the author: 'All my contemporaries as Commanders knew the extent to which he had interfered directly with the operations (in detail) of the Home Fleet during the Norwegian campaign.' This is indeed a widely held belief in the Service. It is shared by the Official Naval Historian of the war, who is more specific:

> . . . the Admiralty frequently intervened directly in the operations of the Home Fleet. The diversion of the destroyers of 'Force WV' from the entrance to Vestfiord [8 April], the orders sent directly to Captain Warburton-Lee on his passage up the fiord to Narvik [9 April] and the cancellation of Admiral Forbes' intended attack on Bergen [9 April] are but three examples of a policy which was, in fact, constantly applied. [This produced] difficulties and uncertainties . . . in November 1939 Admiral Pound reiterated . . . his determination that Commanders-in-Chief should normally be left free to conduct their own operations without constant intervention from Whitehall.
>
> The reader will therefore ask why it was that . . . the Admiralty's actions ran contrary to the First Sea Lord's expressed intentions. There can be no doubt that the powerful personality of the First Lord was a large factor in bringing this about. Mr. Churchill used, during critical periods of naval operations, to spend long hours in the Admiralty Operational Intelligence Centre and the tendency for him to assume direct control therefrom is easily to be understood. Many of the signals sent during such periods bear the unmistakable imprint of his language and personality and, admirable

---

[129] The Edwards diary is at Churchill College; 1/2 is the reference for the 1940 diary.
[130] Grantham's written reply to a questionnaire from McLachlan, 15 July 1967, McLachlan MSS.
[131] *Naval Memoirs*, viii. 14, vii, Pt. 2, p. 229.

though their purpose and intention were, it now appears plain that they sometimes confused the conduct of operations and increased the difficulties of the Commander-in-Chief.[132]

That the Admiralty had intervened seriously in naval operations, particularly in the early stages of the campaign, is an indisputable fact, as is the fact that this caused much resentment in the Fleet at the time. This is not, however, the place to deal with the thorny question of when and how the Admiralty should intervene in fleet operations.[133] We must concern ourselves with the indictment of Churchill's supposed role. A man of strong personality and definite ideas of what should be done can easily give the impression that he is running the show. Yet I can find no hard evidence that Pound was a cipher during the campaign. It was he, rather than Churchill, who effectively quashed Keyes's Trondheim scheme. And note what the ACNS (Foreign) says: 'The Norwegian campaign was such a shemozzle and Pound and Churchill seemed to be having considerable argument that it was difficult for me to keep track.'[134] This hardly suggests a First Lord who was running roughshod over his First Sea Lord. Nor is the Official Historian's serious charge supported by postwar research. Indeed, quite the contrary. Churchill's Principal Private Secretary of those days is

absolutely clear as the result of my researches that the interferences from Whitehall were not Churchill's work, but the spontaneous action of the Naval Staff and in particular Dudley Pound and Tom Phillips, who certainly had good justification. I was confirmed in this view by Ralph Edwards, who had been [D.] D.O.D. (Home) in 1940, and had been promoted to Flag Rank and become Controller by 1954.

The plain fact of the matter was that Dudley Pound, who had recently been C. in C. Med., found it very difficult to keep his hands off the control of the fleet, and he certainly had more and better information. But much suspicion attached to Winston, partly as an echo of the Dardanelles, and partly because it was generally known that he was always in the War Room, to which he was irresistibly attracted. Being aware of the Dardanelles legend, I was very alert to the problem. I am quite satisfied that Winston took scrupulous care not to transgress the proper limits of Naval and Political responsibility, and not to force his view in any professional decision.[135]

Elsewhere Sir Eric Seal writes:

It is perfectly true that he spent a good deal of time in the War Room,

[132] Roskill, *The War at Sea*, i. 201–2. For the unfortunate consequences of the three interventions singled out above, see ibid., pp. 160, 170–1, 173–4.
[133] See above, p. 55.
[134] Blake to McLachlan, 12 Sept. 1967, McLachlan MSS. Churchill and Pound submerged their differences at meetings of the War Cabinet and Military Coordination Committee.   [135] Sir Eric Seal's letter to the author, 24 Aug. 1971.

which had a tremendous fascination for him. To infer from this that he assumed control is, in the circumstances, almost malicious. It is certainly utterly unwarranted, and false. I made a careful search of all the signals sent by the Admiralty between the 7th and 19th April, and there were only two with characteristic marks of Churchill's phraseology, which I may say I am pretty competent to detect! One is an appeal for fuller current information, which was I think dictated in the First Sea Lord's presence, but which was sent off from my office as a personal message, and the other is referred to by Roskill on page 186, who clearly did not recognise the First Lord's hand. It is an appeal to the C.-in-C. [15 April] to reconsider [his strong objections to] the proposed attack on Trondheim ['Hammer'], which contains the characteristic Churchillism '*Pray therefore* consider this important project further.' Roskill omits the underlined [italicized] words, without realising that Pound would never have used this phrase, although his Secretary actually sent the message off.[136]

Seal neatly brings out why the Service, especially officers at the Admiralty, exaggerated Churchill's role in the Norwegian campaign. It was the *impression* the First Lord gave, far more than specific acts of interference with naval operations, that made for

[136] Sir Eric Seal's letter to the author, 8 Sept. 1971. He confined his research to the period 7–19 April because the C-in-C came back to harbour on the latter date, 'and it was evident that Roskill had drawn his (false) conclusion from that period. I am sure that nothing occurred later on to make me change my mind.' Letter of 19 Sept. 1971. Commander G. A. Titterton, who served in the Admiralty Historical Section after the war, has confirmed the substance of Seal's account in a memorandum of 23 June 1966 for the author. He well remembers Seal's visit to the Historical Section when the first volume of *The War at Sea* was published (1954). Seal 'asked for help in a search for documents of the Norway Campaign. He explained that the Prime Minister (as he had again become) was gravely upset at statements being then made implying that he had exercised undue influence on Service Commanders during the War, in particular he was concerned with the Norway Campaign when he was First Lord of the Admiralty. A prolonged search [three days] was made with this Secretary and the personnel of the H.S. Information Room, in which I took part. Every known source was examined, certainly hundreds (possibly thousands, I lost count) of signals, but only *four* signals [Seal confirms there were only two] bore what we may call the Churchillian stamp. ['And these were not in the class of "running" the naval show', the Commander later added.] All these four were signed by the First Sea Lord himself as the sender. No more was heard on this score; one can only surmise that Sir Winston was satisfied with his secretary's report.' Seal reported to Churchill after receiving the Historical Section report: 'It might be thought that Capt. Roskill himself fails to produce evidence adequate to support the conclusion at which he rather more than hints, namely, that the First Sea Lord intended throughout to avoid all interference with Commanders afloat and that you overbore him. . . . There is not the slightest evidence that any operational message issued by the Admiralty did not have the full concurrence of the responsible chiefs of the Naval Staff.' Seal's report to the Prime Minister then referred to the signal from the Admiralty cancelling the attack on Bergen, from which it is clear that it was the First Sea Lord's decision. 'I have a very clear recollection that you spoke to me after lunch saying that the decision to abandon the attack had been pressed on you [by Pound], and that you hoped the decision had been the correct one.' Quoted in Sir Eric Seal's letter to the author, 8 Sept. 1971.

the misunderstanding, and it is quite possible that those writing long after April–May 1940 may have unconsciously blended, as it were, Churchill's methods and policies as First Lord with those of the later period. One of his principal critics at the time, Edwards, later cancelled his diary thoughts. 'It is only fair to record,' Captain Roskill admits, 'that 14 years after he made these diary entries [Roskill quotes the first three on pp. 167–8 above, all with extreme inaccuracy], Admiral Edwards wrote to me that in retrospect he regarded Churchill's interventions in naval operations as insignificant compared to those initiated by Pound.'[137]

* * *

'It was the irony, or fatality, of history', Liddell Hart has observed, 'that Churchill should have gained his opportunity of supreme power as the result of a fiasco to which he had been the main contributor.' Perhaps *a* main contributor would be fairer. It was the 'Norway Debate' in the Commons on 7–8 May, during which Churchill made no attempt to evade his share of responsibility, that led to the downfall of the Chamberlain Government and Churchill becoming Prime Minister on 10 May. Keyes (Member for Portsmouth) played a crucial role in the debate. Attired in all the splendour of an admiral of the fleet, he revealed to a shocked House that the Admiralty had rejected his offer to lead an attack on Trondheim on the ground that the expected success of the Army rendered such a gamble unnecessary. Two months later he took credit for Churchill's elevation. 'I am told my speech was decisive in helping you to get the freedom and power you needed – evidently Chamberlain thinks so, as he cuts me dead!'[138]

'On the day he became Prime Minister men were seen hurriedly erecting barbed wire round the Admiralty and a posse of Royal Marine sentries took up their posts. Wags in the building said that these precautions had been ordered "to prevent Winston coming back" – a harmless enough jest, but one which nevertheless reflected the relief felt in some quarters at his departure from a post where his unorthodox methods had not been universally appreciated.'[139]

Churchill's farewell message to 'the Navy in General' on leaving the Admiralty ran in part: 'I was proud after many years to come

[137] Edwards's letter of 28 July 1954, Roskill, 'Marder, Churchill and the Admiralty, 1939–42', where this passage is relegated to the obscurity of a footnote at the end of the article (p. 53, n. 4). On Roskill's views see further the note at the end of the chapter.

[138] Keyes to Churchill, 4 July 1940, Keyes MSS., 13/13.

[139] Gerald Pawle, *The War and Colonel Warden* (London, 1963), p. 56.

again to the Admiralty in the hour of peril, and the sorrow which I feel on leaving is tempered by feeling I shall not be far away. . . . As Prime Minister and Minister of Defence it will be my duty to watch over your interests and your proceedings.'[140] And this he most certainly did, for in many respects he continued to act as First Lord throughout the war. He retained his close interest in naval matters, nor did his influence on the Navy diminish. His famous map room, organized by Captain Pim, went with him everywhere, which meant that he continued to know the disposition of every ship. The new First Lord, Churchill's appointee, A. V. Alexander, had plenty of bluff common sense, but he was of not more than moderate abilities. Of greater significance, he was a politician of no stature, and one who was not prepared to argue with the Prime Minister. One of Churchill's secretaries has called Alexander, as First Lord, a 'stooge', and an Admiral in a position to know claims that Alexander was 'subservient and terrified of the P.M.' Alexander never stood up to Pound, either. He was, in fact, largely a figure-head and was put at the Admiralty not to interfere with the naval side of the war. Moreover, Churchill continued to keep up a direct contact with the First Sea Lord, as well as with other officers he had got to know well at the Admiralty. He normally spoke to Pound on the telephone in the early hours of the morning—neither ordinarily went to bed until about 3 a.m.—and then Pound would go along punctiliously to see Alexander to tell him what had happened during the day and what the Prime Minister had said. 'Thus,' as Admiral Brockman sums up the position, 'the First Lord was kept in the picture but the Prime Minister and the First Sea Lord ran the naval war.' Admiral Grantham remarks: 'I am sure he thought he could conduct the war at sea far better than anyone else, and that is why he virtually remained First Lord of the Admiralty when he became Prime Minister.'

How can we sum up Churchill's eventful eight months at the Admiralty? His influence on the Navy and the war at sea was in the main extremely beneficial. He imparted a note of urgency to the shipbuilding programme and 'he did much', as Admiral Gretton correctly points out, 'to marry technological development with tactical thought and to ensure that no scientific idea which could be useful in the war at sea was neglected'. His unceasing promotion of an offensive strategy was not an unmixed blessing. As during the First War, he originated a flood of imaginative strategic ideas which led to considerable investigation and hot arguments as

[140] ADM 1/10570.

to their practicability. As President Roosevelt said, 'Winston has a hundred ideas a day, of which at least four are good'.[141] Perhaps four is a high average! Most importantly, Churchill had a unique capacity to keep everybody on their toes and to inspire others well beyond the limits of what they supposed their own capacity to be. In the ultimate verdict on Churchill, as both First Lord and Prime Minister, these gifts may be judged as his greatest contribution of all.

Musings on a Bolt from Olympus

The serious reader will, of course, wish to consult Captain Roskill's provocative, and in places amusing,[142] article, if he is not already familiar with it. He may also wish to re-read what I have said above (pp. 108, 137 n.) on Churchill's rights and responsibilities as First Lord. Roskill's basic criticisms of my original article are two closely related propositions: Churchill all too frequently interfered in professional concerns, especially in strategy and operations; and this was made possible because he had 'a ready, indeed too ready, mouthpiece in the compliant Pound'. Again, 'What he did was to act always through the ready mouthpiece of Pound, thereby preserving the fiction that it was the First Sea Lord who was issuing the orders and directions.' That Churchill involved himself in the war at sea much more than is the wont of civilian First Lords is incontestable, and I have given a number of instances of this. Where I part company with Roskill is, first, in my firm belief that the Churchillian forays into the concerns of the sailors did not apply to naval strategy and operations *while he was First Lord*, except when political considerations were involved. Second, I believe that to impugn the character of the professional head of the Navy in the first four years of the war by accusing him of being too acquiescent, even servile, to Churchill is grossly unjust and, not to put too fine a point on it, is sheer nonsense as well.

Roskill's case is founded on these arguments.

(1) Ralph Edwards's diary entries. This I have dealt with, and I trust disposed of, above (p. 117).

(2) His, Roskill's, personal knowledge of Pound, particularly in 1939–41, when he served on the Naval Staff. 'During the latter period he often used me as his personal emissary to the C-in-C, Home Fleet and other senior officers, and I always reported personally to Pound on return from these missions.' I am not impressed. Roskill was a commander in this period and nowhere near the top echelon in the Naval Staff. Certainly he was in no

---

[141] Once (April 1940?), going over to see Lord Gort in France (he was C-in-C of the British Expeditionary Force), he said: 'I must have two secretaries with me. I am feeling very fertile!'

[142] As in his introductory personal allusion (which leaves a great deal unsaid), his concluding suggestion that the time has not come for a 'reworking' of the Official naval history of the war, and again when he takes me to task for failing to make use of the Forbes Papers at the British Museum and the Alexander Papers at Churchill College. For the good Captain's information, there is no separate collection of Forbes papers at the British Museum—only a file in the Cunningham MSS., of which I made good use; and the Alexander MSS. (except for the *Altmark* paper, above, p. 139) are worthless for Churchill's time at the Admiralty.

position to know what passed between Churchill and Pound, and therefore to have been able to make a perceptive assessment of their relationship.

(3) Pound's 'deferential attitude to Churchill (e.g. always addressing him as "Sir")'. This could give the wrong impression. Admiral Sir Guy Grantham, who was Naval Assistant to Pound during most of the first year of the war (until late May 1940), offers this first-hand testimony of the significance of Pound's 'deferential attitude': 'Anyone in a room with them when Winston stated in exact terms what he considered should be done, might well have been deceived by Pound saying, "Yes, Sir." I think Pound disliked disagreeing with Winston before he had examined any proposal, however wild it might be. Also he probably did not want other people to feel that they did not get on well.' Admiral Waller says of the later period: 'Naturally, Pound would not bring out his opposition, however strong, in front of subordinates: only those at the Chiefs of Staff meetings [over which Churchill presided at times] would actually hear those clashes. One has to judge by what came out for the staff to deal with and the directions given as to the action to be taken, plus of course the nuances of manner in which the matter was talked about. One can tell when the boss is fuming or shrugging his shoulders in resignation. One didn't see the latter!'

(4) '. . . the action of 10th April [in the first Battle of Narvik], which resulted in the loss of two of Warburton-Lee's ships [destroyers] and severe damage to a third would almost certainly have proved unnecessary but for the Admiralty's signal [direct to Warburton-Lee]. . . . the use of the plural in the sentence "we shall support whatever decision you take" can only refer to Churchill *and* Pound. . . . no naval officer, not even Pound with all his readiness to signal orders to distant ships, would have initiated such a signal.' One might perhaps question the wisdom of sending such a signal to a man like Captain B. A. W. Warburton-Lee, for if ever an officer was destined to win a posthumous V.C., it was this same Warburton-Lee. Indeed, one can argue that, given his character and his principles (the soundest principles of naval affairs of 'never lose time' and 'never lose touch'), he would never have hesitated over his decision and would have held back only if he was given a definite order to that effect. But this is not the issue here. This signal is the one specific instance advanced by Roskill of Churchill's interference in operations while he was First Lord. The use of the word 'we' most probably referred to the Board of Admiralty in its collective being, but if, which is unlikely, it referred personally to Churchill and Pound, it need indicate no more than that Churchill and Pound were in agreement, drafted the signal, and sent it. But no, the incident is magnified into a case of the First Lord forcing his First Sea Lord to adopt a course of action against his better professional judgement. This is stretching the known facts a bit, to put it mildly. Let me say here that I have not denied Churchill's important influence on the broad strategy of the Norwegian campaign and on the combined operations—indeed, I have called attention to both. He acted very largely in his capacity as Chairman of the Military Co-ordination Committee. But his interference in *naval operations* in whatever capacity, even in the Norwegian campaign, was minimal, all appearances to the contrary notwithstanding.

(5) Roskill introduces a plethora of illustrations of Churchill's meddling and of Pound's alleged knuckling under in these cases from the later period,

when Churchill was Prime Minister and Minister of Defence. This displays a foggy notion of relevance. My concern was, and remains, as the title of the essay should have made clear, Churchill as First Lord, though I do have a few passing references to the later period.[143] However, since Roskill has made so much of the later period, I now challenge the correctness of his thesis for this period, too. Though Churchill interfered more often in the prosecution of the war at sea after he went to No. 10, I see little evidence of weak and 'compliant' behaviour by Pound. We must accept that Churchill, when Prime Minister and Minister of Defence, regarded himself as the Supreme Commander, as he had every right to do, with the Chiefs of Staff as his professional commanders. All three—Pound, Brooke, and Portal (and Mountbatten later as Chief of Combined Operations) fought him hard. The Prime Minister did on occasion wear Pound down and have his way, as over the dispatch of the *Prince of Wales* and *Repulse* to Singapore in November 1941. But it never came easy, and by no stretch of the imagination can one deduce from this that Pound (any more than the other Service Chiefs) was ever a 'yes' man. He handled Churchill the Prime Minister as he had handled Churchill the First Lord. 'The P.M. is very difficult these days,' he wrote late in 1940, 'not that he has not always been. One has, however, to take a broad view because one has to deal with a man who is proving a magnificent leader and one just has to put up with his childishness as long as it isn't vital or dangerous. Also with a man like that it is not good policy to present him with a brick wall unless it is a thing which is really vital.'[144]

I have consulted with four of the most authoritative witnesses to the Churchill–Pound relationship, including the only living members of Pound's wartime personal staff: Vice-Admiral Sir Ronald Brockman, Secretary to the First Sea Lord, January 1940 to October 1943, Admiral Grantham, Vice-Admiral J. Ashley Waller, Naval Assistant to Pound in 1941–2, and Admiral Sir Henry Moore, VCNS (in succession to Phillips), October 1941–June 1943 (previously, ACNS (Trade), May 1940–October 1941).[145] I would not describe any of these officers as uncritical admirers of Pound. All four categorically deny the truth of Roskill's charge as it applies to their period of service with Pound. The picture that emerges from my correspondence with them is of a tough officer to whom no one could dictate, least of all, Churchill. He had, as I have pointed out, the common sense to know that a frontal collision would only increase Churchill's obstinacy, so that when one of Churchill's 'prayers' arrived, suggesting some operation, possibly but by no means always tactically advisable, and almost always practically impossible from sheer lack of available means, Pound would have the operation (e.g. 'Catherine' in the earlier period and the capture of Pantelleria, the Italian island 150 miles north-west of Malta, in the autumn of 1940) 'appreciated', the forces necessary assessed, the scale of expected losses added, and finally

[143] Speaking of irrelevance, we have another good instance in the pooh-poohing of my statement about the *First Lord's* good relations with the sailors afloat by citing examples of the strained relations between the *Prime Minister* and Cs-in-C.
[144] Pound to Cunningham, 1 Dec. 1940, Cunningham MSS., Add. MSS. 52561. Similarly, Pound to Cunningham, 20 Sept. 1940, ibid. Cf. above, p. 110.
[145] Respectively, letters of 5 May, 4 May, 2 Apr., 1 July 1973, and subsequent correspondence.

G

showing where the forces would have to come from and what their removal would mean. 'Thus', as Admiral Waller sums up the matter, 'Churchill was brought to a point of saying (nearly), "Who thought up this damn-fool project, anyway?" and it was then dead as a dodo.' Admiral Grantham adds to the statement I quoted above (p. 174): 'Once back in his office, Pound would have Winston's suggestions examined, and would then let Winston know whether his ideas were practicable, impracticable or could be met in some other way. At first I had a feeling that Pound was going to give way to Winston out of a sense of loyalty. But it was not so.' Admiral Brockman remembers Churchill circulating a paper to the Defence Committee (Operations) of the War Cabinet from the C-in-C, Bomber Command, Sir Arthur Harris, which had not passed through the Air Ministry. 'Pound wrote a really tough letter to Winston about this and got a tough reply—but the paper was withdrawn. Hardly the action of a supplicant.' Admiral Moore cites this instance when he was VCNS.

Winston had been pressing Pound to use our few battleships from Alexandria in what Pound thought (and I agreed with him) was not a suitable way. This had gone on for several days. Then Winston called a special meeting late one evening. (I think the meeting would have been early in 1942; only the Chiefs of Staff, Pug Ismay, and possibly the Prof [Lindemann] were there; no Ministers.) Pound asked me to come with him. Pound used our well-worn arguments but did not actually say 'no'. We got back to the Admiralty well after one a.m. I said to Pound, 'Well, I suppose in the morning we will get a direct order to send them.' Pound thought a moment or so, and then said, 'What will you bet against [my view] that we never hear about it again.' Pound knew his Winston. We never heard a word about it again!! Winston realized that Pound was not going to give in—Winston wanted to keep Pound as First Sea Lord—so never brought it up again. So Pound could say 'no' his way. This agrees with the advice Pound once gave me: 'Never say a direct "no" to the P.M. *at a meeting.* You can argue against it and as long as you don't exaggerate your case the P.M. will always let you have your say.'

Allowing for the fact that purely Admiralty affairs (e.g. Convoy PQ 17 and the Admiral North case) were not matters of general strategy which affected the three Services, those who attended the COS meetings were in a good position to observe the Churchill–Pound relationship. Thus, Admiral of the Fleet Lord Mountbatten of Burma, who was Chief of Combined Operations and a member of the Chiefs of Staff Committee in 1942–3, has called attention to 'how much Dudley Pound stood up to the Prime Minister, as he did in so many ways. . . . Winston had a tremendous respect for the old First Sea Lord, who was never prepared to give way to the Prime Minister, and who always expressed himself forcibly.'[146] An officer who was in constant

[146] Lord Mountbatten to Admiral J. H. Godfrey, 18 Nov. 1964, Godfrey MSS. Nearly ten years later, Mountbatten reiterated this belief ('I always admired the old boy, the way he stood up'), though with the qualification that he was relying on his own experience, and adding that 'the only time he [Pound] was finally defeated was on the *Repulse* and *Prince of Wales*'. Mountbatten in a conversation with Mr. Richard Hough, 28 June 1973. It is only fair to record Godfrey's reply to Mountbatten's letter

attendance at the COS meetings through most of the war, but who prefers not to be named, writes: 'The description of Pound as a "Yes" man could hardly be further from the truth. Churchill clearly had a high respect for Pound's views and judgement on most naval problems and affairs and I never heard him attempt to overrule Pound—any more than he attempted to overrule the collective views of the three COS. But that respect did not stop Churchill trying to talk them, individually or collectively, out of those opinions, sometimes at great length and with gusto!' My last witness is the former Military Assistant Secretary to the War Cabinet:

> I would not have called Pound a 'yes-man'. He over and over again stated his case in Cabinet, Defence Committee, or Staff Conference [COS plus a few particular ministers] to the P.M.—very well too. What happened outside the meetings is much harder to assess. Only the immediate staff in the Admiralty could give a direct answer [yes indeed: see above] . . . I don't think it is a sound assessment of the situation to say that Pound was simply Churchill's mouthpiece. Often it would be true to say that Pound acquiesced in what Churchill wanted, perhaps because he agreed with it, perhaps through being convinced after a considerable argument, perhaps because it was not worth opposing on unimportant matters when more important matters were under discussion. . . . both as First Lord, and as P.M., W.S.C. and Pound formed a partnership that made mistakes, but which stood the test very well. . . . Pound was never obsequious, that is certain.[147]

The matter of Churchill's intervention in naval operations, especially through his signals to Cunningham, requires an additional word of explanation. The Admiral's *A Sailor's Odyssey* has some sharp digs at the interminable telegrams from the Prime Minister/Minister of Defence. These were ostensibly from the First Sea Lord, but the language was unmistakable and Cunningham was never in any doubt about their origin. Admiral Brockman does not recollect Pound ever reacting strongly against these signals. He believes that some at least of these signals reflected Pound's wishes—that he knew the sure way to get something approved by Churchill was to sell him the idea verbally and then let him draft the necessary 'prayer' or signal as if it were his idea. 'Dudley was first class at this!' But there are two other, and larger, points here which I feel have escaped historians of the war and which put Churchill's role and methods in proper historical perspective.[148]

The first is that the Navy is not an expensive toy for admirals to manipulate and fight a lot of glorious battles; it is, or should be, an instrument of national policy designed and supplied to further the political and strategic

(20 Nov. 1964): 'I think the First Sea Lord won most of his battles about appointments but not about operations, e.g. Plan Catherine and the movement of *Prince of Wales* and *Repulse* to the East.' Godfrey MSS. I consider 'Operation Catherine' an excellent illustration of how Pound went about *blocking* a Churchillian foray into operations! As for sending the two capital ships to Singapore, one swallow hardly makes a summer. Pound regretted his having yielded over the *Prince of Wales* and *Repulse* against his better judgement. He never got over it.

[147] Lieutenant-General Sir Ian Jacob's letter to the author, 13 June 1973.

[148] The discussion of these essential aspects of the top direction owes a great deal to Lieutenant-Commander P. K. Kemp.

requirements of the nation. During the First War most of the admirals were expressing such thoughts as: 'If only the damned politicians would leave us alone to fight our war, we'd be much better off.' A lot of this doctrine lived on into the Second War among naval officers, and I think that Dudley Pound was one of the few senior admirals who realized that the naval war could not be fought in a vacuum. Churchill certainly had a clear idea of the true role of the Navy (and of the other two Services) in the context of grand strategy and national requirements, and made sure that the Navy did not forget it. I think he overdid it, but better that he did than the other way round. At least, he kept everyone on their toes, and kept them on their toes in the right way with a restless search for new methods and new ways of furthering the national requirements in the war as a whole. This, it seems to me, explains his 'interference' or, better, his continual prodding to keep the naval war moving as fast as it could in the direction he thought right to achieve the national aim. And I am inclined to think that the Navy needed it.

The other point arises out of this. Churchill, as well as being a very acute politician, was also a historian of considerable merit. It could not have escaped him that throughout English naval history, when the admirals had been left to their own devices, they had made a mess of things, and that it was only when there had been strong political direction at the top, as in the Seven Years War and the Napoleonic War, that the Navy had really achieved the full measure of its capability. In other wars, with weak political direction, as in the War of American Independence, Crimean War, and World War I up to 1917, it had very largely failed to achieve its potentiality. And I suspect that when Churchill became Prime Minister, he was determined that the necessary strong political control would never be lacking while he occupied the hot seat. So he automatically combined the office of Prime Minister with that of Minister of Defence to give himself the legal right of exercising this control. Although there are bound to be blunders in every war, it strikes me that the British made fewer of them during the last war than in most of the wars of the past. This I would, at least, in part, attribute to the strength of the political control as exercised by Churchill.

J'y suis, j'y reste, or, to borrow Captain Roskill's words (in reference to his *The War at Sea*), 'Re-reading today what I wrote on Churchill, Pound and this matter I see no cause to revise any of it.'

Chapter Five

Oran, 3 July 1940

Mistaken Judgement, Tragic Misunderstanding, or Cruel Necessity?[1]

(Charts 2, 3, 4, 5)

THE British naval attack on the French squadron at Mers-el-Kébir on 3 July, when seen against the vast panorama of the campaigns and battles of the Second World War, is an isolated and relatively minor operation. It would appear at first sight to merit only the briefest attention. Yet, in its origins, execution, and consequences the operation offers the historian a rich harvest of facts and inferences and provides a revealing searchlight on the character of human motivations and relationships. The event has other kinds of attraction for the historian: it has been the subject of continuing controversy and it has many of the elements of Greek tragedy.

[1] The British generally refer to the episode as the 'Oran' affair; the French, with more accuracy, as 'Mers-el-Kébir'. My primary British sources have been these Public Record Office materials: scattered documents in ADM 1, 116, and 199, but especially the pertinent volume of the 'First Sea Lord's Records, 1939–1945' (ADM 205/4), and the War Cabinet minutes ('Confidential Annexes' to the 'Conclusions': CAB 65/12–15) and papers (CAB 66/8–9), Chiefs of Staff minutes (CAB 79/5) and papers (CAB 80/12–15), and the Chiefs of Staff Joint Planning Sub-Committee minutes (CAB 84/2) and papers (CAB 84/14–16). I am assured on the best authority that the Naval Intelligence staff records, which, as with certain other records, have had to be given extended closure for security reasons, add nothing of material substance to the story as revealed in the Cabinet and Admiralty records available in the Public Record Office. However, many of the decisions at that critical time were taken orally on a very high level and are not fully recorded. I have, additionally, made use of the papers of Admirals of the Fleet Sir James Somerville (Churchill College) and A. B. Cunningham, and Admiral J. H. Godfrey. The papers of my good friend the late Commander M. G. Saunders, who had begun to assemble material for a book on the French Fleet from June 1940 through 1942, were useful, as were the recollections of Sir Clifford Jarrett and a number of distinguished officers: Marshal of the Royal Air Force Sir John Slessor, Admiral of the Fleet Sir Algernon Willis, Admirals Sir Charles Daniel, Sir William Davis, Sir Guy Grantham, and Sir Manley Power, Vice-Admirals Sir Ronald Brockman and B. B. Schofield, Rear-Admirals G. K. Collett, E. N. V. Currie, R. M. Dick, and K. H. Farnhill, and Captains K. L. Harkness and the late T. M. Brownrigg.

In the unpredictable course of a great war nothing can be sadder or more shocking than the spectacle of two nations, till very recently allied, directing at each other the weapons of destruction that were intended to repel the common aggressors. Mers-el-Kébir went back to the cataclysm of events following the Dunkirk evacuation (28 May–4 June), when one of the main anxieties of the British War Cabinet centred on the fate of the French Fleet, should the French military resistance collapse. Exposed to the powerful armoured thrusts of the German invaders, the French Army rapidly disintegrated. On 11 June the Government retired to Tours, and on the 14th to Bordeaux, on which day the conquerors entered Paris. By this date the Army was no longer capable of organized resistance, and it was clear that the French might have to negotiate with the enemy. On the 10th, Italy had declared war on Britain and France, bringing a fleet of 6 battleships (2 new, 4 old), 19 cruisers, 49 large and about 70 smaller flotilla craft, and some 100 submarines to Germany's side.

The military deterioration had not affected the French Navy, the second largest in Europe, which remained a disciplined and integrated force under the rigid control of its Commander-in-Chief, Admiral of the Fleet François Darlan. Its main units comprised 5 old 22,000-ton battleships, completed in 1913–16, 3 of which had undergone extensive modernization in 1932–5 (*Bretagne, Provence, Lorraine*—the other two were the *Courbet* and *Paris*); 2 modern battle cruisers (*Dunkerque, Strasbourg*) of 26,500 tons, completed in 1937–8, armed with eight 13-inch guns, capable of 30 knots or better, and at least the equal of the German battle cruisers *Scharnhorst* and *Gneisenau*; 2 powerful battleships of 35,000 tons nearing completion (*Jean Bart, Richelieu*), armed with eight 15-inch guns and designed for a speed of over 30 knots; seven 8-inch-gun cruisers of 10,000 tons; eleven 6-inch (or 6·1-inch) cruisers of 5,800–7,600 tons; 2 aircraft carriers; 28 large destroyers of 2,100–2,800 tons; 26 smaller destroyers; and 70-odd submarines. Except for the older battleships, none of these warships was more than thirteen or fourteen years old, and the latest destroyers were as fast and well armed as any in the world. In general, it was a homogeneous Fleet, the guns and communications equipment of the warships were excellent, and the crews disciplined and well trained: 80 per cent were long-service personnel. The ships, however, were without the latest means of locating both a surface and a submerged enemy that were to play so important a part in the war at sea: radar and asdic, a deficiency that the Royal Navy was in the process of rectifying in its own units. The French ships had already proved themselves in various Allied operations such as the Norwegian campaign, the escorting of Atlantic convoys, mine-laying in the English Channel, and safeguarding sea communications in the Mediterranean. They played a valuable role at Dunkirk, where the smaller ships suffered severe losses.

Co-operation between the two navies had, on the whole, been good, although the First Sea Lord, Pound, the VCNS, Phillips, and the Royal Navy generally did not have too high an opinion of the French Naval Command. Pound had for years been rather contemptuous of the French Navy, as when in the early twenties he said, with deliberate exaggeration to be sure, that it was not worth a hatful of crabs. An officer on Pound's staff relates:

> I had been with him and the other Chiefs of Staff to Paris more than once, for pretty abortive meetings with the French COS, and once we went to Marceau, where the French Naval Operational Headquarters had been established. The purpose of that particular visit was to persuade the French to operate their ships in conjunction with the R.N. They agreed to take over convoy escort duties on the Gib./U.K. run and to help with Atlantic Convoy protection. We thought we had got them to take a really useful part. After one round trip, they withdrew from the Gib. run, saying their ships had to refit. All complete cock, of course, as they had quite a large fleet virtually unemployed. After that the general feeling was that they could not be counted on to do anything worthwhile.[2]

Relations, nevertheless, were generally amicable until the Franco-German armistice.

The capital-ship situation in particular gave the British cause for concern. There was a numerical superiority on paper: Britain— 11 battleships and 3 battle cruisers, with 5 battleships building; Germany–2 pocket-battleships, 2 battle cruisers, with 2 battleships building. But this was deceptive, since a number of the big ships had to be available to escort convoys when the *Scharnhorst* and *Gneisenau* were reported in the Atlantic. At least six battleships

---

[2] An assessment of the French Navy in its nine months of co-operation with the Royal Navy reads in part: 'At sea the French temperament and outlook differed from our own. They were content with fewer days at sea than ourselves, though this is not to say that they did not work to the full extent of their own ideals. The spirit of the Officers and men was excellent, but it took a little time for the British Officers to understand the French point of view. Their arrangements for supervision of tactical and weapon training was inadequate from British standards, and practices and exercises lacked realism. Their standards of night fighting, and of air defence were well below those of the Royal Navy. The French were behind us in technical matters such as wireless and anti-submarine equipment due to lack of funds for development in peace time. If due allowance is made for differences of outlook and temperament, the co-operation given by the French at sea was excellent.' 'Fulfilment of Our Promises to France: Naval Co-operation', a draft Naval Staff paper, *c.* 7 Mar. 1941, approved by the First Sea Lord. ADM 1/11328.

had to keep watch on the six Italian battleships in the Mediterranean. There was no capital-ship margin for the Far East, where a bellicose Japan could not be relied on to remain neutral. The cruiser situation was equally perilous. Using Norwegian and Biscay bases, the German Navy could raise havoc on the ocean trade routes by sending out cruisers, auxiliary cruisers, and submarines. Cruisers were also needed in the Mediterranean to safeguard communications with the Middle and Far East and to watch the Italian Fleet. Most desperate was the destroyer shortage, following the heavy losses in the Norwegian campaign and the Dunkirk evacuation (6 were sunk and 19 damaged). Only a hundred or so were left for convoy duties and to help repel the expected German invasion in the near future. Under these circumstances, the loss of the co-operation of the French Fleet would constitute a serious blow to British hopes of victory. But should that Fleet be added to German and Italian naval strength, it would confront Britain—Churchill does not exaggerate—with 'mortal dangers': the ability of the Royal Navy to retain control of sea communications would be in grave jeopardy indeed. Would the French ask for an armistice and would the armistice include the surrender of the French Fleet? These were the questions that loomed so large in British calculations after Dunkirk.

Already, on 7 June, with the Germans 70 miles from Paris and possibly but a week away from its occupation, the problem of the disposition of the French Fleet in the event of France pulling out of the war was under serious discussion in London. At a meeting in the First Sea Lord's room attended by Pound, Lord Hankey (Chancellor of the Duchy of Lancaster), and Sir Alexander Cadogan and William Strang of the Foreign Office (respectively, Permanent Under-Secretary of State and Under-Secretary of State), the fear was expressed that the Germans would, as part of an armistice, insist that the French Fleet be surrendered. According to Pound, 'the only practical way to deal with the matter was to sink the French Fleet'. What he had in mind was an attempt to persuade Darlan to scuttle the ships *in advance of armistice negotiations*, so that the Germans could not put pressure on the French by threatening to destroy Paris if the Fleet were not handed over. He believed that Darlan might accept the British proposal, as he would hate the thought of surrendering the ships to the Germans, but that he would not agree to send the Fleet into British harbours. It was decided to send Vice-Admiral Sir Geoffrey Blake, the ACNS (Foreign), over to persuade Darlan that, to avoid the ignominy of surrendering the Fleet, it had better be scuttled.[3] In the event, Blake did not go.

[3] Minutes of the meeting, ADM 205/4.

It was on 11 June that the Chiefs of Staff first revealed their concern over the French Fleet in a report to the War Cabinet. It envisaged the collapse of French resistance and stated the main points that Pound had made on the 7th: the Germans would very probably insist on the surrender of the French Fleet before agreeing to an armistice; the French, if they were set on capitulation, would not be likely to agree to their Fleet joining the British; there were but two alternatives: '(*a*) to attempt to persuade as many French ships as possible to join our own Fleet. We cannot expect such efforts to meet with much success; (*b*) if (*a*) fails, to press the French to sink the whole of their Fleet.' It might also be possible to remove or destroy valuable naval equipment from such French bases as Brest and Toulon, to block or destroy French naval bases which might be useful for German and Italian operations, and to secure the use for British forces of such colonial bases as Dakar and Casablanca.[4]

On 15 June, with War Cabinet approval, Pound reverted to a variant of the tack which he had all but dismissed on the 7th as impracticable. He instructed Captain the Hon. Edward Pleydell-Bouverie, Head of the British Naval Mission in France, to secure the immediate transfer of the uncompleted battleships *Richelieu* and *Jean Bart* (at Brest and St. Nazaire, respectively) to the United Kingdom (the Admiralty could supply escorts and tugs), and, as 'a wise precaution', the battle cruisers *Dunkerque* and *Strasbourg* (at Mers-el-Kébir) to Gibraltar. 'Should it become necessary later to transfer other French ships to the United Kingdom, Admiral Darlan could be sure that they would receive a warm welcome and be given every facility.' With this end in view, all spare ammunition, torpedoes, and other armament stores should be embarked forthwith, especially from Cherbourg and Brest, with the help of French ships. 'The main point', said Churchill, 'was to secure the French Fleet.'[5]

From this date the fate of the French warships was the dominant concern of the War Cabinet, Service Chiefs, and Admiralty. The DDOD (H) noted on 16 June: 'There was much talk about the future of the French Fleet. It is desperately important to ensure it doesn't fall into the hands of the enemy. But we mustn't go sinking it out of hand. It'll put us out of court vis-à-vis U.S.A.'[6] The last sentence is significant. At this stage the emphasis was still on friendly

---

[4] COS (40) 444, 'Plans to Meet a Certain Eventuality', CAB 80/12. The Service Chiefs at this date were Pound, Air Chief Marshal Sir Cyril Newall (Chief of the Air Staff), and General Sir John Dill (Chief of the Imperial General Staff).

[5] WM 167 (40), CAB 65/13.   [6] Diary of Captain Ralph Edwards.

persuasion—that the French either send their principal naval units to British ports or sink their Fleet, with the former course preferred.

As the prospect of the French having to conclude an armistice loomed closer, the British sought assurances that the French Fleet would, regardless of developments, not be handed over to the Germans and Italians. On 12 June, as he was leaving the Château du Muguet in Briare, near Orléans, where the Supreme War Council had been meeting, to return to London, Churchill took Darlan aside and asked, 'Admiral, what are you going to do about the fleet? I hope you will never surrender it!' 'There is no question of doing so', Darlan replied emphatically. 'It would be contrary to our naval traditions and honour. We will never hand it over to Germany or Italy. Orders to scuttle will be given in the event of danger.'[7]

The following day, at a conference at the Préfecture in Tours during his last visit to France, Churchill was surprised by the request of the French Premier, Paul Reynaud, that Britain consider allowing him to sign an armistice. 'Under no circumstances', was his response, 'will Great Britain waste time in reproaches and recriminations. But that is a very different matter from becoming a consenting party to a peace made in contravention of the agreement so recently concluded.' The reference was to the Anglo-French declaration of 28 March in which the two Governments 'mutually undertake that during the present war they will neither negotiate nor conclude an armistice or treaty of peace except by mutual agreement'. It would be advisable, Churchill continued, that the French make a formal appeal to President Roosevelt and receive his answer before coming to such a grave decision. The British response to the French request would be determined by the tenor of the President's reply; but Churchill warned that if France announced her intention of suing for a separate peace, 'we shall have a host of problems to look into'.[8] At no point was there any mention of the Fleet,[9] but the French could have been under no

---

[7] Jacques Benoist-Méchin: *Sixty Days that Shook the West: the Fall of France, 1940* (London, 1963), p. 308; ii. 149 in the original French edition, *Soixante jours qui ébranlèrent l'occident, 10 mai–10 juillet 1940* (3 vols., Paris, 1956). I have in most instances quoted from the English edition, which is quite full for the episodes that most directly concern our story. In this instance, however, I have altered the English translation to conform more closely to the original. When material is only in the French edition, I cite that edition, naturally. Benoist-Méchin was a Vichy official.

[8] Benoist-Méchin, *Sixty Days that Shook the West*, pp. 319–21, Major-General Sir Edward Spears, *Assignment to Catastrophe* (2 vols., London, 1954), ii. 209–11. Spears was Churchill's personal representative with the French Premier.

[9] De Gaulle, then Under-Secretary of State for National Defence, is the only witness who states that the Fleet was discussed at Tours. Charles de Gaulle, *War Memoirs. The Call to Honour, 1940–1942* (2 vols., London, 1955), i. 75.

illusion as to its prime position among the '*ensemble de problèmes*'. In the small hours of 14 June Reynaud dispatched an appeal to Roosevelt for American armed intervention; France would be forced to capitulate if the United States would not pledge to enter the war 'in the very near future'.

In the late afternoon of 15 June the French Council of Ministers accepted the famous, or infamous, Chautemps proposal, thereby restoring a measure of unity to a Cabinet badly divided between the pro- and anti-armistice men. The principle of an armistice was accepted by a 13–6 vote, but with strings. A neutral country would inquire of Germany what her armistice conditions would be. If they were honourable, the Government would study them; if not, they would fight on. Reynaud reported on the Council meeting in a telegram to Churchill that evening. In the presence of Spears and the British Ambassador, Sir Ronald Campbell, he began to write: 'The Council of Ministers does not doubt that these [armistice] conditions would in effect be unacceptable, but considers it indispensable that this should be proved beyond doubt . . .' He again asked the British Government to release the French Government from its obligation to enter into no separate negotiations, and he formally declared that if the terms (to be ascertained through the United States) included the surrender of the Fleet, they would be rejected out of hand. If the British Government withheld its consent to this step, given the feelings of the Council he would have to resign. At this point Roosevelt's reply to the French appeal was handed to Reynaud. 'As he read it he grew still paler, his face contracted, his eyes became just slits . . . "Our appeal has failed," he said in a small toneless voice, "the Americans will not declare war." ' The President promised 'ever increasing quantities [of] material and supplies of all kinds', but no more. Only Congress could undertake a military commitment. Reynaud now added this postscript to his telegram to Churchill: 'At meeting held in Tours last Thursday [13 June] it was agreed at your suggestion that the question of authorising a request for an armistice would be reconsidered if President Roosevelt's reply was negative. This eventuality having materialised the question must now be put afresh.' He asked for an answer early in the morning of the 16th.[10]

Sunday, 16 June, was the crucial day. The last of the British troops were being evacuated from France, and the Germans were bombarding the Loire bridges. At the Council meeting in the

[10] Sir Llewellyn Woodward, *History of the Second World War. British Foreign Policy in the Second World War* (3 vols., London, 1970–1), i. 272–3, Spears, *Assignment to Catastrophe*, ii. 265–7.

morning Marshal Pétain, Vice-President of the Council, read out a letter of resignation. He could no longer remain in the Government; an immediate cessation of hostilities was the only way to save the country. He agreed to wait, however, until Churchill's reply to the Chautemps proposal arrived.

The War Cabinet met in the morning to consider the reply to Reynaud's urgent message. They would not accept as sufficient his assurance that the Fleet would not be surrendered. It was the Prime Minister's view that they 'should make it an absolute condition for the granting of our consent that the French Fleet should sail forthwith for British ports pending any discussion of armistice terms. . . . in no circumstances whatsoever would the British Government participate in any negotiations for armistice or peace. . . . President Roosevelt should be sent a copy of our reply, and urged not to act as a mediator in any circumstances unless the safety of the French Fleet was previously secured.' There was apparently unanimous support for this view, with the Admiralty, through the First Sea Lord (the First Lord, A. V. Alexander, was in Scotland), giving strong backing to Churchill's condition about the Fleet.[11] Note that Pound's scuttling idea had been shelved, and that it was Churchill's bolder course that had now been officially adopted.

The telegram to Campbell was dispatched at 12.35 p.m. It gave the Government's 'full consent' to the French to sound out the Germans on armistice terms, 'provided, but only provided, that the French Fleet is sailed forthwith for British harbours pending negotiations. . . . His Majesty's Government being resolved to continue the war wholly exclude themselves from all part in the above mentioned enquiry concerning an armistice.' Spears was 'very perturbed' by the message. It was a mistake, he felt, to do anything in the nature of releasing the French from their agreement. London 'had opened a dangerous door to the defeatists'. Furthermore, the French, especially the Navy, might 'feel insulted by the peremptory condition that they should sail forthwith to British harbours'. In defence of Churchill and the War Cabinet, it must be said that there seemed to be no alternative, since the French Army was by now in a state of complete disintegration. Spears and Campbell delivered the telegram to the Premier early in the afternoon. Reynaud was 'annoyed and took no pains to disguise it'. He feared that it would strengthen the position of the ministers who were backing Pétain's desire for an immediate armistice, and, moreover, that if the French Mediterranean Fleet were withdrawn to British ports, it

[11] WM 168 (40), CAB 65/13.

would open all French North Africa as targets to the Italians. Campbell and Spears left Reynaud's office at 2.30 p.m.

Campbell received a telegram of 3.10, in continuation of the first, at 3.55 p.m. It stated that His Majesty's Government 'expect to be consulted as soon as any armistice terms are received. . . . You should impress on French Government that in stipulating for removal of French Fleet to British ports we have in mind French interests as well as our own and are convinced that it will strengthen the hands of the French Government in any armistice discussions if they can show that the French Navy is out of reach of the German forces.' Again the two Englishmen hustled the message over to Reynaud. All three reacted to it pretty much as they had to the first message.

At about 4.30, while Reynaud was discussing the two telegrams with his visitors, he received a telephone call from de Gaulle in London transmitting the text of a dramatic offer. It was a solemn declaration of complete union between the two countries which had been approved by Churchill and the War Cabinet. The Prime Minister hoped that this far-reaching offer would persuade the French Government to continue the struggle from North Africa. Reynaud was 'transfigured with joy'. He believed his colleagues might accept the new proposal of union at the meeting which was to start at 5 p.m. Encouraged by the prospects, Churchill and the Service Chiefs had arranged that afternoon to embark on a cruiser so as to arrive at Concarneau in Brittany on the morning of the 17th to confer with Reynaud. The British party had actually boarded their special train at Waterloo in the evening of the 16th when the news reached them of a French ministerial crisis, which put an end to the Brittany meeting. For Reynaud, having failed to impress the Council of Ministers with the British proposal, had no alternative, he felt, but to resign. Most of the ministers mistrusted British motives, seeing in the offer of union either a device to delay the armistice or to make France subservient to Britain as a kind of dominion. Reynaud never showed the ministers the two earlier telegrams of the 16th, nor gave them their sense: there was merely a quick allusion to them. Accordingly, the Council did not hear either of the British consent to a French approach for an armistice or of the stipulation about the Fleet. Reynaud had assumed that the offer of union superseded the two telegrams dealing with the Fleet, and Spears and Campbell had assured him that this was the case. When they returned to the British consulate, they found a 4.45 p.m. telegram from the Foreign Office: 'Please suspend action' on the two earlier telegrams. They got a message through to Reynaud during the Council meeting to say that they had been right and that the two telegrams should be considered as 'cancelled'.[12]

The new French Government, headed by the arch-defeatist Pétain, included Darlan, Weygand, and Paul Baudouin, as Ministers of Marine, Defence, and Foreign Affairs, respectively. Darlan retained the post of Commander-in-Chief of the Fleet. Without hesitation, and in breach of the declaration of 28 March, at 12.30 a.m., 17 June, Baudouin asked the Spanish Ambassador to transmit a request to the Germans for armistice terms. At 1 a.m. he informed Campbell of what he had done, while assuring him that the armistice terms would be rejected if they included the surrender of the Fleet. And Darlan told the Ambassador: 'So long as I can issue orders to [the Fleet], you have nothing to fear.'[13] In the afternoon of the 17th Campbell informed Pétain (whom he found quite hopeless: 'Conversations with him are fruitless') that a 'necessary pre-condition' of British assent to a French bid for an armistice was that their Fleet should immediately sail for British ports, so that it would be in British control when the Germans asked for it. Pétain replied rather feebly that the Fleet would never be turned over; in his view it should be scuttled. The Ambassador reminded Baudouin that the British Government expected to be consulted before German terms were accepted. He also reminded French ministers that the 28 March agreement had been concluded on behalf of the French Republic, not any particular Government.

The fresh assurances did not satisfy Churchill, who, with his colleagues, was sure that the Germans would insist on the surrender of the Fleet as a *sine qua non* of an armistice. During the night of 17–18 June he sent a last appeal, a sharp one, to Pétain and Weygand 'not to injure their Ally by delivering over to the enemy the fine French fleet. Such an act would scarify their names for a thousand years of history. Yet this result may easily come by frittering away these few precious hours when the fleet can be sailed in safety to British or American ports, carrying with it the hope and the future and the honour of France.' The message included the promise, inserted at Pound's request, that the Fleet would not be incorporated in the Royal Navy: it would continue to operate freely.[14] But the Pétain Government would neither promise to sail the Fleet to British or American ports, nor to scuttle it. For them the Fleet constituted a stake to play in the negotiations

---

[12] '"Suspended" would have been a better word' is Churchill's laconic comment. The principal British sources on these events of the 16th in Bordeaux are Spears, *Assignment to Catastrophe*, i. 282–5, 289–95, and Woodward, *British Foreign Policy in the Second World War*, i. 275–82.   [13] ibid., pp. 283–4.   [14] ibid., pp. 293–4.

with the Germans: France could not throw away her best card so that another could play it.

The British spotlight from now until the events of 3 July was on Darlan. Churchill afterwards grieved for the Admiral who threw away an opportunity to achieve immortality.

Admiral Darlan had but to sail in any one of his ships to any port outside France to become the master of all French interests beyond German control. . . . He would have carried with him outside the German reach the fourth Navy in the world, whose officers and men were personally devoted to him. Acting thus, Darlan would have become the chief of the French Resistance with a mighty weapon in his hand. British and American dockyards and arsenals would have been at his disposal for the maintenance of his fleet. . . . The whole French Empire would have rallied to him. Nothing could have prevented him from being the Liberator of France. The fame and power which he so ardently desired were in his grasp. Instead, he went forward through two years of worrying and ignominious office to a violent death, a dishonoured grave, and a name long to be execrated by the French Navy and the nation he had hitherto served so well.[15]

The 58-year-old Admiral of the Fleet was without doubt the unchallenged head of the French Navy, whose strength and efficiency he had done so much to build up and maintain since he was appointed Chief of the Navy General Staff at the end of 1937. (He assumed the additional title of C-in-C of the French Fleet when war broke out.) 'He appears to be a typical French sailor, short, sturdy, tanned face and smokes a pipe', wrote Admiral Sir William James after meeting him early in 1940. This 'florid, dapper little officer, unimpressive both in manner and appearance' (as Sir Samuel Hoare described him) was widely regarded in his time as an enigma. He had declared that the Fleet would never be allowed to fall into German hands—to Churchill on the 12th and to Campbell early on the 17th. On the morning of the 15th he had said brusquely to the politician Herriot: 'Is it true that those bastards Pétain and Weygand wish to conclude an armistice? If this is so, do you hear, I am leaving with the fleet.' He had spoken in similar terms on 3 June to Jules Moch, and to the Air Force General d'Astier de Lavigerie on 14 June —that, as he put it to the latter, 'We will fight to the end, and if necessary, I will put the whole fleet under the British flag.'[16] This

[15] Churchill, *The Second World War*, vol. ii. *Their Finest Hour*, pp. 202–3.

[16] Rear-Admiral Paul Auphan, who was Assistant Chief (Operations) of the French Naval Staff, told the Head of the British Naval Mission in Bordeaux sometime before the ships left for North Africa that the *Richelieu* and *Jean Bart* would be sent to the United Kingdom under certain (undefined) circumstances. Pleydell-Bouverie, 'Preliminary Report on the Situation Regarding the Fleet', n.d., ADM 205/4. According

mood quickly evaporated. In the evening of 16 June, when Darlan was about to become a minister in the Pétain Government, he again met Herriot, who assumed that he was planning for the departure of the Government to North Africa. 'No,' Darlan answered. 'A Government that leaves never returns.' 'This Admiral knows how to swim' was Herriot's terse comment![17] The next day Cambon, the French Chargé d'Affaires in London, told a Foreign Office official that the new French Government would 'behave worse than King Leopold' of Belgium—that they ought not to put too much trust in Darlan. They did not, particularly when Darlan emerged as a prime mover of a German armistice.

Overmastering ambition is often cited as one possible explanation of Darlan's volte-face. Amouroux wonders whether Pétain's offer to the self-seeking Darlan to make him 'First Consul' in a revived Consulate had not weakened the Admiral's original intention to take the Fleet to British ports.[18] Loyalty to Pétain may be another partial explanation of Darlan's behaviour. Also, like Weygand, Pétain, and the other defeatists, Darlan was convinced by 17 June that Britain could not survive, and he had accordingly trimmed his sails to the prevailing wind. Then, too, he believed, with the Government, that the Fleet should be retained as a weapon for fighting on, or as a bargaining counter in any armistice or peace negotiations. (It was, in the words of the Press Attaché at the French Embassy in London, 'the means by which the prisoner could blackmail his jailer'.) Another key to understanding Darlan is that, in de Gaulle's words, 'The fleet is Darlan's fief. A feudal lord does not surrender his fief.' Reynaud quotes Darlan as often saying at Vichy: 'I did not create a Fleet to offer it to the British.' Darlan and the French Navy generally were somewhat anti-Royal Navy, though never pro-German. This story is relevant. Admiral Schofield, who was Assistant to the British Naval Attaché in Paris just before the war, writes of a luncheon party to which Darlan had asked him. 'He was an excellent host, but there was no doubt that he was extremely jealous of the position held by the Royal Navy in the world generally. He pointed with pride to the *Dunkerque* and *Strasbourg*

---

to Churchill, as late as the morning of 17 June Darlan had told the French General Georges that he was determined to order the ships to British, American, or French colonial harbours. Churchill, *Their Finest Hour*, p. 202.

[17] Édouard Herriot, *Épisodes, 1940–1944* (Paris, 1950), pp. 64–5, 75, Albert Kammerer, *La Passion de la flotte française* ('Édition définitive', Paris, 1950), pp. 66–7.

[18] Henri Amouroux, *Le 18 Juin 1940* (Paris, 1964), pp. 241–3. The original published source of the incident appears to have been Admiral J. T. Docteur, *La Grande Énigme de la guerre: Darlan, amiral de la flotte* (Paris, 1949), pp. 73–4. The date was 11 June (Docteur gives it incorrectly as 12 June).

and the flotilla of fast and heavily armed destroyer leaders which accompanied them and asked "Have you British anything as good as this?"'[19]

In the late morning of 18 June, after deciding for, then against, sending the Fleet to British ports, the Pétain Government adopted a unanimous solemn and irrevocable decision 'not to let the Fleet fall into enemy hands in any circumstances. If its surrender were included in the armistice conditions they would be rejected out of hand, *however grave the consequences of such a refusal.*'[20] This decision was immediately made known to the British Government. Baudouin, in giving the same assurance to Campbell, explained that the decision had been changed, that is, *not* to send the Fleet to Britain, because the ministers thought that, as a point of honour, France should receive the German terms while her Fleet and Army were still fighting. By this date Churchill had simply lost faith in the word of the French politicians. His harsh statement in the House of Commons on 18 June can have left the new French Government in no doubt that the British still held France to the agreement of 28 March. However, he was momentarily encouraged by the results of a conference between Alexander, Pound, and Darlan at Bordeaux in the afternoon of the 18th.

The First Sea Lord and First Lord came to learn at first hand from Darlan what French intentions were as regards their Fleet. What they heard–they did more listening than talking–left them for the moment optimistic.[21] 'With a warmth unusual in him', Darlan gave an explicit promise that nothing would ever induce him to surrender the Fleet. It would go on fighting until an armistice was called, and if the Germans insisted on its surrender as a

[19] From Admiral Schofield's unpublished memoirs (1951), cited in a letter to the author, 4 July 1972. As French writers see it, however, the jealousy operated in reverse, e.g.: 'For Darlan the truth is simple: England has always been jealous of the increase of our maritime potential. She made every effort to place obstacles to it, by every possible means, in the interwar naval conferences', etc. Benoist-Méchin, *Soixante jours qui ébranlèrent l'occident,* iii. 538.

[20] Benoist-Méchin, *Sixty Days that Shook the West,* p. 396.

[21] My account is derived primarily from the official British record of the conversation by the Deputy Director of Plans, Captain E. G. H. Bellars, who had been present; ADM 205/4. There is some extra detail in Rear-Admiral Paul Auphan and Jacques Mordal (alias for Captain Hervé Cras, French Navy), *The French Navy in World War II* (Annapolis, 1959), pp. 109–10. Auphan had been there. Not in either account is Pound's introductory remark, that if the *Richelieu, Jean Bart, Dunkerque,* and *Strasbourg* sailed to England, they would be received with open arms. Amouroux, *Le 18 Juin 1940,* p. 239, who relied on Pétain's papers and interviews with Auphan for his account of the meeting. Many writers (among them Benoist-Méchin, Docteur, Varillon, Hytier, and Böhme) incorrectly date the meeting on the 19th. (Benoist-Méchin corrected the error in his English edition.)

condition, there would be no armistice. The Fleet would in that case 'fight to the end and anything that escaped would go to a friendly country or would be destroyed'. The British had heard this sort of talk before. But what impressed Pound and Alexander was that the French were continuing hostilities against Italy (the Fleet had bombarded the Italian coast and sunk two submarines) and the measures taken by Darlan to remove the warships from ports about to be seized by the Germans. Darlan said that the *Jean Bart* would probably have to be destroyed, if they could not remove her from St. Nazaire before the 20th, since tide conditions would then not be right for another month;

that the *Richelieu* [at Brest] should have left that day for Dakar and that all other ships that could steam and were in danger, by reason of the enemy advance, of falling into their hands would go to Dakar and the remainder would be destroyed. He suggested America or Canada ultimately for the *Richelieu* on account of working up and final fitting which, if done in England, would subject her to a heavy scale of bombing attack. . . . He stressed the point that any ship which is not fit to take her place in the battle line but can steam will be sent away from French ports and those that can fight will remain at their war stations until other orders are issued.

The First Lord and First Sea Lord took their leave, 'moved, cordial, and apparently satisfied'.[22] They were satisfied that the ships would remain French or be destroyed. They had no doubt of Darlan's complete authority over the Fleet, or his sincerity in undertaking that it would never fall into German hands.[23]

Events quickly seemed to bear out Darlan's assurances. French

[22] Auphan, 'The French Navy Enters World War II', *United States Naval Institute Proceedings*, lxxxii (June 1956), 601. Pierre Maillaud, the well-informed French journalist, learned that Pound had returned from Bordeaux with reassuring news about the French Fleet. Robert Mengin, *No Laurels for de Gaulle* (London, 1967), p. 66. Alexander sent a telegram to Churchill, which, the Prime Minister reported to the War Cabinet on the 19th, gave 'a more encouraging picture of the general situation than we had been led to believe possible'. WM 172 (40), CAB 65/7. But cf. Auphan and Mordal, *The French Navy in World War II*, p. 110: 'Admiral Pound returned immediately to London, where he gave Admiral Odend'hal [Head of the French Naval Mission] the impression of not being too happy over his trip, but the other British officers who had accompanied him were full of confidence.' Darlan's visitors had made a sour impression on him: 'The English gave him the impression of heirs who had come to see if the dying man had indeed made his will in their favour and do not worry about his health.' Kammerer, *La Passion de la flotte française*, pp. 95–6 n., citing a Darlan note of 9 July 1940 in the French naval records.

[23] In the evening of the 19th, Alexander, who had remained in Bordeaux, Lord Lloyd, the Colonial Secretary, and Campbell had called on Pétain and Baudouin. Apart from the usual strong assurances—the Fleet would be scuttled if the armistice terms called for its surrender—which, according to Baudouin, 'seemed to satisfy' the Englishmen—nothing further could be got out of the old Marshal.

Admiralty signals of 18 June ordered that no warship must fall into enemy hands intact. In case of need, the rallying point for any warship or aircraft was to be North Africa. Any warship having difficulty in getting there, and in danger of falling into enemy hands, was to be destroyed or scuttled on orders from higher authority.[24] These instructions were carried out with perfect discipline, as Benoist-Méchin points out. As the Germans advanced along the coast, the French Navy, which showed no sign of disintegration and whose communications remained intact, was able to evacuate almost all its warships and merchant shipping from the Channel and Biscay ports. Some of these ships made for British ports, but the majority, including the modern ships, sailed for French North or West African ports. Thus, of the larger ships, the *Richelieu*, which had just completed her trials, put to sea on the 18th and arrived at Dakar on the 23rd. The *Jean Bart* left the Loire for Casablanca on the 19th. Sloops and smaller patrol vessels unable to put to sea were scuttled at Lorient on the 19th, La Pallice (near La Rochelle) on the 22nd, and Le Verdon (entrance of the Gironde estuary) on the 24th—that is, as soon as German forces reached the outskirts of these ports. The warships based on Toulon (eight cruisers) were not moved, as they were in a less vulnerable port and, moreover, were ostensibly still engaged in hostilities with Italy. Nevertheless, Vice-Admiral Duplat, commanding the Toulon squadron, issued instructions as to how and when ships were to be scuttled.

'In these circumstances', asks Varillon, 'was it fair for Churchill to write in 1949 "that no French warship stirred or put itself beyond the reach of German power"? History is there to answer: in June 1940, *not a single undamaged unit* was captured by the enemy in the ports of Ponant [French Atlantic ports]. And that was not all. For once the ships had been scuttled, the harbour installations were likewise destroyed. In Cherbourg, the arsenal was blown up. In Brest, Lorient and La Rochelle, oil reservoirs, maga-zines, ammunition dumps, workshops, office-blocks, quays, docks— all were ablaze . . .'[25] But the real point, unnoticed by Varillon (and by Benoist-Méchin, who quotes him) is that Darlan failed to keep the British Government informed of these acts. The Admiralty did

---

[24] Telegrams 5025, 5026, 10.40 p.m., 18 June, Assemblée Nationale, *Rapport fait au nom de la commission chargée d'enquêter sur les événements survenus en France de 1933 à 1945* (2 vols., Paris, n.d.), ii. 446. The principal French Admiralty telegrams from 7 through 30 June are in ibid., pp. 436–75. This volume is hereafter cited as *Rapport. Événements*. There are also nine volumes of *Annexes. Dépositions*, the hearings of 1947–51, under the same title (n.d.); cited below as *Rapport. Annexes*. The entire set seems to have been published in 1947–54.

[25] Pierre Varillon, *Mers-el-Kébir* (Paris, 1950), p. 80.

learn about the movements of the *Jean Bart* and the *Richelieu*, but knew little about the scuttlings and demolitions at the naval bases.

Churchill's vain appeal of 15 June to Roosevelt to change his mind about military intervention included this passage: 'Have you considered what offers Hitler may choose to make to France? He may say, "Surrender the Fleet intact and I will leave you Alsace-Lorraine," or alternatively: "If you do not give me your ships I will destroy your towns." I am personally convinced that America will in the end go to all lengths, but this moment is supremely critical for France. A declaration that the United States will if necessary enter the war might save France. Failing that, in a few days French resistance may have crumpled and we shall be left alone.'[26] If Churchill was right over America's ultimate role, he proved wrong as regards Hitler's immediate intentions.

* * *

From his Ardennes headquarters on the morning of 17 June, Hitler announced his 'principles' in framing the armistice conditions to a small circle which included the Chief of the OKW (Supreme Command of the Armed Forces), Colonel-General Keitel, and the Chief of the Operations Staff of the OKW, General Jodl. 'The result of the negotiations must not be jeopardized through excessive [*gespannte*] demands on France.' He then defined the first of his guiding principles: 'The aim of the armistice must be to eliminate France from the war and at the same time create the best possible prerequisites for the further prosecution of the war against England.' Accordingly, the terms to be offered the French must be sufficiently attractive. The fourth principle concerned the Fleet, which 'would be neutralized in some form or another, still to be determined by Hitler. He stressed that there should be no demand for its surrender, because in such an event the Fleet would undoubtedly sail for French overseas territories or escape to England.'[27]

On the same day the German Naval War Staff (*Seekriegsleitung*) presented their requirements for an armistice. The crucial point called for 'securing [*Sicherstellung*] the entire French Fleet', inclusive of all ships under construction. 'French warships to be recalled

[26] Churchill, *Their Finest Hour*, p. 166.

[27] Hermann Böhme, *Entstehung und Grundlagen des Waffenstillstandes von 1940* (Stuttgart, 1966), p. 21. Lieutenant-Colonel (afterwards General) Böhme of the OKW was a reliable witness. Professor Henry H. Adams, in *Years of Deadly Peril* (New York, 1969), p. 187, states that 'the real reason for [Hitler's] softness regarding the French fleet was that he totally failed to appreciate the strategic importance of the Mediterranean'. However that may be, it was not the operative factor as regards the armistice.

immediately to ports designated by Germany and there secured. There they are to remain under the surveillance of the German and Italian navy. Only care and maintenance parties will remain on board. . . . Ammunition and demolition equipment to be discharged. . . . Such ships or vessels specified are to be handed over immediately to German commands. The precise fate of the remaining units of the fleet and the ships to be disarmed will be decided in the peace treaty.'[28] The penultimate sentence appears to have had certain small craft in view. These desiderata were in harmony with Hitler's 'principles' and spelt out some of the specifics that were to go into the naval conditions.

Hitler also decided in the forenoon of 17 June to have a meeting with Mussolini as soon as possible, so as to reach agreement on the conditions to be put to the French. A meeting in Munich was quickly arranged. It was during the night of the 17th–18th, while the train sped to Munich and the staff were busy drafting the German terms, that Hitler elaborated his ideas on Article 8, which covered the fate of the French Fleet. Whether or not he realized that at Bordeaux the British Government representatives were at that moment equally occupied with the same problem, he undoubtedly knew that the French would reject the terms if this clause conflicted with their ideas, as expressed by Pétain and Darlan. He therefore ordered the inclusion of a guarantee that no demand for handing over the Fleet would be made either at the armistice or in the ultimate peace treaty. Instead he wanted to secure the French Government's agreement to neutralize the Fleet by disarming it and laying up the ships in French ports under the supervision of the Axis powers. Hitler put these thoughts before Mussolini in a two-hour meeting on the 18th. He got the Duce to put aside his ambitious programme of territorial occupation (Corsica, Tunis, and France east of the Rhone) and the surrender of the French Fleet and Air Force, all in the interests of a lenient armistice, which would ward off the possibility of the French Fleet joining with the Royal Navy.

The Führer explained in detail what a great increase in strength the French fleet would represent for England, if it were to put itself at Britain's disposal. In certain categories the present strength of the English fleet would thereby be practically doubled or trebled, especially in the case of destroyers. Considering that a convoy protected by six destroyers could no longer be attacked by submarines, one could realize the great advantage which England would derive from use of the numerous French

[28] 'Military Demands of the Naval War Staff in Case of a French Capitulation', 17 June 1940, BA-MA (Bundesarchiv-Militärarchiv) Marinearchiv, III M/1005/2 (Freiburg im Breisgau).

destroyers. It would, therefore, be best to reach agreement with a French government on neutralizing the fleet. This neutralization could be carried out by disarmament in French ports under German or Italian supervision, and as an inducement Germany might offer a guarantee that the entire fleet would be restored to France when peace was concluded. It would also be a favorable solution if the French fleet scuttled itself.[29]

After the Munich conference, Hitler and Admiral Raeder, C-in-C of the German Fleet, met and fixed the naval terms of the armistice. The important thing to remember is that by adopting the simple method of allowing the French to keep nominal possession of a disarmed Fleet in ports under German or Italian control, they believed they would avoid the risk that it might sail for British ports some day and renew the fighting.

At midday on 20 June Pétain received radio instructions from the Germans for the dispatch of an armistice delegation. It reached Compiègne in the afternoon of the 21st. The two delegations met in the nearby forest of Rethondes in the railway coach where Foch had dictated armistice terms to the defeated Germans in November 1918. The German delegation was headed by Keitel; the French, by General Huntziger.

Article 8 of the German terms was the crucial one dealing with the Fleet. It stipulated:

The French war fleet, with the exception of the part permitted to the French Government for the protection of French interests in its colonial empire, is to be assembled in ports to be specified and is to be demobilized and disarmed under German or Italian supervision [*contrôle* in the French text]. The choice of these ports will be determined by the peacetime stations of the ships.

The German Government solemnly declares to the French Government that it does not intend to use for its own purposes in the war the French fleet which is in ports under German supervision [*contrôle*], with the exception of those units needed for coastal patrol and for mine sweeping. Furthermore they solemnly and expressly declare that they have no intention of raising any claim to the French war fleet at the time of the conclusion of peace.

With the exception of that part of the French war fleet, still to be determined, which is to represent French interests in the colonial empire, all war vessels which are outside French territorial waters are to be recalled to France.[30]

At 10.30 p.m., 21 June, Huntziger was able to telephone the dictated terms to Weygand in Bordeaux. He said the delegation

---

[29] *Documents on German Foreign Policy, 1918–1945*, Series D (1937–45) (13 vols., London, Washington, 1949–64), ix. 608. (Series D was terminated with December 1941.) Series D is to be understood in further footnote references.
[30] ibid., p. 673.

found the conditions very severe, but that they contained nothing dishonouring, particularly in regard to the Fleet. He then read out the text. Although the German renunciation of any claim to the Fleet removed the main barrier to an honourable armistice, a meeting of the Council of Ministers at 2 a.m. on the 22nd decided to make two counter-proposals. That on the Fleet asked that the first paragraph of Article 8 should read: 'The French war fleet, with the exception of the part permitted to the French Government for the protection of French interests in its colonial empire, after demobilization and landing of their ammunition under German or Italian supervision, will be based on French African ports. Ship complements should not exceed half the ordinary peacetime complements.'[31] The French alterations had two purposes: to limit the extent of German and Italian *contrôle*, and, still more important, to place the ships beyond the reach of the Germans. A large proportion of them were based on Cherbourg, Brest, and Lorient, which would, under the armistice terms, lie in the occupied zone. But the reason Huntziger gave the Germans for the change in bases was that French warships assembled in Atlantic or Channel ports would be exposed to British air attacks and that by shifting them to African ports the French would be bringing them to safety. Keitel's first reaction was to turn down the modification categorically. He noted 'with regret that the French delegation seemed to be losing sight of the generosity of the offer as a whole in trivial discussions on separate points. There was therefore no need for a formal amendment of the text of the treaty, and the German delegation refused the French request.'[32]

Keitel's position was later somewhat softened: 'The removal to North African ports was refused and the text of the treaty was adhered to. On the other hand it was pointed out that the demand to direct the ships to their peacetime stations was a "should" provision ["*Soll*"-*Bestimmung*]. The Armistice Commission would reserve the right to order exceptions to this in cases where there was reason to do so.'[33] The practical effect of the German reply was

[31] The French text is given in Woodward, *British Foreign Policy in the Second World War*, i. 331.

[32] 'Record of the Second Day's Negotiations on the Armistice at Compiègne on June 22, 1940', *Documents on German Foreign Policy*, ix. 665–6.

[33] Unsigned, undated memorandum which Hencke, the representative of the German Foreign Ministry on the Franco-German Armistice Commission at Wiesbaden (established in accordance with the provisions of Article 22), referred to on 6 July as 'the explanatory notes to the Armistice Treaty (answers to French questions during the negotiations in Compiègne), which according to the Führer's instructions did not form part of the treaty, but were binding for the German side'. *Documents on German Foreign Policy*, ix. 676 n., 678. The French record of the German reply is:

to leave open the possibility that the French would be permitted to keep some, perhaps all, of their ships in African ports or in the unoccupied zone of France (Toulon). Admiral Auphan suggests that it was German prestige and *amour-propre* that explain why they would not accept any modifications in their draft.

The French Government accepted the armistice terms at about 6.30 p.m., 22 June, an hour before a German ultimatum was due to expire, and the armistice was signed at 6.50. It was not to come into force until six hours after the French had concluded an armistice with the Italians (Article 23). The French delegation flew to Rome in the early hours of 23 June; an Italian agreement was signed at 7.15 p.m. on the 24th. The German Article 8 and the Italian Article 12 were inherently identical. A cease-fire went into effect on all fronts at 12.35 a.m., 25 June.

In fact, no important warship was disarmed in French Atlantic ports, if only because no such ships remained in these ports when the armistices were concluded. Indeed, their return to these ports while Anglo-German hostilities continued would have been against both German and French interests. Thus, the ships, apart from those which had fled to England, remained in the ports where they happened to be when the armistices came into force, namely, at the bases of Toulon, Oran/Mers-el-Kébir, Bizerta, Algiers, and Alexandria.

The British Ambassador spent the 22nd acquiring information on the armistice proceedings at Compiègne and registering vehement pleas for the rejection of the German terms. Neither the assurances of Darlan, Pétain, and Baudouin that the British need have no qualms about the Fleet—it would sabotage or scuttle itself if the Germans made any attempt to capture it—nor the French counter-proposal on Article 8, satisfied Campbell. He vainly protested that once the Germans got hold of the ships for purposes of supervising their demobilization and disarmament, they would not let them go. Campbell learned in the evening that the armistice had been signed. Somewhat precipitously and on his own initiative, he departed at midnight for England with his entire staff. It was unfortunate that he left Bordeaux at a time when accurate information on the changing situation and a prompt and free exchange of viewpoints were more than ever needed in London

'The proposed modification is not accepted for insertion in the convention. The Germans do not refuse to contemplate acceptance of the proposal made, but they consider that it is a measure of application falling within the competence of the Armistice Commission.' Woodward, *British Foreign Policy in the Second World War*, i. 331. I detect no significant substantive differences between the two versions.

and Bordeaux. Matters were worsened on the 23rd with the resignation of the French Ambassador, Corbin, who was disenchanted with the policy of his Government. Although the Chargé d'Affaires, Cambon, remained in London until 5 July, when the French formally broke off relations, there was a *de facto* cessation of Anglo-French diplomatic relations from 23 June. Communications between the two Governments became increasingly uncertain, and with it inevitably came misunderstanding.

The departure of the British Naval Mission with Campbell is an important aspect of this breakdown in communications. It

took away the last direct means of liaison between the French Admiralty and the British Admiralty. After that, the French Admiralty at Bordeaux would be able to communicate with London only by telegram through the roundabout and uncertain Spanish communication system. Article 14 of the Franco-German armistice convention required the sealing of French naval radio stations from the moment the armistice took effect. In consequence French Admiralty messages were to take an average of 35 to 40 hours to reach their addressees through other means of communication. Sometimes the lapse was as much as three days! Thenceforth communication between the French Admiralty and Admiral Odend'hal, its sole liaison with the British in London, took on many of the one-sided aspects of a dialogue between two deaf persons.[34]

Pound was dependent on Odend'hal for information, and Odend'hal was dependent on slow, uncertain, and often garbled messages from Bordeaux via Spain.

*   *   *

The German naval terms were known to the War Cabinet when it met at 9.30 p.m. on the 22nd, but not that an armistice had been signed. The First Sea Lord informed the ministers that Darlan had appointed a committee of four admirals (not correct) to take charge if he was unable to exercise his command freely, and had enjoined them to fight to a finish, hold defended ports against the enemy, and not accept any orders from a foreign government.[35] For Pound

---

[34] Auphan and Mordal, *The French Navy in World War II*, p. 118.

[35] The information had just been received from the British Naval Liaison Officer in Bizerta. The actual message (in three parts, 1.30, 1.35, 1.40 a.m., 20 June) appeared over Darlan's code name of 'Xavier 377', which had authenticated his signature since 17 June. The telegram was addressed to all the principal flag officers in command and to Odend'hal in London. After establishing the succession of the command of the Navy (Admirals de Laborde, Esteva, Abrial, and Gensoul, in that order), Darlan had directed these flag officers, or those who might succeed them, to: 'Fight fiercely to the end so long as a legal French Government independent of the enemy has not given orders to the contrary; disobey all other governments; no matter what orders are received, never abandon a warship intact to the enemy.' Nos. 5057, 5058, 5059, *Rapport. Événements*, ii. 454.

'this information was in accordance with Admiral Darlan's previous assurances and showed that he had taken all possible steps to safeguard our interests'. Churchill could not accept this.

> In a matter so vital to the safety of the whole British Empire we could not afford to rely on the word of Admiral Darlan. However good his intentions might be, he might be forced to resign and his place taken by another Minister who would not shrink from betraying us. The most important thing to do was to make certain of the two modern battleships *Richelieu* and *Jean Bart*. If these fell into the hands of the Germans, they would have a very formidable line of battle when the [battleship] *Bismarck* was commissioned next August. Against these fast and powerful ships we should only have *Nelson*, *Rodney* and the older battleships like *Valiant*. *Strasbourg* and *Dunkirk* would certainly be a great nuisance if they fell into the hands of the enemy, but it was the two modern ships which might alter the whole course of the war. . . . at all costs *Richelieu* and *Jean Bart*, particularly the former, must not be allowed to get loose.

He had no compunction about using force against the two battleships. 'If the captains refused to parley, they must be treated as traitors to the Allied cause. The ships might have to be bombed by aircraft from *Ark Royal* or they must be mined into their harbours and naval forces stationed outside to prevent the minefields being swept up. In no circumstances whatever must these ships be allowed to escape.' The Prime Minister, however, fell in with the suggestion of the Foreign Secretary, Lord Halifax, that they 'should exhaust every means of persuasion before using force', but he stressed that they must not take their eyes off the main object—'that in no circumstances must we run the mortal risk of allowing these ships to fall into the hands of the enemy. Rather than that, we should have to fight and sink them.' Pound singled out Admiral Esteva (Admiral, South), at Bizerta, as the key person to be won over. He commanded all French naval forces in the Mediterranean, was one of Darlan's heirs, and the French captains would be sure to refer any proposals to him.

The War Cabinet decided that, 'with a view to the vital need for obtaining control of the French Navy', the First Lord and First Sea Lord should send an appeal to Darlan and Esteva, and the Admiralty should make certain that the *Richelieu* and *Jean Bart* did not leave Dakar and Casablanca, respectively. As the meeting was ending, news arrived that the French had signed an armistice, but the details were not yet known.[36] From this time the War Cabinet position was that French actions counted for more than French

[36] WM 176 (40), CAB 65/13. The actual text appears to have been known by the 24th.

words, and the moderates outside the War Cabinet, who included Alexander and Pound, were slowly but surely swept along in Churchill's wake.

No time was lost in carrying out the attempts at persuasion. Alexander and Pound sent messages to Darlan in the small hours of 23 June via the British destroyer *Beagle* at Bordeaux. (Apparently she had been sent there to demolish harbour and petroleum installations in the Gironde River.) Both messages were in the nature of final appeals and offered Darlan the choice between having his Fleet continue the struggle at the side of the Royal Navy, or, if it ceased to fight, of sending it to British ports to make certain the ships would not fall into the hands of Britain's enemies. Pound's message was couched in more personal terms and made the point that if Article 8 was 'anything like the original German version it is likely to be a grave additional burden to our winning the war'. If the Germans once got control of such ships as the French battle cruisers or modern battleships, they would find a pretext to delay their demilitarization and, later, an excuse to incorporate them in their own Fleet.[37]

'Admiral Darlan was greatly perplexed by these two messages', write Auphan and Mordal, above all because only five days earlier their authors had, in their meeting with him, 'not laid down any conditions and had spoken to him in an entirely different vein. He had already pledged that in no case would the French ships be utilized by the Germans, and had issued the necessary orders to insure this. As for the armistice, it had been signed the evening before, and there was nothing the Navy could do about it. Short of leaving immediately on the British destroyer to join De Gaulle, Darlan really could not see what was expected of him.' The Captain of the *Beagle* radioed back to the Admiralty: 'No satisfactory answer obtainable. Am leaving Bordeaux now.'[38] This left the Esteva ploy, which, we shall see in a moment, was broadened in scope.

The War Cabinet met three times on the French Fleet problem during 24 June—at noon, 6 p.m., and 10.30 p.m.[39] At the first two meetings it was reported that the senior officers of the *Jean Bart*, which was being observed by the destroyer *Watchman*, were apathetic, and the Admiral, Africa, at Casablanca, Ollive, had declared he would take orders only from the legal government of France, but that there was a good spirit among the more junior officers and the possibility of persuading some of the crews to sail

---

[37] ADM 205/4.
[38] Auphan and Mordal, *The French Navy in World War II*, pp. 118–19.
[39] WM 178, 179, 180 (40), CAB 65/13.

their ships to British ports. As for the *Richelieu,* which was being watched by the heavy cruiser *Dorsetshire,* the attitude of her Captain was 'one of deep depression and anxiety. The position was very delicate, and the only hope seemed to be a pronouncement from some form of recognised government in North Africa.' The attitude of Admiral Gensoul, commanding the Atlantic Fleet (Force de Raid) at Mers-el-Kébir, was that he would obey the orders of the legal government of France so long as one existed. 'The morale of Force de Rade [Raid] was comparatively high, and it was unlikely that the Admiral would be bluffed. If *Dunkerque* and *Strasbourg* had to be tackled by force, it would be a difficult proposition. The harbour defences at Oran [Mers-el-Kébir] were powerful, and owing to the position of the ships, they could not be torpedoed from the air in harbour.'

The afternoon War Cabinet reached no final decision on the course of action *vis-à-vis* the French Fleet, but it was agreed they should do all they could to 'get hold of' the four big ships, or, failing that, to make sure they were scuttled. The early evening meeting featured a long discussion on the course of action to secure the French ships. The point was made—it was to become the leitmotiv of the whole British case for strong action—that:

Whatever assurances the French might have received from the Germans, we could not prevent the enemy obtaining possession of the ships unless they were either scuttled or taken in possession by us. It would be a great temptation to Germany to use some pretext of non-fulfilment of the terms of the armistice to seize the ships when they came into ports under German or Italian control, to be demilitarised. Moreover, the terms of Article 8 of the armistice left it open to the Germans to take as much as they wanted of the French Fleet for 'coast surveillance and mine-sweeping.' No reliance whatever could be placed upon the safeguards in this Article. The best hope therefore lay in a French Government being set up in North Africa, whose orders French Officers might be prepared to accept. But the prospects of this were none too bright. If we were to stop the ships being handed over, we should have to act quickly.

This was because the Franco-German armistice would go into effect six hours after a Franco-Italian armistice had been signed. The Germans 'might at once fly over personnel to the North African French ports'.

The meeting discussed two alternatives: they could 'take immediate action to ensure that the main units of the French Fleet did not fall into the hands of the enemy. If necessary, we should not scruple to use force to secure this end.' Or they could allow the French Fleet to go to the ports as provided in Article 8, and 'watch events closely, being prepared to take action at once if we saw any risk that the ships would fall into German hands'. In this case an ultimatum would be sent to the French Government, demanding that the ships be scuttled within a specified time, 'otherwise we should be forced to take action by force against them'. The War Cabinet instructed the Prime Minister and the Foreign Secretary to draft such an ultimatum, and the First Lord to secure a Naval Staff appreciation of the action which would be involved if it were found necessary to use force against French warships not under British control, and to consider what fresh fleet dispositions were required.

The main business of the late evening War Cabinet was the presentation and discussion of the Naval Staff appreciation. These were the principal points made by the First Sea Lord: The moment they made any attempt to seize or sink French ships, the crews of the other ships 'would probably become actively hostile, thus reducing our chances of securing more than a small part of the Fleet. In addition the Germans would at once take more stringent measures to get possession of the remaining ships.' They should concentrate on eliminating the capital ships rather than the submarines, if the use of force became necessary, since Italy was expected to have five or six capital ships in a few months' time. Were two French capital ships to be added to that force, 'we should find ourselves unable to leave our Fleet in the Eastern Mediterranean and should need to augment our force at Gibraltar in order to keep this Italian Fleet within Mediterranean waters'. If Spain joined the Axis powers, capital ships would be required for convoys, which would make it impossible to maintain effective control of the western exits from the Mediterranean. The most important units to be eliminated were the battle cruisers *Dunkerque* and *Strasbourg* of the Force de Raid, which squadron was reported to be in a new harbour near Oran (Mers-el-Kébir), under the protection of 6-inch shore batteries. The British force available to deal with this squadron consisted of the battle cruiser *Hood*, battleship *Resolution*, and aircraft carrier *Ark Royal*. Aircraft from the *Ark Royal* could bomb the Force de Raid, but they could not carry out torpedo attacks in the harbour. 'The only real chance of success lay in a surprise attack carried out at dawn and without any form of prior notification. The operation might well result in the loss or partial disablement of both our battleships, and we should then, in consequence, be badly handicapped in dealing with the *Richelieu* and *Jean Bart*.' Whereupon Pound expressed an opinion which revealed once more his extreme reluctance to proceed to extreme measures:

. . . the probable loss of our 2 ships seemed a heavy price to pay for the elimination or partial elimination of Force de Rade [Raid]. Admiral Darlan and other French Admirals had maintained the consistent attitude that in no circumstances would the French Fleet be surrendered, and it would seem more likely that we should achieve our object by trusting in these assurances rather than by attempting to eliminate units of the French Fleet by force. He did not therefore recommend the proposed operation.

The lively discussion that followed focused on the Force de Raid. It was brought out that, to have any chance of success, the operation must be a complete surprise; if it resulted in the loss or disablement of two capital ships, they would be in danger of losing the command of the Western Mediterranean; it was possible that the Italian Fleet might appear off Oran 'to take delivery' of the Force de Raid; and most importantly: 'The decision to order the destruction of people who had only 48 hours before been Allies would be hard to make. If French sailors were to be killed in action with the British Fleet, the French and German Governments would declare that England was making war on France and the sympathy of the entire French Empire would probably be lost to us.' Churchill admitted that an operation to destroy the Force de Raid would prove very costly and might not succeed; anyhow, the *Jean Bart* and *Richelieu* mattered the most, and, unarmed as they were, it should be easy to secure them once they left the shelter of their ports. There was considerable discussion of a Foreign Office draft of an ultimatum to the French Government demanding that steps be taken forthwith to sink those ships which might be in danger of falling into enemy hands, but nothing was decided. (The proposed ultimatum was not sent, but Churchill used most of it in his statement to the Commons on 25 June. See below, p. 214.) The First Lord made the sensible suggestion that no ultimatum be sent if the operation at Oran was to be carried out, for a surprise attack was essential. After this exhaustive discussion, the War Cabinet 'deferred a decision as to the action to be taken in regard to French naval units generally, other than those in British control, until it was seen how the situation developed in the light of the Franco-Italian Armistice terms'.

There was another reason for postponing a decision. Between 23 and 27 June, while the War Cabinet marked time, there was a concerted attempt by the Admiralty to determine the attitude of French naval officers, with the special purpose of judging the likelihood of French warships continuing to co-operate with the Royal Navy. In the afternoon of the 23rd the Admiralty instructed Admiral North at Gibraltar (Flag Officer Commanding North Atlantic) to proceed to Oran and contact Esteva and Gensoul.

Admiral Sir Dudley North was in his later career as much a courtier as a naval officer, in that he had commanded H.M. Yachts under three kings (1934–9). Although universally popular—he was an extremely pleasant person—he was no great shakes as regards brain power, leadership, or personality. In addition to finding out what the French Fleet in the western Mediterranean was likely to do, North was to ascertain the berthing positions of the French ships, 'in case it might be necessary to take drastic action against them'.[40] Esteva had left for Bizerta when North arrived in Oran on the morning of the 24th. This, with the judgement of Commander Collett, the British Naval Liaison Officer to the French Atlantic Fleet, that Esteva would obey any orders from Darlan short of handing the ships over to the enemy, convinced the Admiralty there would be no point in trying to catch up with him. Accordingly, they instructed North to see only Gensoul. His twenty-minute interview with the French Admiral in his flagship, the *Dunkerque*, was painful and unsatisfactory. Gensoul, 'like all his brother officers appeared to be in a state of stupefied misery'. He was on the verge of tears several times. He made it clear that he intended to obey the orders of a legally constituted French government while it existed, but would fight on if there were no such government. Although he would not hear of turning his ships over to the British or of joining them, he gave North his word of honour that, on orders from Darlan (messages of 20, 22 June), under no circumstances would he surrender his ships intact to the Germans or the Italians. 'He repeated his assurance several times, and I must say that I believed him.' 'Behind it all,' North wrote after the war, 'and I can't remember whether he actually said so, there was, I am convinced, in the Frenchmen's minds the thought that England's collapse was only a matter of a week or two.' Therefore, giving the English their Fleet would be 'silly'.[41]

North's report to the Admiralty, sent at 2 p.m., 24 June, was available at the third War Cabinet meeting that evening. The next morning Pound telegraphed to the Admiral: 'Do you consider that there would be any prospect of French ships at Oran surrendering

[40] 24 June, WM 178 (40).

[41] North to Admiral Sir Herbert Richmond, 23 Oct. 1945, Richmond MSS., 7/4. 'We parted on quite friendly terms. He looked utterly dejected, and I felt keenly for him. We shook hands on the quarter-deck, the trumpets sounded "Aux Champs" again, and the band played the Admiral's salute to a British admiral for the last time. At the quay, where my destroyer *Douglas* was berthed, the captain of the dockyard told me in perfect English that he was ashamed of his Government and that he wished to apologize. He wished me the best of luck.' Noel Monks, *That Day at Gibraltar* (London, 1957), pp. 20–1, quoting from North's papers.

to us if British force arrived off port and summoned them to surrender?' North's reply was that from his interview he was 'sure they would not surrender'. Other reports at about this time bore out North's findings.

Collett had left the *Dunkerque* very soon after Darlan had on the 24th (following the signing of the Italian armistice) ordered all liaison officers to be disembarked. 'As I left the quarter deck of *Dunkerque*, I think almost all the officers were on deck to see me off and they all insisted on shaking me by the hand, wishing me good luck and saying how much they wished that they were coming with me. It is not surprising, therefore, that I was most anxious to convey to Their Lordships the feeling that they had expressed, and my personal opinion, that they would never let their ships be taken over by the Germans.'[42] Gensoul detailed a destroyer specially to take him to Gibraltar, and there Collett wrote his report. Gensoul was, he said, 'a cool headed man' with 'unswerving' loyalty to Darlan, whose orders he would follow to the very end. The officers, too, were loyal to their Commander-in-Chief, Darlan, but 'they all resent the train of events and very many are willing to offer their services to us if the French Fleet ceases to exist'. As for the men, the majority, comprising the active service ratings and some reservists, were willing to continue the fight. The *Dunkerque* and *Strasbourg*, as well as the small ships, were in this group. On the other hand, it was doubtful if the old battleships *Provence* and *Bretagne* (the latter mistakenly given as the *Lorraine*, which was in Alexandria), with a high proportion of reservists, would continue. 'For them the war is over and they want to return to their wives and families . . .'

To summarise, the majority of the fleet will fight, but it is essential to find a leader with initiative who will go against the Bordeaux government. The general faith in Maréchal Pétain is marked and all consider that he knows what is best for France, although they bitterly resent his decisions. . . .

When I left the Fleet I was convinced that the ships would never be turned over intact to the Germans and even more definitely not to the Italians. The orders for scuttling and/or wrecking the ships had been issued.

Whether this state has since been modified in view of our threatening attitude, I am not able to judge. . . .

I am convinced that we shall gain nothing by threats or attempts at coercion. France is fighting for 'La Liberté' and if this is to be denied them in their fighting forces they will not play.

It is a situation that requires very delicate handling on account of the touchy French character, especially in moments of stress.[43]

---

[42] Rear-Admiral G. K. Collett's letter to the author, 16 Aug. 1972.
[43] 'Review of Situation by Commander Collett', n.d. (26 June?), ADM 205/4.

C. S. Holland, Captain of the *Ark Royal*, reported on the attitude of French senior officers whom he had interviewed at Casablanca between 24 and 26 June. His belief was that Ollive had 'little strength of character, is completely defeatist in his present frame of mind and the only assurance he showed was that of an absolute obedience to any orders received from Darlan. . . . He expressed the opinion that our only course of action was to sue for the best terms we could as soon as possible. He did, however, as did all other senior officers, assert that no French man of war would be used against us.' De Laborde, late Admiral, West, at Brest, a fine officer with the reputation of being a fighting man and 'absolutely straight', assured Holland that he would implicitly obey all orders received; but he added that the Germans and Italians would not be allowed to use French naval units against the British. Rear-Admiral Moreau, another fighting officer with a reputation for honesty, 'seemed compelled by loyalty to his Chief to obey any orders which are given to him, although it was obvious that the idea of not going on fighting was most distasteful to him. . . . he hoped to see the day when France will again be fighting by our side. He said there were many officers and men who were more than willing to break away and fight with us. He also said that he thought any attempts at coercion or use of force on our part to detach the units would have a bad effect.' Holland also reported, after meeting in Casablanca with the former Naval Liaison Officers at Brest (Commander Mackay) and Casablanca (Commander Mackintosh), that there was 'a strong party of more junior officers and regular service ratings who wish to go on fighting. What they require is a leader. If one were to appear, it is considered quite possible that the situation would greatly change for the better, and ships might even be brought over to British ports. But this would only be on the understanding that they fought as French units under the French flag as heretofore.' Holland's conclusion agreed with Collett's: 'The present feelings amongst the officers are those of bewilderment, humiliation, and disparagement [*sic*]. They are more touchy than ever as regards their honour and freedom of action, and I would suggest that the situation requires most delicate handling to get them to fight willingly with us.'[44]

Finally, there were two reports from the former Head of the British Naval Mission in France, Pleydell-Bouverie. Among the salient facts that stood out in the experience of his last days in France were that the Fleet and its commanders had great faith in Darlan and would obey his orders in all circumstances; that the

---

[44] 'Review of the Situation by Captain C. S. Holland', n.d., ADM 205/4.

H

Government was entirely concerned with stopping the war; and that there was considerable fear among the officers and men about the consequences to their families if they failed to obey the armistice terms. 'The conclusion that I come to from these facts is that it seems likely that the French Fleet will be ordered by Admiral Darlan to its "Home Ports", there to be disarmed under the terms of the Armistice but that insufficient preparation will have been made for the eventuality which is almost certain to happen.' What action could be taken to prevent the French Fleet going to its home ports? There were two answers: the setting up of a French government in Africa, which would take control of the Fleet, or British naval action to prevent the Fleet from reaching its home ports. He had no opinion on the feasibility of the former. The latter possibility 'bristles with difficulties and it is quite certain that political reaction of such a course might be adverse and be very far reaching'.[45] In a second report Pleydell-Bouverie pointed out that the first possibility was ruled out, since the latest telegrams indicated that the three officers who might have given a strong lead, i.e. continued the war from North Africa, Generals Noguès and Mittelhauser and Admiral Godfroy, had all come into line with the Bordeaux Government. He now expected that the Fleet stationed outside metropolitan France would do what it was told, which would be to return to ports in France.[46]

It was obvious to the Admiralty and War Cabinet by 27 June that they could not expect to secure the co-operation of the French Fleet. A sense of honour, compounded of loyalty to the legal government of France and even more to their Commander-in-Chief, who was 'a kind of fetish to the French Navy', was a powerful deterrent to independent action by the Admirals and the other senior officers. It was also appreciated in London that fear of German reprisals against the families of Frenchmen who continued the struggle, and the belief that Britain herself would collapse in the near future, were other considerations that made it extremely unlikely that any substantial part of the French Navy would fight on the British side. Although the British liaison officers were convinced that the French Navy was firmly resolved to maintain its independence, they were 'not believed, or only in a half-hearted way. CNS did not dare to gamble on its being true'.[47] Forcible measures to neutralize the

---

[45] 'Preliminary Report on the Situation Regarding the French Fleet', n.d. (26 June?), ADM 205/4.

[46] 'Report on the Situation of the French Overseas Possessions', 27 June, ADM 205/4.

[47] Admiral Godfrey's comments on Auphan and Mordal's *The French Navy in World*

French Fleet outside metropolitan French ports seemed to be the only alternative to standing by and seeing these ships return to home ports for demobilization and probable German seizure in the near future.

The intensified anti-English feelings in Bordeaux were an important factor in the British loss of confidence in French assurances. A series of official statements issued in London after the signing of the German armistice stoked this Anglophobia. On the morning of the 23rd Churchill issued a statement over the BBC which began: 'His Majesty's Government have heard with grief and amazement that the terms dictated by the Germans have been accepted by the French Government at Bordeaux. They cannot feel that such, or similar terms, could have been submitted to by any French Government which possessed freedom, independence, and constitutional authority.' He called on 'all Frenchmen outside the power of the enemy' to aid the British Government in its task of achieving victory, so that the greatness of France and the freedom of her people would be restored. The broadcast had the opposite effect to what was intended. It antagonized far more Frenchmen than it roused to take up arms against the Germans. Pétain fired off an angry protest the next day in a broadcast to the French people, and it was now that he brought the notoriously anti-British Pierre Laval into his Government. France, Pétain broadcast on the 25th, had been forced to surrender, but her Government 'will still be free'. The French were exasperated by the British support of de Gaulle, who was now in London, rallying the 'Free French'. On the 23rd he announced over the BBC that a French National Committee would be formed in agreement with the British Government, resolved to maintain French independence, honour her alliances, and contribute to the Allied war effort. The following day he appealed to Frenchmen 'to join up with those who still want to fight'. On 28 June the British Government announced their official recognition of de Gaulle as 'the leader of all Free Frenchmen, wherever they may be, who rally to him in support of the Allied cause'.

The continual British attempts to subvert senior French officers from their allegiance to Bordeaux was another powerful irritant, as was the British decision (25 June) to blockade the whole of metropolitan France. Of course, there were the older French grievances centring on the alleged modest British contributions to the land campaign, especially their refusal to send extra aircraft, which might have stopped the German armoured advance, and their

War II (a passage on p. 123), enclosed in Godfrey to Cunningham, 17 Nov. 1959, Godfrey MSS.

bitterness over the *sauve qui peut* attitude which, they claimed, underlay the British 'desertion' of their Ally and the decision to retreat to Dunkirk. And always, on the British side, was the anger over the French negotiating the armistices in violation, as they saw it, of the solemn pact not to conclude a separate armistice or peace except by mutual agreement. The British Government had agreed to relieve the French Government of their obligations only on condition that their Fleet be immediately sent to British ports. The French Government had, in Neville Chamberlain's words, 'behaved abominably'.

Bordeaux's Anglophobia was noted in London and served to harden feelings there. As Pleydell-Bouverie summed up the situation (27 June):

> It must be realised that anglophobia is very strong in the Pétain Government, and that every attempt is made to discountenance anybody with leanings towards England and to prevent them from having any communications with us. I know of several who have been, practically speaking, driven out of the country and more than one Naval Officer with whom I was upon intimate terms I now know to have been forbidden under any circumstances to see me. This leads me to the conviction that Admiral Darlan and several others of his Staff who outwardly used to meet me on the frankest of terms are no longer any friends of ours.

Relations between the two navies very naturally soured after the German armistice, though there was much personal sympathy with Odend'hal, who conducted himself with much dignity in a difficult situation. He was, however, rather roughly treated by the Admiralty and is said to have protested bitterly when certain restrictions were placed on him and his Mission until their return to France in mid-July. One incident in particular rankled and created a most unfavourable impression in French naval circles. Rear-Admiral Chalmers had the painful task of delivering a letter from Pound to Odend'hal in which the First Sea Lord demanded that he return all ciphers, plans of minefields, and secret information in his possession. The demand shook Odend'hal up. He was almost in tears as he pleaded, 'Don't you trust me?' Odend'hal was an admirer of the Royal Navy and has been described as 'a nice old cup of tea with very agreeable manners, and was a man of complete integrity'. Darlan and the French Admiralty gave him practically no latitude and used him as little more than a post office.

Specific French naval grievances focused on the British refusal to permit the French ships in British ports and at Alexandria to leave for French ports. Over 200 French war vessels of every type, including the old battleships *Paris* and *Courbet*, had taken refuge in British ports, mainly Plymouth and Portsmouth. In the evening of 21 June, with the signing of the German armistice imminent, Darlan ordered all warships and merchant ships in Great Britain to depart for a Mediterranean or North African port. The Admiralty at first, in the afternoon of the 22nd, were perfectly agreeable, then changed their mind that night, and the naval authorities at the ports found a variety of pretexts to prevent the French ships from leaving. On the 25th Odend'hal relayed Darlan's displeasure to Pound in person. The Admiral had been 'sadly impressed in learning that the British Admiralty opposed the departure of the French warships now in the United Kingdom ports; such a position, if maintained, could only be considered as unfriendly to the French Government. Therefore, Admiral Darlan requests me to ask you most pressingly to alter your decision at an early date.'[48] There was no alteration. Happenings at Alexandria fanned Darlan's extreme displeasure.[49]

In June 1940 a French squadron, 'Force X', consisting of the old

[48] ADM 205/4, French Admiralty to Odend'hal, No. 5147, 24 June, *Rapport. Événements*, ii. 466. In a message of 12.45 p.m. on the 24th to all maritime prefects and admirals afloat Darlan (signing himself 'Xavier 377') confirmed his instruction of 20 June to scuttle. 'Armistice clauses will be notified to you *en clair* by other means. I am taking advantage of this last message that I can transmit in code to inform you of my thoughts on this subject. 1. Demobilized warships should remain French under French flag in French metropolitan or colonial ports. 2. Secret precautions for scuttling should be taken so that enemy or foreign power seizing a ship by force will be unable to use her. 3. If armistice commission responsible for interpreting text should decide otherwise than in first paragraph, upon execution of this decision, warships should, without further orders, be taken to the United States or scuttled, if there is no other means of denying them to the enemy. In no circumstances must they be allowed to fall into enemy hands intact. 4. Ships thus taking refuge abroad must not be used for war operations against Germany or Italy without orders of Commander-in-Chief French Naval Forces.' Nos. 5143, 5144, 5145, ibid. Another authoritative French source adds 'with reduced crews' after 'under French flag'. French writers, Kammerer among them, assert that Odend'hal communicated this message to the Admiralty on 25 June. There is nothing to substantiate this in the Admiralty or War Cabinet records. There has apparently been a confusion between the telegrams of 12.45 p.m. and 1.50 p.m. It was the contents of the latter which were conveyed to Pound, as the Admiralty records and Odend'hal's telegram of 5.05 p.m., 25 June, to the French Admiralty (Varillon, *Mers-el-Kébir*, p. 84) show. If Odend'hal received the earlier message, he did not mention its contents, in particular paragraph 3, to Pound on the 25th. It was not until 3 July, on the eve of the fleet action at Mers-el-Kébir, that the British learned of Darlan's message of 24 June. But even if Pound had had knowledge of paragraph 3, it would not have changed anything, because he supposed that the Fleet, *once it returned to metropolitan ports* under Article 8, could not scuttle itself in case of need. (Anyhow, he was aware of the provisions for scuttling in Darlan's message of 20 June.) It would have been still more inconceivable to Pound that the disarmed ships with reduced crews in metropolitan ports could, in case of danger, have sailed for the United States.

[49] The episode that follows is based on a memorandum of 8 Sept. 1966 from the late Captain T. M. Brownrigg, who was Admiral Cunningham's Master of the Fleet at that time.

battleship *Lorraine*, 3 heavy cruisers, 1 light cruiser, 3 destroyers, and 1 submarine, under Vice-Admiral René Godfroy, formed an integral part of the Mediterranean Fleet under Admiral Sir Andrew Cunningham. The British force (about 20 June) included 4 battleships (*Warspite*, flag), an aircraft carrier, 7 cruisers, 24 destroyers, and 12 submarines. The relations between the two Admirals were cordial; they trusted each other. Moreover, Godfroy was an Anglophile and, now a widower, had been married to a Scotswoman. When the French collapse became imminent (16–17 June), the C-in-C decided to take the whole fleet, British and French, to sea on an offensive operation against the Italians (a bombardment of Augusta (Sicily) and a raid on the Straits of Messina, if a sweep of Italian communications with Libya produced no important results). The major impulse for the operation sprang from a desire to hit back at the Italians for the bombing of Malta. But there appears also to have been a hope that a successful operation would demonstrate the Allied command of the sea and raise the spirits of Godfroy and his men, so that they would continue to fight on the British side even if the French Government surrendered. Godfroy was keen to show how the French could fight. Late on 22 June, as the fleet was preparing to sail, Cunningham received a signal from the Admiralty telling him that the French were signing an armistice with the Germans and that, therefore, the operation must be cancelled for fear that Force X would sail on to France. The Master of the Fleet took the signal to the Admiral, who turned over in his bunk and said, 'Nelson is not the only Admiral with a blind eye; show it to me in the morning.' About three hours later, however, when the fleet had just begun to leave harbour, he came out to the bridge and said, 'Master, that was a political decision: return to Alex.' The fleet was bitterly disappointed.

On 23 June the French Admiralty informed Godfroy that, if an armistice were signed with Italy, he was 'to cease all operations or hostile acts' and sail for a French port, provisionally Bizerta. During the night of 24–25 June, Godfroy received instructions to proceed without delay to Bizerta. Upon informing Cunningham of his intention, the latter replied: 'Deeply regret to inform you that I yesterday received orders not to allow your squadron to leave Alexandria.' The two Admirals reached a gentleman's agreement on the 26th–27th, Cunningham giving his word that he would not try to seize the French ships, and Godfroy promising not to put to sea without previously notifying the British Admiral.

Darlan was not at all happy when he heard of the arrangement at Alexandria, as it was in violation of the armistice agreement, which called for all French ships to return to France. 'To agree to some of them remaining immobilized in Alexandria', remarks Benoist-Méchin, 'was to risk giving the Germans the impression that the French government was trying to shirk the armistice conditions—at the very moment when negotiations concerning the retention of the fleet in North Africa were about to open in Turin and Wiesbaden.'[50] Darlan voiced his annoyance over the retention of Force X in a message to Odend'hal on the 26th, which reached London the next day. It was, Odend'hal wrote to Pound, Darlan's

foremost desire not to widen the gap between Great Britain and France. The French Admiralty understood the disappointment which the British felt when they saw France compelled to come to terms; they eagerly wish for a British victory. . . . But crippled France asks to be treated not as an enemy but as a neutral Power. Admiral Darlan states that there never was any question of such unfriendly treatment in the course of his conversations with you in Bordeaux. I have therefore been instructed to ask you most pressingly for instructions from the British Admiralty to allow the sailing of Force X from Alexandria, of the French ships from the United Kingdom ports and the liner *Pasteur* from Halifax.[51]

Pound saw Odend'hal that evening (27 June). He was blunt.

. . . the one object we had in view was winning the war and that it was as essential for them as for us that we should do so. That all trivialities such as questions of friendship and hurting people's feelings must be swept aside. That though there was not the slightest doubt that we should win the war it is essential that we should prevent, as far as possible, the scales being weighted any further against us at the present time. I asked him to ask Admiral Darlan to remember this whenever anything occurred which seemed to him unfriendly. As Admiral Darlan has wished to protest against the retention of their ships at Alexandria, Portsmouth, Plymouth, and *Pasteur* at Halifax, he asked whether, if their ships attempted to leave Alexandria, they would be fired on and I replied 'Yes,' and now that Admiral Darlan knows about it and taking into account the reasons for our action, the responsibility for any incident would rest on him.

Pound added that many French officers seemed to think they were going to be permitted to retain the ships in French colonial ports. But this, he pointed out, would not conform to the original German terms, and the Italian and German terms regarding the Fleet had to be the same. The First Sea Lord wanted the naval terms of the Italian armistice at the earliest possible moment.[52]

*   *   *

[50] Benoist-Méchin, *Sixty Days that Shook the West*, p. 487.   [51] ADM 205/4.
[52] ibid. The document, though undated and unsigned, was undoubtedly written by Pound after he had seen Odend'hal. On the 28th Odend'hal was able to send

The serious deterioration in Anglo-French relations is essential background to the War Cabinet's momentous decision of 27 June. Churchill set the stage for it when he spelt out the practical consequences of Article 8 in his famous Commons speech of 25 June:

This Article . . . says that the French Fleet, excepting that part left free for the safeguarding of French interests in the Colonial Empire, shall be collected in ports to be specified and there demobilised and disarmed under German or Italian control. From this text it is clear that the French war vessels under this Armistice pass into German and Italian control while fully armed. We note, of course, in the same Article the solemn declaration of the German Government that they have no intention of using them for their own purposes during the war. What is the value of that? Ask half a dozen countries what is the value of such a solemn assurance. Furthermore, the same Article 8 of the Armistice excepts from the operation of such assurances and solemn declarations those units necessary for coast surveillance and mine-sweeping. Under this provision it would be possible for the German Government to reserve, ostensibly for coast surveillance, any existing units of the French Fleet. Finally, the Armistice can at any time be voided on any pretext of non-observance, and the terms of Armistice explicitly provide for further German claims when any peace between Germany and France comes to be signed. Such, in very brief epitome, are the salient points in this lamentable and also memorable episode, of which, no doubt, a much fuller account will be given by history.[53]

I must stress here the problem in semantics caused by the use of the term *contrôle* in the French text of the armistice. The word appears twice in Article 8. (See above, p. 196.) The British consistently translated it as 'control', which in English means 'the power of directing and restraining'. The *Oxford English Dictionary* (1933) gives as the first meaning: 'The fact of controlling, or of checking and directing action; domination, command, sway.' This is a much stronger meaning than it has in French, where *contrôle* means no more than 'administrative verification', 'inspection', or 'checking'. This is certainly how the French interpreted it—that the Germans and Italians would *oversee* the demobilization and disarming, *not that they would have operational authority over the ships.*[54] The word in the German text, *Kontrolle*, also connotes supervision

Phillips the authentic naval terms of the Italian armistice. (They had appeared in *The Times* on the 26th.) On 28 June the Foreign Office received an urgent request from Bordeaux that Force X be allowed to obey their orders and leave for French ports. The Foreign Office reply was similar to Pound's: they regretted they could not accede, since H.M. Government could not rely on German and Italian promises not to use the ships against Britain. ADM 1/10321. The reply had been authorized by the War Cabinet on the 28th.

[53] Hansard, 5th series, ccclxii, cols. 304–5.
[54] This 'control' was in fact applied by commissions composed of a few dozen officers and secretaries, which would have been quite incapable of seizing the disarmed ships by force even with reduced crews.

—a supervision that guaranteed that all demobilization and disarmament measures were in accordance with the armistice terms. The British appeared to believe that it was not only the disarming of the ships which would be 'controlled' by the Germans and the Italians, but that it would be the ships themselves that would go over to the 'control', that is, be under the authority, of the enemy. This would take place in ports controlled by them, where they would be tempted not just to demobilize and disarm the ships, but instead, under some pretext, to seize them by force or by a ruse. Pound told a high-level Admiralty conference on 29 June: 'A situation could be visualised in which the Germans would remove the guns from the French ships and not destroy them. They would then pretend that the Armistice terms had not been carried out, and would replace the guns and put the ships into commission again.'[55]

The continued and almost mechanical repetition by Darlan, Reynaud (when Premier and later, on 24 June, at Pétain's request), Baudouin, President Lebrun, and Pétain that the Fleet would never be handed over to Germany or allowed to fall intact into German hands, and that in the last resort it would be destroyed, had no influence on the decision-makers in London. There can be little question about the sincerity of the French leaders, and above all Darlan, in their determination that the ships must remain French and must be scuttled if in imminent danger of German seizure. But the War Cabinet did not feel as confident about it as they would have liked. They thought that Darlan was no longer a free agent after the German armistice. The succession arrangement showed that the Admiral had anticipated on 20 June that his hands would shortly be tied. By the 27th it was believed that Darlan was virtually a prisoner of the Germans.[56] There was, moreover, some question about the friendliness of Darlan's feelings towards Britain.[57]

---

[55] ADM 205/4. I have found no direct evidence of this consideration, but it could be that the British authorities believed that Hitler's recollection of the Scapa Flow precedent of June 1919 would spur him to seize the French ships before they could be scuttled to prevent a take-over.

[56] Butler states that 'the Admiralty had evidence, moreover, that the Germans were in possession of French naval codes and were issuing instructions to French ships purporting to come from Darlan'. Butler, *Grand Strategy*, ii. 221. For this reason, even if Darlan's signals to the French Fleet had been passed on, the British were not prepared to take his assurances at face value.

[57] A copy of Darlan's 26 June message to the French Fleet (No. 3158, *Rapport. Événements*, ii. 471, quoted more fully below, p. 241 n.) included this warning: 'To respond to the appeals of outside interested parties would lead to our metropolitan territory becoming a German province. Our former allies are not to be listened to. Let us think French, let us act French.' This signal fell into British hands (possibly on 27 June). ADM 199/826. The above passage was later held up as proof that Darlan had repudiated his one-time Allies and would no longer consider their interests.

They had a good line on his Anglophobia, which suggested to them that he might well cave in to German pressure to surrender the Fleet.[58]

Even assuming that Darlan's intentions were of the best, what did that signify? As the VCNS later argued: 'While having no reason to doubt Admiral Darlan's good faith, it was clear that events might put it beyond his power to control the future of the Fleet if it was not handed over to us. Further, when vital matters which might govern the whole future of the world were at stake, it could not be accepted that the British Government could place itself in a position of having to rely on the word of one man, however much they trusted him.'[59]

In the last analysis, the British position was founded on the belief that, with the armistices in force and the French laying down their arms, they would be powerless to keep their word. No matter what precautions they took, once the ships were under German and Italian control, they could not carry out scuttling and sabotage measures in the occupied ports.

Churchill told Cordell Hull in December 1941 that 'since many people throughout the world believed that Britain was about ready to surrender, he had wanted by this action [Mers-el-Kébir, 3 July] to show that she still meant to fight'.[60] Some writers have suggested that this represents Churchill's *ex-post-facto* reasoning. But we have positive evidence that in *his* mind, at least, there were

[58] Darlan had by the end of June become 'intensely bitter against Great Britain', as the American Ambassador reported. It was almost with glee that he declared that the British were finished: he was 'absolutely certain that Great Britain would be completely conquered by Germany within 5 weeks unless Great Britain should surrender sooner'. When the Ambassador observed that 'the French would like to have England conquered in order that Germany might have as many conquered provinces to control as possible and that France might become the favorite province, he smiled again and nodded'. 'Under no conditions', Darlan went on, according to the Ambassador, 'would he send the fleet to England since he was certain that the British would never return a single vessel of the fleet to France and that if Great Britain should win the war the treatment which would be accorded to France by Great Britain would be no more generous than the treatment accorded by Germany.' William C. Bullitt to Secretary of State Hull, 1 July, reporting his conversations of that day with Darlan and other leading figures in the French Government. *Foreign Relations of the United States, 1940* (5 vols., Washington, D.C., 1955–61), ii. 462–9, for the whole of this fascinating document. The telegram was not received in Washington until 10 July. There was nothing in it that would have raised eyebrows in Whitehall had its contents been known on 1 July.

[59] Phillips's minute of 23 Apr. 1941, ADM 199/826. Early in 1941 the Chiefs of Staff asked the Admiralty to prepare a statement for the French Fleet on the decisions that had led to the Oran and Dakar episodes. An important objective was to smooth away the memories of those unhappy events. The points made in the minutes on the drafts of the leaflet constitute a good résumé of the British case.

[60] *The Memoirs of Cordell Hull* (2 vols., New York, 1948), i. 799.

prior to the action important political fruits to be plucked from a bold and determined policy. His Principal Private Secretary has left an authoritative record of what was in Churchill's mind:

He was convinced that the Americans were impressed by ruthlessness in dealing with a ruthless foe; and in his mind the American reaction to our attack on the French Fleet at Oran was of the first importance; as a clear demonstration that we were in deadly earnest about our intention to fight on alone, and that we were prepared to go to all lengths in so doing. This ruthlessness did not come naturally to the British, and he had to force it on many of his colleagues and associates over here; especially the Admirals, who were reluctant to fire on their erstwhile comrades-in-arms. But it was Churchill's policy; he was firm and impetuous in its favour, and it was the force of his personality which pushed it forward.[61]

And, though the evidence here is not so clear, he probably expected that a bold stroke, should it come to that at Mers-el-Kébir, would fire up public opinion at home on the eve of the expected invasion, when morale needed stimulating.

There was good reason for urgency in settling the problem. With the collapse of France, British fortunes were at their nadir. Britain and the Commonwealth stood alone, with the Germans poised in the Low Countries and along the Channel and Atlantic coasts of France, ready to intensify the attack on merchantmen carrying vital supplies to Great Britain—and ready to invade. The War Cabinet and Chiefs of Staff regarded a German invasion attempt as imminent. 'Certainly everything is as gloomy as can be. Probability is that Hitler will attempt invasion in next fortnight. As far as I can see, we are, after years of leisurely preparation, completely unprepared.' So ran Cadogan's diary entry on 29 June. On 1 July he noted: 'This is the zero hour for Hitler's invasion of England—the actual date favoured by the tipsters being about 8 July.'[62] The invasion threat underscored the imperative need to settle the French Fleet problem swiftly, so that the naval force detailed for its solution could be recalled to Home waters with no loss of time.[63]

[61] Sir Eric Seal's unpublished autobiography.

[62] David Dilks (ed.), *The Diaries of Sir Alexander Cadogan, 1938–1945* (London, 1971), p. 308.

[63] See below, p. 225 for the opinion of the Chiefs of Staff on this point. The British Naval Historical Section afterwards called attention to two incidents in the Mediterranean which from an operational point of view brought out the necessity to terminate this period of indecision. The first occurred on 23 June, when 3 Italian battleships, 4 cruisers, and 10 destroyers were sighted to the south of Sardinia, steaming eastward. This information reached the Admiralty on the 26th. Then, on 25 June, three Italian destroyers bombarded the road near Sollum (Egypt, at the Libyan frontier). That evening Cunningham signalled to the Admiralty: 'Operations

The British Government would not have proceeded against the French Fleet had there been any question about America's approval of a strong policy. The Americans shared British apprehensions. They had a profound interest in the French ships not falling under the control or into the possession of the Germans—for the sake of British survival and American national security. (Note that a substantial part of the United States Fleet was in the Pacific at this time.) They received assurances similar to those the French gave the British, and put no greater trust in them than did the British. Undersecretary of State Sumner Welles told the French Ambassador in Washington (the Comte de Saint-Quentin) on 24 June that the armistice 'apparently threw the entire [French] fleet directly into German hands'.[64] The American concern was expressed to the Bordeaux Government in unequivocal terms. The Secretary of State informed the French Ambassador (27 June) that it was 'naturally a matter of great importance to us if France hands to Germany a cocked gun to shoot at us'.[65] The Ambassador reported to his Government that the British Government had consulted the American Government and received its approval. Two American scholars comment:

Nothing has been found in the State Department files to substantiate this statement, and it may be doubted whether any officials of the Department, excepting possibly Mr. Hull and Mr. Welles, knew anything of the project in advance. But the President certainly did, as may be seen from a handwritten note of Lord Lothian's [British Ambassador in Washington] on the British situation report sent to Mr. Roosevelt on July 4, 1940. This note read: 'You will see that Winston Churchill has taken the action in regard to the French Fleet which we discussed and you approved.'[66]

presently seriously impaired because of the uncertainty which reigns concerning French squadrons.' Naval Historical Branch (Ministry of Defence) records.

[64]   *Foreign Relations of the United States, 1940,* ii. 460.

[65]   *The Memoirs of Cordell Hull,* i. 796. 'As the President and I minutely scrutinized the wording of Article VIII of the armistice terms, relating to the fleet, we could not but be anxious. If the Germans were to superintend the dismantling of the French warships, they could also seize them. As for German promises not to use the French Fleet for their own war purposes, they were worth less than an oat.' Ibid., p. 795.

[66]   William L. Langer and S. Everett Gleason, *The Challenge to Isolation, 1937–1940* (New York, 1952), p. 573, citing the Roosevelt Papers for the Lothian note. There is confirmation of the American advance approval, albeit indirectly, in the War Cabinet minutes of 29 June. Halifax stated that Welles 'had said that in the view of the American Government, the surrender of the French Fleet was the most degrading surrender in history. The United States Government had been given most explicit undertakings that the Fleet would not be surrendered. It seemed safe to assume that any action which we might take in respect of the French Fleet would be applauded in the United States.' WM 187 (40), CAB 65/13. A telegram from the Ambassador was read to the War Cabinet which met at midday on 3 July, six hours before fire was opened on the French fleet at Mers-el-Kébir: The President had 'volunteered the

In his Commons speech of 25 June Churchill had declared that 'neither patience nor resolution will be lacking in the measures they [H.M. Government] may think it right to take for the safety of the Empire'. By the 27th it was plain that the French would not fight in North Africa and that their Fleet was resigning itself to the terms of the armistices. The decisive War Cabinet met at noon, 27 June. There was unanimous agreement to force the issue.[67] 'Public opinion', the minutes read, 'was strongly insistent that we should take action on the lines of the measures taken at Copenhagen against the Danish Fleet.'[68] There was no concern over the *Jean Bart* at Casablanca (the *Watchman* had her under observation) or the *Richelieu* at Dakar (the aircraft carrier *Hermes*, seaplane carrier *Albatross*, and two armed merchant cruisers were keeping an eye on her). The French ships in British ports posed no pressing problem, and it was anticipated that Cunningham's superior force could neutralize Force X. 'The real question at issue was what to do as regards the French ships at Oran.' The situation was very different there. At Oran in western Algeria lay a conglomeration of smaller vessels: torpedo-boats, submarines, etc.; but the near-by

suggestion that His Majesty's Government might offer to convoy all the French officers and men back to France under a flag of truce, give them a year's pay, delay undertaking to return the ships and their equipment to a free France after the war was over. I asked him whether that meant that American opinion would support forcible seizure of these ships. He said certainly. They would expect them to be seized rather than that they should fall into German hands and that he would do everything in his power to help this solution. He said that he had offered to buy the Fleet from the French before the Reynaud Government fell but that there was nobody from whom he could buy it today.' WM 192 (40), CAB 65/14.

[67] As claimed by Churchill in the Commons on 4 July: '. . . there was not the slightest hesitation or divergence among them.' The War Cabinet at this date consisted of Churchill, Neville Chamberlain (Lord President), Lord Halifax (Foreign Secretary), and two representatives of the Labour Party, Clement Attlee (Lord Privy Seal) and Arthur Greenwood (Minister without Portfolio). Nine others were present on the 27th: the First Lord, the Service Chiefs, the Air Secretary (Sir Archibald Sinclair), the Home Secretary (Sir John Anderson), the Dominions Secretary (Lord Caldecote), the C-in-C, Home Forces (General Sir Edmund Ironside), and the Foreign Under-Secretary (Sir Alexander Cadogan). Churchill had added on 4 July that 'the three Service Ministers, as well as men like the Minister of Information [Duff Cooper] and the Secretary of State for the Colonies [Lord Lloyd], particularly noted for their long friendship with France, when they were consulted were equally convinced that no other decision than that which we took was possible'.

[68] Wrote Churchill in *Their Finest Hour* (p. 206): 'The War Cabinet never hesitated. . . . This was a hateful decision, the most unnatural and painful in which I have ever been concerned. It recalled the episode of the destruction of the Danish fleet at Copenhagen by Nelson in 1801; but now the French had been only yesterday our dear Allies, and our sympathy for the misery of France was sincere. On the other hand, the life of the State and the salvation of our cause were at stake. It was Greek tragedy. But no act was ever more necessary for the life of Britain and for all that depended upon it.'

protected naval base at Mers-el-Kébir gave shelter to the cream of the French Navy, the powerful Atlantic Fleet (Force de Raid), which had moved from Brest at the end of April as a precaution against Italy's entry into the war. It comprised the modern battle cruisers *Dunkerque* and *Strasbourg*, two older battleships, a seaplane carrier, and six large destroyers.

The War Cabinet of 27 June discussed three alternative strategies: (1) mining the ships in with magnetic mines, which could be done right away by aircraft from England (they would have to land near by after the operation, perhaps in Tunisia) or, if they were prepared to wait three days, by aircraft from the *Ark Royal*; (2) a strong fleet (it could be off Oran by 3 July) would demand that the French ships be demilitarized under British control, or that they sail for British ports, or that they sink their ships within three hours or face British bombardment; (3) two submarines could be stationed outside the port to sink any ships that came out. The Prime Minister was opposed to the minelaying operation, since he thought it unlikely that the French squadron would leave Oran immediately. He and the War Cabinet preferred the second alternative, to be carried out on 3 July, and this is what was agreed to 'in principle'. Internment in American ports was an option that might be offered to the French. The precise course of action on the 3rd was not spelt out, but the First Lord and First Sea Lord were instructed to take in hand at once the plans for the operation.[69] In the evening of 30 June the War Cabinet accepted the Prime Minister's proposal that the operation at Oran take place on 3 July rather than wait until the 5th, when the battleship *Nelson* could take part, because it was wiser not to send her away from Home waters in view of the invasion threat. The Oran operation should be contemporaneous with steps to establish full control of the French ships in British ports and at Alexandria.[70]

There can be no question that Churchill initiated, and was the driving force behind, 'Operation Catapult', as the Mers-el-Kébir operation was named.[71] He had from the start advocated a bold course and had carried an initially hesitant War Cabinet and Admiralty with him by strength of will. The ACNS (Trade) at the time feels 'quite certain that Winston was the prime mover', and the then Director of Plans at the Air Ministry says: 'The fact was that WSC was determined on it, and bounced us into it.'[72]

---

[69] WM 184 (40), CAB 65/13.   [70] WM 188 (40), CAB 65/13.
[71] 'Catapult' was to be extended to all points where French warships were accessible to action by the Royal Navy, but in particular at Oran and Mers-el-Kébir.
[72] Admiral Sir Harold Burrough's and Marshal of the Royal Air Force Sir John

It is the belief of the Principal Private Secretary to the First Lord that 'there was unanimity—and spontaneous unanimity—among Winston, Dudley Pound, and AVA [Alexander] that no other conclusion was possible'.[73] Alexander and Pound had by this date overcome their earlier doubts and were now almost as adamant as Churchill that no risk should be run that the Germans might achieve control of the French battle fleet. We must remember that, in the last analysis, the decision lay with Churchill and Pound. The First Sea Lord's policy stemmed from the simple concept that 'the best place for the French fleet is at the bottom of the sea'.[74] To Pound's non-political mind, the elimination of as much of the French Fleet as possible seemed an obvious precaution. 'His thinking', Admiral Godfrey tells us, 'did not take into account trends of opinion or ultimate consequences. No one was less able to understand or believe the French, and the only man of knowledge who stuck up for them was Holland and one or two of our liaison officers with the French fleet, and this source was regarded as tainted. The warning of Lord Tyrrell [the Ambassador in Paris, 1928–34] that Darlan was a twister may also have influenced the First Sea Lord.'[75] Pound's Secretary 'seldom saw the First Sea Lord so determined as he was then'.[76] Pound, nevertheless, was more prepared than was Churchill to seek a solution short of the use of force, on which more below. The VCNS, Phillips, had his doubts. In the opinion of his Assistant Secretary, he was 'alive to the dangers but was not, I think, as alarmed as Churchill evidently was. He could not believe that the French Navy would voluntarily put itself at the disposal of the Germans, and if it did not and the Germans were nonetheless able to get control of the French ships with their seagoing and fighting efficiency unimpaired, would the Germans be able to find trained crews to man them?' Moreover, Phillips shared

Slessor's letters to the author, 18 Sept., 7 Aug. 1972, respectively. Less kindly, the DDOD (H) wrote: 'W.C. wants to take drastic action for the glorification of W.C. and the discomfiture of his erstwhile friends. He always was the protagonist of France and feels their defection badly.' Edwards's diary, 1 July.

[73] Sir Clifford Jarrett's letter to the author, 12 Aug. 1972.

[74] As uttered in the presence of the DNI, Rear-Admiral J. H. Godfrey. Godfrey to J. P. L. Thomas (First Lord of the Admiralty), n.d. (late Mar. 1954), Godfrey MSS. However, 'Pound's remark was not meant literally. He had a way of oversimplifying complex subjects . . .' Godfrey to Admiral of the Fleet Lord Cunningham of Hyndhope, 7 May 1954, Godfrey MSS.

[75] Godfrey's comments on Auphan and Mordal's *The French Navy in World War II* (a passage on p. 122).

[76] Vice-Admiral Sir Ronald Brockman's letter to the author, 22 May 1972. A document in the Beaverbrook MSS. (box 16, folder XII), a note of a conversation Alexander had with Beaverbrook in 1960, confirms his initial opposition to an attack on the fleet. I am thankful to Mr. A. J. P. Taylor for bringing this document to my attention.

the strong feelings of the Admirals at Gibraltar (see below) about the danger of antagonizing the French.[77]

All discussions held and decisions made were at the very top level: Churchill and the War Cabinet, with the close involvement of the First Sea Lord and, to a lesser extent, the First Lord. There is no evidence that the Naval Staff (except for the hasty appreciation on 24 June), the Joint Planners, or even the Chiefs of Staff were asked their opinion about the strategic necessity, military feasibility, or military consequences of 'Catapult' prior to 27 June. On the 28th, that is, *after* the decision 'in principle' had been made, Churchill asked the Admiralty for an appreciation by 30 June of the consequences which would be likely to follow from the projected naval action, if it came to that. Pound turned the request over to the Joint Planning Sub-Committee of the Chiefs of Staff, which reported on the 29th, after a rather hurried consideration of the operation: 'With Germany and Italy already against us, with the possibility that Japan may come in in the near future, and with France no longer an ally, it is clear that the possibility of French hostility can only be viewed with the greatest concern.' They outlined the military consequences which might arise as a consequence of the destruction by force of French warships, among them: (1) the effect on American opinion of 'vigorous action of the kind now contemplated' would be good. 'Moreover, America is very apprehensive of the fleet under German control.' (2) If France adopted a hostile attitude, the enemy would acquire four light cruisers and four destroyers presently in metropolitan France. 'This reinforcement is not of great importance, but there is an evident possibility of further reinforcement by forces in French North Africa and colonial ports which might escape our clutches.' This applied especially to submarines, destroyers, and light cruisers. The augmentation of the German Navy by French destroyers and light cruisers which managed to escape would be a serious matter, since 'the Germans are very short of these, a fact which makes operations in home waters much less difficult for us than they would otherwise be'. But the conclusion of the Joint Planners was that the real danger of active French hostility outbalanced any advantages in destroying French ships. 'We cannot gauge the French re-actions to the proposed naval action against their ships. At the worst the French re-actions might be extremely serious and would then immensely complicate the already heavy task. If, therefore, there is a genuine danger that the action proposed would lead to the active hostility of France and of her colonial possessions,

[77] Rear-Admiral K. H. Farnhill's letters to the author, 22 Sept., 10 Oct. 1972.

we do not consider that the destruction of these French ships by force would be justified.'[78]

The Chiefs of Staff considered the Joint Planners' paper at their afternoon meeting on 30 June. The Directors of Plans were present. One gathers that their conclusions did not sit well with the Service Chiefs, who after a full discussion asked the Planners to redraft their report in the light of the discussion and submit it to the War Cabinet for its meeting later that day.[79] No such paper was submitted. Instead, as we shall see in a moment, the Chiefs of Staff prepared their own.

The two living members of the Joint Planning Sub-Committee, Admiral Sir Charles Daniel and Marshal of the Royal Air Force Sir John Slessor, are in complete agreement that the Joint Planners had no enthusiasm for 'Operation Catapult' and made no bones about their dislike of it. Phillips did not ask Daniel's view of the Oran operation until about an hour before fire was opened! 'I was opposed to it, because I felt that although we sank one or two heavy ships, we should find all the French commerce destroyers, e.g. cruisers and submarines, at war with us. Here I was wrong. I also felt Darlan would not allow the French Fleet to fall into German hands.'[80] Slessor says it is an 'understatement' that the Joint Planners had no enthusiasm for the operation. 'Anything that involved real risk of active French hostility in anything other than merely local affairs—like Syria and Dakar—understandably worried us severely. We were doubtful whether "Catapult" could be completely successful—and it was not. Anyway it was a rushed decision and we did not like it.'[81]

The Naval Staff, who, apart from the First Sea Lord and the VCNS, were scarcely involved, shared the feelings of the Joint Planners, if we may judge from Captain Edwards's diary entries: 'I'm afraid we're going to make a mess of this difficult problem. My own view is that we've bungled so much that the position is almost impossible for us [to] either trust them or take drastic action. The result will be for us to lose 'em all.' 'To attack the French Fleet seems to me open to all sorts of possibilities & on the face of it I'm bitterly opposed to this course of action.' 'I gather we're committed

[78] COS (40) 505 (JP), 'Implications of Action Contemplated in Respect of Certain French Ships', CAB 80/14. The Joint Planners were the three Service Ds of P, Captain C. S. Daniel, Air Commodore J. C. Slessor, and Brigadier I. S. O. Playfair.

[79] COS (40) 200th meeting, CAB 79/5. The Service Chiefs were still Pound, Air Chief Marshal Sir Cyril Newall, and General Sir John Dill.

[80] Daniel's letter to the author, 21 Apr. 1972.

[81] Slessor's letter to the author, 7 Aug. 1972. See also his *The Central Blue*, p. 299.

against all the advice of the Naval Staff to attack the French Forces at Oran.'[82]

The Service Chiefs, however, gave the War Cabinet full backing. Their position, as well as that of the three Vice-Chiefs of Staff, who were present at a grand review of the situation in the evening of 30 June,[83] was stated in a paper which summed up the discussion and which deserves to be quoted *in extenso* as the one full statement of the attitude of the Service Chiefs:

The following action is open to us with regard to the French Fleet—

(a) To ask the French Navy to join with us actively against Germany.

(b) To ask them to come to our ports on the understanding that they would not be used against the Germans unless the latter break the terms of the Armistice.

(c) To induce the French to demilitarise their Fleet to our satisfaction, i.e. under our supervision and inspection.

(d) To induce the French to scuttle their Fleet.

(e) On the assumption that (a), (b), (c) and (d) prove unsuccessful, to take no forcible action in the hopes that events will somehow turn in our favour, e.g. by the terms of the Armistice being faithfully carried out.

(f) In the last resort to take action against the French Fleet at Oran.

We have given most careful consideration to the implications of taking action against the French Fleet at Oran and, after balancing all the arguments both for and against such action, we have reached the conclusion on balance that the operations contemplated should be carried out.

In reaching this conclusion we have studied the following main considerations:—

(a) The likelihood of the French ships falling into the hands of the Germans, if the action is not taken.

(b) The balance of capital ship strength which would eventuate if Germany obtained possession of the ships.

(c) The effect which the action contemplated would have on the home defence situation, having regard to the probability of imminent invasion.

(d) The effect on the general situation, if as a result of our action, France becomes hostile.

The Likelihood of the French Ships falling into the hands of Germany.

In the light of recent events[84] we can no longer place any faith in French

---

[82] 30 June, 1, 2 July. Cunningham sent a message to the Admiralty on 30 June deploring the use of force at Oran 'if it can possibly be avoided. . . . the whole of the friendly French element may be alienated, and in particular I would mention the effect in North Africa where friendly attitude may greatly affect naval operations later on.' Cunningham of Hyndhope, *A Sailor's Odyssey*, p. 245.

[83] COS (40) 201st meeting, CAB 79/5. The Vice-Chiefs of Staff were Phillips, Air Marshal R. E. C. Peirse, and Lieutenant-General Sir R. H. Haining.

[84] '"Recent events" must have included the collapse of the will to resist in North

assurances, nor could we be certain that any measures, which we were given to understand the French would take to render their ships unserviceable before reaching French metropolitan ports, would, in fact, be taken. Once the ships have reached French metropolitan ports we are under no illusions as to the certainty that, sooner or later, the Germans will employ them against us.

The balance of Capital Ships Strength.

If it could be assumed that the French capital ships were effectively demilitarised or otherwise disposed of, our present capital ship strength *vis-a-vis* that of the Germans and the Italians combined is not unsatisfactory.

If, however, the two French battle cruisers were to fall into the hands of the Germans apart from such other heavy ships as they might acquire, and we were to suffer a reduction of capital ship strength as a result of submarine or air attack the situation would be extremely serious.

The effect of the Operations on the Home Defence Situation.

The over-riding consideration which we have placed in the forefront of our discussions has been the importance of ensuring, as far as possible, the concentration of the maximum possible naval strength in home waters to meet the imminent threat of invasion. We are informed by the Chief of Naval Staff that the implications, on the situation at home of the detachment of the force to the Mediterranean for the operations contemplated, were fully taken into account before their despatch, and the risks were considered acceptable. It is the intention of the Admiralty to retain a force of heavy ships in the Western Mediterranean, whether or not action is taken against the French Fleet. Should it be decided not to carry out the operations against the French Fleet it would be possible for one heavy ship and from four to six destroyers to return to home waters.

Although we agree that any avoidable dispersion of force, which militates against the concentration of the maximum strength available in the United Kingdom, is highly undesirable, we are prepared to accept the detachment of the force referred to above for the operations against the French Fleet.

In this connection it is important to note that simultaneously with the action against the French Fleet at Oran, it is the intention to seize all the French warships, at present in British ports. These include a large number (approximately 100) of small craft of various sizes and categories. Amongst this number are 12 destroyers which could, within a short space of time, be put into service and would be of considerable value for convoy operations on the trade routes.

We are faced with grave issues at home. It is therefore of paramount importance that the uncertainty regarding the French Fleet should be dissipated as soon as possible in order that the ships now shadowing the French Fleet can be released for operations elsewhere.

Africa and Syria, the rebuff sustained by Mr. Duff Cooper [Minister of Information] and General Lord Gort at Rabat [26 June, when General Noguès, the Governor-General of French Morocco, refused to see them], and a mendacious account, issued from Bordeaux, of the British Government's behaviour in the past.' Butler, *Grand Strategy*, ii. 222.

French Hostility.

We realise that the action contemplated may result in France becoming actively hostile to us. In weighing up the implications of this possibility, we take the view that if we carry out our intention of including France in the blockade, it will only be a matter of time before the French become, in any case, actively hostile.

In our view, the implications of hastening French hostility are not such as to over-weigh our previous arguments.

Conclusion.

To sum up, we consider that, from the military point of view, Operation 'Catapult' should be carried out as soon as possible.[85]

This statement was decisive. There was to be no turning back, and the alternatives to be presented to the French had been formulated.

There was at this time a most important development on the French side. In the afternoon of the 27th, Darlan, concerned over the threatening attitude of Britain, asked Odend'hal to inform the Admiralty 'to abstain from any judgement' on the armistice terms until the conclusion of the talks at the armistice commissions. 'In particular request already made to immobilize the fleet in non-occupied French ports will in all probability be agreed to. I repeat that fleet will remain French or will not exist.'[86] The message did not reach London until the 29th. There is no record that Odend'hal acted on it. The same day, at the first meeting of the Italian armistice commission in Turin, Admiral Duplat, the leader of the French delegation, proposed that the French warships should be disarmed in the unoccupied Mediterranean ports, namely in Toulon and North Africa. The Italians agreed, subject to German concurrence. This was understandable, since the ruling desired by the French was entirely dependent on a German concession—that they waive their claim for the return from the Mediterranean of those ships whose home bases were in Atlantic ports. At 2.30 p.m. on the 30th, before the Germans had acted, Darlan telegraphed Odend'hal: 'Italian Government authorizes stationing of the fleet with half crews in Toulon and North Africa. I have firm hopes that it will be likewise with the German Government, whose reply we are now awaiting. Under these conditions all English pretexts for detaining our forces are without foundation, and I beg of you to insist on our warships and merchant ships being released.'[87] The message reached Odend'hal on 1 July in garbled form. All that he

[85] COS (40) 510, 'Implications of Action Contemplated in Respect of Certain French Ships. Aide Mémoire', 30 June, CAB 80/14.

[86] (Nos. 5185, 5186) *Rapport. Événements*, ii. 472.

[87] (No. 5202) ibid., p. 473.

reported to Phillips on the morning of 1 July was that he had received a telegram from Darlan 'asking that we [the British Government] should reserve final judgment until the details of the armistice conditions were known. Discussions on the armistice conditions were starting at Wiesbaden on the 1st July, and the conditions in regard to the French Fleet were to be dealt with first.'[88] The fact is that the German armistice commission at Wiesbaden had quickly given their consent on the 30th to what had been agreed at Turin. The practical effect was that all the bases of the French Fleet would lie outside the German occupied zone, thus ruling out the Atlantic ports of Cherbourg, Brest, Lorient, and St. Nazaire. The Germans had now formally accepted the modification of Article 8 requested by the French at Rethondes. Incidentally, it was on this day, 30 June, that the French Government left its latest temporary capital, Clermont-Ferrand, and set itself up in Vichy as the Government of Unoccupied France.

Would it have made any difference had the War Cabinet and Admiralty known the precise situation on 1 July as regards the critical armistice article? I doubt it. They had been aware since 22 June that the French were hoping to be allowed to retain and demilitarize their ships in French colonial ports. On the 27th and again on the 29th Odend'hal had reported that Pound would have been satisfied if the ships were kept in North African ports, far from enemy occupied areas. '. . . the British Admiralty would consider such an internment as offering some guarantee.'[89] Although Pound might have accepted such an arrangement, Churchill would never have agreed to this as sufficient. Thus, he had greeted the news of the Phillips–Odend'hal meeting with the revealing remark that the 'discussions [at Wiesbaden] as to the armistice conditions could not affect the real facts of the situation'. These were probably the worth of German promises and the belief that not even Toulon and North African ports could be regarded as beyond the reach of Hitler's forces.

Auphan and Mordal claim that the plans for 'Operation Catapult' predated the signing of the German armistice, and Michel says: 'Actually, the English decision was very firm and dates from 17 June.'[90] This is not the case. All that happened before the

[88] The quoted material is the paraphrase of the message in WM 190 (40), CAB 65/14. This War Cabinet met at 6 p.m. on 1 July.

[89] Varillon, *Mers-el-Kébir*, pp. 85–6, and material in Naval Historical Branch (Ministry of Defence) records. There is no confirmation of this in the official British records.

[90] Auphan and Mordal, *The French Navy in World War II*, p. 117, Henri Michel, *Vichy Année 40* (Paris, 1966), p. 235.

armistice was that Churchill had approved Pound's decision on 17 June to send the battle cruiser *Hood* and the aircraft carrier *Ark Royal* to Gibraltar in order 'to watch over the fate of the French Fleet'. The force would also take over the duties of the French squadron at Mers-el-Kébir.[91] The two ships arrived at Gibraltar on the 23rd. It was not until the 28th, that is, after the War Cabinet decision to proceed with 'Catapult', that 'Force H' was officially constituted from these two capital ships and the battleships *Valiant* (that veteran of Jutland, which arrived at Gibraltar on 2 July) and *Resolution* (there since 10 June). On 26 June the Admiralty instructed North to 'institute air patrol as continuous as possible' between Oran and Toulon, since they expected that the *Dunkerque* and *Strasbourg* might be sent to Toulon. (This, indeed, was Darlan's plan.) On 29 June the submarines *Proteus* and *Pandora* were directed to patrol off Oran and Algiers, respectively, but not to attack, and on the 30th the Vice-Admiral, Aircraft Carriers (L. V. Wells, *Ark Royal*), was ordered to establish a destroyer patrol 30 miles west of Oran, and to capture and take to Britain the two French battle cruisers, should they proceed to the westward.

*   *   *

At 3.30 in the afternoon of 27 June, after the War Cabinet, the First Sea Lord informed Vice-Admiral Sir James Somerville that he was to command Force H. Its initial task would be 'to secure the transfer, surrender or destruction of the French warships at Oran and Mers-el-Kébir, so as to ensure that these ships could not fall into German or Italian hands'. Pound stated in categorical terms that no concessions were to be made: the French must accept the British terms or face the consequences.

The 58-year-old Somerville was one of the great personalities of the Navy. He possessed unusual charm, a quick brain, and exceptional energy, and was a fine seaman in all senses (thus, he was

[91] The First Sea Lord had at first contemplated the entire evacuation of the eastern Mediterranean, transferring Cunningham's fleet to Gibraltar in order to hold the western exit to the Mediterranean, without which the protection of the vital Atlantic trade would become very difficult. Churchill 'reacted strongly against any such proposal at the present time. . . . [It] would involve grave reactions in the Dominions, and would expose our forces in the Middle East to the risk of annihilation, & the Canal to the risk of falling into Italian hands. It would also have a profound influence on the Middle East as a whole. Turkey and Greece would disappear finally from our side even before the Battle of Britain was fought.' Memorandum of a meeting on 17 June (6 p.m.) between Churchill, Pound, and Phillips—unsigned but in the hand of the Principal Private Secretary to the First Lord, Jarrett. Alexander MSS., 5/4/26. Cunningham also registered a vigorous protest that day when apprised of the Admiralty's proposal. No more was heard of it.

well versed in modern technology) and a natural leader of men. 'His humanity, sympathy, and unfailing sense of humour greatly endeared him to the men', Taprell Dorling has written. 'He knew their thoughts and could speak their language.' Nearly everyone loved serving under him, officers and men both, although he could be tough if crossed! His sense of humour and high spirits had won him the sobriquet of 'Naughty James'. (He had prefaced a BBC broadcast early in 1940 with a characteristic aside: 'Good God, they've given me a bottle of water to drink!') An unusual feature of his career is that, while C-in-C, East Indies, he was invalided home early in 1939, a medical board having diagnosed tuberculosis. Although he obtained a Harley Street opinion to the contrary, to his great indignation the Admiralty placed him on the retired list on grounds of ill health. He was brought back immediately war broke out to head up the work at the Admiralty on the development of radar, which job was later expanded into AA weapons and devices. He also played an important role in the Dunkirk evacuation. The origin of his appointment to command Force H lies in the consideration, as stated by Pound afterwards, that 'the force for the Oran business had to be collected in a hurry, and a Flag Officer of experience, who was immediately available in London, selected, even though he was on the Retired List'. A special reason for Somerville's appointment may have been his considerable experience on the Mediterranean station, including the command of the destroyer flotillas there as Rear-Admiral (Destroyers), Mediterranean Fleet, in 1936–8.

Following his interview with Pound on 27 June, Somerville gaily burst into his office, quickly packed his belongings, and left with a 'Goodbye, boys—look after yourselves. I am stepping out!' The next thing they knew he was back at sea, approaching North Africa. On the evening of the 27th Somerville entered in his diary: 'Absolutely grand to get a sea job at last.'[92] He had no premonition of playing a principal role in a grand tragedy. At a subsequent interview on the 27th with Pound and Alexander it was explained to him that, although 'every preparation was to be made to employ force . . . it was hoped that the necessity would not rise. The opinion I held after this meeting was that the French collapse was so complete and the will to fight so entirely extinguished, that it seemed highly improbable that the French would, in the last resort, resist by force the British demands.'[93] And this view he continued

[92] Somerville MSS., 1/31.
[93] Somerville, 'Report of Proceedings: F.O. Force "H"—28th June to 4th July 1940', 26 July 1940, Somerville MSS., 7/19. (Hereafter cited as 'Report of Proceedings'.)

to hold almost until he opened fire. Unknown to him, the feeling at the Admiralty was that force would probably have to be employed.[94]

Somerville and his staff embarked from Spithead in the light cruiser *Arethusa* on the 28th, arriving at Gibraltar at 5.45 p.m. on the 30th. The Admiral transferred his flag to the *Hood*, then plunged into a series of conferences on 'Catapult'. First he saw his old friend Dudley North, who expressed grave concern at the use of force against the French Fleet. North was certain that the French would not hand their ships over intact to the Germans or Italians, and that they would fight, were force threatened by the British. It seemed to him 'that an action which must result in the killing of many Frenchmen by Englishmen was bound to have a far reaching deleterious effect on our long and difficult road to ultimate victory'.[95] The forthcoming operation was discussed at a meeting of flag officers and captains and other commanding officers on board the *Hood*. 'The view I held,' Somerville reported, 'and which was shared by others present at the meeting, was that it was highly improbable that the French would use force to resist our demands.'[96] A classic example of wishful thinking! 'The faces of the Admirals and other officers round the table were a picture. The news that they were probably going to be ordered to fire on their late allies, now crushed and ashamed, was utterly repugnant to all of them. So much indeed was it so, that several of them came to me and protested and asked if this mad idea couldn't be stopped. One of them,

His intense aversion to the use of force must have been strengthened by his interception in the afternoon of 30 June, when *en route* to Gibraltar, of Cunningham's message to the Admiralty (above, p. 224 n.) expressing strong opposition to the use of force at Oran. Alexander's version of Somerville's mood on the 27th should be noted. 'He understood clearly the position and what had to be done. He said to me in my room at the Admiralty: "I quite recognise that, however repugnant this job may seem, the Government know it has got to be done, in the interests of the safety of the nation."' Viscount Alexander of Hillsborough (as he then was) in the Lords, 26 July 1954, Hansard, 5th series (Lords), clxxxix, col. 96.

[94] Thus, Pound's signal to Cunningham on the 28th, which prompted the latter's of the 30th: 'As soon as adequate force has been collected at Gibraltar, drastic action against ships at Oran will probably be taken.' 'Selection of Signals Relating to the Disposal of the French Fleet. 1940', Cunningham MSS., Add. MSS. 52569.

[95] 'Extracts from a letter from Admiral Dudley North', n.d., North to Richmond, 23 Oct. 1945, Richmond MSS., 7/4. It was on this occasion that North, after reading his copy of the orders for 'Catapult', pencilled across the envelope: 'Should be Boomerang, not Catapult.' Monks, *That Day at Gibraltar*, pp. 22–3. North offered a quixotic suggestion facetiously: 'Winnie must be mad. I see what he's after but this is a bloody silly way of going about it. Why not send me a decent yacht, let me fill it up with champagne and pretty Wrens, and I'll sail in and get the French myself.' Warren Tute, *The Deadly Stroke* (London, 1973), p. 57.

[96] 'Report of Proceedings.'

indeed, refused duty when it came to the point.'[97] At the conclusion of this meeting, North, 'Nutty' Wells, and Holland (Captain, *Ark Royal*) expressed vigorous opposition to the use of force. It would be 'disastrous'; besides, there was little danger of the French allowing their ships to fall into German hands.[98] Somerville got more of the same the next morning (1 July) from Holland and from two officers who until recently had been liaison officers attached to the French fleet in the Mediterranean—Lieutenant-Commanders A. Y. Spearman and G. P. S. Davies.

Somerville had already received an Admiralty message of 2.25 a.m., 1 July, which instructed him to be prepared for 'Catapult' on the 3rd and gave him four alternatives to be put to the French: (1) to bring the ships to British harbours and fight with the British; (2) to sail their ships to a British port; (3) to demilitarize their ships to British satisfaction; (4) to sink their ships.[99] Now, at 12.20 p.m. (1 July), 'very impressed' by the views he had just heard, Somerville communicated them to the Admiralty, together with certain alternative proposals:

I have had further opportunity to discuss situation with Holland, Spearman and Davies and am impressed by their view that use of force should be avoided at all costs.

They consider now that armistice terms are known there is distinct possibility of French accepting first alternative. To achieve this and, in accordance with their experience of French, they propose Holland arrives 0800 and signals in P/L [plain language, i.e. not ciphered] addressed to the Admiral: 'The British Admiralty have sent Captain Holland to confer with you. The British Navy hopes their proposal will enable you and your glorious French Navy once more to range yourself side by side with them. In these circumstances your ships would remain yours and no one need have anxiety for the future. A British fleet is at sea off Oran waiting to welcome you.'

One hour after Holland enters harbour, Force H arrives off Oran, repeats same message addressed to French Admiral using signal projectors turned on as many ships as possible. This is to ensure purport of message is received by officers and men other than the French Admiral.

If French refuse first alternative they consider second alternative must be amended as follows: French to proceed to sea with a minimum steaming party, i.e. demilitarised, and allowing themselves to be captured by Force H. Strictly ensuring ships being returned intact to France on completion of hostilities. France can plead they acted under force and that unable to contest British action.

[97] North to Richmond, 23 Oct. 1945.

[98] 'Report of Proceedings', Somerville's diary, 30 June.

[99] These were the alternatives in the Chiefs of Staff *aide mémoire* of 30 June (above, p. 224). The signals exchanged between the Admiralty and Somerville are, with an exception or two, in 'Report of Proceedings'.

Third and fourth alternatives to be in form of invitation to French.

They hold strongly that offensive action on our part would immediately alienate all French wherever they are and transfer a defeated ally into an active enemy. They believe our prestige would be enhanced if we withdrew from Oran without taking offensive action.

These views based on very recent contact with French naval authorities. Unless Their Lordships have more definite and contrary information I consider proposals merit very careful consideration.

Very early reply requested as possible acceptance of first or second alternative depends on immediate action.[100]

He was promptly rapped over the knuckles for his trouble, a peremptory telegram reaching him in the evening of 1 July that it was 'the firm intention of H.M.G. that if the French will not accept any of the alternatives which are being sent you their ships must be destroyed. The proposals in your 1220/1 are not therefore acceptable.'[101] 'So that's that' was Somerville's terse comment in his diary. He was still not unduly upset, because: 'I felt at this time that, although there was a possibility that the French might be prepared to fight, it was improbable that they would do so under the conditions which would obtain at Oran. At the worst, they might fire a few token shots before abandoning their ships.'[102]

The War Cabinet met at 6 p.m. on 1 July, with Pound and Phillips present, for a short discussion on whether to include the third of the alternatives (demilitarisation) suggested by the Chiefs of Staff in their *aide mémoire*. A compromise resulted.

On the one hand, it was argued that any steps of demilitarisation which could be carried out in a short time could probably also be fairly quickly repaired. The essence of the present plan was quick action.

On the other hand, the First Sea Lord took the view that demilitarisation was the measure which was most likely to appeal to the French Navy. If their ships were demilitarised, they would hope to get them back after the war.

The view taken on this point was that, while we should not offer demilitarisation, the Flag Officer should be authorised to accept it if the other alternatives were refused, in order to avoid bloodshed.

The last paragraph referred to a *French* offer to accept demilitarization—that is, it depended on French initiative. The text of the instructions to Somerville was prepared and approved (see below).

[100] Naval Historical Branch (Ministry of Defence) records.

[101] ADM 1/10321.

[102] 'Report of Proceedings.' The officers of the *Hood*, when informed that day that the operation was about to be ordered, were 'absolutely appalled at the prospect. It was the one time in my life I have seen Admiral Somerville really worried.' Letter from Admiral Sir William Davis (he was the Commander, i.e. Second-in-Command, of the *Hood*) to the author, 14 Jan. 1974.

It was agreed that the Prime Minister and the First Lord would meet at 10 p.m. to settle the final wording of the message to be handed to Admiral Gensoul and the supplementary instructions to Somerville, the latter to consist of the answers to be used to meet Gensoul's arguments in any discussion between the British and French naval authorities.[103]

In the early hours of 2 July the Admiralty telegraphed four 'most secret' messages to Somerville.[104] The first (1.03 a.m.) contained his final instructions for dealing with the French warships at Oran and Mers-el-Kébir. The alternatives superseded those of 2.25 a.m., 1 July (above, p. 231). The first and second alternatives were the same as in the previous instructions, though with extra trimmings; the third was a replacement of the former third alternative; the fourth was the same. Additionally, demilitarization at Mers-el-Kébir was stated to be acceptable, subject to a time proviso, *if suggested by the French* after refusing the four alternatives. The text reads:

(*A*) French Fleet at Oran and Mers el Kebir is to be given four alternatives:–

(1) To sail their ships to British Harbours and continue to fight with us.

(2) To sail their ships with reduced crews to a British port from which the crews would be repatriated whenever desired.

In the case of Alternatives (1) and (2) being adopted, the ships would be restored to France at the conclusion of the war or full compensation would be paid if they are damaged meanwhile.

If French Admiral accepts alternative 2, but insists that ships should not be used by us during the war you may say we accept this condition for so long as Germany and Italy observe the Armistice terms, but we particularly do not wish to raise the point ourselves.

(3) To sail their ships with reduced crews to some French port in the West Indies such as Martinique.

After arrival at this port they would either be demilitarised to our satisfaction or, if so desired, be entrusted to United States jurisdiction for the duration of the war. The crews would be repatriated.

(4) To sink their ships.

(*B*) Should the French Admiral refuse to accept all of the above alternatives and should he suggest that he should demilitarise his ships to our satisfaction at their present berths, you are authorised to accept this further alternative provided that you are satisfied that the measures taken for demilitarisation can be carried out under your supervision within six hours and would prevent the ships being brought into service for at least one year, even at a fully equipped dockyard port.[105]

---

[103] WM 190 (40), CAB 65/14.
[104] CAB 65/8.
[105] French naval authorities have commented on this condition: 'It is not easy

(C) If none of the above alternatives are accepted by the French you are to endeavour to destroy ships in Mers el Kebir but particularly *Dunquerque* and *Strasbourg*, using all means at your disposal. Ships at Oran should also be destroyed if this will not entail any considerable loss of civilian life.

If the French accepted the first alternative, their ships were to go to a United Kingdom port; if the second, also to a United Kingdom port, unless the French preferred Gibraltar. A separate operation against the French naval force at Algiers was ruled out because of the strength of the defences there.

The second message (1.08 a.m.) gave Somerville the text of the communication to be made to the French Admiral. It had gone through various drafts and represented a 'marriage' of Churchill's draft with the Admiralty's last draft.[106]

His Majesty's Government have sent me to inform you as follows:—

They agreed to the French Government approaching the German Government only on the condition that *before* an armistice was concluded the French Fleet should be sent to British ports to prevent it falling into the hands of the enemy. The Council of Ministers declared on the 18th June that before capitulation on land the French Fleet would join up with the British Navy or sink itself.[107]

to see what "measures of demilitarisation" that complied with these demands could have been taken in under six hours other than a complete scuttling.' Naval Historical Branch (Ministry of Defence) records.

[106] Documents in ADM 1/10321 give some idea how the text had evolved. The final draft was designed to avoid too much emphasis on broken pledges. And so there was deleted from an early draft: 'The French Government, having signed the armistices, must presumably order the Fleet to French metropolitan ports. We do not doubt Admiral Darlan's good faith and we are sure that he would do his utmost to fulfil his pledge but the fact remains that the French Government is now, unfortunately, in a position where it is not possible to resist German and Italian pressure.' Also deleted (at the end of the second paragraph): 'Admiral Darlan promised the First Lord and First Sea Lord on same day [18 June] that French Fleet would never be surrendered to the enemy', and a variant of this. It popped up, however, among the 'suggestions' made to Somerville (see below).

[107] 'This sentence, alone,' says the Official Historian of the Mediterranean theatre, 'is misleading. The information given to the British Ambassador in Bordeaux on 18th June was that the Council of Ministers had been discussing the action they would take if presented with terms requiring the French Fleet to be surrendered. This contingency did not arise, so the "declaration" never became operative.' Major-General I. S. O. Playfair, *The Mediterranean and Middle East* (4 vols., London, 1954–66), i. 133 n. The British, however, continued to stress this point. Thus, in Phillips's minute of 23 Apr. 1941 (p. 216 n., above): '. . . the French Government had given a solemn undertaking not to make a separate peace. When they began to crack they approached us as to whether we could release them from this undertaking. The British Government, after due consideration, agreed to release the French from this undertaking on the condition that they would send their Fleet to our ports. It was understood that this condition was accepted but in the event nothing but unimportant

Whilst the present French Government may consider that the terms of their armistices with Germany and Italy are reconcilable with these undertakings, H.M. Government find it impossible from our previous experiences to believe that Germany and Italy will not at any moment which suits them seize French warships and use them against Britain and her allies. The Italian armistice prescribes that French ships should return to metropolitan ports and under the armistice France is required to yield up units for coast defence and minesweeping.

It is impossible for us, your comrades up till now, to allow your fine ships to fall into the power of the German or Italian enemy. [Deleted: 'Yet this is what must happen under the terms of the Armistice signed by the Government at Bordeaux.'] We are determined to fight on to the end, and if we win, as we think we shall ['may' in an early draft, altered to 'shall' by the Prime Minister!], we shall never forget that France was our ally, that our interests are the same as hers, and that our common enemy is Germany. Should we conquer we solemnly declare that we shall restore the greatness and territory of France. For this purpose we must make sure that the best ships of the French Navy are not used against us by the common foe.

In these circumstances H.M. Government have instructed me to demand that the French Fleet, now at Mers El Kebir and Oran, shall act in accordance with one of the following alternatives:—

(*a*) Sail with us and continue to fight for victory against the Germans and Italians.

(*b*) Sail with reduced crews under our control to a British port. The reduced crews will be repatriated at the earliest moment.

If either of these courses is adopted by you, we will restore your ships to France at the conclusion of the war, or pay full compensation if they are damaged meanwhile.

(*c*) Alternatively if you feel bound to stipulate that your ships should not be used against the Germans or Italians unless these break the armistice, then sail them with us with reduced crews to some French port in the West Indies, Martinique for instance, where they can be demilitarised to our satisfaction, or be perhaps entrusted to the United States, and remain safe till the end of the war, the crews being repatriated.

If you refuse these fair offers I must with profound regret require you to sink your ships within six hours.

Finally failing the above I have the orders of H.M. Government to use whatever force may be necessary to prevent your ships from falling into German or Italian hands.

Ismay, the Deputy Secretary (Military) of the War Cabinet, who was present when the message was drafted, captures some of the

units of the French Fleet, which could not go elsewhere, came to our ports, and in the place of this sure guarantee all we received was a statement from Admiral Darlan that he would never let the French Fleet fall into enemy hands.'

poignancy of the moment: 'To kick a man when he is down is unattractive at any time; but when the man is a friend who has already suffered grievously, it seems almost to border on infamy. To Churchill, with his deep love of France, it must have been an agonising moment. But he never flinched.'[108]

The third message (1.13 a.m.) offered Somerville 'suggestions' which were intended only as a 'guide' in case of a discussion with the French Admiral:

On 18th June Darlan gave a personal promise to 1st Lord and 1st Sea Lord that French Fleet would never surrender *to the enemy*.

The French may argue that they will scuttle if Germans or Italians attempt to seize the ships even in French metropolitan ports. But with French Army disarmed and the Fleet laid up with reduced crews under German or Italian surveillance, there can be no certainty that, however resolute the attempt to destroy or sink any particular ship, it would be possible to forestall seizure by the enemy.

Officers and men of any units fighting on with us will receive British rates of pay, pensions etc.

Our recent naval successes against the Italians show that vigorous action which would be possible with continued French collaboration would have greatest value in undermining Italian will to fight. We have now sunk or captured 10 Italian submarines certain and 5 possible and sunk a destroyer —all in about a fortnight.

It is a delusion to believe that France can be restored by co-operation with Axis. Armistice terms are not peace terms and Mein Kampf shows what treatment Hitler has in store for France. Whatever is left to France, if anything, will only be held on sufferance until Germany is defeated. How much better therefore to fight on with us for restoration of French Empire.

If French Admiral replies to first overture by saying we have no need to worry since all arrangements have been made, you should reply 'How can we be sure that this will be effective? You may be relieved from your command, pressure may be put on families of ships companies and so on. The Ships companies may in any case be unwilling to scuttle in a French Port for fear of immediate reprisals by the enemy. Therefore you must put your intentions into effect now and at this port, when the blame will fall on us and not on your ships companies.'

The fourth message (2.28 a.m.) offered the Vice-Admiral 'general instructions', should he meet the French fleet at sea.

What we particularly require is that *Dunquerque* and *Strasbourg* should not get into enemy control. Other modern units are important but less so.

If the French Fleet is either in visual signalling distance or in sight of your aircraft some means must be found to order them to stop and if they fail to do so action must be taken to force them to do so either by gunfire or air striking force.

[108] *The Memoirs of General the Lord Ismay* (London, 1960), p. 149.

Once they have stopped, action must be taken as if they were in harbour except that should they finally suggest demilitarisation you should only accept on condition that they return to Oran.

On the morning of 2 July Somerville held a conference of all flag and commanding officers to discuss the orders for 'Catapult'. They were framed in rather general terms, since the precise situation could not be foreseen, and focused on Mers-el-Kébir.[109] 'Phase I' would be the use of 'persuasion and threats as may be found expedient', to inform the French of the alternatives. Phase II would follow if the French refused to accept any of the alternatives and the Admiral had, accordingly, to use force. In the first stage of Phase II they would 'show the French that we are in earnest by the firing of a few rounds or by the dropping of bombs [by *Ark Royal* aircraft] close to, but not actually hitting, French ships'. The hope was that, their morale destroyed, the French crews would abandon their ships. The second stage would follow if it became necessary to undertake the destruction or sinking of the French ships. 'If the French offer organised and spirited resistance, it may be necessary to develop a full offensive with all the means at our disposal on French ships, shore batteries, etc. . . . ceasing fire as soon as it is apparent that the French have ceased to resist. . . . If, on the other hand, no organised French resistance is encountered, the destruction of French ships will be undertaken with more deliberation and greater economy of ammunition and torpedoes, available reserves of which are at present very limited.' Ships still afloat would be sunk by demolition parties from destroyers. Somerville had decided against laying magnetic mines at Mers-el-Kébir, 'except as a last resort', since he felt this would prevent the French Admiral from accepting the first or second alternatives (and the third, too); also, it would prevent the entry of British destroyers with the demolition parties. As it turned out, he did use mines. As for Oran, since gunfire would cause severe civilian casualties, the facet of 'Catapult' concerned with it spoke only of an aircraft bombing attack on the harbour to destroy morale and induce the crews to abandon their ships, to be followed by demolition parties from a destroyer.

The orders provided for full precautions throughout the operation against Italian, as well as French, submarine and air attack. If important Italian surface units were met, Force H would engage them, if necessary postponing operations against the French fleet. The only possible evidence of Italian interference came at 10.47 p.m.

[109] 'Operation Orders for Operation "Catapult"', 1 July, enclosure No. 3 to 'Report of Proceedings'.

on 2 July, when a torpedo exploded ahead of the destroyer *Vortigern* in 36° 12½' North 3° 4·6' West. This was about 100 miles east of Gibraltar. Two destroyers hunted the submarine for 65 minutes without success.

*　　*　　*　　-

At 5 p.m. on 2 July Force H was clear of Gibraltar harbour and steaming towards Oran, 195 nautical miles away. The Vice-Admiral made a general signal to Force H, soon after leaving, explaining the purpose of their mission.[110] 'Boys a bit rusty but not bad', Somerville's 2 July diary entry reads. 'Kept cruisers and all inside A/S screen as submarine attack most probable. Signal from Alexander to me from one Somerset man to another.' This may be the signal which Churchill asked the Admiralty to send that evening: 'You are charged with one of the most disagreeable and difficult tasks that a British Admiral has ever been faced with, but we have complete confidence in you and rely on you to carry it out relentlessly.'[111] At 1.35 a.m., 3 July, Somerville received an Admiralty message stating that, although there was no time limit for the acceptance of the British demands, it was very important that the operation be completed during daylight hours on the 3rd.

At 3 a.m., 3 July, the Vice-Admiral sent the destroyer *Foxhound* on ahead. The operation orders called for her, with Captain Holland on board, to arrive off Mers-el-Kébir at about 7 a.m. He would act as British emissary in view of his long and recent association with the French Navy. With him were Lieutenant-Commanders Spearman and Davies. Permission having been requested and received for the *Foxhound* to enter, she anchored at 8·05 a.m. at the entrance to the Mers-el-Kébir channel outside the net defences. When the French look-outs reported that a British destroyer had just anchored, and when, an hour later, the rest of Force H appeared on the horizon, 'most of our men supposed that this squadron was on its way to search for the Italian forces and that the first round in the fight for the naval domination of the Mediterranean was soon going to be fought'.[112] Force H had, in addition to the *Hood*, *Valiant*, and *Resolution* (all carried eight 15-inch guns), and the *Ark Royal* (30 torpedo/spotter/reconnaissance aircraft and 24 fighters), the light cruisers *Arethusa* and *Enterprise*, and 11 destroyers.

[110] Captain K. L. Harkness, who commanded the destroyer *Fearless* in Force H, is 'fairly sure the signal also ordered or at least encouraged C.O.s to explain these intentions to their ships' companies. This would have been typical of Admiral Somerville, who always liked the sailors to know what was going on.' Harkness's letter to the author, 14 Sept. 1972.

[111] Churchill, *Their Finest Hour*, p. 209.   [112] Varillon, *Mers-el-Kébir*, pp. 97–8.

V*a* Admiral Sir Andrew Cunningham, C-in-C, Mediterranean Fleet, 1939–42

V*b* Captain Cedric Holland, Commanding HMS *Ark Royal*, 1940–41

VI Vice-Admiral Sir James Somerville, Commanding 'Force H', 1940–42, in his cabin with his Siamese cat 'Figaro', who always accompanied Somerville on board his ships

The French squadron at Mers-el-Kébir (about three miles to the west of Oran harbour) comprised, as we have seen, the new battle cruisers *Dunkerque* (flag of Vice-Admiral Gensoul) and *Strasbourg*, the two old battleships *Bretagne* and *Provence*, the seaplane carrier *Commandant Teste*, and six large destroyers. (At Oran was a mélange of 10 torpedo-boats, 6 sloops, 5 patrol-boats, 2 minesweepers, and 6 submarines, only three immediately ready and one at 72 hours' notice. In the case of the other two, the torpedoes were unprimed— that is, the pistols had been withdrawn from the warheads—and their high-pressure air chambers needed topping-up.) The French ships were fuelled, fully manned, and at six hours' notice to sail. The main shore defences consisted of a battery of four 7·5-inch guns mounted on the hill of Santon, a thousand feet high, a mile to the west of the harbour, and a battery of three 9·2-inch guns near Cape Canastel, which was five miles north-east of Oran. An anti-submarine net boom protected the harbour entrance. A 30-foot high mole, which extended half a mile from the shore, with a further half-mile still being built, and the 100-foot-high Fort Mers-el-Kébir afforded some protection to the side armour of the ships inside the harbour from short-range fire. The half mile of mole under construction had a line of A/S nets each side of it in case what was being built was not yet enough. The outer of these nets turned south and, incorporating a gate 600 feet wide, beyond which the barrier branched into two parallel lines of nets, about 1,200 feet apart, headed towards the shore between Oran and Mers-el-Kébir. Naval aviation consisted of 12 aircraft; army aviation, about 50 heavy aircraft and 50 fighters. The crews of the naval aircraft had had no training in sea operations, that is, they lacked experience against ship targets.

The prologue to the drama consisted in the attempts to persuade the French Admiral to accept one of the British alternatives. A word on the two principal actors is essential at this point. Captain Cedric Holland, in his 51st year, was known to his many friends as 'Hooky' because of his pronounced Roman nose. Of medium height and thickset, he lacked the commanding presence of, say, a Howard Kelly or a W. W. Fisher; but he was, all the same, a delightful person of considerable natural charm who was immediately welcome in any society. Persistence was his forte—he threw himself heart and soul into any task given him. He had been a most successful Naval Attaché in Paris (1938–40), was quite fluent in French, if spoken with an English accent (he used both English and French on the 3rd), and was on excellent terms with all the French naval officers, from Darlan down. Admiral Schofield, who was Holland's

I

Assistant in Paris, is 'quite certain there was no one else in the Royal Navy in a better position to conduct the delicate negotiations at Oran. He had met Admiral Gensoul before the war, so they were not strangers, and this should have made the negotiations easier.'[113] But with all his assets Holland was perhaps not the ideal choice.

He had for some time been going through an emotional experience [later wrote the DNI of that time, Admiral Godfrey], an upheaval, which distorted, as I thought, his estimation of the French: he saw everything French through rose-tinted spectacles. This was all right so long as France was a co-operative ally, but when the split came—Pétain v. de Gaulle—Holland seemed to me to lose his balance. Holland, I may say, was a great personal friend of mine and we discussed these matters (including the cause of his emotional disturbance) with great frankness. . . . I reached the conclusion in May that Holland's judgment about French affairs had become gravely impaired and was, in my opinion, useless, and, of course, I told Pound, and told him why. . . . I did not tell James [Somerville] 'why', I merely said that I felt that Pleydell Bouverie would be a more satisfactory and tough person to deliver an objectionable message to Gensoul. James listened to what I had to say, but chose Holland. . . . Neither do I know if Pound and James Somerville ever discussed Holland's suitability, taking into account his love for the French, his wish to think the best of them, and to let them off lightly. . . . Holland was not 'tough' enough to get his message through, somehow, to Gensoul.[114]

In fact, Holland hated the task he was given at Mers-el-Kébir and knew that his French friends would feel that he was acting traitorously. He tried to avoid having to do it, but he was told he had to go in. His friends at the Admiralty and in the Fleet felt sorry for him and bitter at Churchill, though actually it was Somerville's idea that he undertake the mission.

The 59-year-old Vice-Admiral Marcel Gensoul, the short, stocky, and ponderous commander of the Force de Raid, described himself in his postwar testimony (see below) as having been, prior to the Mers-el-Kébir action, 'one hundred per cent pro-English! . . . I have always had a great admiration for the English. I am a Protestant and I have always liked everything that was English.' Gensoul is a classic example of one of the two basic types of admirals. There are those who never put a foot wrong, who are intelligent, sober, and diplomatic, who are admirable staff officers and who work their way slowly, but surely, to the top, mainly in peacetime. And there are those who have fire in their bellies, are born leaders, are rebels against the Establishment, but with their courage and determination only come into their own in time of war. Gensoul was one of the former. He was an excellent staff

[113] Schofield's letter to the author, 4 July 1972.
[114] Admiral J. H. Godfrey to Cunningham, 7 May 1959, Godfrey MSS.

officer and had a pleasant personality, but he did not really command the respect of his officers and men. He was no leader, in the true sense of the word. A 'yes-man', devoted without reservation to Darlan, he was not prepared to depart from the brief of his superior if his views were in conflict with it. Admittedly, Gensoul was in one of the toughest spots a naval commander has ever had to face, and, like any officer in the world, he owed allegiance to his Commander-in-Chief.[115]

With Holland's request for permission to enter the port went a message to Gensoul (7.09) for the purpose of 'disseminating the reason of the arrival, and giving some indications as to the proposals so that the Lower Deck should get to know of them since it was thought that Admiral Gensoul might otherwise keep the matter secret'. The message, sent in French and *en clair*, read: 'The British Admiralty has sent Captain Holland to confer with you. The British Navy hopes that their proposals will enable you and the valiant and glorious French to be on our side. In these circumstances your ships would remain yours and no one need have any anxiety for the future. A British Fleet is at sea off Oran waiting to welcome you.'[116]

Minutes after the *Foxhound* had anchored, the Admiral's barge

---

[115] The last message from Darlan must have fortified Gensoul's resolve to give unswerving obedience to his wishes. On 26 June, in response to allegations in Free French Radio, London, Darlan told the Fleet that the naval clauses of the two signed armistices contained nothing dishonouring in them. 'Await receipt from me of complete texts and minutes of the discussions which diminish their severity on various points ... Once and for all I repeat that we are keeping all our warships and all our planes belonging to our naval air service, that the size of our service is not to be limited and that our enemies have solemnly undertaken not to touch our navy in the peace treaty. As losers, what more can we hope for? It now remains to carry out the signed conventions honestly and with dignity. To do otherwise would bring about the definitive ruin of our country, gravely wounded by defeat. To respond to the appeals of outside interested parties would lead to our metropolitan territory becoming a German province. Our former allies are not to be listened to. Let us think French, let us act French. ...' No. 3158, *Rapport. Événements*, ii. 471.

[116] My account of the pourparlers and action on 3 July and the aftermath is based on 'Report of Proceedings: F.O. Force "H"–28th June to 4th July 1940', 26 July 1940 (already cited) and its continuation, 'Report of Proceedings: F.O. Force "H"– 4th July to 6th July 1940', 29 July 1940, Somerville MSS., 7/19, 7/3, respectively; Holland's 'Narrative of Events at Oran on 3rd July, 1940', 11 July 1940 (enclosure No. 4 in Somerville's first Report); 'Force H. Diary of Events. From Wednesday, 3rd July 1940', ADM 1/10321, which contains a précis of the messages exchanged between Somerville and the Admiralty; Gensoul's testimony to the Parliamentary Investigating Committee, 28 June 1949, *Rapport. Annexes*, vi. 1897–1916; Gensoul's reports of 9, 19 July 1940 (copies in the possession of Mr. Warren Tute); and Naval Historical Branch (Ministry of Defence) records. The times in my narrative are British Summer Time, which was one hour ahead of Greenwich Mean Time. French sources use GMT.

arrived alongside with his Flag-Lieutenant, Bernard Dufay, on board. Holland, who thought his old friend had come to take him to the *Dunkerque*, was annoyed when informed that Gensoul was too busy to see him but would accept any documents via Dufay, and would send his Chief of Staff if he had verbal proposals to make. Holland pleaded that the Admiral should receive him. Getting nowhere, he sent a message back with Dufay that he carried proposals which could only be delivered to the Admiral in person, with verbal clarification. Gensoul's reply was to signal the *Foxhound* (8.45) to sail immediately. The reason he gave after the war was that his orders were not to enter into any communication with the English. Also, it is apparent that he had taken umbrage at the message which had accompanied Holland's request to enter port. 'The English may consider this as bringing friendly pressure to bear, but the presence of a British Fleet comprising three battleships and an aircraft carrier is something else. This proposal that I should sail my Fleet and join them merits no further examination. And a British Fleet at large off Oran is a menace. I will not be threatened in this way. I've told the British destroyer to get out at once.'[117] The *Foxhound* weighed anchor and gave the appearance of complying with the request to sail, while Holland, in a daring move, embarked with Spearman and Davies in the *Foxhound*'s motor-boat and headed for the *Dunkerque* (9.05). They were met halfway between the inner boom and the mole by the Admiral's barge with Dufay on board. The two boats made fast to a buoy about 200 yards from the net defences of the harbour. Informed that the Admiral would not see him, Holland handed Dufay the British proposals in a sealed envelope addressed to Gensoul and said he would wait there for a reply. The Admiral, who received the proposals at about 9.35 a.m., was unable to accept any of the British alternatives.

At about 10 the Flag-Lieutenant was back at the buoy with the Admiral's written reply confirming the assurances he had given to Admiral North that the French ships would in no circumstances be allowed to fall into the hands of the Germans or the Italians, and adding: 'In view of the substance and form of the veritable ultimatum which has been sent to Admiral Gensoul, the French warships will meet force by force.' Holland then sat down with Dufay and discussed the matter 'as old friends'. He emphasized that Darlan's hands were tied, as proven by his own signal of 20 June regarding the succession. Dufay had to admit that no

[117] Tute, *The Deadly Stroke*, p. 83, relying on interviews with officers who were on board the *Dunkerque*, including Dufay.

message from Darlan with the special code signature had arrived for some days. Holland begged him to stress this point to the Admiral. Dufay left with the typescript notes which Holland had previously prepared for his anticipated interview with Gensoul.

Dufay returned at 11.09 with the COS, Captain Danbé, who handed Holland a curt written reply from the Admiral. It confirmed his first written message, repeated his resolve 'to defend himself by every means at his disposal', and drew Somerville's 'attention to the fact that the first shot fired at us will result in immediately ranging the entire French Fleet against Great Britain, a result which would be diametrically opposite to that sought by H.M. Government'.[118] Since the Admiral seemed determined not to see him, a sorely disappointed Holland returned to the *Foxhound*. On arrival on board at about 11.25 he read Somerville's message of 10.46 asking that he inform Gensoul that his ships would not be allowed to leave harbour unless the British terms were accepted. (Somerville, who had arrived off Oran at 9.10 a.m. and was being kept *au courant* by Holland, had received reports from reconnaissance aircraft that the French ships were preparing for sea.) Holland immediately sent the message in by Spearman, who handed it to Dufay on board the *Dunkerque* at 11.40. Towards noon the *Foxhound*, which had remained close in to the inner boom, proceeded to a position outside the outer net boom in order to avoid having to run the gauntlet of the shore batteries if hostilities started.

Foxhound's signals (11.46, 12.01), summarizing Gensoul's second written reply and indicating the apparent intention of the French ships to put to sea, were received in the *Hood* at 12.27. Somerville now ordered the mining of the entrance to the port in order to discourage the escape of the French ships. (The Admiralty had at 10.45 a.m. given him discretion to lay magnetic mines to prevent the French ships from leaving the harbour.) The mining of the main channel was carried out by seaplanes, five magnetic mines being laid at about 1.30 (the French charts show only four) in and just outside the gate in the A/S net boom, which was normally the only entrance to, and exit from, the harbour. To mine the harbour entrance before the negotiations were seriously started was a mistake. The French afterwards charged that this was the first belligerent act: it merely stiffened their resistance and, as we shall see, the mining was quite insufficient. In the meantime, Somerville had informed the Admiralty (12.31) that, as Gensoul had refused

[118] At this point Holland is supposed to have told Danbé, 'Allow me to say as one officer to another, that in your place my answer would have been no different.' Naval Historical Branch (Ministry of Defence) records.

the British terms and stated he would fight, he was prepared to open fire at 1.30. He also twice signalled Holland asking if he saw any alternative. Reluctant to press matters home, he was happy to accept Holland's suggestion (1.32) that the *Foxhound* move in to V/S touch (which she did at 1.40) and ask Gensoul if there was any further message before resorting to force. At 2.19 Holland received the Vice-Admiral's signal of 1.58 asking Gensoul to hoist a large square flag at the masthead if he accepted the British terms, otherwise fire would be opened at 3 o'clock. The signal was passed to the *Dunkerque*. With the French giving no indication of leaving harbour, Somerville notified Gensoul that he now had until 3.30 to accept the terms or abandon the ships. Holland received the message at 2.50, but he did not pass it to Gensoul, for some ten minutes earlier he had received his signal of 2.30 that he was now ready personally to receive the British delegate for 'honourable discussion'. Somerville debated 'whether this was merely an excuse to gain time, but decided that it was quite possible Admiral Gensoul had only now realised it was my intention to use force if necessary'. He gave Holland permission to proceed inshore, and at 3.06, accompanied by Davies, Holland embarked in *Foxhound*'s motor-boat at a point just clear of the minefield. It was not until about 4.15 that Holland, after transferring to the Admiral's barge just inside the net defences, arrived on board the *Dunkerque*. On the way in, considerable interest was taken by all ships' crews, who in many cases stood to attention while the boat passed. Holland noted: 'All ships were in an advanced state of readiness for sea. All directors and control positions were manned, and all director range-finders in tops of battleships were trained in the direction of our fleet. Tugs were ready by the stern of each battleship. Guns were trained fore and aft.' He was piped over the side of the flagship and received by the COS.

What had caused Gensoul to change his mind? The explanation he gave after the war was this: 'When I saw that about an hour before the end of the time limit that had been granted to us things were going to get worse, when I saw a British plane come and drop magnetic mines in the exit channel, I said to myself: "It is really incredible, horrible, to think that we are going to find ourselves fighting with the English, that we are going to exchange gunfire with them! It was absolutely necessary to gain time. All time gained would perhaps allow one to find a solution other than that of cannon."' It was at that moment that he agreed to receive Holland.[119] It was not so much that he expected to find a solution.

[119] Gensoul's testimony, *Rapport. Annexes*, vi. 1901.

Every minute gained allowed his ships to prepare for rapid weighing and for action, and enabled the coastal and shore AA batteries to rearm, the submarines at Oran to replace the pistols on their torpedoes, and the naval and military aircraft to equip themselves. Moreover, he needed time in order to receive instructions from Darlan.

Gensoul had earlier in the day sent two radio messages to the French Admiralty. The first, at 9.45 a.m., read: 'British force comprising 3 battleships, 1 aircraft carrier, cruisers and destroyers off Oran. Ultimatum sent: sink your ships within six hours or we shall force you to. Reply: French ships will meet force with force.' The second message, at 1.20 p.m., was a fuller report of the situation:

First English ultimatum was: either to join English Fleet or destroy ships within six hours to prevent their falling into German or Italian hands. Have replied: 1. The latter eventuality is not anticipated. 2. Shall defend myself by force. 3. First shot fired will have the effect of setting the entire French Fleet against Great Britain, a result diametrically opposed to that desired by the British Government. English reply: If you weigh without accepting British propositions, which are reasonable and honourable, I shall regretfully open fire. Captain Holland, who has served as intermediary, has indicated that disarmament of the Force de Rade [Raid] at Mers-el-Kébir would appear to give a basis for an arrangement. This with all due reservations.

Thus, Gensoul's second message was no more accurate as to the British alternatives than his first, in that he did not report the third proposal made to him, namely, to take his ships to the West Indies, although that alternative seems at first sight to be close to the instructions given in point 3 of the French Admiralty message 5143 of 24 June (above, p. 211 n.). It prescribed, in the event of the enemy trying to take possession of French ships, that they should without further orders be taken to the United States.

In reality [as French naval authorities have correctly pointed out], the British proposals and the [French] Admiralty instructions, while both envisaging the dispatch of the ships to the West Indies, referred to totally different situations. It was only in the event of the armistice commissions interpreting the armistice terms in a way that would have led to a surrender of our ships to the Germans or the Italians that this departure for the United States was to take place, whereas the British were demanding this departure when no menace to our warships existed and nothing in the conduct of our enemies justified it. Sailing to the West Indies or the United States under these conditions would have entailed breaking the armistice just as much as acceptance of one or the other of the first two British propositions.[120]

[120] Naval Historical Branch (Ministry of Defence) records. In 1949, when examined by the Parliamentary Investigating Commission, Gensoul agreed that he probably should have summarized the British ultimatum in a more precise fashion. He may

Indeed, *all* the British alternatives entailed a violation of the armistice. The chances of getting the approval of the German Armistice Commission would have been slight, and had the French accepted one of the alternatives, it would inevitably have resulted in the German invasion of the unoccupied zone of France and perhaps the extension of the war to North Africa. This was, in fact, in the back of Darlan's mind.

We must return to the narrative. Holland and Davies were shown into the Admiral's cabin, where Gensoul, Danbé, and Dufay awaited them. Gensoul received Holland very formally, frigidly almost, though the two were old friends. The atmosphere was tense from the moment the Admiral began to talk, as both men realized that failure to arrive at a satisfactory formula must lead to tragedy. Nor did the suffocating heat of the cabin make for a relaxed atmosphere.

'The Admiral', Holland relates, 'was clearly extremely indignant and angry at the course of events.' If it was the British aim to ensure that the French Fleet should not be used against them, he insisted that the resort to force would not achieve this.

We might sink his ships at Oran but we should find the whole of the rest of the French Navy actively against us. He was angry at the sudden presentation of terms which he considered as an ultimatum, and also at the laying of mines at the entrance to the harbour which he pointed out prevented him in any case from being able to accept or carry out the three terms (*a*), (*b*), (*c*) [above, p. 235], and he rejected out of hand the idea of sinking his ships forthwith, saying it was impossible to abandon the ships at a moment's notice and he reiterated his former statement given to Admiral North that he would sink his ships to prevent them from falling into German or Italian hands.

I explained most carefully to him that the British Government were un-

have been wrong, he admitted, but one had to consider his position at that time. Communication with the French Admiralty was very difficult, consequently he felt he had to keep his telegrams brief. But his main point was that the ultimatum aspect of the British proposals overshadowed everything in his mind. As soon as he read the ultimatum, 'I said to myself: "It just isn't possible! Here is an ultimatum presented to me at gunpoint which is completely inadmissible from every point of view."' Again, '. . . my first telegram gives only the end of the ultimatum, which, in my mind, summarized the whole. The overall ultimatum being unacceptable, I sent the ultimatum itself, that is, the end of the paragraph.' *Rapport. Annexes*, vi. 1898, 1899. Gensoul was later violently castigated, by one-time members of the Vichy Government among others, for his misleading messages, which had not disclosed all the British alternatives. For instance, Weygand thought that an agreement could have been reached on the third proposal. But Charles-Roux, the Secretary-General of the Foreign Ministry, did not think it would have changed the Government's attitude. This is my feeling, too. The ultimatum was couched in such terms that even if Darlan had known all the British proposals, to have accepted any one would only have been at the cost of both his own face and the face of the French Navy he had done so much to build up.

able to accept this latter statement as a sufficient guarantee that the ships would not fall into enemy hands and so be used against us. Although we trusted his word and the similar promises given by Admirals Ollive, de Laborde and Esteva that they would do everything possible to prevent their ships falling into enemy hands, we could not trust the Germans or the Italians who would by treachery do all they could to achieve this end. Admiral Gensoul, however, would not listen to this argument and said he was convinced that steps taken were adequate to sink his ships whatever happened. I pointed out that by sinking his ships, he would be anyway breaking the terms of the Armistice, and by his own action. Should he accept any one of the terms we had offered to him that morning, he would be acting under 'Force majeur' and the blame for any action taken would rest on us. To this, he replied that, so long as Germany and Italy abided by the Armistice terms, and allowed the French fleet to remain with reduced crews, flying the French flag in a French Metropolitan or Colonial port, he would do the same, and not until Germany or Italy had broken their promises would he break the terms laid down, and that these were his orders signed by Admiral Darlan.

Holland then explained that unless Gensoul accepted the British terms, Somerville would, in response to his orders, have to use force. At this point Gensoul produced a copy of Darlan's orders of 24 June (above, p. 211 n.).

Apart from laying down clearly what steps were to be taken to prevent ships from falling into enemy hands, they mentioned also sailing the French Fleet to the U.S.A., and that ships were not again to operate actively against Germany or Italy.

This appeared to be so close to the term (*c*) laid down that there seemed to be a chance to persuade the Admiral to accept this latter one.[121]

Time was getting very short. It was by then 1700.

Admiral Gensoul however, remained stubborn, and would not give way further, except to state that steps had been taken to commence the reduction of crews that morning[122] by demobilising a certain number of reservists.

I again pointed out that Admiral Somerville must obey his orders and use force unless the terms were accepted to our satisfaction immediately, to which Admiral Gensoul reiterated that the first shot fired would alienate our two navies and do untold harm to us, and that he would reply to force

---

[121] After reading the famous signal of 24 June and passing it on to Davies, Holland is said to have remarked with emotion: 'If only we had known of this before it might have made all the difference.' Anthony Heckstall-Smith, *The Fleet That Faced Both Ways* (London, 1963), p. 97, apparently derived from Davies. Benoist-Méchin has the same incident, source not indicated: *Sixty Days that Shook the West*, p. 502. Gensoul in his 9 July report says that Holland was struck [*frappé*] by the third point in the 24 June message, and adds: 'I confirmed, besides, that I was ready to undertake to disarm our ships in Mers-el-Kébir'. More on the latter in a moment, but I would establish here that Gensoul's phrasing would seem to indicate an interest in pursuing point 3. But Holland's report leaves the distinct impression that Gensoul would not jump through this loophole.

[122] Actually, the day before. See below.

by force. Asked if he had received any answer from his Government to the message he had sent that morning, he rather unconvincingly replied that the answer was 'resist by force'.

But it was at about this time that a message from the French Admiralty (2.05 p.m.) reached Gensoul (5.18), and he showed it to Holland.[123] We must go back.

Gensoul's first message (9.45 a.m.) was received at 11.56 a.m. at Nérac (80 miles south-east of Bordeaux), the temporary site of the French Admiralty, which was being transferred to Vichy in central France. Rear-Admiral Le Luc, Chief of Staff to Darlan, was the only senior officer left there. He at once ordered the 3rd Squadron at Toulon (4 heavy cruisers, 3 divisions of destroyers) to raise steam, then passed Gensoul's message to Captain Négadelle, who was with Darlan in Clermont-Ferrand. At 12.50 p.m., acting in accordance with Darlan's orders, Le Luc directed all ships in the western Mediterranean, especially the 3rd Squadron and the Algiers squadron (6 cruisers), to raise steam and proceed to Oran to meet force with force. Gensoul's second message reached Nérac at 1.30. It was immediately telephoned to Clermont-Ferrand, and at 2.05, at Darlan's order, Le Luc transmitted this reply to Gensoul *en clair* by W/T: 'Inform British intermediary that Admiral of the Fleet has ordered all French forces in Mediterranean to rally to you immediately ready for action. You are empowered to give orders to these forces. You will meet force with force. Call in submarines and aircraft if necessary. Armistice Commissions have been informed.'

Returning to the Admiral's cabin in the *Dunkerque*, we find that Gensoul now 'confirmed that he was ready to promise to disarm his ships at Mers-el-Kébir'. To recapitulate his position, he wrote out a pencilled statement of the orders he intended to obey and handed it to Holland:

1. The French fleet cannot do otherwise than apply the clauses of the Armistice, on account of the consequences which would be borne by Metropolitan France.

2. It has received definite orders [*ordres formel*], and these orders have been sent on to all commanders, in order that if after the Armistice there is risk of the ships falling into enemy hands, they would be taken to the United States or scuttled. (See Admiralty message of 24 June.)

3. These orders will be carried out.

4. Since yesterday, 2 July, the ships now at Oran and Mers-el-Kébir have begun their demobilisation (reduction of crews). Men from North Africa have been disembarked.

[123] Naval Historical Branch (Ministry of Defence) records, and Gensoul's 9 July report and his postwar testimony. This is not mentioned in Holland's Narrative.

Holland drafted a brief signal in plain language for Somerville, which Gensoul had transmitted by searchlight to the *Foxhound*. It summed up what appeared to be the Admiral's final position: 'Admiral Gensoul says crews being reduced and if threatened by enemy would go Martinique or U.S.A. Can get no nearer.' Barely had it been sent when, at 5.25, as Holland and Davies were preparing to leave the *Dunkerque*, Gensoul was handed an ultimatum. Again we must go back.

The Admiralty had intercepted the 2.05 signal from the French Admiralty to Gensoul and had at once (4.14) radioed Somerville that he must settle matters quickly, as he might have reinforcements to deal with. (They had at 4.10 received Somerville's signal of 2.59 stating that Gensoul had agreed to receive Holland, and that action had been postponed, as the Vice-Admiral thought the French were weakening.) The Admiralty signal was received in the *Hood* at 4.46, and at 5.12, without waiting for the conclusion of the discussion in the *Dunkerque*, Somerville had signalled Gensoul, by wireless and searchlight, that if none of the alternatives was accepted by 5.30 p.m., the French ships would be sunk. Since Holland's last message (above), which he received at 5.29, did not in his view comply with any of the three alternatives, Somerville ordered the air striking force to fly off and the ships to stand in towards the coast.[124]

Gensoul read the ultimatum in silence and handed it to Holland. The leave-taking of the British party was, Holland reported, 'friendly, and from the Admiral, more friendly than our reception. Even at that stage I did not believe that he was certain that fire would be opened.' Dufay and Holland were in tears as they saluted each other and said their farewells. As Holland and Davies went over the side (5.35), they heard the bugles sound 'Action Stations'. They transferred to the *Foxhound*'s motor-boat some minutes later. It was clear of the net defences and about a mile to seaward when fire was opened. When some fifteen miles from Oran, a British destroyer picked them up (7.35).[125]

[124] Holland's Narrative gives a different sequence of events towards the end: Somerville's ultimatum–Holland's last signal–Gensoul's written statement. I have followed the sequence presented in Naval Historical Branch (Ministry of Defence) records, which strikes me as being more plausible: Gensoul's written statement–Holland's signal–Somerville's ultimatum, and I have also used the times given in the latter account. Holland has the ultimatum arriving at 5.15 and his leaving the *Dunkerque* at 5.25. The ship's company of the *Hood* had been kept informed of the progress of the negotiations. The officers hoped against hope that it would not be necessary to use force; the men were a bit more phlegmatic, and a few were heard to say 'Did they not let us down, so why complain?' Admiral Sir William Davis's letter to the author, 14 Jan. 1974. And see below, p. 268.

[125] Captain Harkness writes: 'To everyone's horror, the French opened fire on

In summarizing the day's events, Holland put the onus for the failure of his mission on Gensoul, who had made it impossible for him to carry out his scenario:

The action of Admiral Gensoul in refusing to see me on arrival made the task of reaching a peaceful solution in the short time available extremely difficult since he received the terms by letter through the hands of an intermediary, this eliminating all possibility of a friendly interview and amicable discussion. Had I been able, as was my intention, to present the case verbally . . . I feel a peaceful settlement might have been arrived at. . . .

I would then have outlined the three proposals that I was instructed to make and discussed them in a friendly spirit. If, after this, he had not accepted one of the three terms, I would have requested him to sink his ships within six hours. Finally, should he have refused even to do this, but not until then, I would have informed him that H.M. Government would be obliged to use force if he did not comply with any of the terms proposed. In this way, the proposals would have come to him gradually, and my considered opinion is that he might have accepted one of them.

As it was, he took the proposals in the form of an ultimatum and for this reason, together with the national dislike of the French for being rushed into negotiation, he became stubborn and would not listen to argument, though, as the day wore on, he did gradually take up a less uncompromising attitude.

When I boarded the *Dunkerque*, I still had a faint hope that it was not too late for a peaceful settlement.[126]

Holland probably had done the best that was possible, given the circumstances of inflexible demands, a time limit, Gallic pride, and an Admiral who, in the French military tradition, had an unquestioning loyalty to the orders of a leader and who in any case would never have dreamed of taking any great decision on his own. And yet one may speculate whether, as Admiral Godfrey has maintained, Holland 'dilly-dallied in a way a tougher man would not', and whether Gensoul might have reacted more reasonably (from the British point of view) had a flag officer been sent as

her. I thought at the time (and still think) they must have been shore-based guns, because the splashes were "singles" and not salvos. As soon as she came under fire, the destroyer bringing out "Hooky" immediately started to zig-zag and lay a smoke-screen. The moment the smoke-screen (parallel to the shore) became effective, she turned away and rejoined Force H without being hit. I cannot remember if she flew a white flag [she did], but we all felt she was morally entitled to do so and we were greatly shocked that our so-recent allies should think otherwise.'

[126] Holland talked very little about Oran with his wife other than to say that he felt he could have won the day if he could have had another two hours with Gensoul, whom he described as 'an obstinate old codger'. Mrs. Holland, in a conversation with Admiral Schofield; the latter's memorandum for the author, 4 July 1972. Holland was undoubtedly highly strung and felt things deeply. Schofield believes that Oran 'took years off his life'.

emissary. Holland was only a captain, and the French could be very touchy on such points. In some ways Somerville would have been ideal. Indeed, Admiral Cunningham, in a postwar letter, expressed the view that Somerville, with his remarkable powers of persuasion ('It took a wide awake man to resist James's blandishments') should himself have gone to see Gensoul, taking Holland as interpreter.[127]

Somerville in his Report speculated whether the use of force might have been avoided had Gensoul agreed at once to meet Holland. He pointed out that Gensoul's final offer was very close to the third British alternative. It

differed, unfortunately, in the proviso that the action proposed would not be carried into effect *unless* there was a danger of the French ships falling into the hands of the enemy.

Admiral Gensoul claimed that this danger was not imminent; we maintained that it was. I believe that given more time Captain Holland might have succeeded in converting Admiral Gensoul to our point of view. At the actual time when the French Admiral made his offer, it was already too late, since French reinforcements were approaching and the orders of His Majesty's Government were explicit that a decision had to be reached before dark.

I consider that Captain C. S. Holland carried out his most difficult task with the greatest tact, courage and perseverance. That he failed in his mission was not his fault—that he so nearly succeeded is greatly to his credit.[128]

It is possible that a little patience and diplomacy might have achieved the desired result far more satisfactorily than the resort to violence. But haste was implicit in 'Catapult' from the beginning, Somerville's ships being needed closer to home on still more urgent tasks. Yet, when everything has been said, I consider it extremely improbable that, even if Gensoul had signalled a full summary of the British terms, and there had been more time for discussion, anything short of a direct order from Darlan would have changed his mind on 3 July. As he testified afterwards, he could not accept any of the alternatives, since he believed that if he had, he would

[127] Cunningham to Godfrey, 17 May (1954), Godfrey MSS. 'You see how it is', Gensoul had commented when informed that Holland was the British emissary. 'Last week they sent me Admiral North, today they send me a Captain. Next time it will be a Petty Officer.' Tute, *The Deadly Stroke*, p. 76.

[128] 'Of course, I don't know all the facts,' he had written earlier, 'but, from what Holland tells me, it does appear that if Gensoul had not been given an ultimatum we might have brought him round. He evidently had doubts whether Darlan was still a free agent and in view of Darlan's last certified orders, that the ships were *not* to fall into German hands, it does seem just possible that we might have brought him round to demilitarising at Martinique.' Somerville to ? (probably Vice-Admiral Sir Geoffrey Blake, the ACNS (Foreign)), 7 July, Somerville MSS., 7/28.

have been completely disavowed by his Admiralty. He had no right to break an armistice which had been accepted by the legal government of France. But the crucial consideration for him was the British 'threat, with guns pointing at us', which, 'from the point of view of France and the honour of the flag', made the British conditions 'inadmissible'.[129]

There is one important might-have-been. The War Cabinet met at 11.30 a.m. on the 3rd. Signals from Force H had made it clear that Gensoul would not see Holland and that the latter had handed in the letter with the British terms and was awaiting a reply. Another signal, timed at 10.58 and received at 11.30, said that the French reply was not expected before 11.30. It was at this juncture, with the prospect of a deadlock, that Pound, who was at this meeting, drafted a signal authorizing Somerville to offer the French Admiral alternative (B) (above, p. 233), namely, to accept immediate demilitarization at Oran.[130] *This, as it developed, was precisely what Gensoul offered in his final statement.* Had Holland been authorized to offer this alternative by the time he boarded the *Dunkerque*, a happy resolution of the whole problem would have been quite possible. But it was not to be. The War Cabinet considered the First Sea Lord's draft proposal, but turned it down for a reason that, at first sight, almost defies belief.

The War Cabinet were reminded that the instructions issued had been that demilitarisation should not figure among the alternatives offered, but might be accepted, subject to certain conditions, if volunteered by the French. The question arose whether a signal should now be sent instruct-

[129] I put these two questions in writing to the 92-year-old Admiral on 5 September 1972: '(1) If you could relive your experiences of that unhappy day, is there anything you would do differently? (2) If there had been no time limit imposed by the British for the satisfactory conclusion of the negotiations, would there, in your judgement, have been a chance of a peaceful settlement?' His reply was prompt and crisp: 'First, considering everything, my course of action would be the same, the fundamental reason being not to break the Armistice which had just been concluded, with all the dramatic consequences that would result for France and the French, and not having in my possession, moreover, the elements necessary to arrive at a different judgement. Second, until the very last moment, I hoped for a peaceful solution, and it is for that reason that I avoided making any movement to sail, or even opening fire on British aircraft which were coming to drop mines in the channel: thus putting myself in a position of inferiority in regard to the British force, allowing it to choose its own moment and its own formation for opening fire. But given the orders sent to his ships by Prime Minister Churchill and the action already taking place, against the French ships, in the British ports, there was, in fact, no hope of seeing this aggression end peacefully. And if there was, on that day, a stain on a flag, it most certainly was not on ours!'

[130] 'Force H. Diary of Events.' The First Sea Lord had pressed for this at a War Cabinet on 1 July. See above, p. 232. But Holland had exceeded his instructions when he suggested this possibility to Gensoul. See above, pp. 233, 245.

ing our representative to include among the alternatives offered demilitarisation of the ships to our satisfaction.

The War Cabinet decided: 'That demilitarisation not having been included in the alternatives first offered, we should not offer it now, *as this would look like weakening.*'[131]

Churchill writes of the 'manifest emotion' at the Admiralty as events unfolded on 3 July. There was even more 'manifest emotion' in Force H as zero hour neared. An officer on Somerville's staff tells us that 'from the Admiral downwards our heart was not in the job. It was repugnant to all of us to kill several thousand French sailors who until recently had been our friends and allies.'[132] Never in the long annals of the Royal Navy had a commander found himself in a more distasteful situation. Somerville hated the whole business, and at the same time he was left with insufficient daylight to do the job 'properly'.

*   *   *

Having been instructed from London to brook no delay, and his final ultimatum having expired at 5.30, Somerville reluctantly ordered fire to be opened at 5.54 p.m. at 15,000 yards (maximum visibility) from the north-west with aircraft spotting. The French capital ships and carrier were moored stern-on to the mole, with the other ships moored on the west side of the harbour. A minute later Gensoul ordered the fire returned—the first time in 125 years (since Waterloo) that British and French forces had fired at each other. The French were trapped in the confined waters of the harbour, where they could neither manœuvre nor bring their guns fully to bear on their attackers. Their fire was largely blanked by Mers-el-Kébir fort, and their ships were severely handicapped in attempting to return the fire while slipping their cables and manœuvring to put to sea. Somerville later paid tribute to the 'gallantry' shown by the French, but the contest was brief and unequal. Fire from the French warships achieved no direct hits, although one or two salvoes from the battleships straddled the British ships. (Some fragments struck the *Hood*.) Their fire soon eased off, then ceased at 6.04. The British salvoes (thirty-six 15-inch salvoes were fired) soon found their mark. Within minutes a salvo of three shells hit the *Dunkerque*, putting one gun turret out of

---

[131] WM 192 (40), CAB 65/14. Italics mine! This is, of course, not the first time that *amour propre* has played a vital role in international relations. At 12.35 p.m. a telephone message to Somerville from 'The First Sea Lord in Cabinet' (presumably telephone to Gibraltar and signal on from there) informed him that the draft proposal had not been approved.

[132] Vice-Admiral Sir Gordon Hubback's letter to the author, 18 May 1967.

action, destroying one of the main generators, so that electric power failed at once, damaging one of the boiler rooms, and wrecking the hydraulic machinery which controlled the watertight doors. Unable to continue the fight, the *Dunkerque* steamed to the far end of the harbour and dropped anchor off the harbour of St. André (6.13). Several 15-inch hits on the *Bretagne* caused a heavy internal explosion as she was moving away from the quay. Ablaze from the bridge aft, she suddenly capsized (6.09) with the loss of over a thousand officers and men. The *Provence* fired several salvoes but received so many hits that she had to be beached. A 15-inch shell blew the stern off the destroyer *Mogador*, which miraculously stayed afloat and was able to anchor in shallow water, a sitting duck.

In response to repeated wireless and searchlight signals requesting that he cease fire, Somerville broke off the action at approximately 6.10.[133] He had no desire to prolong the agony and he wanted to give the French the opportunity to abandon their ships, which he expected them to do, and thus avoid further loss of life. At the same time he turned 16 points to port together, withdrawing westward to take up a position from which, if necessary, he could renew the bombardment without causing casualties to men proceeding ashore in boats. He also wished to avoid damage from the powerful shore batteries, whose fire (especially that of Santon) was becoming increasingly accurate and was beginning to straddle his ships; and he deemed it prudent to stand out to sea to avoid a possible attack from any submarines that might succeed in leaving Oran, or a possible surprise attack by aircraft under cover of the pall of smoke that lay between his ships and the shore. At 6.35 Somerville signalled to the French: 'Unless I see your ships sinking I shall open fire again.'

Since the French were aware of the magnetic mines in the harbour entrance, Somerville 'felt quite positive that no attempt would be made by them to put to sea'. He had miscalculated, for the *Strasbourg* took advantage of Gensoul's foresight, as well as the confusion and smoke, to escape along the coast, past Oran, well clear of the British magnetic mines. Directly after the mines had been dropped, Gensoul had ordered the Naval Command at Oran to demolish the part of the double A/S boom (made of nets hung on buoys) that was south of the gate to form an additional channel between the regular gate and the shore. This had been done immediately by sinking the buoys with machine-gun fire.

[133] The time is given as 6.04 in his Report, 6.10 in Playfair, and 6.12 in an authoritative French account.

There was, then, plenty of room, up to three cables or more in width, and with plenty of water, south of the normal gate. Preceded by five destroyers, the *Strasbourg* steamed eastward, then north-eastward, at 28 knots, close under the land, emerging by the Canastel channel and rounding the Cap de l'Aiguille without difficulty. At 6.20, to his 'intense surprise', Somerville received a report from one of *Ark Royal*'s aircraft that one 'Dunkerque' had left harbour and was steering east. The Admiral did not take the report seriously until he received confirmation from an aircraft at 6.30, whereupon he altered course to the east and gave chase (6.38). 'The resultant delay in commencing the chase,' he candidly admitted in his Report, 'though not appreciably affecting the situation, could have been avoided.' He also admitted to a tactical error in not keeping to the north-east of Oran, between Oran and Toulon, rather than to the west, to ensure that he could intercept any fleeing French ships, if his assumptions that French resistance had ceased and that the mines were an effective barrier proved wrong.

When Somerville realized that only one battle cruiser was at sea, the *Hood* and light craft proceeded ahead (6.43), leaving the two battleships to follow unscreened. Six Fairey Swordfish aircraft from the *Ark Royal*, each armed with four 250-lb. SAP (semi-armour-piercing) bombs and escorted by Blackburn Skuas were sent after the fleeing *Strasbourg*. (The versatile Swordfish were biplanes which gave a splendid account of themselves in the war. They were known as TSRs, standing for torpedo, spotting, and reconnaissance. The Skuas were erratic fighter–dive bomber monoplanes.) They made a bombing attack (7.45–7.54 p.m.), and then six Swordfish armed with torpedoes attacked (8.55 p.m., 20 minutes after sunset). One hit was believed to have been scored in each attack. Despite chase at utmost speed, by 8.20 p.m. the Frenchman was reported to be 25 miles ahead of the *Hood*, and the chase was now abandoned. At 8.25 course was altered to the westward. The *Strasbourg* and four of her consorts reached Toulon in the evening of 4 July, the fifth arriving the next day. Two other destroyers from Oran had broken out and reached Toulon about the same time, as did the six cruisers from Algiers and, on 5 July, the *Commandant Teste*.

Somerville signalled the Admiralty at 8.21 that he was unable to engage the battle cruiser before dark and was withdrawing to the westward, and that the torpedo-bombers would be attacking shortly. This message was received at 9.10. The Admiralty ordered him (9.56) to pursue the battle cruiser if she were winged by the torpedo attack. Somerville was by then on his way back to

Gibraltar. On arrival the next day he sent the Admiralty his reasons for abandoning the chase:

> *Dunkerque* [*Strasbourg*] reported about 25 miles ahead.
> Algiers force including 8 cruisers would probably join her about 2030. Sun had set placing me at tactical disadvantage.
> V & W Class destroyers had insufficient fuel for prolonged chase and night operations necessary to destroy *Dunkerque*.
> Without H.M.S. *Resolution* and H.M.S. *Valiant* I had no margin of strength. H.M.S. *Resolution* and H.M.S. *Valiant* were without screen.
> I assumed Their Lordships did not wish me to incur serious loss especially of destroyers in these operations, in view of future requirements in Western Mediterranean.[134]

Somerville's original plan had been to reach a position approximately 60 miles WNW. of Mers-el-Kébir at 4.30 a.m., 4 July, from where he would launch an air attack at dawn to finish off the ships remaining afloat in the harbour. At 6.30 a.m., however, Admiral Wells reported that fog had forced him to abandon the attack. In view of this, and a wireless message he had received from Gensoul the preceding evening—'Warships at Mers-el-Kébir are out of action. I have ordered the crews to evacuate the ships'—Somerville gave up his plan and shaped course for Gibraltar, arriving at 7 p.m. on the 4th.

The day's operations had cost Force H three Swordfish and two Skuas, but all crews were rescued but for one of the Skuas. The other casualties were one officer and one rating slightly wounded in the *Hood*, which ship had suffered 'negligible material damage'.

Back at Gibraltar, Somerville immediately had his ships completed with ammunition and fuel, ready, if required, to proceed to Dakar and carry out operations against the *Richelieu*. At 10.40 p.m. (4 July) he informed the Admiralty that aircraft observation was unable to determine the extent of the damage to the *Dunkerque*, but that she was definitely aground, lying on an even keel. The Admiralty directed him early on the 5th to renew the bombardment, unless he was certain that the *Dunkerque* could not be refloated and repaired in less than a year. This was to take precedence over the operation against the *Richelieu*. Plans were drawn up for the final disposition of the partially disabled ship, 'Operation

---

[134] 'Force H. Diary of Events.' A slightly different explanation is given in Somerville's Report. It includes these points: 'The prospects of locating and engaging the French battlecruiser at night were small.' 'The speed of advance was too high to allow the destroyers to spread.' 'Unless *Hood* was in a position to support the advanced forces, the latter would be numerically much inferior to the French. This support could not be assured under night action conditions.' He expected the Algiers force, which he knew to be at sea, to join the *Strasbourg* soon after 9 p.m.

Lever', which was to be carried out at 9 a.m., 6 July, by Force H, less the *Resolution* and a destroyer.[135] But then Somerville realized that 'Lever' would involve considerable further loss of French lives, including civilians, as the *Dunkerque* was quite close to the town of St. André, and that this would provoke the French to far more active measures against British ships. Given the already difficult situation in the western Mediterranean and the absence of indications that the French had any immediate intention to move the *Dunkerque*, the Vice-Admiral asked if some compromise could be reached concerning her demilitarization to avoid further bloodshed (6 p.m., 5 July). He was 'much relieved' when the Admiralty decided to have torpedo-bombers carry out the second attack on the *Dunkerque*. There was far less risk to life in such an attack, particularly since Gensoul had stated at the time of the first attack that the ships had been evacuated. The Admiralty approved (2.24 a.m., 6 July). Force H had sailed from Gibraltar at 8 p.m. on the 5th.

The attack was launched when Force H was about 90 miles from Oran, at 5.15 a.m., 6 July. Three waves (6–3–3) of low-flying Swordfish torpedo-bombers attacked the hapless *Dunkerque*. Eleven torpedoes in all were fired. The first attack, achieving complete surprise, met no opposition. Four hits were thought to have been made on the starboard side amidships. The second attack, in the face of hot AA fire, supposedly scored one certain and two possible hits on the starboard side. The third attack, which met heavy AA opposition and interference from fighter aircraft, scored one doubtful hit on the port side. All aircraft returned safely. Force H returned to Gibraltar at 6.30 p.m., 6 July.

Somerville was satisfied with the results. One of the six or seven hits had apparently caused a large explosion which enveloped the *Dunkerque* in smoke. 'I think she can now be written off for this war.'[136] And to his wife (6 July): 'The ship must be completely knocked out so that filthy job is over at last.' Later, however, in his Report, he said that he was satisfied that the attack had put the *Dunkerque* out of action for at least a year. This conclusion was correct: the damage was due to the bombardment of 3 July and an explosion on the 6th. But we now know that no torpedo actually hit and damaged the *Dunkerque*. Five or six may have found their mark without exploding. A torpedo in the first wave exploded under the stern of the patrol-boat *Terre Neuve*, thirty yards to the

---

[135] The British 'believed, because of the ill-advised broadcast of Admiral Estéva, boasting that the *Dunkerque* had hardly been hit, that the ship had not been sufficiently damaged'. Adrienne D. Hytier, *Two Years of French Foreign Policy: Vichy, 1940–1942* (Geneva, Paris, 1958), p. 63.   [136] Somerville to ? (Blake?), 7 July.

starboard of the *Dunkerque*, and sank her. A torpedo in the second wave hit the wreck of the *Terre Neuve*, setting off her 44 depth charges. The seven tons of TNT triggered by the explosion opened a great breach in the *Dunkerque*'s hull and killed or wounded 4 officers and 150 men. It was the heavy explosion in the *Terre Neuve*, which sent up a column of smoke and spray over 600 feet high, that convinced Somerville that the battle cruiser was 'sufficiently damaged'.

The action at Mers-el-Kébir on 3 July was timed to follow directly the surprise seizure of the 200-odd French warships and naval auxiliaries lying in British Home ports, mainly in Plymouth (the old battleship *Paris*, 2 light cruisers, 2 destroyers, etc.) and Portsmouth (the old battleship *Courbet*, 2 light cruisers, 5 torpedo-boats, etc.). For the most part these ships represented 'only rubbish from the Northern ports', as the C-in-C, Portsmouth, Admiral Sir William James, described them. They had arrived on 19 June and following days. A conference at the Admiralty on 29 June had settled on the *modus operandi*. The important thing was that bloodshed must be avoided, if possible, to which end the operation must be kept a complete secret.[137] At Portsmouth, Admiral James employed a ruse to get the ships within the harbour and seizing distance: they were anchored at Spithead, and the C-in-C had no ships strong enough to deal with them if they resisted. The French Admiral was persuaded to bring his ships in with the argument that the water space he was occupying was needed for some experiments.

The take-over, by large British forces sent on board the ships before daylight on 3 July, took the ships' companies by complete surprise. The Portsmouth operation was a total and bloodless success, if a most unpleasant task for those who carried it out.[138] At Plymouth, unfortunately, blood was shed: two British officers and a seaman and a French officer were killed, when the large

---

[137] The War Cabinet discussed the problem of how to obtain control of these ships. 'It was very undesirable that any action should be taken which might appear like sharp practice. For this reason, it was desirable that a party arranged for the night of Tuesday, 2nd July, should be cancelled. At the same time, it was important to take steps to avoid the risk of these ships being sunk in our harbours.' In the end, the War Cabinet decided to leave the methods for obtaining control of the ships to the Admiralty in the light of the discussion. 6 p.m., 1 July, WM 190 (40), CAB 65/14.

[138] The Commodore, R. N. Barracks, Portsmouth, Harold Walker, was in charge. A few days later, when Churchill visited Portsmouth, he spoke to Walker about the operation at Portsmouth. With a wry smile, he said something like this: 'A great act of treachery. Nothing has been more successful since the massacre of St. Bartholomew's Eve [1572]'! Admiral Sir Harold Walker's letter to the author, 19 Jan. 1970.

submarine *Surcouf* offered resistance. In Churchill's judgement, 'the whole transaction showed how easily the Germans could have taken possession of any French warships lying in ports which they controlled'.[139]

Ostensibly, the War Cabinet, in sanctioning this operation, was concerned only that these ships must be prevented from joining the Axis fleets, should that be the intention of the Pétain Government. It is difficult to see how the French ships could have put to sea, hemmed in and carefully watched as they were. Admiral James says it would have been easy to prevent the French ships at Portsmouth weighing anchor. Dockyard-men to work the hawsers, pilots, etc., all were required. If any of the ships had tried to make a dash for it, they would have been stopped at the boom. If, when they were at Spithead, the Admiral had decided to return to France, the minefields and the forts on the Isle of Wight would easily have stopped them. 'But I do not think anyone contemplated them sailing.' Indeed, he had no orders what he was to do if the French ships sailed.[140] No, I believe that the reason for seizing the ships was in order to make use of them at a time when there was a desperate need for more anti-submarine craft. (See above, p. 225.) The French crews, which totalled about 12,000 men, were given the choice between staying on and serving with the Free French Forces, or returning to France. Those who elected to remain— about 3,000 by November 1940—formed the Free French Naval Forces (FFNF, which had come into being on 28 June), helping to man the ships suitable for convoy escort work. The Royal Navy commissioned a number of the seized ships of military value under the White Ensign for a variety of purposes. The two old battleships, one manned by the British, the other by the FFNF, were used as AA ships in British harbours.

What is difficult to understand, let alone condone, was the treatment of the sailors who chose not to fight on under the British. They and their officers were interned in separate camps in the Isle of Man and near Liverpool, respectively. The men were treated virtually as prisoners of war behind barbed wire, living in miserable conditions and subjected to moral pressure to join the Free French movement. On the other hand, they were not exactly angelic in their own behaviour. 'Serious complaints of marauding, damage, theft, and indiscipline' gave much trouble to the British military authorities who were responsible for them.[141] The latter were

[139] Churchill, *Their Finest Hour*, p. 207. Alexander had said the same thing over the BBC on 4 July.

[140] Admiral James's letter to the author, 22 Dec. 1972.   [141] FO 371/24358.

delighted when, at the end of 1940, the majority were repatriated to the unoccupied zone of France in British and French ships. It would be foolish to pretend that their unhappy experience in England, combined with their fury over Mers-el-Kébir, encouraged them to join de Gaulle's movement. They were anti-British and pro-Vichy, and remained loyal to Darlan, their Commander-in-Chief. The callous treatment of the internees exacerbated the outraged feelings of many Frenchmen.

Entirely different was the situation at Alexandria, where it early became apparent that the Admiralty and the man on the spot were approaching matters from a very different point of view. To Cunningham it was a question of how to win over erstwhile and highly esteemed colleagues and avoid force, whereas from the other end the whole atmosphere was one of how best and most quickly to get possession of the French ships. Another lively consideration with the Admiral was that of safeguarding the local population and buildings and the dockyard port installations, all of which would inevitably suffer greatly if he resorted to force. He particularly felt that this latter consideration was carrying little weight in Whitehall, and that there was also little appreciation of the fact that to him and his officers and men, who had been on active service at sea, and that so recently, with the French ships, the use of force against their former allies in order to seize these ships would seem highly dishonourable.

Cunningham strongly opposed (30 June) the Admiralty's suggestion of 29 June that Force X should be seized on 3 July, simultaneously with the execution of 'Catapult'. He realized that any forcible attempt to seize the ships would only result in their being scuttled at their moorings and causing unacceptable obstruction in the harbour. The Admiralty replied (1 July), giving him three options on the 3rd, in this order of desirability: (1) he could obtain the French ships for his own use if this could be achieved without bloodshed; (2) the ships could remain at Alexandria in a non-seagoing condition with skeleton crews, with the British Government responsible for pay and upkeep; (3) the ships were to be sunk at sea. On Cunningham's invitation Godfroy arrived in the *Warspite* at 7 a.m. on the 3rd. His 'demeanour was entirely helpful and cordial,' wrote Cunningham, 'though we could realize, and see, the strain under which he was labouring'. When Godfroy left an hour later, it was Cunningham's impression that he would accept the second alternative. But Godfroy's written reply, received at noon, declared for the third alternative. 'It alone is reconcilable with our sense of honour.' Cunningham was very disappointed, as he felt that acceptance of the second alternative would mean that eventually the ships would join the British. He 'cast round in his mind for some solution to the terrible impasse'.

He came up with one in the afternoon which was acceptable to Godfroy because it did not call upon him to reduce his crews. He would discharge the oil from his ships and land the warheads from his torpedoes. To Cunningham's surprise and anger, his report of the progress made drew this signal from the Admiralty (received at 8.15 p.m.): 'Admiralty note that oil fuel is being discharged by French ships. Reduction of crews, especially key ratings, should however begin at once by landing or transfer to merchant ships, before dark tonight. Do not, repeat NOT, fail.'

It is a perfect example [Cunningham testily wrote in his autobiography] of the type of signal which should never be made. Apart from being quite unhelpful, it showed no comprehension whatever of the explosive atmosphere at Alexandria or the difficult conditions in which we were working. It filled me with indignation. Moreover, while ordering us to take action before dark, it was sent off from the Admiralty at a time which was after sunset at Alexandria. As it was impossible to implement it we ignored it completely. At the time I did not believe that signal emanated in the Admiralty, and do not believe it now.[142]

One has no more doubt than Cunningham had who was behind this signal, which was so alien to naval methods and so wounding to the man in charge. As Rear-Admiral R. M. Dick, who was on the Admiral's staff, has observed, 'It was only the extreme moral courage of Cunningham in ignoring this signal that saved the day. There were, incidentally, few who would have had this strength of mind and it is indeed an example of the dangers of interference from on high.'[143]

A more serious complication followed. Godfroy, having heard of the ultimatum to Gensoul and having received a French Admiralty message that he 'Weigh immediately and leave Alexandria with all your ships, using force if necessary', stopped the discharge of oil fuel 'pending events'. Cunningham had three courses of action, now that they were back where they had started. He could (1) attempt to capture the ships, (2) sink them at their moorings, or (3) demand that Godfroy either surrender them or intern them, failing which the ships would be sunk. Cunningham rejected (1) because the French force would be on the alert and (2) as being likely to result in useless bloodshed on both sides and possible

---

[142] Cunningham of Hyndhope, *A Sailor's Odyssey*, p. 250, where 'key ratings' in the Admiralty message is rendered, obviously incorrectly, as 'by ratings'.

[143] Admiral Dick's letter to the author, 3 Aug. 1968.

damage to his ships and to Alexandria as a fleet base (both fleets were in Alexandria harbour), while at the same time probably causing French ships to be sunk in 'awkward places in a crowded harbour', so bottling up the harbour for weeks or months. His decision, which he signalled to the Admiralty shortly after midnight, was to carry out the third alternative on the 5th.

Worse followed later that morning (4 July). Godfroy had heard of the action at Mers-el-Kébir. He now repudiated his undertaking, reserved his freedom of action, and had his ships raise steam and train their guns on the British ships. Apparently, he was resolved to put to sea, even at the risk of a battle. What followed was a masterstroke of diplomacy. Cunningham took advantage of the six to eight hours he knew the French needed to be ready to sail. A message, composed in French, was flashed several times to Godfroy's ships. 'In it', Cunningham writes, 'we set out the helplessness of their situation; our sincere desire not to fight with or kill any of them if they tried to get away; and the generous terms the British Government offered which we assured them could be accepted without loss of dignity or honour.'[144] To supplement this effort, large blackboards with the same message were displayed in boats that steamed round the French ships. Finally, captains of British ships visited the captains of French ships (each British ship served as host to a French ship) and reasoned with them. Cunningham refused to be hustled by an Admiralty message that he take his ships to sea, issue Godfroy an ultimatum, and be prepared to engage the French from seaward, or, alternatively, if the French were believed to be short of food and water, that he might try to starve them into surrender. 'On no account should the risk be taken of a battle inside the harbour.'[145] Cunningham's appeal to the French officers and men over their Admiral's head produced results. In mid-afternoon Godfroy came on board the *Warspite* and made it clear that he was yielding to overwhelming force. An agreement was concluded which settled the crisis: all fuel oil was to be discharged immediately from the French ships; they were to disarm themselves, landing the obturating pads (an essential part of the breech-block mechanism) of their large guns, the spares of the breech-blocks and the firing mechanism of small guns, and all warhead pistols, at the French Consulate General; and the ships'

---

[144] Cunningham of Hyndhope, *A Sailor's Odyssey*, p. 253.
[145] WM 193 (40), CAB 65/14. Churchill had 'deprecated' the alternative course, because 'a quick solution of the problem must be reached. It was most important for the Eastern Mediterranean Fleet to regain its mobility and the spectacle of a deadlock in the harbour would do great harm to Egyptian opinion.'

companies were to be reduced. Defuelling and disarming was completed on 5 July. On 9 July the French agreed to a reduction to one-third of full complement. An expanded agreement based on the understanding reached on the 4th was signed on the 7th.[146]

Cunningham's tactful but firm handling of a delicate situation had shown what could be achieved without bloodshed and came as a great relief to the War Cabinet and the Admiralty. Alexander and Pound sent the Admiral a warm personal message: 'After what must have been a most trying and anxious time your negotiations have achieved complete success. We offer you our most sincere congratulations. The Prime Minister also wishes his congratulations to be sent to you.'[147] Cunningham has justly paid tribute to Godfroy, 'who, throughout this painful episode, and placed in an unprecedented and most difficult situation, conducted himself as an honourable if obstinate man'. The French on their part have been equally generous to Cunningham. As expressed by

[146] Not a little of the credit should go to Captain R. M. Dick, who was Cunningham's staff officer for Policy and Plans, and Commander Philippe Auboyneau, the French Liaison Officer to Cunningham, who dealt mainly with Dick. Auboyneau initially lived in the British flagship and went to sea in her. But when France collapsed and the attitude of the French became uncertain, he believed that it was his duty to be on board his own flagship, and he went back to her. (He may have done so to try and cajole the French into coming over to the British side.) It so happened that the telephone between the buoys of the two flagships was never disconnected. This made it possible for Dick to get Auboyneau on the line and to initiate negotiations after a certain hesitation on the part of the latter. Thereafter the two officers were able to telephone each other and to meet at this lower level without fully committing their masters, who were, of course, fully aware. This telephone line made much of the subsequent events possible. Had such interchanges been possible at Mers-el-Kébir, events just might have developed differently. Auboyneau, incidentally, joined the Free French Navy in August 1940.

[147] However, the Prime Minister bristled when Cunningham proposed to offer to guarantee that the French ships would not be seized unless Germany or Italy broke the armistice terms. (Cunningham's purpose was to avert the danger of scuttling and to expedite the discharge and repatriation of the crews.) 'It is', the Prime Minister insisted, 'undesirable to give the guarantee . . . above all merely for the sake of expediting the departure of crews, or preventing scuttling by a promise. Please see my other Minute addressed to you the other night about wheedling the skeleton crews when they are on board. What action have you taken on this? We want all these ships very much, and we must not inhibit ourselves by needless undertakings. Now that we have them in our power, we must certainly not let them go. How are we to define a German breach of the Armistice? They will do whatever they think fit under its very elastic terms, and the Petain Government will not dare to protest. We are not parties to the Armistice, and cannot relate any action of ours to a breach of its conditions. On no account let the Admiral give any further guarantees. I trust he has not done so already.' Cunningham to Admiralty, 6, 7 July, Churchill's minute to the First Sea Lord and First Lord, 7 July, ADM 199/1930, ADM 116/4413. On 7 July, however, Cunningham signed an agreement with Godfroy under which, *inter alia*, the French ships would not be scuttled and the British would not attempt to seize them by force.

Auphan and Mordal, 'No French sailor will ever forget the chivalry and the intelligence which Admiral Cunningham displayed in arriving with Admiral Godfroy at a solution to the crisis of July 3.'

The situation after Mers-el-Kébir was extremely confused, as various instructions were issued regarding the action British forces were to take if they encountered French warships. The War Cabinet took the position (4 July) that their object was still to prevent French naval units falling into German hands, if possible without bloodshed. Therefore, when French ships were met at sea, they were to be signalled to 'heave-to' and offered the same terms as had been offered to Gensoul. If the signal or the terms were not complied with, action should be taken to seize the ships or, if necessary, to sink them.[148] In other words, the policy was to give the French ships warning before attacking. Accordingly, the Admiralty instructed Somerville (10.05 p.m., 4 July): 'Ships must be prepared for attack, but should not fire the first shot.' Since his earlier instructions spoke of the necessity to seize or destroy French ships, he asked whether the new instructions applied to the submarines off Algiers and Oran. (They had orders to attack all French warships, but they were intended to cover only the period of the Mers-el-Kébir operation.) Upon receiving confirmation that this was the case (8.45 p.m., 5 July), Somerville informed the *Proteus* and *Pandora*. It was too late. They had remained on patrol when Force H had returned to Gibraltar on 4 July. At 2.58 p.m., 4 July, *Pandora* (off Algiers) sighted what she thought was a cruiser—actually, the minelaying escort vessel *Rigault de Genouilly*, *en route* from Oran to Bizerta. *Pandora* fired four torpedoes at 3,800 yards, obtaining two certain hits and sinking the French ship (4.32). The news of the sinking arrived at the Admiralty late in the night of 4–5 July. Since it was deemed imperative that the French understand the true position, Phillips awakened Odend'hal during the night to apologize for the torpedoing, which, he said, was due to the British commander having gone beyond his orders.

The War Cabinet on the morning of 6 July discussed the policy to be adopted *vis-à-vis* French warships. The point was made that unrestricted attack might lead to French retaliation, which could result in considerable damage by their submarines to British ships. 'It was explained that our present policy had been designed to deal primarily with the four modern capital ships, and it had been realised that we could not hope to get possession of all the smaller French ships and submarines. The Naval Staff felt that it would be unsound to risk war with France for the sake of dealing with these

[148] WM 193 (40), CAB 65/14.

smaller and less important ships.' It was decided that the First Lord should send Odend'hal a supplementary statement of their general policy regarding French ships along these lines: 'Orders to all British warships meeting French warships are that they are on no account to open fire without giving sufficient warning to enable alternatives to be considered which would avoid bloodshed.'[149]

But the situation called for further clarification. In accordance with Admiralty thinking, that 'the further maintenance of the present state of tension between the French Navy and ourselves is very undesirable and might even lead to war with that country', a new policy was worked out and was communicated to Odend'hal on 14 July:

(1) No further action will be taken against French ships in French Colonial or North African ports; but we must reserve the right to act against French warships proceeding to enemy controlled ports.

(2) As regards French submarines, we shall follow the rules first generally accepted in the Nyon Convention, viz:

    (i) that submarines found submerged outside certain limited areas to be agreed upon will be treated as hostile, and

    (ii) that submarines on the surface outside the same areas will be treated as hostile unless accompanied by a French surface warship.[150]

Adoption of this policy was made easier by the fact that the *Richelieu* had been dealt with and *Jean Bart* could not complete for a considerable period.

The *Richelieu* still lay at Dakar. On 7 July a task force under Acting Rear-Admiral R. F. J. Onslow in the small aircraft carrier *Hermes*, with two cruisers, arrived off the port and presented the Governor-General with what the French Admiralty afterwards called 'a shameful ultimatum'. It was rather similar to the Oran proposals. The Governor-General ignored the ultimatum, whereupon a motor-boat from the *Hermes* was sent into the harbour (2 a.m., 8 July). It dropped four depth charges under the *Richelieu*'s stern, which failed to explode because of the shallow depth. The boat was lucky to return unmolested to the *Hermes*. At dawn six torpedo-bombers from the carrier delivered an attack. One torpedo exploded, which evidently set off the depth charges. The resulting damage to the *Richelieu*'s hull took the best part of a year to repair with the limited local resources. But the battleship was never completely neutralized. Her powerful armament remained intact and

---

[149] WM 195 (40), CAB 65/14.

[150] ADM 205/4. The Nyon Convention of September 1937, signed by nine powers, dealt with piracy in the Mediterranean in connection with the Spanish Civil War.

was to play a major role in the repulse of the attempt to land Free French forces at Dakar in September 1940.

Action was contemplated against the *Jean Bart* at Casablanca. It was Churchill's idea that Force H be sent there to dispose of the battleship and other ships in the port. A destroyer would present the Admiral with the choice of scuttling or demilitarizing the ships, failing which Force H would destroy them with gunfire.[151] The Admiralty decided that this operation could wait, after North had reported (9 July) that the *Jean Bart* would pose no threat for a long time: she had no main armament ammunition on board, only two of her eight 15-inch guns were manned, and practically no fittings or equipment were in place.[152]

Somerville's Report expressed satisfaction with the 'good station-keeping and handling of ships and the promptness with which signals were executed. This is all the more creditable since the ships of Force "H" had no previous opportunity of working together as a squadron.' He was also pleased with the gunnery, which 'appeared to be accurate and effective . . .'. What he really thought was probably more accurately reflected in his letter to the Admiralty of 7 July: 'The gunnery and fleet work leave a lot to be desired and the destroyers are not capable of night search at present.'[153] If the gunnery results were not better, it was at least in part due to the exceptionally poor visibility. The French ships had begun to raise steam about midday, and their smoke, together with the haze along the coast, made the tops and upper works of the ships in the harbour practically impossible to range on. When the squadron opened fire, therefore, the observation of fall of shot was most difficult, and it became almost impossible after the first hits were obtained. The hit on the *Bretagne* caused a large column of smoke to rise in the air which hung over the whole harbour. Add the smoke from other explosions and fires. Air spotting was most difficult. One of the lessons rubbed home by the action was this 'difficulty of observation of fire under action conditions. It was of course accentuated in this case by the haze and the fact that the ships were not moving and the smoke remained all around

[151] Churchill to Pound, 9 July, ADM 205/6.

[152] Naval Historical Branch (Ministry of Defence) records. Captain Roskill offers as the possible reason the proposal was not carried out the fact that 'shortly after the Oran operation Admiral Somerville was ordered to take his ships north from Gibraltar to attack French shipping in the Biscay ports'. *The War at Sea*, i. 272. That operation, incidentally, did not take place.

[153] Letter to ? (Blake?). It was indeed a heterogeneous force. Edwards, the DDOD (H), had remarked of the capital ships and cruisers: 'They couldn't be a more ill-assorted party. None of 'em can concentrate with the other.' Diary, 29 June.

them. The smoke from the big explosion obscured practically everything inside the harbour.'[154]

* * *

At Mers-el-Kébir on 3 July the curtain had fallen on a scene of destruction and desolation which constituted a bitter and most painful memory for all the participants, whether French or British. It was an experience that they never wished to recall. The slaughter of the sailors of one nation by those of another when both had until so recently been loyal comrades in arms against a common enemy 'left an extremely unpleasant taste in our mouths', as the Gunnery Officer of the *Hood* put it. 'Our', as will be explained, referred to the officers, more particularly the senior officers. Somerville himself was sickened by the whole affair. 'Fear I've made a mess of this lousy operation', he confided to his diary on the night of 3 July. He wrote to his wife without restraint the next day, as Force H headed for Gibraltar:

Afraid I shall get a colossal raspberry from the Admiralty for letting the Battlecruiser escape and not finishing off more French ships—we disposed of three or four big ships in the harbour I believe. In fact I shouldn't be surprised if I was relieved forthwith. I don't mind because it was an absolutely bloody business to shoot up these Frenchmen who showed the greatest gallantry. The truth is my heart wasn't in it and you're not allowed a heart in war.

But, as I warned the Admiralty, I think it was the biggest political blunder of modern times and I imagine will rouse the whole world against us.

Still, if it brings me back to you it will be some consolation, though I hate the idea of being regarded as the 'unskilled butcher of Oran' or something like that. Those are my reactions at the moment and I thought you'd like to know. It *was* a hateful business, but the French Admiral played me up all right by delaying and playing on my feelings to avoid killing a lot of Frenchmen.

I was quite determined that I would not have any of my destroyers sunk or big ships seriously damaged in this beastly operation and I succeeded. Wonder if anyone will think I had cold feet? Shouldn't be surprised. But the truth was that the action left me quite unmoved, I just felt so damned angry at being called on to do such a lousy job. I never thought that they would fight in spite of what the French Admiral said. Hooky Holland acted as our delegate and I am quite sure put up the best possible case for accepting our terms. But the French were furious that we did not trust them to prevent the ships falling into German hands.

I am sure myself we could have trusted them but even if we didn't I'd sooner that happened than that we should have to kill a lot of our former

---

[154] Lieutenant-Commander E. H. G. Gregson (Gunnery Officer of the *Hood*) to Commander R. A. Currie, 24 July 1940; copy in the author's possession.

allies. We all feel thoroughly dirty and ashamed that the first time we should have been in action was an affair like this.

But I feel sure I shall be blamed for bungling the job and I think I did. But to you I don't mind confessing I was halfhearted and you can't win an action that way. . . .

He continued in the same vein in a letter on the 5th:

You will have had a bellyful of my name on the wireless and in the papers and it all disgusts me because it is connected with this filthy business. And now I've got to do some more of it and kill a lot more French sailors and probably a lot of civilians as well. I feel thoroughly depressed and unclean. Of course I'm only carrying out my orders but that doesn't seem to make it any better.

Contrary to my expectations I got a signal from the First Lord and DP [Pound] with which Winston asked to be associated saying that whilst they were sorry I did not put *Dunkerque* in the bag, they congratulated me on [the] measure of success achieved. I replied thanking [them] but saying that my repugnance to causing loss of French lives induced me to seize first excuse for ceasing fire and that by doing so I failed to achieve my task which was to definitely destroy *Strasbourg* and *Dunkerque*.

I have now sent a message saying that further loss of French lives must inevitably provoke the French Navy into immediate and hostile action.

Dudley North is in entire agreement with me that the bombardment on Wednesday was bad enough, but to continue further action would be disastrous. Andrew Cunningham has said the same. It's all too bloody for words and I curse the day I was landed with this appointment. It all seemed so rosy and it has all been so horrible.

Poor Hooky Holland is so upset that he's asked to be relieved of his command in *Ark Royal*. I persuaded him to withdraw it but have sent on a letter to the Admiralty saying in all fairness he ought to be relieved as the strain of it all after his close association with the French must inevitably prove too much for him. . . .

Finally, on the 6th:

I hear from the Press that the French Government have severed diplomatic relations so what the hell have we gained by this monstrous business? I still simply can't understand how their minds are working at home. None of us can. It doesn't seem to worry the sailors at all as 'they never 'ad no use for them French bastards.' But to all of us Senior Officers it's simply incredible and revolting.

If I didn't feel that in war one can only have one loyalty and that is to the King and Government I shouldn't hesitate to ask to be relieved at once. But I feel it would be wrong and a stab at the country if I did.

Well I don't know what other butcher's work awaits me, but as things are it looks as if the French will actually declare war on us by now so then at least they will be legitimate enemies.[155]

The Governor and C-in-C, Gibraltar, Lieutenant-General Sir Clive

[155] Somerville's letters to his wife are in the Somerville MSS., 3/22.

Liddell, expressed his deep concern to the War Office (4 July): His garrison was 'perturbed and bewildered' by the events of 3 July, which 'may clearly affect adversely the morale of the garrison'.[156] The same day North felt compelled to relieve his conscience by placing on record in a long signal to the Admiralty the strong feelings against the use of force which he had felt and expressed to Somerville in the days preceding 'Catapult'.[157] He received an icy blast in reply (17 July):

... the opinions of Senior Officers are always of value before an operation is carried out; but once the operation has taken place Their Lordships strongly deprecate comments on a policy which has been decided by the Admiralty in the light of factors which were either known or unknown to officers on the spot.

In this case Their Lordships were never under the delusion that the French Fleet would not fight in the last instance, and this fact was taken fully into consideration in the preliminary deliberations. . . .

Their Lordships fully realised how repugnant the operation would be to all officers concerned, but they cannot allow such considerations to influence decisions in war and are surprised that comment of the kind received should be made.

The reply had been 'authorised and sent' by the First Lord. It was not enough, for (he wrote Churchill) he had 'suggested to the First Sea Lord that it should be for consideration to supersede F.O.C.N.A. [Flag Officer Commanding North Atlantic] but he does not think there is a strong enough case for this'.[158]

North had the last word—of a sort—(6 August), when he expressed 'deep regret' that his remarks on 'Catapult' had provoked the 're-proof' from Their Lordships. 'I did not intend my notes to be read as a criticism of the decision to carry out the operation.' He added that his 'dislike of the operation arose not from sentimental attachment to our late allies, but from strong doubts as to its effect on the

---

[156] 'Selection of Signals Relating to the Disposal of the French Fleet. 1940.'

[157] The entire correspondence thus initiated is in the Alexander MSS., 5/4/35, 5/4/42, 5/4/43, 5/4/47.

[158] Alexander's minutes to Pound, 15 July, ADM 1/19178, and Churchill, 17 July (with a copy of the Admiralty letter to North of that day), ADM 1/19177, also Alexander MSS., 5/4/43. Churchill's response to the latter minute, on 20 July, was: 'It is evident that Admiral Dudley North has not got the root of the matter in him, and I should be very glad to see you replace him by a more resolute and clear-sighted Officer.' ADM 1/19177. North, we shall see, was not replaced at this time. Captain Roskill maintains ('Marder, Churchill and the Admiralty, 1939–42', p. 51) that 'it was certainly Churchill who demanded the immediate relief' of North, and suggests that Alexander was merely doing Churchill's bidding. He adds: 'This is one of the rare examples of Pound standing up to Churchill.' Letting the last sentence pass, the content and dates of the three minutes make it evident that it was Alexander, not Churchill, who, rather surprisingly, had taken the initiative in the matter.

course of the war. I fully realise that if the war is to be won, there is no room for false scruples or for sentiment . . .' It is evident that the First Lord and the Prime Minister, anyway, had lost confidence in North. The episode contributed to his downfall in October 1940, when he was superseded, following the unmolested passage of a French squadron from Toulon through the Straits of Gibraltar (11 September). (These ships were a factor in the failure of the expedition to occupy Dakar on 23–25 September.)

Mers-el-Kébir raises the age-old problem of the proper relationship between statesmen and commanding officers. Where is the dividing line between one's conscience and the duty to obey a debatable political directive? The circumstances of Mers-el-Kébir, and Dakar afterwards, provide an excellent background for an examination of this rather delicate and ever topical question. But I shall not attempt it here.

When the Prime Minister walked into the House of Commons in the afternoon of 4 July, there was complete silence, 'the silence of suspension'. He proceeded to report 'with sincere sorrow' the measures taken on the 3rd to prevent the French Fleet from falling into German hands. It was a chivalrous speech, with both a regretful tinge and a note of cheerful confidence at the end. He began by criticizing the one-time Ally. 'The least that could be expected was that the French Government, in abandoning the conflict and leaving its whole weight to fall upon Great Britain and the British Empire, would have been careful not to inflict needless injury upon their faithful comrade, in whose final victory the sole chance of French freedom lay, and lies. . . . what might have been a mortal injury [the signing of the armistice] was done to us by the Bordeaux Government with full knowledge of the consequences and of our dangers . . .' He dealt quickly with the events at Portsmouth, Plymouth, and Alexandria, then turned to 'the most serious part of the story', the 'melancholy action' at Mers-el-Kébir. Here, after outlining the course of events, he paid tribute to the French, whose 'ships were fought, albeit in this unnatural cause, with the characteristic courage of the French Navy, and every allowance must be made for Admiral Gensoul and his officers who felt themselves obliged to obey the orders they received from their Government and could not look behind that Government to see the German dictation'. He concluded with a reference to the impending Battle of Britain and a pledge that Britain would fight on. 'The action we have already taken should be, in itself, sufficient to dispose once and for all of the lies and rumours . . . that we have the slightest intention of entering into negotiations . . . with the German and

VII*a* Vice-Admiral Marcel Gensoul, C-in-C, Atlantic Fleet (Force de Raid), 1938–40

VII*b* Admiral of the Fleet François Darlan, C-in-C, French Fleet, 1939–40, Minister of Marine, 1940–42

VII*c* General view of Mers-el-Kébir shortly before 3 July

VIII*a* The *Bretagne* on fire after the bombardment and beginning to sink

VIII*b* Admiral Gensoul at the funeral of the 'victims' of the action at Mers-el-Kébir, held on 5 July 1940 (see p. 275)

Italian Governments. We shall, on the contrary, prosecute the war with the utmost vigour by all the means that are open to us until the righteous purposes for which we entered upon it have been fulfilled.'[159]

The Times Parliamentary Correspondent observed: 'It is not often that the House is so deeply moved. The Prime Minister's speech matched a theme which had the qualities of a Greek tragedy, and it will live as one of the most memorable in the history of Parliament.' Churchill, in his war memoirs, says 'the House was very silent during the recital'. In fact, according to *The Times* report, he was interrupted by 'cheers' or 'loud cheers' some twenty times. At the end of the speech, members in all parts of the House and the visitors in the galleries, forgetting parliamentary decorum, rose spontaneously for two or three minutes and 'the Chamber rang with sustained cheers'. Order papers and handkerchiefs were waved like mad. It was, says Churchill, 'a scene unique in my own experience'. Tears poured down his cheeks as he took his seat. He left the House 'visibly affected'. One of his secretaries recorded in his diary, 'I heard him say to Hore Belisha: "This is heartbreaking for me".'[160]

Benoist-Méchin claims: 'Nearly all Britain's newspapers treated the Royal Navy's action as a noble exploit.'[161] I can find no such note in the principal London dailies and weeklies, but rather warm approval of the action and praise of Churchill and the Navy, mixed with profound regret. *The Times* declared (5 July): '. . . the British squadron won a melancholy victory. . . . There can be little pleasure in contemplating this defeat of enemies whom we believe to be at heart our friends, and who were fighting, not for their country, but for a point of honour, which was rooted in the dishonour of their political chiefs.' For the organ of the Labour Party, the *Daily Herald* (5 July), Mers-el-Kébir was a bitter and most disagreeable necessity. 'Our sorrow for the French sailors who suffered in the Mediterranean action—the Battle of the Brothers—is almost beyond the scope of words. Their dilemma was as cruel as ours. . . . We are proud of the British Government for its fearless and terrible decision, and of the Navy which carried out that decision. . . .*It had to be.*' 'HORRIBLE—BUT NECESSARY' began the leader of the Liberal *News Chronicle* (5 July). '. . . there is no effective counter to the total war which Hitler has declared on mankind except the use of

---

[159] Hansard, 5th series, ccclxii, cols. 1043–51.
[160] John Colville, in his introduction to Tute, *The Deadly Stroke*, p. 17.
[161] Benoist-Méchin, *Sixty Days that Shook the West*, p. 510. De Gaulle, in his *War Memoirs* (i. 97), writes of 'the way they [the British] gloried in it'.

K

total methods ourselves. To be weak is to be destroyed. . . . If the French Fleet had been allowed to fall intact into German hands, we might have lost the war.' 'An Inexorable Duty' was the title of the leader in the Conservative *Daily Telegraph* (5 July), and *The Observer* asserted (7 July), 'The world's annals know no stranger case of human reluctance and relentless necessity.' These are representative press opinions.

Nor did the sailors celebrate Mers-el-Kébir as 'a glorious exploit'. The inconclusive results of the action and, for most, the fratricidal combat, served only to depress further those at the Admiralty whose hearts had never been in the operation. Thus, Edwards, in his diary (4 July): 'The more information that arrives the less do I like the French Med. affair. We have pushed 5 8" cruisers & innumerable 6" straight into the hands of our enemies. Furthermore the *Dunkerque* will soon be ready for sea again.' One young naval officer exclaimed to a Frenchman who worked at de Gaulle's headquarters, 'I am ashamed of what we have done!'[162] Here and there, at the Admiralty and afloat, an approving voice was raised, the line being that it had been a time for forceful action, that too much was at stake, the command of the sea, to permit any trust in the armistice promise that the French Fleet would remain French.

For a day or two there was a distinct possibility that the French would declare war on Britain. Darlan's first reaction had been to issue an order at 8 p.m. on 3 July that French warships were to attack all British ships met. In the morning of 4 July Pétain, Darlan, Laval, and Baudouin met in the Marshal's office to discuss the situation, now that the details of Mers-el-Kébir were in. An enraged Darlan declared in a trembling voice, 'I have been betrayed by my brothers-in-arms. . . . They did not believe in my word.' All he had on his mind was revenge.[163] He had already, on his own initiative, instructed the *Strasbourg* and the cruiser squadron which had been based at Algiers to launch a surprise attack on Force H, then on its way back to Gibraltar. Laval supported Darlan. Baudouin, with Pétain's backing, succeeded in cooling tempers somewhat. 'Let us at least allow ourselves time to think. The attack on our fleet is one thing, war is another.' The operation was shelved. The full Council of Ministers, which met later in the morning, decided

[162] Mengin, *No Laurels for de Gaulle*, pp. 93–4. Mengin saw no Englishman who 'ever dreamed of making of the tragedy "a glorious victory"'. Ibid., p. 95. General Spears (then Churchill's liaison officer with de Gaulle) wept unashamedly when the news of the action came through.

[163] Why Mers-el-Kébir should have come as such a dreadful surprise to Darlan is a mystery. His post-armistice telegrams had forewarned the Fleet of a possible clash with their one-time Allies.

to hold in abeyance any form of reprisal, but accepted the Foreign Minister's suggestion that the *de facto* break in diplomatic relations with Britain since 23 June be made official. But Darlan persuaded them to approve an air bombardment of Gibraltar. What amounted to no more than a symbolic bombing was carried out by three naval bombers from French Morocco in the early morning hours of 5 July, when twelve bombs were dropped on Gibraltar, and two other aircraft unsuccessfully attacked battleships at anchor. Darlan wisely refrained from further useless hostile acts, and on 5 July contented himself with a broadcast warning that 'All British ships approaching to within less than 20 sea miles of the French coast are open to attack'. This replaced the order of the evening of 3 July. However, he had another flare-up after the second attack at Mers-el-Kébir (above, pp. 257–8) and the sinking of the *Rigault de Genouilly* (above, p. 264). At the Council of Ministers on the morning of the 6th he outlined with passion a Franco-Italian naval operation to free Force X, and on the 8th, after the attack on the *Richelieu*, he proposed a military expedition against Freetown in the British colony of Sierra Leone. The Foreign Office quashed these operations with the argument that they would at once create a state of war. Nothing came of a Darlan proposal of the 8th for another air bombardment of Gibraltar.

The War Cabinet had accepted the risk of war with the French when they sanctioned the use of force at Mers-el-Kébir. There was 'general agreement' at a late evening meeting of the Defence Committee (Operations) on 3 July that 'there was a strong likelihood that the French Government would in the very near future declare war against us', and the next day the Admiralty told flag officers that 'we may be at war with France shortly'.[164] On the same day, in accordance with instructions, the Joint Planners submitted a draft report to the Service Chiefs on the 'Implications of French Hostility'. They thought it 'conceivable' that the French, egged on by the Germans and Italians, might undertake active operations against the British. There was little to fear from any action that the French Army and Air Force might take, as it was 'likely to be ill organised, sporadic', but 'the action of French naval forces may add considerably to our commitments'.

It is clear that, with the increased forces now at the disposal of our

---

[164] DO (40) 19th meeting, CAB 69/1, Roskill, *The War at Sea*, i. 309. On becoming Prime Minister, Churchill had replaced the Military Co-ordination Committee with a Defence Committee, in two panels, 'Operations' and 'Supply', presided over by himself. The other members of the former were the Service ministers (when the occasion required), the Chiefs of Staff, the Secretary of the War Cabinet (Sir Edward Bridges), and Ismay.

enemies, our naval position vis-a-vis the combined German, Italian and French fleets is a difficult one. At present it does not seem likely that French and Italian or French and German ships will co-operate in attack on any of our forces, but rather that French Units will concentrate with the object of making their way to ports in France, resisting any attempt to stop or divert them. If these French ships reach their home ports, it still is not certain that they will necessarily be able to operate effectively against us, as such action might lead to trouble with the crews. On the other hand once under German control, it is certain that ruthless persuasive methods will be employed to ensure obedience to German demands. . . .

It follows that it is important to prevent wherever and however possible, French ships getting back to France. Operations are now in train to prevent this, but our forces available for this purpose are limited. . . . Concurrently with these operations a full blast of propaganda both by wireless, using French Cyphers, and by broadcast should be directed on the French Fleet to break their spirit to fight against us, and, should this fail, to confuse, mislead and disorganize any concentrated movements or operations.[165]

In accordance with a COS directive (5 July) to widen the scope of the report, the Joint Planners drew up a revised and expanded draft report on 9 July which became with (on the whole minor) changes the position of the Chiefs of Staff on 16 July. The latter report began with the blunt statement: 'Recent events have made it clear that we may have to face in the near future the active hostility of the French.' The most serious military effects included 'a considerable added Naval commitment due to the altered balance of Naval strengths', since these French naval forces were still at large: a battle cruiser (damaged), an aircraft carrier, 12 cruisers, 32 destroyers, and 44 submarines. (These units did not include the forces at Dakar and Casablanca.) 'We cannot say what action the French naval forces will take, as this will probably depend upon the state of morale of their crews. The Germans have, however, virtually released the French fleet from the demilitarisation terms of the armistice, and the French naval forces have shown that they are prepared to engage our own naval forces if ordered to do so.' Apart from fleet operations in the Mediterranean, the most probable course of French naval action would be surface and submarine operations against British trade, which could be a serious menace in the Atlantic. In the event of French hostility, British naval counter-action would take three forms: destruction of French naval units outside the Mediterranean and prevention of any further units from breaking out into the Atlantic; to this end, so far as French surface ships were concerned, a powerful capital ship force would be based at Gibraltar; destruction of the facilities at

[165] COS (40) 529 (JP), CAB 80/14.

Casablanca and especially Dakar.[166] Fortunately for the British and the Free World, Vichy did not declare war.

*   *   *

Churchill had stated in the House of Commons on 4 July: 'I leave the judgment of our action, with confidence, to Parliament. I leave it to the nation, and I leave it to the United States. I leave it to the world and to history.' I can hardly speak for Clio; yet after an interval of a third of a century and the release of the documents it is possible for the historian to arrive at a few conclusions.

The French have never ceased to refer to Mers-el-Kébir as a 'massacre' without justification. (Portsmouth, Plymouth, and Alexandria did not provoke the same intense reactions.) A number of Englishmen have agreed that it was a tragic mistake—Cyril Falls, the distinguished military historian, for one. British naval officers who were critical, notably Somerville and Cunningham, saw no reason to change their minds as the years passed that Mers-el-Kébir had been a mistaken policy. It was the latter's

considered opinion at the time that it was almost inept in its unwisdom. It would at once add to our enemies, and later on, when the war turned in our favour, as I never doubted it would, and we wanted all the help the French could give us, they might well remember our action against their fleet and the slaughter of their sailors and refuse to help us.

I could not believe the French would surrender their fleet to the Germans or Italians. . . . Nothing that has happened in the intervening years has altered my opinion . . .[167]

Unquestionably, the unhappy episode embarrassed the British in their prosecution of the war. French anger against their former Allies was stoked by the publication on 7 July of the French casualties at Mers-el-Kébir on 3 and 6 July. They showed 1,297 officers and men (47 and 1,250, respectively) killed and missing, and 351 wounded (14 and 337), for a total of 1,648. The *Bretagne* alone had lost 36 officers and 976 petty officers and men, or a total of 1,012. The *Dunkerque* was next with 210 officers and men. The dead of 3 July were buried in the cemetery at Mers-el-Kébir on 5 July. 'In an emotion-laden speech, delivered beside the line of coffins, Admiral Gensoul said: "You had promised to obey your superiors in whatever they might command you to do for the honour of the Flag and the greatness of the arms of France. If there is a stain on a flag today, it is certainly not on yours."'[168] The Vichy Government

[166] COS (40) 543, 'Implications of French Hostility', CAB 80/14. The report dealt with a number of other considerations pertaining to the defence of the Empire such as the diversion of shipping.

[167] Cunningham of Hyndhope, *A Sailor's Odyssey*, pp. 244–5.

[168] Benoist-Méchin, *Sixty Days that Shook the West*, p. 511. Cf., as regards the last

used the 'massacre' of Mers-el-Kébir as an effective piece of anti-British propaganda. The film of the cemetery at Mers-el-Kébir with its 1,200-odd graves and crosses was often shown on the screen in France, and on 3 July 1941 a memorial service was held throughout France to commemorate the 'martyrs'. The 'massacre', with its appalling toll, unquestionably encouraged the revival in many a Frenchman of a centuries-old animosity towards England which had been dormant since the two nations had last confronted one another in action at Waterloo. 'Perfide Albion' once again!

It was to have been expected that the British attack would have a profound psychological effect on the officers and men of the French Navy, who until so recently had proved themselves loyal Allies of the Royal Navy. Mers-el-Kébir embittered the French Navy, as Gensoul had predicted. Robert Murphy, who was the American Chargé d'Affaires in Vichy, relates how in the following weeks 'French naval officers bitterly told me that the British always had been jealous of the French Navy, always were looking for a chance at international conferences to weaken it, and now had seized the moment when France was knocked out by Hitler's Germany to destroy a large part of the helpless French fleet'.[169] In the French Navy, as well as in the North and West African colonies, the memory of Mers-el-Kébir lingered on, acting as a spur to the resistance at Dakar in September 1940, when the Anglo–Free French forces were repulsed, and since injured pride has a long memory, it may even account for the unexpected French naval resistance to the Anglo-American landings in North Africa (November 1942), which cost the Allies many lives. It was not until after the landings that there was a gradual healing of the breach.

The indignation at the British action spread far beyond the Navy, and there can be little doubt that it caused many a Frenchman out-

---

sentence, Gensoul's letter to the author, above, p. 252 n. The fact that British shells had killed so many hundreds of French naval officers and men was concealed from the British public, although Churchill in the House of Commons (4 July) had expressed the fear that the loss of life 'must have been heavy'.

[169] Murphy, *Diplomat among Warriors* (London, 1964), p. 78. Some weeks after the action, Somerville received a sharp letter of rebuke signed by the officers of the *Dunkerque*. (See reproduction opposite.) It lashed him for 'defiling the glorious flag of St. George with an indelible stain'. Somerville's immediate response to the letter and the accompanying returned mementoes was that he did not think 'any appropriate reply or acknowledgement can be forwarded except, perhaps, as suggested by Admiral North, a gift of thirty pieces of silver'. Somerville to Admiralty, 20 Aug. 1940, ADM 199/826. Lord Ismay writes, 'He pretended to take the rebuke lightheartedly, but I am sure that it cut him to the quick.' Ismay, *Memoirs*, p. 150. The Admiral's family confirm that he was very upset when he received this testimonial from the French Navy.

*Le Commandant et les Officiers du DUNKERQUE
vous font part de la mort, pour l'honneur de leur
pavillon, les 3 et 6 Juillet 1940, de neuf officiers et de
200 hommes de leur batiment.*

*Ils vous retournent les souvenirs ci joints, qu'ils
tenaient de leurs camarades de combat de la Marine
Royale britannique, en qui ils avaient placé toute leur
confiance.*

*Et ils vous expriment à cette occasion toute leur
amère tristesse et leur dégout de voir que ces camarades
n'ont pas hésité à souiller le glorieux pavillon de
S.ᵗ Georges d'une tache ineffaçable, celle d'un assassinat.*

*Ont signé : C.V. Seguin Cᵈᵗ du D.K _ C.F. Tanguy Cᵈᵗ en S.ᵈ _ C.F. Simon Chef du S.ᵗᵉ Securité.
C.C. Lecreux Chef du 3ᵉ Conduite du Navire _ L.V. du Gardin _ L.V. Biseau _ L.V. Labvigne_ L.V. Ligiot
L.V. d'Hennezel _ L.V. Fontaine _ E.V. 1ᵉʳᵉ cl. de Bonaffos de la Tour _ E.V. 1ᵉʳᵉ cl. Jourdan
E.V. 2ᵐᵉ cl. Delegue _ E.V. 2ᵐᵉ cl. Putz _ I.M.C. 2ᵐᵉ cl. Booh _ I.M. P.ⁿᵉ Fauveder _ I.M. 1ᵉʳᵉ cl. Borey
I.M. 1ᵉʳᵉ cl. Chef d'Hotel _ I.M. 2ᵐᵉ cl. Lecroq _ I.M. 2ᵐᵉ cl. Leroux _ I.M. 2ᵐᵉ cl. Denoyelle_
O.E. 2ᵐᵉ cl. Grall _ O.E. 2ᵐᵉ cl. Pellem _ O.E. 2ᵐᵉ cl. Gouzard _ Medecin Ppal Barges. C.3ᵐᵉ cl. Pelois
E.V. 2ᵐᵉ cl. Cambon _ E.V. 2ᵐᵉ cl. Le Doaré _ E.V. 2ᵐᵉ cl. Autric_ Chir. Dentiste 2ᵐᵉ cl. Loriot.
E.V. Chemlier _ Legrand _ Le Bouhlillon Ray _ Giacomi _ L.ᵗᵉ V. d'Hennezel_Millet_Cheminat_Cassugaa.*

The 'round robin' from the captain and officers of the *Dunkerque* sent to Admiral
Somerville in 1940 after the action at Mers-el-Kébir.

side metropolitan France to hesitate before joining the Free French forces. De Gaulle has shown how 3 July undermined the Free French movement:

> In spite of the pain and anger into which I and my companions were plunged by the tragedy of Mers-el-Kébir . . . I considered that . . . our duty was still to go on with the fight. . . .
> But it was a terrible blow at our hopes. It showed at once in the recruitment of the volunteers. Many of those, military or civilian, who were preparing to join us, turned on their heels then. In addition, the attitude adopted towards us by the authorities in the French Empire and by the naval and military elements guarding it, changed for the most part from hesitation to opposition. Vichy, of course, did not fail to exploit the event to the utmost. The consequences were destined to be grave as regards the rallying of the African territories.[170]

The Free French Naval Forces were hit especially hard. By 3 July some 10 or 12 naval officers and 400 sailors had joined. Without doubt many more would have followed but for Mers-el-Kébir. As stated above, only about 3,000 of the 12,000 men quartered in the camps were recruited by November 1940.

Mers-el-Kébir had other important results that worked against British interests. The Germans already had the Dunkirk slogan, 'The English will fight to the last Frenchman'. And now the English had slaughtered the French seamen in harbour. The German press, reported *The Times* on 5 July, 'exploded in anger at what flaring headlines in the evening newspapers [4 July] describe as a "cowardly British attack on the French Fleet"'. The first official German comment (4 July) asserted that 'all crimes in history pale before this new act of piracy of the British Government'. The Germans, however, allowed the opportunity to slip by. The only attempts to exploit Mers-el-Kébir, it would seem, took the form of a display in French ports of propaganda posters illustrating the sinking of the *Bretagne,* and in Paris of posters 'depicting a French sailor, his wife and new-born baby standing with tragic expressions on their faces amidst the ruins, menaced by a brutal British officer and with captions such as "Remember Oran!" "Thus ends the *Entente Cordiale!*" "The English did this!"'[171]

---

[170] De Gaulle, *War Memoirs,* i. 97. He had no choice himself but to condone the action in a broadcast of 8 July. Vice-Admiral Émile Muselier, commanding the Free French Navy, 'went straight to the First Sea Lord, Sir Dudley Pound, and told him flatly that if any more blood was shed between English and French sailors he would ask to be interned. He demanded, and obtained, an agreement for indemnification for the wives, children, and families of the victims of Mers-el-Kebir.' Mengin, *No Laurels for de Gaulle,* p. 93.

[171] Vice-Admiral Friedrich Ruge, *Sea Warfare, 1939–1945* (London, 1957), p. 83, Tute, *The Deadly Stroke,* pp. 205–6.

Actually, Hitler was pleased with the turn of events. He told Ciano at a conference in Berlin on 7 July that 'it had been very fortunate that the Duce and he [the Führer] had not insisted on the surrender of the French fleet. One would never get the French fleet that way. But now, by this intelligent handling of the fleet question, England and France had been made mutual enemies. This eased the situation considerably, in particular for Italy, and improved the situation in the western Mediterranean as well as the position of the Axis Powers in respect to Franco.'[172] Hitler was so impressed with the French willingness to oppose their former Ally by force that he made an important concession to them. On 3 July the French delegation at Wiesbaden had intimated that, under the circumstances, the Germans might be prepared to stop the disarmament of French warships. The next day, in response, the Armistice Commission informed the French delegation that Hitler had 'expressed his understanding [*Verständnis*] for the steps taken by the French Government. He has further stated that the assurances given for the French fleet in article 8 of the Armistice Agreement gain in importance with respect to a fleet that is prepared to resist unjustified and dishonoring seizure by other powers. The German Armistice Commission . . . is prepared to postpone the execution of those provisions of the Armistice Agreement that are incompatible with the reported French measures, until the situation is clarified.'[173] The practical result was the suspension of Article 8.[174] The Germans in effect granted the French request that they be allowed to keep their ships in full commission with ammunition and fuel, and the French recalled those in Oran and Algiers to the strongly defended base at Toulon, where they would be safer from British encroachment. Auphan and Mordal bring out the significance of the concentration of the bulk of the French Fleet in Toulon:

If it had not been for the aggression of the British, the principal French squadrons would have remained in North Africa, out of reach of the Germans. Under the original applications of the armistice, there would have been only one naval force based in European France, and that would have been merely 'a police division,' made up of light craft. But with the ports of Casablanca, Mers-el-Kebir, Algiers, etc., all directly on the coast, at the mercy of another British attack, the remaining capital ships of the

---

[172] *Documents on German Foreign Policy*, x. 148; similarly, Malcolm Muggeridge (ed.), *Ciano's Diplomatic Papers* (London, 1948), p. 376.

[173] *Documents on German Foreign Policy*, x. 124.

[174] The work of the Armistice Commission to date was summarized on 13 July, with the entry under Article 8 reading: 'Completely suspended at the moment.' Ibid., p. 203.

French Navy—including the *Dunkerque* when she was temporarily repaired —took cover under the protection of the powerful coastal batteries of Toulon. They thus came nearer to the German forces in the Occupied Zone.

The French Navy, driven out of its Atlantic bases by the Germans, and then out of its African bases by the English, had nowhere to go but Toulon. And there, by their very nearness, they offered a constant temptation to the Germans—a temptation to which the Germans finally succumbed on November 27, 1942, when they attempted to get their hands on it.[175]

Did the gains to Britain offset the serious disadvantages of provoking a rancorous hostility in France, turning the French Navy against Britain, and driving the French squadrons to Toulon? There are two considerations here: the effect on the naval balance of power and the moral effect. The naval balance sheet showed that still at large were the following French naval units: 1 battle cruiser (damaged), 1 aircraft carrier, 4 cruisers 8-inch, 8 cruisers 6-inch, 32 destroyers, 44 submarines. In addition, at Dakar and Casablanca were 1 battleship (*Jean Bart*, 77 per cent complete), 1 cruiser 6-inch, 10 destroyers, 17 submarines, and 11 armed merchant cruisers. Against this 'accretion to enemy strength' the British had seized in Home ports: 2 battleships (old), 5 destroyers, and 8 submarines ('although difficulties in manning and maintenance may limit their usefulness'), and had immobilized in Alexandria 1 battleship, 3 cruisers 8-inch, 2 cruisers 6-inch, 3 destroyers, and 1 submarine.[176] On balance, it is not clear that the actual gain to the British was greater than the potential gain to the enemy. As Admiral Richmond asked:

Was the gain of depriving the enemy of the problematical help of two, or even of four, heavy ships—if all at Oran had been eliminated—worth the candle? The margin of British capital ship superiority was undoubtedly unduly low; but if there were a possibility that the French navy might be used against Britain, did the act effectively diminish the danger? or did it tend to increase the risk of such action? The destruction of even four heavy ships would not destroy French sea power, for France still possessed a fine body of cruisers, heavy and light, a large flotilla of destroyers, many of them of great power, numerous submarines, and her air forces. In the condition in which Britain then stood, short of cruisers, short of destroyers, threatened with a struggle in defence of her sea communications in which these four types of vessel would play a far larger part than the battleship or battlecruisers, it was surely unwise—to put the matter on no higher level than mere expediency—to provoke a resentment which might tip the scales, in a delicately balanced political situation, in the enemy's favour. There had been more than one, among them Napoleon, who in their day had

[175] *The French Navy in World War II*, p. 139.
[176] The figures are from COS (40) 543, 16 July 1940. Omitted from the Dakar/ Casablanca figures, no doubt in error, was the *Richelieu*.

considered that Britain had lost more by incurring the active hostility of Denmark than she had gained by the capture of the Danish navy in 1807; but whereas it was then practically the entire Danish navy that had been taken, the Oran affair accounted for no more than this small fraction of the navy of France. To be sure it was in accordance with those schools of thought which estimated naval strength wholly in terms of battleships and had so belittled the importance of cruiser and flotilla craft that the number of those vessels had been fantastically reduced.[177]

Richmond's argument refers only to the action at Mers-el-Kébir, and takes no account of the immobilization of the capital ships at Alexandria, Casablanca, and Dakar, and the damage to the *Richelieu,* which are perhaps relevant.

At any rate, the Admiralty and Churchill viewed the situation differently. For them all that mattered was the capital-ship position and they had no doubt about the crucial gains made. Britain had 14 capital ships (including one on long refit); Italy had 6 and Germany 1 or 2. France, before 3 July, had 9 (5 'Bretagne' class, 2 'Dunkerques,' the *Richelieu,* and *Jean Bart*). '. . . the transfer of this powerful modern capital fleet to the enemy might have altered the whole balance of naval strength, with incalculable results to our cause.' As a result of the measures taken on and since 3 July, 'this grave anxiety' had been removed. The British had captured two 'Bretagnes' in Home ports, and a third was under control at Alexandria; they had sunk one and badly damaged and immobilized another at Mers-el-Kébir. They had knocked out one battle cruiser for some time; the other had escaped and was presumably in Toulon, but only after having been hit by a torpedo, which would immobilize her for some time. (The *Strasbourg* was in fact un-damaged: no hits were made by either the aerial bombs or torpedoes.) The *Richelieu* was heavily damaged and the *Jean Bart* would not be operational for some months. Altogether a satisfactory state of affairs.[178]

As for the moral effect, the strong action at Mers-el-Kébir showed

[177] Admiral Sir Herbert Richmond, *Statesmen and Sea Power* (London, 1946), pp. 358–9.

[178] Alexander's minute, 9 July, to Churchill, Alexander MSS., 5/4/38, and his statement in the House of Commons, 9 July, Hansard, 5th series, ccclxii, cols. 1089–90. The repairs of the *Dunkerque* were not completed until February 1942, when she was sent to Toulon with five destroyers as escort. The *Provence* left Mers-el-Kébir in November 1940 for Toulon with a destroyer escort. The three capital ships at Toulon, *Strasbourg, Dunkerque, Provence,* were among the ships scuttled there in November 1942. (See below.) The *Richelieu* left Dakar for the United States in January 1943 and, after quick repairs, joined the British Home Fleet in November 1943. Early in 1944 she joined the Eastern Fleet at Trincomalee for operations against Japan. The *Jean Bart* remained at Casablanca and was not completed until after the war.

the United States and the world Britain's determination to continue the struggle at all costs and whatever the odds. To this extent at least one of Churchill's principal reasons for sanctioning the use of force was justified. As he explained afterwards:

> The elimination of the French Navy as an important factor almost at a single stroke by violent action produced a profound impression in every country. Here was this Britain which so many had counted down and out, which strangers had supposed to be quivering on the brink of surrender to the mighty power arrayed against her, striking ruthlessly at her dearest friends of yesterday and securing for a while to herself the undisputed command of the sea. It was made plain that the British War Cabinet feared nothing and would stop at nothing. This was true. . . .
>
> Immense relief spread through the high Government circles in the United States. The Atlantic Ocean seemed to regain its sheltering power, and a long vista of time opened out for the necessary preparations for the safety of the great Republic. Henceforth there was no more talk about Britain giving in.[179]

At Chequers the following January, Harry Hopkins, the President's confidant, told John Colville that Oran had convinced Roosevelt, in spite of Ambassador Kennedy's defeatist opinions, that the British would continue the fight, as Churchill had promised, if necessary for years and alone.[180]

When the French Ambassador delivered Pétain's message to Roosevelt on 4 July, which declaimed that 'nothing could justify this hateful aggression, in view of the repeated assurances that French naval forces would never be used against Britain',[181] the President replied: 'Even if there were only the most remote possibility of seeing your Fleet pass into German hands, the British Government had reason to act as it did. I would not have acted otherwise. I am a realist.'[182] American press, political, and naval opinion approved the British action as a hard but necessary decision and as demonstrating Britain's will to victory.[183]

---

[179] Churchill, *Their Finest Hour*, pp. 211–12.

[180] Colville in Tute, *The Deadly Stroke*, p. 17.

[181] *Foreign Relations of the United States, 1940*, ii. 469–70.

[182] François Charles-Roux, *Cinq mois tragiques aux affaires étrangères* (Paris, 1949), p. 130.

[183] This 'great stroke', in the opinion of the American Military Attaché in London, 'should show the Dominions and the United States that, after all the defeatism in France and elsewhere, the British mean to win . . .' Journal, 4 July 1940, James Leutze (ed.), *The London Journal of General Raymond E. Lee, 1940–1941* (Boston, Toronto, 1971), p. 12. A conspicuous exception was Secretary of State Hull, for whom Mers-el-Kébir was a 'tragic blunder'. *The Memoirs of Cordell Hull*, i. 798. Elsewhere the opinion of neutrals, with one or two exceptions, was distinctly favourable. They did not think the British could have done anything else, or they admired the resolution with which the action was carried out, or they regarded it as solid evidence that

There is no way of estimating the importance of the moral factor. It may, in the long run, have proved decisive and therefore would by itself constitute sufficient justification for Mers-el-Kébir. The answer is less clear as regards the strategic, or balance-of-naval-power, factor, which, it must be emphasized, was the dominant consideration that led to Mers-el-Kébir. Was there, in fact, a sound basis for the extreme anxiety of Churchill, the War Cabinet, and the Service Chiefs that the Germans might get their hands on the French Fleet? Certainly not on French initiative. No evidence has come to light that would justify the fear that the French were not to be trusted. Vichy never showed the slightest inclination to surrender the Fleet. On this vital point Darlan and Pétain did not fail their erstwhile Allies; the thought of handing the ships over never so much as occurred to them. Yet, the Germans might have seized the ships, despite all French plans to scuttle them. Here, too, the record shows that British fears were exaggerated. Who can fail to be moved by Darlan's *cri de coeur* three weeks before his assassination, three weeks after the Germans had invaded and taken over unoccupied France, and one week after the French fleet at Toulon had scuttled itself to forestall a German attempt to get possession?[184]

the British intended to carry on the war to their utmost power—or some combination of these positions. In the case of the Turks, their Foreign Minister was 'entirely in sympathy with our action and this is the prevailing view here—not excluding members of the French Embassy who admit that it was the only thing to do'. Only in Madrid and Tokyo was opinion, as one would expect, violent in its condemnation of Britain; but the Japanese Navy 'understood and regarded [the action] as inevitable'. The Swedish press was critical, although the majority of Swedish naval opinion considered that their Navy would in similar circumstances have acted as had the Royal Navy. Cabled replies (8–10 July) from the British Naval Attachés in Tokyo, Madrid, Stockholm, Bucharest, Belgrade, Lisbon, Rio de Janeiro, and Santiago de Chile, in response to the DNI's request of 8 July for the reactions to Oran; also a report from the Ambassador to Turkey (6 July). FO 371/24231. Even the Italians, although hardly approving of Mers-el-Kébir, were impressed with British toughness, Ciano noting that the action 'proves that the fighting spirit of His Britannic Majesty's fleet is quite alive, and still has the aggressive ruthlessness of the captains and pirates of the seventeenth century'. 4 July 1940, Malcolm Muggeridge (ed.), *Ciano's Diary, 1939–1943* (London, 1947), p. 274. He undoubtedly had the Elizabethan Age in mind, post-dating it a century!

[184] In November 1942 there were some eighty warships at Toulon, representing 'the most modern, the most powerful half' of the French Fleet. Pursuant to a directive of December 1940, which called for the immediate seizure of unoccupied France and of the French Fleet and Air Force in case of an uprising in French Africa, the Germans struck after the Allied landings in North Africa (8 November) with local French collaboration, and the ceasefire ordered by Darlan (then in Algiers) on the 10th. They occupied the Free Zone (11 November), but when they moved on Toulon, with a view to seizing the fleet, the French, in accordance with long-standing plans for such a contingency, scuttled 77 of the ships, including the 3 capital units, 7 cruisers, and 32 destroyers. A few submarines escaped. At Bizerta on 8 December

He believed he had acted with the greatest loyalty to his war comrades. The letter began:

Dear Mr. Prime Minister,

On June 12, 1940, at Briare, at the Headquarters of General Weygand, you took me aside and said to me: 'Darlan, I hope you will never surrender the Fleet.' I answered you: 'There is no question of doing so; it would be contrary to our naval traditions and honour.' The First Lord of the Admiralty, Alexander, and the First Sea Lord, Pound, received the same reply on June 17 [18], 1940, at Bordeaux, as did Lord Lloyd. If I did not consent to authorise the French Fleet to proceed to British ports, it was because I knew that such a decision would bring about the total occupation of Metropolitan France as well as North Africa.

I admit having been overcome by a great bitterness and a great resentment against England as the result of the painful events which touched me as a sailor; furthermore it seemed to me that you did not believe my word. One day Lord Halifax sent me word by M. Dupuy that in England my word was not doubted, but that it was believed that I should not be able to keep it. The voluntary destruction of the Fleet at Toulon has just proved that I was right, because even though I no longer commanded, the Fleet executed the orders which I had given and maintained, contrary to the wishes of the Laval Government.[185]

This is the quintessence of the French case—that events proved that the British should have taken the French Navy and Government at their word when they solemnly declared and reiterated that they would never permit a French warship to fall intact into German hands. This would have spared the one-time Allies the tragedies of Mers-el-Kébir and Dakar, and the blood shed in the North African landings of November 1942. Churchill as much as admits the validity of Darlan's argument: '. . . he vehemently claimed that he had kept his word. . . . It cannot be disputed that no French ship was ever manned by the Germans or used against us by them in the war. [But see below.] This was not entirely due to Admiral Darlan's measures; but he had certainly built up in the minds of the officers and men of the French Navy that at all costs their ships should be destroyed before being seized by the Germans, whom he disliked as much as he did the English.'[186]

The French have the better of the argument when they look at the record of what followed 3 July. The British case must stand on how the situation looked to their responsible leaders *at the time*. From this point of view, and eschewing the luxury of hindsight,

the Germans were able, through an ultimatum backed with overwhelming force, to prevent any scuttling and to take over the entire decrepit force (9 old submarines, a badly damaged large destroyer, and 7 small surface craft of no great value).

[185] Churchill, *Their Finest Hour*, pp. 203–4. He might have mentioned Vichy's successful rejection of all German requests (the first on 15 July 1940) to use French North African bases for U-boats or raiders.   [186] ibid., p. 203.

a good case can be made for the proposition that, to quote Sir Llewellyn Woodward, the British 'could not shrink from desperate remedies to meet a desperate situation'. The decision-makers could not know for certain what French and German intentions were, and the stakes were too high to warrant taking any chances. Nothing less than certainty would do. Both the political and Service Chiefs saw no escape in the last resort from the powerful and distasteful necessity of crippling the French Fleet. The German promise in the armistice terms not to seize the French ships for their own use was a pretty weak safeguard against a tipping in the balance of naval strength. Although no Germans were within hundreds of miles of Oran, and there was no immediate danger from that quarter in July 1940, we must remember that the British expected that the ships of the Force de Raid would sail to their home ports in metropolitan France for demilitarization under German 'control'. On a matter of life and death for Britain and her Empire the British refused to rely on either the goodwill of the Pétain régime or its ability to keep the Fleet out of enemy hands. The Anglophobe sentiments of Darlan, Pétain, Laval, and other leading members of the French Government were well known, as was their expectation that Britain's days were numbered—that, in Weygand's famous words, 'Her neck would be wrung like a chicken's'.

And yet, if only some effort had been made in London to examine the question of the French Fleet from Hitler's viewpoint, there would have been cause to wonder whether his own interests would be served by demanding its surrender or attempting to seize it. Although the British were haunted by the fear that the Germans would get possession of the French capital ships and man them with German crews, neither Hitler nor his naval adviser ever contemplated this. On the contrary, we know that Hitler had decided to treat the French Fleet leniently in the armistice terms in order to discourage it from sailing for British ports, and in this he was successful. He, rightly, thought that if the French destroyers went over to join the British, they would provide a valuable addition to her hard-pressed anti-submarine forces and to that extent would hinder the U-boat campaign in the Atlantic. He would have been satisfied if the French Fleet had been scuttled. At no time did he or Raeder advocate demanding or seizing the major units of the French Fleet. Admiral Dönitz, who was in command of the U-boats in 1940, had nothing to do with such matters as the disposition of the French Fleet. But he never heard of any intention to take over and man the French ships. He does not think that the Naval Command had any such intention, since it was, he says, impractical, politically and from the personnel point of view.[187] Nor is there any evidence in the war diary of the German Naval Staff that the naval leaders seriously considered this.

It may be plausibly argued that the British could not have known what the German intentions *vis-à-vis* the French Fleet were and therefore had to be prepared for the worst. Yet the Admiralty should have been able to estimate with a measure of accuracy how long it would have taken the enemy to render the French ships serviceable (the French sailors would never have manned their own ships to fight under German orders), and this would have given them a better line on German intentions in regard to the French Fleet. The British Naval Staff appreciation that, if the French capital ships fell into German hands, it would be some two months before the enemy fleet could employ them efficiently (and about three months before the Italians could do so)[188] is extremely flattering. It is true that German naval personnel expanded to five times its prewar size within two years; but trained key personnel, the specialists, could not be procured as quickly. There was a serious shortage of sailors and specialists in the non-commissioned and petty officer ranks. After the campaigns in Norway and France, the German Navy did not know how to provide the indispensable forces to protect the newly conquered coasts. Personnel were needed, to quote a few examples, for additional patrol-boats, submarine-hunting groups, minesweeping flotillas for the Dutch and Danish coasts, floating AA batteries, repair ships for the U-boat arm, enlarging of auxiliary minesweeping flotillas, harbour protection flotillas (90 boats), the build-up of the U-boat fleet, flotillas for coast protection (180 units), establishment of a motor-boat division for Norway, the Western area, and German coastal area (400–500 units), and so forth and so on.[189] It seems to me that the upshot of

---

[187] Grossadmiral Karl Dönitz's letter to the author, 7 Sept. 1972.

[188] 24 June, WM 180 (40), CAB 65/13. The Naval Staff had, to be sure, produced the estimate on but a few hours' notice.

[189] War diary volumes of the German Naval War Staff, BA-MA Marinearchiv, Case 1502, Skl. IIIa, 4–4, and Case 1504, Skl. IIIa, 6–3, 6–4. We know that in 1941 the Naval Staff contemplated taking cruisers out of service in order to provide for personnel badly needed elsewhere in the Fleet, and that the U-boat arm always felt a shortage of manpower. It is significant, too, that the Germans did not make much use of the French warships that fell into their hands. There was little of the French Navy left in the Atlantic or Channel ports which the Germans occupied in 1940, except for those units under construction or paid off. The main German interest at this time seems to have centred on merchant ships and/or such shipping as could be brought into use as auxiliaries for minesweeping, escort, and coastal patrol. It was not until after the occupation of the whole of France that the Germans employed a few small ex-naval vessels for these tasks. Again in 1943, after the Italian capitulation, one or two former French torpedo-boats that had been taken over in the

this and other archival material pertaining to the disposition of captured French ships under construction is that there was no plan on the German side for manning and putting into service any of the French capital ships. They would have found it impossible to provide the necessary specialists (they were all needed by the German Fleet itself) and to train crews in the use of French equipment. If considered at all, any seizure of French capital units was probably thought to be unrealistic. The attempted seizure of the Toulon fleet in 1942 was designed to prevent these ships from joining the Allies.

Let us suppose the Germans had available the large number of trained officers and ratings to man the ships. It would not have paid them to attempt the technically complex business of manning foreign ships with German crews. The need to master all the complicated instruments marked in a foreign language is one factor. Another is that some degree of French sabotage of machinery would have been practically certain. Those most competent to judge are agreed that it would have been at least eighteen months before the ships could have been made serviceable, even assuming there had been no personnel problem.

The Admiralty appear not to have made any study of these factors. On the basis of a hasty Naval Staff appreciation, it was assumed that the Germans would be able to make efficient fighting units of captured French ships within a few months. Whether NID or the Plans Division of the Admiralty or the Joint Planners could have determined the full dimensions of the German naval personnel problem and analysed with some degree of accuracy the German capabilities in rendering serviceable units of the French Fleet is another matter. But there is no evidence that the attempt was even made. Neither Marshal of the Royal Air Force Slessor nor Admiral Daniel remembers that the Planners or the Naval Staff ever attempted to make such an appreciation, and it is the 'strong impression' of the officer who was responsible for French Fleet movements at NID that no such analysis was made by NID.[190] There was, then, mistaken judgement of German intentions and

Italian port of La Spezia were put to use by the Germans for routine tasks. These also had a short and ineffectual career. The Germans made no use of the ships captured at Bizerta, and neither they nor the Italians did much with the thirty-seven or so ships that were refloated at Toulon. Few were put into condition. See Auphan and Mordal, *The French Navy in World War II*, pp. 264 n., 270–1, 313–16, Naval Historical Branch (Ministry of Defence) records, *Laufende Kriegsgliederung der Kriegsmarine*, BA-MA Marinearchiv, Skl. Qu II Org.

[190] Slessor's letter of 7 Aug. 1972, Daniel's of 4 Aug. 1972, and Commander A. P. Barrow-Green's of 4 Aug. 1973 to the author.

capabilities as there was of French intentions and capabilities. The result was the precipitate action of 3 July.

What of the misunderstandings? Were they tragic? That is, would it have made any difference had the War Cabinet known either of the German concessions in regard to Article 8 (30 June), or of Darlan's unequivocal orders to prevent the ships falling into enemy hands, or if Gensoul had reported all the British propositions in their ultimatum? None, as I have pointed out: they had no practical importance, hence were not tragic. As for Article 8, the British would not trust Hitler's word. Regarding Darlan's orders, again I quote Woodward: '. . . the British Government had been told only in general terms of these instructions [Darlan's of 24 June], and, in view of the failure of the French to fulfil so many of their engagements, could not be sure that this particular order had been given, or that, if given, it would be carried out by a French authority which was under German control or that the Germans would not employ some trick to foil the French intentions.'[191] Concerning Gensoul, I have stated that the misunderstanding stemming from his handling of the British ultimatum was not of crucial importance.

The French have always held that 'one man and one man alone' must bear the responsibility for Mers-el-Kébir. There can be no cavilling over Churchill's primary responsibility. It took extra-ordinary moral courage on his part to act as he did in the face of the attitude of those charged with carrying out the operation, his own extreme abhorrence to the enterprise, and the possible serious results. Yet he did not shrink from a stern and painful decision, for, as he told the House of Commons on 4 July, they had to 'look with particular attention to our own salvation'. Benoist-Méchin cuts to the heart of the matter: 'Churchill's great argument, to which he always returns, is "that it was necessary that England survive". We do not deny it. But one would wish that he had not transformed this concern, so legitimate in his eyes when it was a question of his country, into an unforgiveable crime when it was a question of our country.'[192] Therein lies the real tragedy of Mers-el-Kébir. It was a case of right against right, for which reason there can never be a conclusive answer to the question whether the events of 3 July were justified. All that one can say—at least, this is my considered opinion—is that 'Catapult' was a mixed blessing for the British, yet necessity had dictated their harsh course of action. In the context of the situation on 3 July 1940, with the information available to the Government, that action is both intelligible and defensible.

[191] Woodward, *British Foreign Policy in the Second World War*, i. 404 n.
[192] Benoist-Méchin, *Soixante jours qui ébranlèrent l'occident*, iii. 383.

Index

All officers and titled people are indexed under the highest rank and title attained. Ships are indexed under 'Warships', British, etc. 'Mers-el-Kébir' is generally to be understood where 'Oran' is cited.

Abrial, V.-Adm. Jean Charles (1879–1962): and succession to command of French Navy, 199 n.

Addison, 1st Viscount (Christopher Addison, 1869–1951): on convoy system, 42

Aircraft, British: in Dardanelles operation, 4–11, 17 n., 19, 28; as convoy escort in First War and afterwards, 44–5; role in Second War, 45, 142; and minesweeping, 50–1; interwar development, 55–7, 101; and Ethiopian Crisis, 86 n., 101–2, 'Royal Marine', 131–6 passim, 'Catherine', 142, 144, 145, Norwegian campaign, 160 n., 166 n., 'Catapult', 255, 256, 'Lever', 257–8, attack on Richelieu at Dakar, 265

Alanbrooke, Field-Marshal, 1st Viscount (Alan Francis Brooke, 1883–1963): relations with Churchill when Prime Minister, 175

Alexander, A. V.: see Alexander of Hillsborough

Alexander of Hillsborough, 1st Earl (Albert Victor Alexander, 1885–1965): 186, 219 n.; reports on Naval Wire Barrage, 111 n.; as First Lord, 172; and disposition of French Fleet pre-Oran, 191–2, 200, 201, 203, 204, 220, 221, 222, 234 n., 284; on Somerville's appointment to command Force H, 230; and wording of messages for Gensoul, Somerville, 233, last message to Somerville, 238; on take-over of French ships in Home ports, 259 n.; congratulates A. B. Cunningham, 263, Somerville, 268; and post-Oran policy re French warships, 265, North's criticism of Oran action, 269–70; on results of Oran, 281

Allen, Capt. George Roland Gordon (1891–): on impact of Churchill's arrival at Admiralty (1939), 106–7

Altmark Episode: 137, 139–40, 152

Anderson, Sir John: see Waverley

Appleyard, Acting Cdr. (RNVR) Rollo (1867–1943): and 'law of convoy size', 45–6

Attlee, 1st Earl (Clement Richard Attlee, 1883–1967): 219 n.

Auboyneau, Adm. Philippe Marie Joseph Raymond (1899–1961): and disposition of Force X, 263 n.

Auphan, R.-Adm. Gabriel Adrien Joseph Paul (1894–): and disposition of French Fleet pre-Oran, 189 n.; on German armistice negotiations, 198

Avon, 1st Earl of (Robert Anthony Eden, 1897–): and Ethiopian Crisis, 67, 85 n., 89, 96, 97–8, 99, 100, southern Irish bases, 125

Bacon, Adm. Sir Reginald Hugh Spencer (1863–1946): on the Narrows (Dardanelles) forts, 29 n.

Baldwin of Bewdley, 1st Earl (Stanley Baldwin, 1867–1947): and Ethiopian Crisis, 65, 67, 81–2, 99–100 n.

Ballantrae, Brig., Baron (Life Peer) (Bernard Edward Fergusson, 1911–): on interwar combined operations, 52–3, submitting papers to higher authority, 60 n.

Baltzer, Cdr. Hermann (1888–1967): on Dardanelles operation, 31

Barnard, V.-Adm. Sir Geoffrey (1902–): on China squadron in Ethiopian Crisis, 71–2 n.

Barrow-Green, Cdr. Andrew Patrick (1910–): on German plans re French Fleet, 287

Baudouin, Paul (1895–1964): seeks armistice, 188; on disposition of French Fleet pre-Oran, 191, 192 n., 198, 215; reaction to Oran, 272–3

Beatty, Adm. of the Fleet, 1st Earl (David Beatty, 1871–1936): 61; on Naval Staff, 35; and Dogger Bank action, 55 n.; saves Admiralty Historical Section, 61

Beaverbrook, 1st Baron (William Maxwell Aitken, 1879–1964): relations with Churchill, 111

Bellairs, Cdr. Carlyon (1871–1955): and lessons of First War, 57–8 n.

Benoist-Méchin, Jacques, Baron (1901–): 193; on Darlan and Royal Navy, 191 n., Force X, 213, British press reaction to Oran, 271; criticizes Churchill's 'great argument', 288

Blackett, Baron (Life Peer) (Patrick Maynard Stuart Blackett, 1897–): and ocean convoy statistics, 45

Blake, V.-Adm. Sir Geoffrey (1882–1968): assessment, 59; on loss of *Hood*, 116 n., Norwegian campaign, 166, 169; and disposition of French Fleet pre-Oran, 182

Boswell, Capt. Lennox Albert Knox (1898–): and Dardanelles operation, 1 n., 17 n.; on Turkish mines in Dardanelles, 17, de Robeck, 22, fast minesweepers, 25, 26 n., the missed opportunity at Dardanelles, 32, interwar convoy exercises, 39 n.

Bracken, 1st Viscount (Brendan Bracken, 1901–58): relations with Churchill, 111

Brand, Capt. Eric Sydney (1896–): and Scapa Flow's defences, 51

Brockman, V.-Adm. Sir Ronald (1909–): on interwar convoy exercises, 39 n., Churchill–Pound relations, 172, 175, 177, Pound and Oran, 221

Broome, Capt. John Egerton (1901–): on efficacy of asdic, 40 n.

Brownrigg, Capt. Thomas Marcus (1902–67): 211 n., 212

Bullitt, William Christian (1891–1967): reports conversation with Darlan, 216 n.

Burrough, Adm. Sir Harold Martin (1888–): on Churchill and Oran, 220

Butler, Sir James Ramsay Montagu (1889–): on Churchill and COS, 163–4

Cadogan, Sir Alexander George Montagu (1884–1968): 219 n.; and disposition of French Fleet pre-Oran, 182; on imminence of invasion, 217

Caldecote, 1st Viscount (Thomas Walker Hobart Inskip, 1876–1947): 219 n.

Cambon, Roger-Paul-Jules (1881–1970): 199; on Pétain Government, 190

Campbell, V.-Adm. Gordon (1886–1953): and Q-ships in Second War, 49, 153

Campbell, Sir Ronald Hugh (1883–1953): 189; and disposition of French Fleet pre-Oran, 185, 186–8, 191, 192 n., 198, 234 n.; leaves Bordeaux, 198–9

Carden, Adm. Sir Sackville Hamilton (1857–1930): and Dardanelles operation, 6, 9, 11, 15; comforts de Robeck, 16 n.

'Catapult', Operation: decided on, 219; alternative strategies, 220, 233–7; orders for operation, 237; 3 July action at Oran, 253–6; *and see* Oran

'Catherine', Operation: 140–7, 150, 175, 177 n.

Cazalet, V.-Adm. Sir Peter Grenville Lyon (1899–): on efficacy of asdic, 41 n.

Chalmers, R.-Adm. William Scott (1888–1971): 210

Chamberlain, Arthur Neville (1869–1940): 131, 163, 219 n.; and Ethiopian Crisis, 98, Churchill as First Lord (1940), 107, southern Irish bases, 125, 'Royal Marine', 135–6, Norwegian campaign, 155, 158; fall of his Government, 171; chastises French Government over armistice, 210

Charles-Roux, François Jules Henri (1909–61): on Gensoul's message to French Admiralty, 246 n.

Chatfield, Adm. of the Fleet, 1st Baron (Alfred Ernle Montacute Chatfield, 1873–1967): 84; emphasizes night-action training, 37; attitude towards staff as C-in-C, 37, naval air, 56; and Ethiopian Crisis, 65–71 *passim*, 74–84 *passim*, 87, 88, 90, 91, 93, 94, 97, 100, 101, 103, 104; assessment, 75–6; on Eyres-Monsell, 76; and air power, 85, 86, Military Co-ordination Committee, 149 n., 163

Cherwell, 1st Viscount (Frederick Alexander Lindemann, 1886–1957): 114, 176; and Naval Wire Barrage, 115

Chetwode, Field-Marshal, 1st Baron (Philip Walhouse Chetwode, 1869–1950): on Navy's attitude towards air power, 86 n.

Churchill, Sir Winston Leonard Spencer (1874–1965): 50 n.; and Dardanelles operation, 2, 14–15, 19, 21, 22, 29, 52; on consequences of Scapa Flow's inadequate defences, 51; establishes Historical Section of Staff, 60; becomes First Lord (1939), 105–6; effect of appointment on Admiralty and Fleet, 106–7; love of job, 107–8; his rights and responsibilities as First Lord, 108, 137 n.; and relations with professional advisers, 108–9, Pound, 109–11, 137, 141–7, 149–50, 168–71, 172, 173–8, officers afloat, 111–12; and personnel questions, 112–13, food production, 113–14, defensive devices, 114–17, construction policy, 117–19, A/S warfare, 119–22, statistics of U-boat losses, 122–4, southern Irish bases, 124–5, Mediterranean strategy, 126, Home Fleet base problems, 126–30, itch for the offensive, 130, 140, offensive devices, 130–1, 'Royal Marine', 131–7, River Plate operation, 137, 138–9, signals anecdote, 137–8 n., *Altmark* episode, 139–40, 'Catherine', 140–7, air threat, 142–3, 156, 157, 166, 167, Norwegian campaign (including background), 147–71, Military Co-ordination Committee, 163, 273 n.; wartime appointments, 165–6 n.; relations with Tom Phillips, 167; becomes Prime Minister, 171; leaves Admiralty, 171–2; maintains close interest in Navy, 172; evaluation of his time at Admiralty, 172–3; his rights as Prime Minister, 175; his role and methods in historical perspective, 177–8; and disposition of French Fleet pre-Oran, 182–94 *passim*, 200, 201, 203, 204, 209, 214, 216–22 *passim*, 227, 230 n., 283, 288, naval movements pre-Oran, 228; opposes evacuation of eastern Mediterranean, 228 n.; and wording of messages for Gensoul and Somerville, 233, 234, 235, 252 n., last message to Somerville, 238; on feelings at Admiralty on 3 July 1940, 253, take-over of French ships in Home ports, 258 n., 259; and Force X, 261, 262 n., 263 n.; congratulates Cunningham, 263; proposes attack on *Jean Bart* at Casablanca, 266; congratulates Somerville, 268; and North's criticism of Oran action, 269; Oran statement in Commons, 270–1, 275, 276; on results of Oran, 281, 282;

receives poignant letter from Darlan, 284; held responsible for Oran by French, 288

Ciano, Count (Conte Galeazzo Ciano di Cortellazzo, 1903–44): 279; reaction to Oran, 283 n.

Clark-Hall, Air Marshal Sir Robert Hamilton (1883–1964): and Dardanelles operation, 6 n.

Clerk, Sir George Russell (1874–1951): on Hoare-Laval Plan, 100 n.

Collett, R.-Adm. George Kempthorne (1907–): on attitude of French naval officers pre-Oran, 205, 206, 207

Colville, John Rupert (1915–): on Churchill's Commons speech on Oran, 271

Colvin, Adm. Sir Ragnar Musgrave (1882–1954): on convoy between wars, 41–2

Commerce Protection, British: in Italian war plan, 104, Second War, 119–26, in event of French hostility, 274–5; *and see* Convoy System, Northern Mine Barrage, Q-ships

Convoy System: 36, 48; attitudes towards convoy between wars, 38–44; and asdic between wars, 40–1, 47 n.; in Second War, 44, 182; and air escort in First War and afterwards, 44–5, 'law of convoy size', 45–6; convoy escort dispositions, 47; and Ethiopian Crisis, 104; Churchill's attitude towards, in Second War, 119–21

Cooper, Alfred Duff: *see* Norwich

Corbin, Charles (1881–): 199

Cork and Orrery, Adm. of the Fleet, 12th Earl of (William Henry Dudley Boyle, 1873–1967): and 'Catherine', 141, 142, 144–5, 147, Norwegian campaign, 160, 162, 164–5, 168

Courtney, Air Chief Marshal Sir Christopher Lloyd (1890–): and Ethiopian Crisis, 66

Cowie, Capt. John Stewart (1898–): on magnetic mines, 49, Northern Mine Barrage, 122 n.

Creasy, Adm. of the Fleet Sir George Elvey (1895–1972): on efficacy of asdic, 41 n., Churchill as First Lord (1940), 124 n.

Creswell, Capt. John (1895–1973): expands *Naval War Manual*, 36; on convoy system between wars, 42 n., what was lacking in 1939, 57

Cunliffe-Lister, Sir Philip: *see* Swinton
Cunningham of Hyndhope, Adm. of the
Fleet, 1st Viscount (Andrew Browne
Cunningham, 1883–1963): 147; and
use of staff as C-in-C, 37, Admiralty
centralization, 54; on *Fighting Instructions* in Second War, 54 n.; protests
at Tripoli bombardment, 55; and
Ethiopian Crisis, 79, 80, 81, 86, 102,
relations with Churchill (Second War),
117; and disposition of Force X,
212, 219, 260–4; on Mediterranean
strategy, 217–18 n.; deplores use of
force at Oran, 224 n., 230 n., 268,
275; and evacuation of eastern Mediterranean, 228 n.; on negotiations at
Oran, 251
Cunningham, Adm. of the Fleet Sir John
Henry Dacres (1885–1962): and use
of staff, 37

Daladier, Édouard (1884–1970): and
'Royal Marine', 136
Danbé, V.-Adm. Jules Julien Lucien
Henri (1887–1957): and Oran negotiations, 243, 244, 246
Danckwerts, R.-Adm. Victor Hilary
(1890–1944): and 'Catherine', 143 n.
Daniel, Adm. Sir Charles Saumarez
(1894–): on 'Catherine', 143 n.,
'Catapult', 223, German plans *re*
French Fleet, 287
Dardanelles Operation: 37, 105, 147;
arouses controversy, 1–2; fundamental
errors before the operation, 2; Turkish
defences, 2–4; disadvantages of the
fleet, 4; air-spotting in the naval pre-
liminaries, 4–11, 21; failure of the
minesweepers, 11–15, 16–18, 24; de
Robeck succeeds Carden, 15; naval
attack of 18 March, 16; Turkish
morale after the attack, 18; de Robeck
against further naval attack, 19–23;
the new minesweeping organization,
23–5; combined operation of April,
25–6; prospects of a fresh naval
attack in April, 26–32; Gallipoli phase,
52
Darlan, Adm. of the Fleet Jean Louis
Xavier François (1881–1942): 180,
206, 210, 239, 260; and 'Royal
Marine', 134, disposition of French
Fleet pre-Oran, 182, 183, 184, 188,
189–92, 193, 195, 198, 199–200,
201, 204, 205, 207, 208, 211, 212–13,

215–16, 226–7, 228, 234 n., 235 n.,
236, 241 n., 246, 251 n., 283–4, 285,
288; becomes Minister of Marine,
188; regarded as a 'twister', 221;
and Oran negotiations, 241 n., 245,
246 n., 247, 248; reaction to Oran,
272–3
Davies, Cdr. George Philip Sevier (1904–
68): opposes use of force at Oran, 231;
and Oran negotiations, 238, 244, 246,
247 n., 249
Davis, Adm. Sir William Wellclose
(1901–): on feelings in Force H pre-
Oran, 249 n.
Decoux, V.-Adm. Jean (1884–1963): and
Ethiopian Crisis, 90
de Gaulle, Gen.: *see* Gaulle
de Robeck, Adm. of the Fleet Sir John
Michael, 1st Bt. (1863–1928): and
Dardanelles operation, 2, 14, 15, 16,
17 n., 18–23, 24 n., 26 n., 28, 29
Derry, Thomas Kingston (1905–): on
air power in Norwegian campaign,
166 n.
de Valera, Eamon (1882–): and
southern Irish bases, 125
Dewar, Capt. Alfred Charles (1875–
1969): proposes Admiralty Historical
Section, 60–1
Dewar, V.-Adm. Kenneth Gilbert Bal-
main (1879–1964): on minesweeping
crews in Dardanelles operation, 14,
and lessons of First War, 58–9
Dick, R.-Adm. Royer Mylius (1897–):
on interwar convoy exercises, 39 n.,
Churchill's interference with A. B.
Cunningham, 261; and disposition of
Force X, 263 n.
Dill, Field-Marshal Sir John Greer (1881–
1944): 183 n., 219 n., 233 n.; on
Italian Army in 1935, 77 n., Chur-
chill, 166 n.
Djevad Pasha: on Dardanelles operation,
31
Dönitz, Adm. of the Fleet (Grossadm.)
Karl (1892–): on disposition of
French Fleet, 285–6
Drax, Adm. the Hon. Sir Reginald Aylmer
Ranfurly Plunkett-Ernle-Erle- (1880–
1967): anticipates post-First War re-
form, 34
Dreyer, Adm. Sir Desmond Parry (1910–
     ): on convoy system between wars,
42 n.
Dreyer, Adm. Sir Frederic Charles

(1878–1956): 165–6 n.; suggests tactical school, 35; and U-Boat Investigation Committee, 124 n.

Drummond, Sir Eric: *see* Perth

Dufay, Lieut. Bernard Jacques Marie (1907–?): and Oran negotiations, 242–3, 246, 249

Duplat, Adm. Émile André Henri (1880–1945): and disposition of French Fleet pre-Oran, 193, 226

Edelsten, Adm. Sir John Hereward (1891–1966): on pre-war A/S plan, 44; work as Deputy Director, Plans, 145

Eden, Sir Anthony: *see* Avon

Edwards, Adm. Sir Ralph Alan Bevan (1901–63): on Churchill's intervention in naval operations, 167–8, 169, 171, 173; and disposition of French Fleet pre-Oran, 183; on Churchill and Oran, 221 n., prospects for 'Catapult', 223–4, composition of Force H, 266 n., Oran action, 272

Ellington, Marshal of the RAF Sir Edward Leonard (1877–1967): assessment, 76; on Italian Air Force, 77 n.

Enver Bey: and Dardanelles operation, 31

Enver Pasha (1881?–1922): and Dardanelles operation, 31

Esteva, Adm. Jean-Pierre (1880–1951): and succession to command of French Navy, 199 n., disposition of French Fleet pre-Oran, 200, 201, 204, 205, 247; broadcasts result of Oran action, 257 n.

Ethiopian Crisis: genesis, 64–5; admonitions of COS, 65–6; precautionary measures, 67–73; the League adopts sanctions, 73–4; Britain attempts to achieve military *détente*, 74; possibility of Italian attack, 75; Chatfield dominates Admiralty and COS, 76; Chatfield's views on strategy, 77; fleet comparisons, 77–8; British confidence if war came, 79–80; naval war plan, 80–1, 101–4; Chatfield's feelings about war, 82–3; a strong sanctions policy and British interests, 83–5; the Far Eastern factor, 83–4 n.; air threat, 85–7; problem of fleet efficiency, 87–8; French naval co-operation, 88–94; and Rhineland Crisis, 94–6; end of crisis, 96–9; reflections, 99; lessons, 100–1

Evans, Adm. Sir E. R. G. R.: *see* Mountevans

Eyres-Monsell, Sir Bolton: *see* Monsell

Falls, Capt. Cyril Bentham (1888–1971): on Oran, 275

Farnhill, R.-Adm. Kenneth Haydn (1913–): on Phillips and disposition of French Fleet, 221–2, Somerville and pre-Oran signal, 238 n.

Fergusson, Brig. Sir Bernard: *see* Ballantrae

Fisher, Adm. of the Fleet, 1st Baron (John Arbuthnot Fisher, 1841–1920): 105, 111, 113, 147; and Dardanelles operation, 2, 21; relations with Army, 37

Fisher, Adm. Sir William Wordsworth (1875–1937): emphasizes night-action training, 37; assessment, 59, 79–80; and Ethiopian Crisis, 68, 69, 70 n., 78 n., 79–80, 81, 82, 86, 87, 100 n., 102, 103

FitzGerald, R.-Adm. John Uniacke Penrose (1888–1940): and 'Royal Marine', 134

Forbes, Adm. of the Fleet Sir Charles Morton (1880–1960): 130; and Home Fleet base problems, 51, 126, 128, 129; on *Fighting Instructions*, 54; and Ethiopian Crisis, 66 n., relations with Churchill (1939–40), 112, Northern Mine Barrage, 122, *Altmark* episode, 140, Norwegian campaign, 157, 162, 165, 166, 168, 170

Force X (French): disposition of, 212, 219, 260–4, 273

Fraser of North Cape, Adm. of the Fleet, 1st Baron (Bruce Austin Fraser, 1888–): on Churchill's return to Admiralty, 106; and 'Royal Marine', 132, 'Catherine', 143

French Fleet: in Dardanelles operation, 16, 22 n.; and Ethiopian Crisis, 74, 78–9, 88, 89–94 *passim*, 99; and Churchill's Mediterranean strategy, 126; strength and efficiency (1940), 180–1, 182; relations with Royal Navy, 181; *and see* Force X, Oran

Gamelin, Gen. Maurice Gustave (1872–1958): and 'Royal Marine', 133–4, 135

Gaulle, Gen. Charles André Joseph Marie de (1890–1970): and disposition of French Fleet pre-Oran, 184 n., offer of Anglo-French union, 187; on

Gaulle (*cont.*):
Darlan, 190; launches Free French movement, 209; on British reaction to Oran, 271 n., undermining of his movement by Oran, 260, 278
Geddes, Sir Eric Campbell (1875-1937): suggests study of 1914-18 reforms, 34
Gensoul, Adm. Marcel-Bruno (1880-1974): 261, 264, 270; and succession to command of French Navy, 199 n.; pre-Oran attitude, 202, 204, 205, 206; assessment, 240-1; and Oran negotiations, 233, 241-52, 267, 288, 3 July action, 253, 254, 256, 257; reaction to Oran, 275, 276
German Fleet: 182; and Ethiopian Crisis, 95, 96; capital-ship strength (1940), 181; and disposition of French Fleet, 221, 285-7; *and see* Submarines, German
Gheel, Lieut.-Col.: and Dardanelles operation, 16
Godfrey, Adm. John Henry (1888-1971): 283 n.; on Major W. W. Godfrey, 19, Keyes, 23, Naval Staff College, 35; promotes co-operation of Operations and Intelligence, 37; on Churchill as First Lord (1939-40), 109, 114; and statistics of U-boat losses, 123; on Churchill and River Plate operation, 138 n., 'Catherine', 143, Norwegian campaign, 164, 165, Churchill, Phillips, and air threat, 167 n., Churchill-Pound relations, 168, 176-7 n., Pound and disposition of French Fleet pre-Oran, 208, 221, Holland as negotiator at Oran, 240, 250
Godfrey, Gen. Sir William Wellington (1880-1952): and Dardanelles operation, 19
Godfroy, V.-Adm. René-Émile (1884-): 208; and A. B. Cunningham, 212, 260-4
Goodall, Sir Stanley Vernon (1883-1965): and trench-cutting tank, 131
Goodenough, Adm. Sir William Edmund (1867-1945): lectures on First War, 35
Gort, Field-Marshal, 6th Viscount (John Standish Surtees Prendergast Vereker, 1886-1946): and rebuff in Morocco, 225 n.
Grantham, Adm. Sir Guy (1900-): on Italian Fleet in Ethiopian Crisis, 79, Pound as C-in-C, Mediterranean, 80,

confidence of Mediterranean Fleet during Ethiopian Crisis, 81, Churchill-Pound relations, 137, 138, 168, 172, 174, 175, 176
Greenwood, Arthur (1880-1954): 219 n.
Gregson, Acting Cdr. Edward Hilleary Gelson (1904-41): on visibility in Oran action, 266-7, distaste of officers for action, 267
Gretton, V.-Adm. Sir Peter William (1912-): on interwar Mercantile Convoy Instructions, 39 n., convoy escort dispositions, 47; on Churchill's interest in personnel matters, 113 n., trench-cutting tank, 131, technological development, 172
Grey of Fallodon, 1st Viscount (Edward Grey, 1862-1933): and Dardanelles operation, 29

Haining, Gen. Sir Robert Hadden (1882-1959): 224 n.
Halifax, 1st Earl of (Edward Frederick Lindley Wood, 1881-1959): 151, 219 n.; and *Altmark* episode, 139-40, Norwegian campaign, 151, 155, disposition of French Fleet pre-Oran, 200, 203; on U.S. and disposition of French Fleet, 218 n., 284
Hall, Adm. Sir William Reginald (1870-1943): and Dardanelles operation, 16 n., 29, 30; lectures on First War, 35; and 'Room 40', 55 n.
Hamilton, Gen. Sir Ian Standish Monteith (1853-1947): and Dardanelles operation, 19, 20-1, 30
Hankey, Col., 1st Baron (Maurice Pascal Alers Hankey, 1877-1963): on Dardanelles operation, 2; and Ethiopian Crisis, 65, 84 n., French Fleet in June 1940, 182
Harkness, Capt. Kenneth Lanyon (1900-): on French firing on British motorboat (3 July), 249-50 n.
Harris, Marshal of the RAF Sir Arthur Travers, 1st Bt. (1892-): 176; on Tom Phillips and air threat, 167 n.
Harwood, Adm. Sir Henry (1888-1950): and River Plate operation, 138
Henderson, Adm. Sir Reginald Guy Hannam (1881-1939): assessment, 59
Heneage, R.-Adm. Algernon Walker (1871-1923): and Dardanelles operation, 24-5, 26 n.

Herriot, Édouard (1872–1957): 189; on Darlan, 190

Hitler, Adolf (1889–1945): 43, 44, 99, 154, 166, 217, 288; on disposition of French Fleet, 194–6, 215 n., 285; reaction to Oran, 279

Hoare, Sir Samuel: *see* Templewood

Holland, V.-Adm. Cedric Swinton (1889–1950): on attitude of French naval officers pre-Oran, 207; pro-French attitude, 221; opposes use of force at Oran, 231; emissary to French Fleet at Oran, 231, 239–52, 267; assessment, 239–40; effect of 3 July, 268

Hopkins, Harry Lloyd (1890–1946): on Roosevelt's reaction to Oran, 282

Hubback, V.-Adm. Sir Arthur Gordon Voules (1902–70): on 'Catherine', 143, 147, feelings in Force H pre-Oran, 253

Hull, Cordell (1871–1955): concern over French Fleet, 218; reaction to Oran, 282 n.

Huntziger, Gen. Charles (1880–1941): and German armistice negotiations, 196–7

Inskip, Sir Thomas: *see* Caldecote

Intelligence, British Naval: and Dardanelles operation, 12, 15–16 n.; cooperation with Operations, 37; 'Room 40', 55 n.; 'Cinderella of Naval staff', 84 n.; and U-boat losses (1939–40), 123, Oran, 179 n.

Inter-Service Relations: 37–8, 52–3, 56

Ironside, Field-Marshal, 1st Baron (William Edmund Ironside, 1880–1959): 131, 151 n., 219 n.; and Norwegian campaign, 155–6, 159, 165, 166

Ismay, Gen., 1st Baron (Hastings Lionel Ismay, 1887–1965): 163, 176, 273 n.; on Oran ultimatum, 235–6, *Dunkerque's* officers' rebuke of Somerville, 276 n.

Italian Fleet: 54, 180–1, 203; and Ethiopian Crisis, 73 n., 77, 78, 79, 80, 81, 84 n., 86 n., 102–3, 104; and Churchill's Mediterranean strategy, 126; strength in June 1940, 180; actions in June 1940, 217 n.; possible submarine attack on Force H, 237–8

Jacob, Lieut.-Gen. Sir Edward Ian Claud (1899–): on Churchill and Naval Wire Barrage, 115 n., 'fury of his

concentration', 140, Norwegian campaign, 164, relations with Pound, 177

James, Adm. Sir William Milbourne (1881–1973): on Chatfield, 76, Ethiopian Crisis, 76, 100 n., Churchill as morale builder, 107 n., Keyes and Norwegian campaign, 160 n., Cork and Norwegian campaign, 165 n., Darlan, 189; and take-over of French ships in Home ports, 258, 259

Japanese Fleet: 48; and fleet air arm, 56, Ethiopian Crisis, 84 n.

Jarrett, Sir Clifford George (1909–): on Oran decision, 221

Jellicoe, Adm. of the Fleet, 1st Earl (John Rushworth Jellicoe, 1859–1935): lectures on First War, 35; and 1914–15 operations, 55 n.

John, Adm. of the Fleet Sir Caspar (1903–): on interwar convoy system, 39 n., 41, obsession with a fleet action, 48, interwar naval air development, 56–7, promotion criteria, 59

Jutland, Battle of: 1, 35, 36, 37, 48, 54

Keitel, Field-Marshal Wilhelm (1882–1946): and French armistice negotiations, 194, 196, 197

Kennedy, Joseph Patrick (1888–1969): 282

Keyes, Adm. of the Fleet, 1st Baron (Roger John Brownlow Keyes, 1872–1945): 165–6 n; and Dardanelles operation, 10, 12–13, 19, 20, 21, 23, 24 n., 26, 52; assessment, 23; and Norwegian campaign, 159–62, 169, downfall of Chamberlain Government, 171

Keyes, Lady (Eva Mary Salvin Bowlby, m. 1st Baron, 1882–1973): and Norwegian campaign, 160

Kitchener, Field-Marshal, 1st Earl (Horatio Herbert Kitchener, 1850–1916): and Dardanelles operation, 28, 29, 30; relations with Navy, 37

Knocker, Group-Capt. Guy Mainwaring (1899–1971): and interwar combined operations, 53

Laborde, Adm. Jean Joseph Jules Noël de (1878–?): and succession to command of French Navy, 199 n.; pre-Oran attitude, 207, 247

Lambe, Adm. of the Fleet Sir Charles Edward (1900–60): on Churchill–Pound relationship, 110

Langley, V.-Adm. Gerald Maxwell Bradshaw (1895–1971): assessment, 59

Laval, Pierre (1883–1945): and Ethiopian Crisis, 67, 71, 74, 75, 89–90, 92, 93; enters Pétain Government, 209; reaction to Oran, 272; and disposition of French Fleet pre-Oran, 285

Law, Andrew Bonar (1858–1923): and lessons of First War, 57

Lawson, Cdr. Harold Fergusson (1901–41): on loss of *Hood*, 116 n.

Leach, Capt. John Catterall (1894–1941): on loss of *Hood*, 116 n.

Lebrun, Albert (1871–1950): on disposition of French Fleet pre-Oran, 215

Lee, Gen. Raymond Eliot (1886–1958): reaction to Oran, 282 n.

Le Luc, V.-Adm. Maurice Athanase (1885–1964): orders reinforcements to Oran (3 July), 248

'Lever', Operation: 256–8

Lewis, Capt. Roger Curzon (1909–): and magnetic mines, 49–50

Liddell, Gen. Sir Clive Gerard (1883–1956): concern over Oran action, 268–9

Liddell Hart, Capt. Sir Basil Henry (1895–1970): on Montgomery-Massingberd, 76, admirals and battleships, 85–6, Ethiopian Crisis, 99 n., Churchill becoming Prime Minister, 171

Liman von Sanders, Gen. Otto Viktor Karl (1855–1929): on Dardanelles operation, 20 n.

Limpus, Adm. Sir Arthur Henry (1863–1931): on Dardanelles operation, 16 n.

Lindemann, F. A.: *see* Cherwell

Litchfield, Capt. John Shirley Sandys (1903–): on Churchill as First Lord (1939–40), 107–8, 151 n.

Little, Adm. Sir Charles James Colebrooke (1882–1973): and Churchill *re* personnel questions, 112–13

Lloyd, 1st Baron (George Ambrose Lloyd, 1879–1941): and disposition of French Fleet pre-Oran, 192 n., 219 n., 284

Lothian, 11th Marquess of (Philip Henry Kerr, 1882–1940): on U.S. foreknowledge of Oran, 218, Roosevelt and disposition of French Fleet, 218–19 n.

MacDonald, James Ramsay (1866–1937): and Ethiopian Crisis, 83

Mackay, Capt. Ronald Gordon (1901–): on pre-Oran attitude of French Navy, 207

Mackesy, Maj.-Gen. Pierse Joseph (1883–1956): and Norwegian campaign, 156, 162, 164–5

Mackintosh, Capt. Kenneth (1902–): on pre-Oran attitude of French Navy, 207

McLachlan, Donald Harvey (1908–71): on German breaking of naval cipher, 71 n., NID, 84 n., Churchill and U-boat loss statistics, 123

MacLean, V.-Adm. Sir Hector Charles Donald (1908–): on interwar convoy exercises, 39 n.

MacLeod, Maj.-Gen. Minden Whyte-Melville (1896–): and interwar combined operations, 53

Madden, Adm. of the Fleet Sir Charles Edward, 1st Bt. (1862–1935): 61

Malkin, Sir Herbert William (1883–1945): and 'Royal Marine', 132–3

Mansergh, V.-Adm. Sir Cecil Aubrey Lawson (1898–): on First War Historical Section monographs, 61

Maund, R.-Adm. Loben Edward Harold (1892–1957): and interwar combined operations, 53

Merten, V.-Adm. Johannes (1857–1926): and Dardanelles operation, 11, 18

Mitchell, Adm. Francis Herbert (1876–1946): 1 n.

Mittelhauser, Gen. Eugène Désiré (1873–1949): 208

Monsell, Cdr., 1st Viscount (Bolton Meredith Eyres-Monsell, 1881–1969): assessment, 76; and Ethiopian Crisis, 83, 84–5, 87, 90, 92

Montgomery-Massingberd, Field-Marshal Sir Archibald Armar (1871–1947): assessment, 76; and Ethiopian Crisis, 83–4 n.

Moore, Adm. Sir Henry Ruthven (1886–): on Churchill–Pound relations, 175, 176

Moreau, V.-Adm. Jacques Hector Claude François (1884–1952): pre-Oran attitude, 207

Morgenthau, Henry (1856–1946): on Dardanelles operation, 18 n., 30

Mountbatten of Burma, Adm. of the Fleet, 1st Earl (Louis Francis Albert

Victor Nicholas Mountbatten, 1900–): relations with Churchill when Prime Minister, 175; on Churchill–Pound relations, 176

Mountevans, Adm., 1st Baron (Edward Ratcliffe Garth Russell Evans, 1881–1957): 165–6 n.

Murphy, Robert Daniel (1894–): on effect of Oran on French Navy, 276

Muselier, V.-Adm. Émile Henry (1882–1965): reaction to Oran, 278 n.

Mussolini, Benito (1883–1945): 109, 112, 161; and Ethiopian Crisis, 65, 67, 73, 74, 77, 85 n., 89, 99, 100 n., French armistice, 195, 279

Négadelle, R.-Adm. Jean Louis (1896–1944): 248

Newall, Marshal of the RAF, 1st Baron (Cyril Louis Norton Newall, 1886–1963): 183 n., 219 n., 223 n.; on Home Fleet's base, 127

Nicholl, R.-Adm. Angus Dacres (1896–): on Churchill as First Lord (1939–40): 115, 116, 147

Noble, Adm. Sir Percy Lockhart Harnam (1880–1955): and A/S warfare, 44

Noguès, Gen. Charles Auguste Paul (1876–1971): 208; rebuffs British in Morocco, 225 n.

North, Adm. Sir Dudley Burton Napier (1881–1961): 251 n.; on attitude of French naval officers pre-Oran, 204–6, 246; assessment, 205; opposes use of force at Oran, 230, 231, 268; on *Jean Bart* at Casablanca, 266; critical of Oran action, 269–70; on French rebuke of Somerville, 276 n.

Northern Mine Barrage: 50, 121–2

Norwegian Campaign: 53, 55, 119 n., 136, 137, 147–71

Norwich, 1st Viscount (Alfred Duff Cooper, 1890–1954): on Montgomery-Massingberd, 76; and Ethiopian Crisis, 87, Oran, 219 n., rebuff in Morocco, 225 n.

Odend'hal, V.-Adm. Jean Hernest (1884–1957): 192 n., 199; treatment by Royal Navy post-armistice, 210; and pre-Oran contacts with Admiralty, 211, 213, 213–14 n., 226–7, sinking of *Rigault de Genouilly*, 264, new British policy *re* French warships, 265

Oliphant, Sir Lancelot (1881–1965): and Ethiopian Crisis, 100 n.

Oliver, V.-Adm. Robert Don (1895–): and Scapa's defences, 129–30

Ollive, Adm. Emmanuel Lucien Henri (1882–1950): pre-Oran attitude, 201, 207, 247

Onslow, Capt. Richard Francis John (1896–1942): attacks *Richelieu* at Dakar, 265

Operations: *see* under specific name: 'Catherine', etc.

Oran (Mers-el-Kébir): 179–80, 263 n.; background to 'Catapult': capital-ship situation, 181–2; problem of disposition of French Fleet, 182–217; U.S. facet, 218–19; the die is cast, 219–20; role of Churchill, Pound, Alexander, Phillips, 220–2, Naval Staff, Joint Planners, COS, 222–6; modification of armistice Article 8, 226–7; British fleet movements, 227–8; Somerville assumes command of Force H, 228–31; alternatives for dealing with French fleet at Oran, 231–3; Somerville's final instructions, 233–7; Force H sails, 238; fleet and defences at Oran, 239; Holland and Gensoul, 239–41; Oran negotiations, 241–53; the action, 253–6; second attack (6 July), 256–8; British post-Oran policy *re* French warships, 264–5; British reactions to Oran, 267–72; French reactions to Oran, 272–3, 275–8; British study 'implications of French hostility', 273–5; German reactions to Oran, 278–9; gains and disadvantages to Britain, 280–3; the French case, 283–4; the British case, 284–5; the German aspect, 285–8; résumé, 288

Oswald, Capt. George Hamilton (1901–71): on Churchill as First Lord (1939–40), 115 n., 116 n.

Ouvry, Cdr. John Garnault Delahaize (1896–): and magnetic mines, 49–50

Peirse, Air Chief Marshal Sir Richard Edmund Charles (1892–1970): 128, 224 n.

Perth, 16th Earl of (James Eric Drummond, 1876–1951): and Ethiopian Crisis, 72, 78 n.

Pétain, Marshal Henri Philippe (1856–1941): 196; urges armistice, 186, 189, 190; becomes Premier, 188; and

Pétain (*cont.*):
  disposition of French Fleet, 188, 195, 198, 215, 283, 285; relations with Darlan, 190; and loyalty of French Fleet, 206, post-armistice broadcasts, 209; reaction to Oran, 272, 282

Phillimore, Adm. Sir Richard Fortescue (1864–1940): chairs Post-War Questions Committee, 34

Phillips, Maj.-Gen. Charles George (1889–): and Norwegian campaign, 156

Phillips, Acting Adm. Sir Tom Spencer Vaughan (1888–1941): 139, 145, 213–14 n., 224 n., 227, 228 n., 232; and lessons of First War, 57; and Ethiopian Crisis, 102 n., new construction, 118, A/S warfare, 121; on Churchill's Mediterranean strategy, 126; and 'Catherine', 143, Norwegian campaign, 155, 158, 169, air threat, 166–7; on French Navy, 181, Darlan, 216; and 'Catapult', 221–2, 223; on French assurances *re* their Fleet, 234–5 n.; apologizes for torpedoing of *Rigault de Genouilly*, 264

Picton-Phillips, Lieut.-Col. Peter (1903–51): and interwar combined operations, 53

Pim, Capt. Sir Richard Pike (1900–): 172; on Churchill–Pound relationship, 110

Plate, River, Battle of: 137–9

Playfair, Maj.-Gen. Ian Stanley Ord (1894–1972): 223 n.; on French assurances *re* their Fleet, 234 n.

Pleydell-Bouverie, Capt. Hon. Edward (1900–51): and disposition of French Fleet pre-Oran, 183; on pre-Oran attitude of French Navy, 207–8, 210

Portal of Hungerford, Marshal of the RAF, 1st Viscount (Charles Frederick Algernon Portal, 1893–1971): relations with Churchill when Prime Minister, 175

Pound, Adm. of the Fleet Sir Alfred Dudley Pickman Rogers (1877–1943): 50 n., 127, 183 n., 223 n.; on submarine tactics in interwar exercises, 46 n., fleet action against Japanese, 53; and Ethiopian Crisis, 80; relations with Churchill, 109–11, 137, 141–7, 149–50, 168–71, 172, 173–8; and dummy ships, 114, new construction, 117–18, A/S warfare, 120, 121, 122 n., statistics of U-boat losses, 123, Home

Fleet base problems, 128, 129, 'Royal Marine', 132, 134, River Plate operation, 138–9, 'Catherine', 141–7, Norwegian campaign (including background), 149–50, 157, 160–1, 162, 166, 167, air threat, 166, 167; relations with A. V. Alexander, 172; opinion of French Navy, 181; and disposition of French Fleet pre-Oran, 182, 183, 186, 188, 191–2, 199–200, 201, 203–4, 208, 211, 213, 215, 219 n., 220, 221, 222, 223, 225, 227, 234 n., 284, treatment of Odend'hal, 210, naval movements pre-Oran, 228; contemplates evacuation of eastern Mediterranean, 228 n.; appoints Somerville to command Force H, 228, 229; contemplates 'drastic action' at Oran, 230 n.; and demilitarization of French fleet at Oran, 232, 252, 253 n., Holland as negotiator, 240; congratulates A. B. Cunningham, 263, Somerville, 268; and North's criticism of Oran action, 269, Free French reaction to Oran, 278 n.

Power, Adm. Sir Manley Laurence (1904–): on interwar staff work, 37, efficacy of asdic, 40 n., submarine tactics in interwar exercises, 46 n., conservatism of Admiralty, 59–60

Pownall, Lieut.-Gen. Sir Henry Royds (1887–1961): on Ethiopian Crisis, 66 n., 69 n., 100–1, Military Coordination Committee, 149 n.

Q-Ships: in two wars, 49, and Norwegian strategy, 153

Raeder, Adm. of the Fleet (Grossadm.) Erich (1876–1960): and disposition of French Fleet, 196, 285

Ramsay, Adm. Hon. Sir Alexander Robert Maule (1881–1972): assessment, 59; and Ethiopian Crisis, 101

Ramsay, Adm. Sir Bertram Home (1883–1945): and use of staff, 37

Reynaud, Paul (1878–1966): and 'Royal Marine', 135, 136, German armistice, 184, 185, 186, 187; on Darlan, 190, disposition of French Fleet, 215

Rhineland Crisis: and Ethiopian Crisis, 94–6, 99

Richmond, Adm. Sir Herbert William (1871–1946): anticipates post-First War reform, 34; and lessons of

First War, 57–9; on results of Oran, 280–1

Roosevelt, Franklin Delano (1882–1945): 184, 186, 194; on Churchill's resourcefulness, 173; and French appeal for armed intervention, 185, disposition of French Fleet pre-Oran, 218–19 n.; reaction to Oran, 282

Roskill, Capt. Stephen Wentworth (1903–): on Geddes's suggestion to study 1914–18 reforms, 34, interwar convoy exercises, 38–9, consequences of Scapa Flow's inadequate defences, 51, interwar combined operations, 52, loss of *Hood*, 116 n., value of southern Irish bases, 125 n., Norwegian campaign, 157 n., 163, Churchill-Pound relations, 168–9, 170, 171, 173–8 *passim*, proposed action against *Jean Bart* at Casablanca, 266 n., proposed relief of North post-Oran, 269 n.

Rosyth: as fleet base in Second War, 127–8

'Royal Marine', Operation: 131–7, 154

Royle, Adm. Sir Guy Charles Cecil (1885–1954): and 'Royal Marine', 134

Sandford, Capt. Francis Hugh (1887–1926): and Dardanelles operation, 23, 24 n.

Saunders, Cdr. Malcolm George (1896–1967): on 1917–18 U-boat operations, 39–40

Scapa Flow: as fleet base, 51–2, 126–30

Schofield, V.-Adm. Brian Betham (1895–): on interwar convoy exercises, 39 n., Darlan, 190–1, Holland as negotiator, 239–40, 250 n.

Seal, Sir Eric Arthur (1898–1972): 106 n., 139; on Churchill as First Lord (1939–40), 130, Churchill-Pound relations, 169–71, Churchill and Oran, 217

Servaes, V.-Adm. Reginald Maxwell (1893–): on Churchill and loss of *Royal Oak*, 127

Shakespeare, Sir Geoffrey Hithersay, 1st Bt. (1893–): on/and Churchill as First Lord (1939–40), 106 n., 108, 113–14

Sinclair, Sir Archibald: *see* Thurso

Slessor, Marshal of the RAF Sir John Cotesworth (1897–): on Tom Phillips, 167 n., 'Catapult', 220, 223, German plans *re* French Fleet, 287

Smuts, Field-Marshal Jan Christiaan (1870–1950): relations with Churchill, 111

Somerville, Adm. of the Fleet Sir James Fownes (1882–1949): 269; and use of staff, 37; assessment, 59, 228–9; on Tom Phillips, 167; appointed to command Force H, 228, 229; attitude towards use of force at Oran, 229–30, 232 n.; conferences at Gibraltar, 230–1; makes alternative proposals to Admiralty, 231–2; receives four Admiralty messages (2 July), 233–7; discusses orders for 'Catapult', 237; sails for Oran, 238; and Holland as negotiator, 240, Oran negotiations, 243–4, 247, 249, 251, 252, 253 n., 3 July action, 253–6, 6 July action, 256–8, Admiralty instructions post-Oran, 264; on efficiency of his ships, 266; deplores Oran, 267–8, 275; rebuked by *Dunkerque*'s officers, 276 n., 277

Souchon, Adm. Wilhelm (1864–1933): and Dardanelles operation, 28 n., 31

Spearman, Lieut.-Cdr. Alexander Young (1904–42): opposes use of force at Oran, 231; and Oran negotiations, 238, 243

Spears, Maj.-Gen. Sir Edward Louis, 1st Bt. (1886–1974): 184 n.; and disposition of French Fleet pre-Oran, 185, 186–8; reaction to Oran, 272 n.

Stanhope, 7th Earl (James Richard Stanhope, 1880–1967): as First Lord, 107

Stanley, Lord (Edward Montagu Cavendish Stanley, 1894–1938): on convoy system, 42–3

Strang, 1st Baron (William Strang, 1893–): and disposition of French Fleet pre-Oran, 182

Strategy, British Naval: enshrined in *Naval War Manual*, 36; effect of Jutland on, 48; *and see* 'Catapult', 'Catherine', Ethiopian Crisis, 'Royal Marine'

Submarines, German: in First War, 38, 40, 46, 148, Second War, 45 n., 46–7, 49, 50, 121–6, 145, 146, 150, 163; *and see* Convoy System

Swinton, 1st Earl of (Philip Cunliffe-Lister, 1884–1972): and Ethiopian Crisis, 85

Tactics, British Naval: foundation and

Tactics (*cont.*):
    work of Tactical School, 35–6, 54 n.;
    interwar improvements, 36–7, 38;
    effect of Jutland, 48; *Fighting Instruc-*
    tions, 53–4
Talbot, V.-Adm. Arthur George (1892–
    1960): and A/S warfare, 121, statis-
    tics of U-boat losses, 123–4
Templewood, 1st Viscount (Samuel John
    Gurney Hoare, 1880–1959): and
    Ethiopian Crisis, 66, 71, 73, 74, 75,
    82, 85 n., 89, 92, 100; on Darlan, 189
Thomson, V.-Adm. Evelyn Claude Ogilvie
    (1884–1941): and Scapa Flow's de-
    fences, 51
Thurso, 1st Viscount (Archibald Henry
    Macdonald   Sinclair,   1880–1970):
    219 n.
Titterton, Cdr. George Arthur (1890–
    ): and Churchill's role in Norwegian
    campaign, 170 n.
Tovey, Adm. of the Fleet, 1st Baron (John
    Cronyn Tovey, 1885–1971): and sink-
    ing of *Bismarck*, 55
Trenchard, Marshal of the RAF, 1st
    Viscount (Hugh Montague Trenchard,
    1873–1956): and divided control of
    Fleet Air Arm, 56
Turkish Fleet: in Dardanelles operation,
    16, 28, 31
Tyrrell, 1st Baron (William George
    Tyrell, 1866–1947): on Darlan, 221

United States Navy: 33 n., 44; and fleet
    air arm, 56
Usedom, Adm. Guido von (1854–1925):
    15 n.

Vansittart, 1st Baron (Robert Gilbert
    Vansittart, 1881–1957): and Ethiopian
    Crisis, 66–7, 100 n.
Vian, Adm. of the Fleet Sir Philip (1894–
    1968): and *Altmark* episode, 139–40

Waller, V.-Adm. John William Ashley
    (1892–   ): on Churchill–Pound rela-
    tions, 174, 175, 176
Wangenheim, Baron (Freiherr) Hans von
    (1859–1915): on Dardanelles opera-
    tion, 18 n., 31 n.

Warburton-Lee, Capt. Bernard Armitage
    Warburton (1887–1940): and Nor-
    wegian campaign, 168, 174
Warships, British*: *Abdiel* (ML): 50–1 n.;
    Achilles (CR): 97; *Albatross* (SC): 219;
    Anson (*Jellicoe*) (B): 117; *Arethusa*
    (CR): 238; *Ark Royal* (SC): 1 n., 5, 6–7,
    9, 10, 11, 17 n.; *Ark Royal* (AC): 200,
    203, 220, 228, 237, 238, 255; *Beagle*
    (TBD): 201; *Belfast* (CR): 51, 129 n.;
    Conqueror (B): 117, 118, 119; *Cornwallis*
    (b): 10; *Cossack* (TBD): 139; *Courage-*
    ous (AC): 68, 118; *Coventry* (CR): 86;
    Curlew (CR): 86; *Dorsetshire* (CR): 202;
    Duke of York (B): 117; *E-15* (SM): 25;
    Enterprise (CR): 238; *Foxhound* (TBD):
    238, 241, 242, 243, 244; *Glorious* (AC):
    118; *Hermes* (AC): 219, 265; *Hood*
    (BC): 71, 74, 96, 100 n., 114, 116 n.,
    117, 203, 228, 230, 238, 253, 255,
    256; *Howe* (*Beatty*) (B): 117, 118;
    Inflexible (BC): 2, 4, 16, 27; *Irresistible*
    (b): 16; *King George V* (B): 117, 119 n.;
    Lion (B): 117, 119; *Nelson* (B): 51, 114,
    117, 200; *Ocean* (b): 16; *Pandora* (SM):
    228, 264; *Prince of Wales* (B): 63,
    116 n., 117, 119 n., 175, 176–7 n.;
    Proteus (SM): 228, 264; *Queen Eliza-*
    beth (B): 4, 5, 6 n., 7–8, 16, 19, 27, 28;
    Renown (BC): 71, 74, 96, 114, 117,
    130; *Repulse* (BC): 63, 117, 130, 175,
    176–7 n.; *Resolution* (B): 69, 203, 228,
    238, 256, 257; *Revenge* (B): 87; *Rodney*
    (B): 117, 130, 200; *Royal Oak* (B): 51,
    127, 129; *Suffolk* (CR): 167 n.; *Sydney*
    (CR): 97; *Temeraire* (B): 117, 119;
    Thunderer (B): 117, 118, 119; *Valiant*
    (B): 200, 228, 238, 256; *Vanguard*
    (B): 119; *Vengeance* (b): 10; *Warspite*
    (B): 212, 219; *Watchman* (TBD): 201
Warships, French: *Bouvet* (b): 16, 18;
    Bretagne (B): 180, 206, 239, 254, 266;
    275, 278; *Commandant Teste* (SC): 239,
    255; *Courbet* (B): 180, 210–11, 258,
    259; *Dunkerque* (BC): 180, 183, 190,
    191 n., 200, 202, 203, 220, 228, 236,
    239, 253–4, 256, 257–8, 268, 272,
    275, 280, 281 n.; *Jean Bart* (B): 180,
    183, 189 n., 191 n., 192, 193, 194,
    200, 201, 203, 204, 206, 219, 265,

* Abbreviations: AC: aircraft carrier; B: battleship; b: pre-dreadnought battleship; BC: battle cruiser; CR: cruiser; ML: minelayer; SC: seaplane carrier; SM:
submarine; TBD: destroyer.

266, 280, 281; *Lorraine* (B): 180, 206, 212; *Mogador* (TBD): 254; *Paris* (B): 180, 210–11, 258, 259; *Provence* (B): 180, 206, 239, 254, 281 n.; *Richelieu* (B): 180, 183, 189 n., 191 n., 192, 193, 194, 200, 202, 203, 204, 219, 256, 265, 273, 280 n., 281; *Rigault de Genouilly* (ML escort vessel): 264, 273; *Strasbourg* (BC): 180, 183, 190, 200, 202, 203, 206, 220, 228, 236, 239, 254, 255, 256, 268, 272, 281; *Surcouf* (SM): 259; *Terre Neuve* (patrol boat): 257–8

Warships, German: *Bismarck* (B): 55, 115, 116 n., 119 n., 200; *Gneisenau* (BC): 180, 181; *Graf Spee* (B): 138; *Graf Zeppelin* (AC): 119 n.; *Scharnhorst* (BC): 180, 181; *U-47* (SM): 51, 127; *U-702* (SM): 122

Warships, Italian: *Miraglia* (AC): 84 n.

Warships, Japanese: *Mikuma* (CR): 84 n.; *Mogami* (CR): 84 n.

Warships, Turkish: *Barbarossa* (b): 6 n., 8; *Breslau* (CR): 28 n., 31 n.; *Goeben* (BC): 28 n., 31

Waters, Lieut.-Cdr. David Watkin (1912–): on interwar convoy system, 38, 'law of convoy size', 46 n.

Waverley, 1st Viscount (John Anderson, 1882–1958): 219 n.

Welles, Sumner (1892–1961): 135; concern over French Fleet, 218

Wells, Adm. Sir Lionel Victor (1884–1965): and pre-Oran dispositions, 228; opposes use of force at Oran, 231; abandons attack on French ships at Oran, 256

Wemyss, Adm. Sir Rosslyn: *see* Wester Wemyss

Wester Wemyss, Adm. of the Fleet, 1st Baron (Rosslyn Erskine Wemyss,

1864–1933): and lessons of First War, 34; starts Naval Staff College, 35; approves Admiralty Historical Section, 61

Weygand, Gen. Maxime (1867–1965): 188, 196, 285; urges armistice, 189, 190; criticizes Gensoul for misleading message, 246 n.

Whitworth, Adm. Sir William Jock (1884–1973): on Churchill as First Lord (1939), 107

William II, Emperor (1859–1941): and Dardanelles operation, 15 n.

Williamson, Group-Capt. Hugh Alexander (1885–): and Dardanelles operation, 1 n., 7; on employment of seaplanes at Dardanelles, 5, 6, 9, 10

Willis, Adm. of the Fleet Sir Algernon Usborne (1889–): on work of Tactical School, 36, interwar convoy exercises, 39 n., *Fighting Instructions* in Second War, 54 n.

Wilson, Adm. of the Fleet Sir Arthur Knyvet, 3rd Bt. (1842–1921): relations with Army, 37

Woodward, Sir Ernest Llewellyn (1890–1971): on *raison d'être* of Oran, 285, 288

World War I, Lessons of: defects revealed by war, 33–4; early postwar prospects, 34–5; interwar achievements, 35–8; convoy lessons ignored, 38–47; the Jutland syndrome, 47–8; Q-ships, 49; magnetic mines, 49–50; paravane, 50; Northern Mine Barrage, 50; aircraft in minesweeping, 50; Scapa Flow's defences, 51; combined operations, 52–3; tactics, 53–4; problem of centralization, 54–5; naval aviation, 55–8; reasons for neglect of First War lessons, 57–63

THE MAPS

Large-scale versions of the maps that follow
can be downloaded from the book's page
on the publishers' websites.

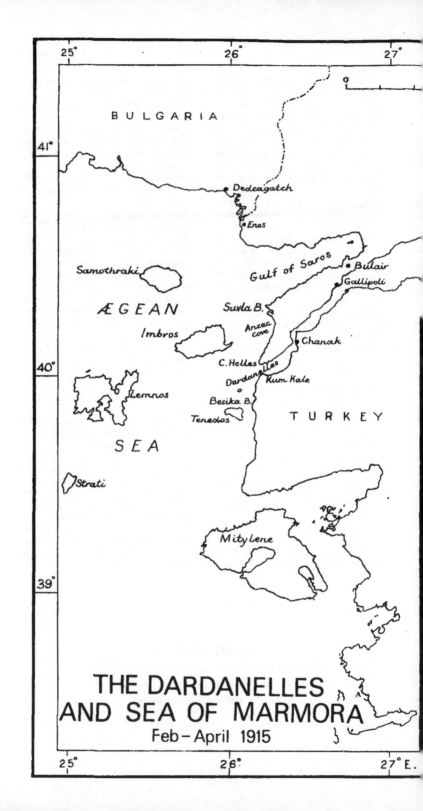

THE DARDANELLES
AND SEA OF MARMORA
Feb–April 1915

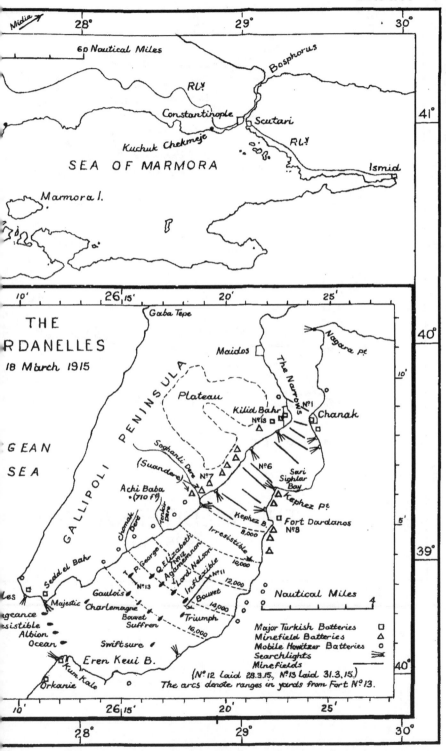

CHART 1

Midia →

60 Nautical Miles

RLᵞ

Bosphorus

Constantinople Scutari

Kuchuk Chekmeje RLᵞ

Ismid

SEA OF MARMORA

Marmora I.

THE
R DANELLES
18 March 1915

GEAN
SEA

Gaba Tepe

GALLIPOLI PENINSULA

Maidos

The Narrows

Nagara Pt.

Plateau

Kilid Bahr
Nº13

Chanak
Nº1

Soghanli Dere
(Suandere)

Nº7

Nº6

Sari Sighlar Bay

Achi Baba
(710 fᵗ)

Yenikeui Dere

Chanak Dere

Seddel Bahr

Kephez B.
8,000

Kephez Pt.

Irresistible

Fort Dardanos
Nº8

10,000

P. George
Q.Elizabeth
Agamemnon
Lord Nelson
Inflexible
Nº11
12,000
Bouvet
14,000
Triumph
16,000

Nº13

Gaulois
Charlemagne
Bouvet
Suffren

Nautical Miles
4

Majestic

les

Swiftsure

Major Turkish Batteries ☐
Minefield Batteries △
Mobile Howitzer Batteries
Searchlights
Minefields

geance
esistible
Albion
Ocean

Eren Keui B.

Kum Kale

Orkanie

(Nº12 Laid 28.3.15, Nº13 Laid 31.3.15.)
The arcs denote ranges in yards from Fort Nº13.

THE MEDITERRANEAN
1935–40

CHART 2

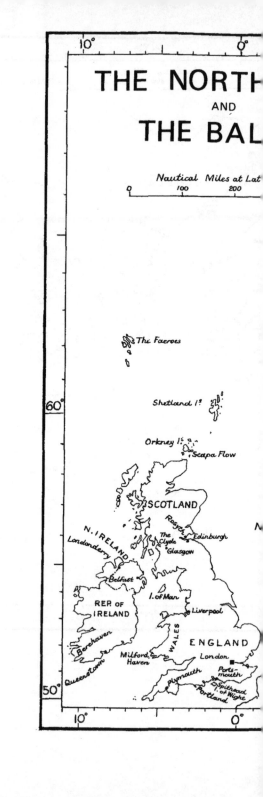

THE NORTH

AND

THE BAL

Nautical Miles at Lat

0   100   200

The Faeroes

Shetland Is.

Orkney Is.

Scapa Flow

SCOTLAND

Rosyth

N. IRELAND   The Clyde   Edinburgh

Londonderry   Glasgow

Belfast

REP. OF   I. of Man
IRELAND   Liverpool

WALES

ENGLAND

Berehaven   Milford   London
                    Haven

Queenstown   Plymouth   Ports-
                                   mouth

                    Portland   Spithead
                                   I. of Wight

60°

50°

10°   0°

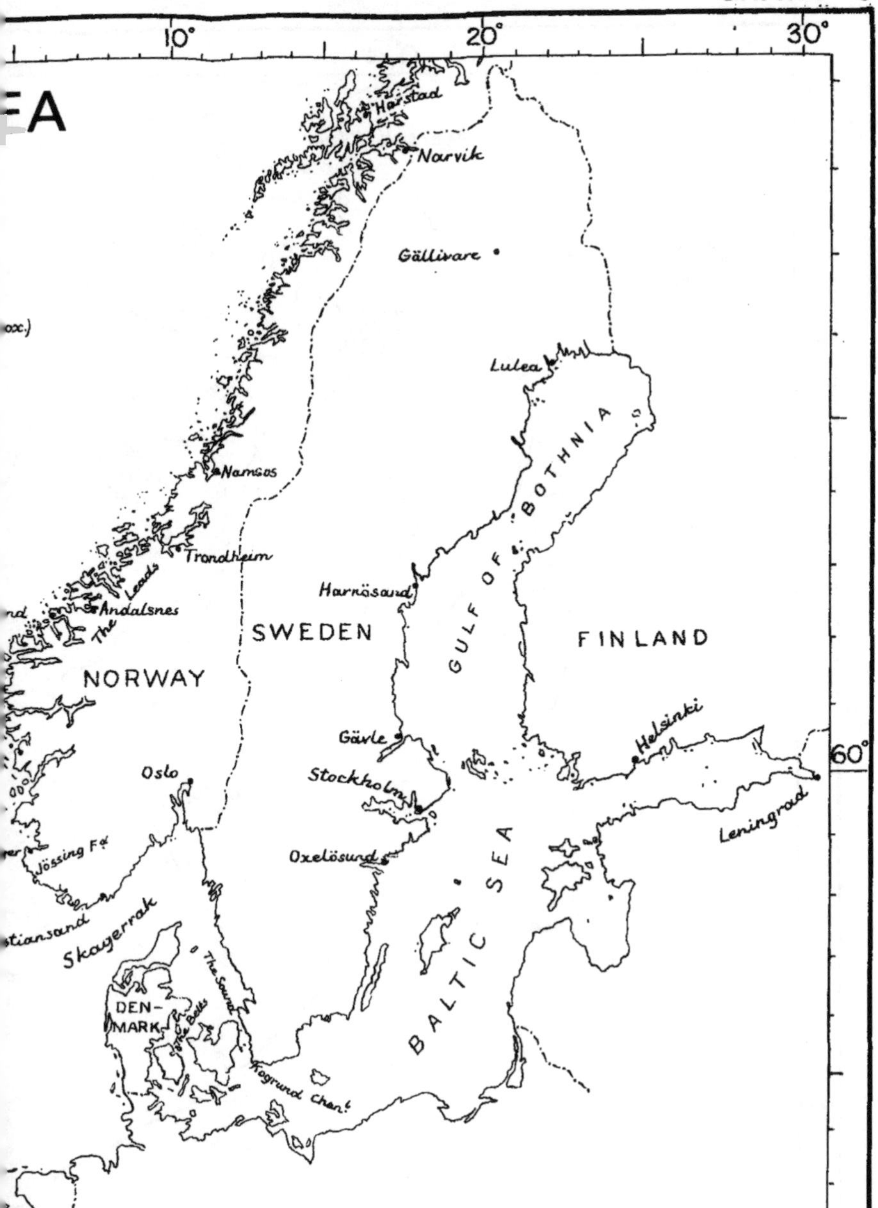
10°
20°
30°
EA
Harstad
Narvik
Gällivare
oxc.)
Lulea
Namsos
Trondheim
The Leads
Andalsnes
GULF OF BOTHNIA
Harnösand
SWEDEN
FINLAND
NORWAY
Gävle
Helsinki
60°
Oslo
Stockholm
Leningrad
Jössing Fd
Oxelösund
BALTIC SEA
stiansand
Skagerrak
The Sound
DEN-
MARK
The Belts
Kogrund Chan.
GERMANY
ETHER-
ANDS
50°
10°
20°
30°

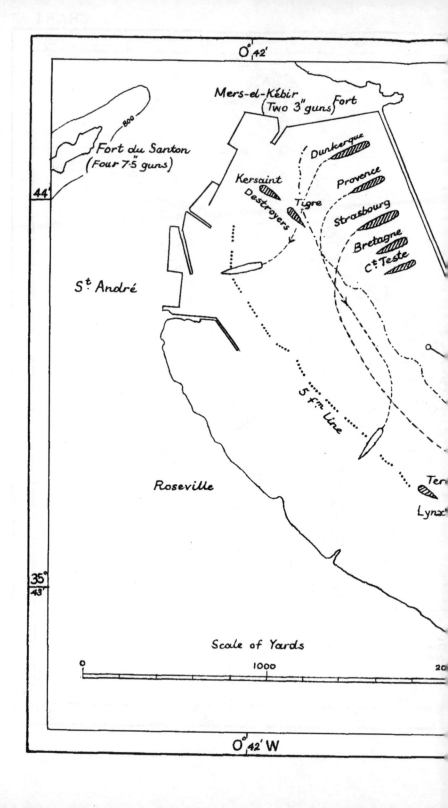

CHART 4

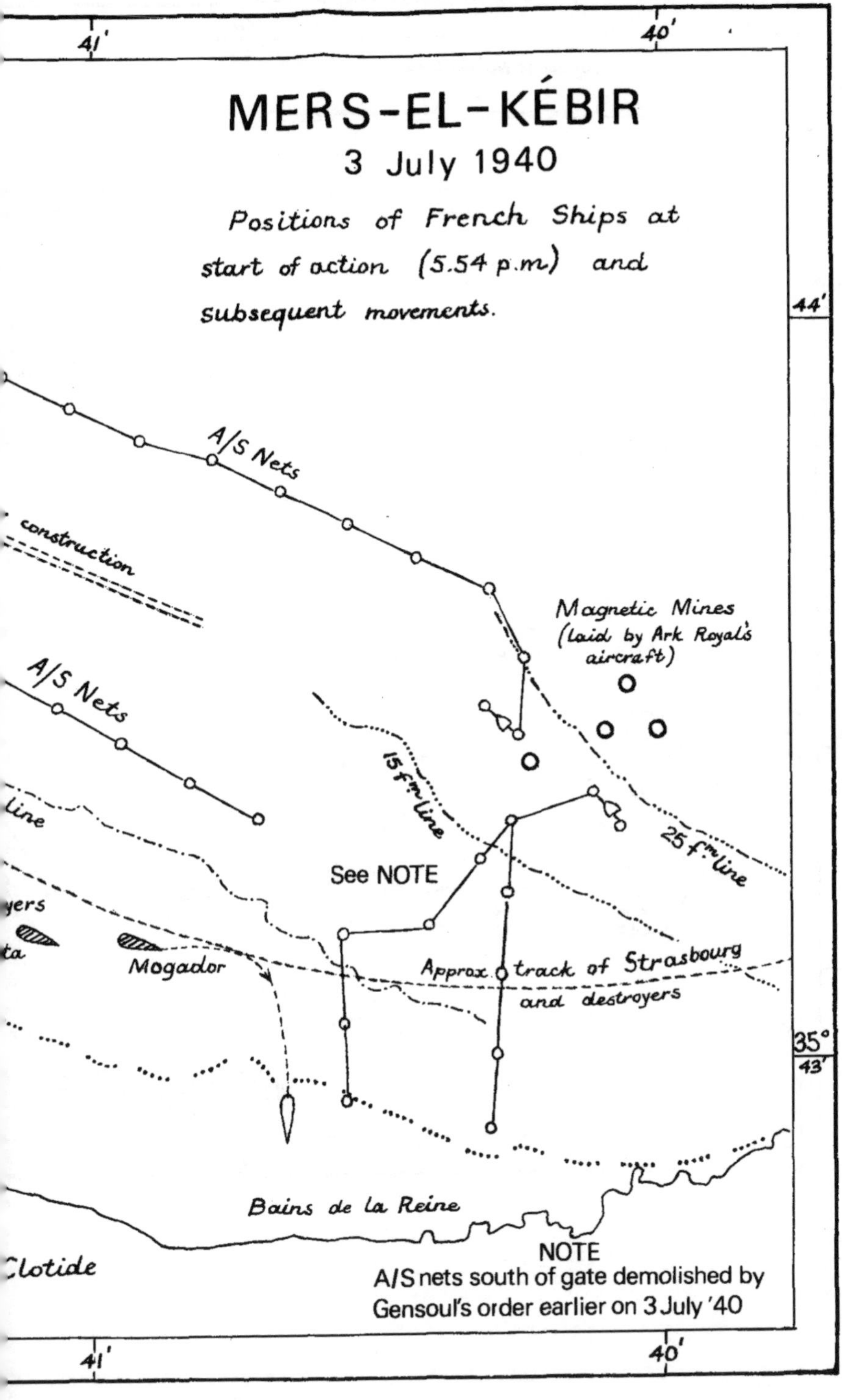

MERS-EL-KÉBIR
3 July 1940

Positions of French Ships at start of action (5.54 p.m) and subsequent movements.

41'

40'

44'

A/S Nets

construction

A/S Nets

Magnetic Mines
(laid by Ark Royal's aircraft)

15 fm line

See NOTE

25 fm line

line

yers

ta

Mogador

Approx track of Strasbourg and destroyers

35°
43'

Bains de la Reine

Clotide

NOTE
A/S nets south of gate demolished by Gensoul's order earlier on 3 July '40

41'

40'

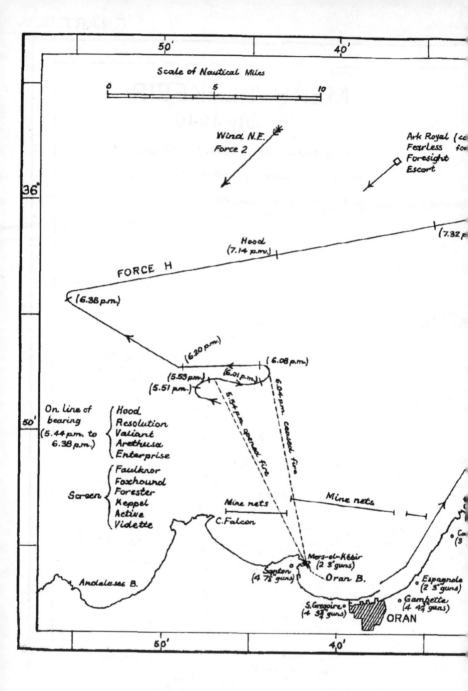

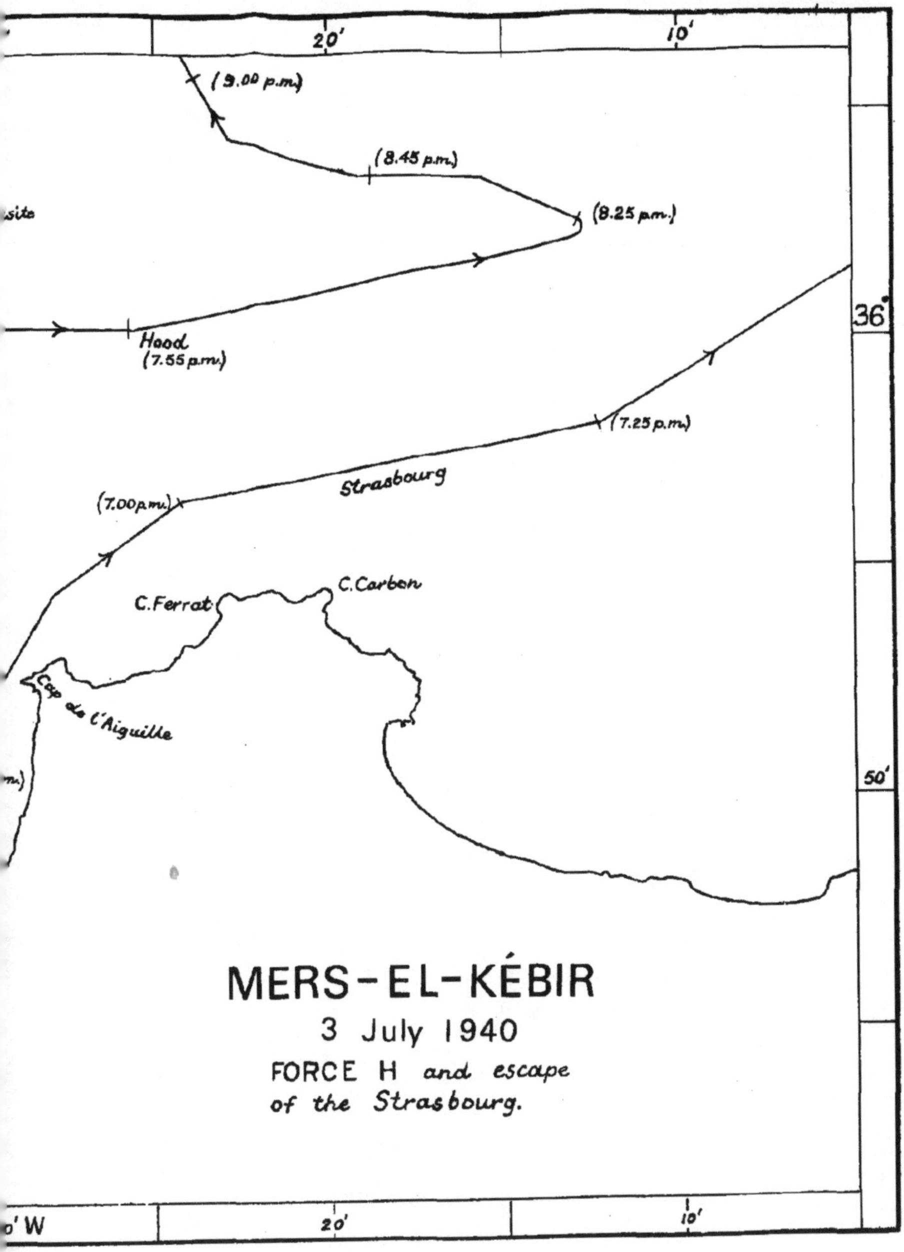

CHART 5

20'

10'

(9.00 p.m.)

(8.45 p.m.)

(8.25 p.m.)

site

36°

Hood
(7.55 p.m.)

(7.25 p.m.)

(7.00 p.m.)   Strasbourg

C. Carbon

C. Ferrat

50'

Cap de l'Aiguille

m.)

MERS-EL-KÉBIR
3 July 1940
FORCE H and escape
of the Strasbourg.

o' W

20'

10'